LAW & MENTAL HEALTH PROFESSIONALS
FLORIDA
SECOND EDITION

Law & Mental Health Professionals Series

Bruce D. Sales and Michael Owen Miller, Series Editors

ALABAMA: Bentley, Reaves, and Pippin
ARIZONA, 2ND ED.: Miller, Sales, and Delgado
CALIFORNIA: Caudill and Pope
CONNECTICUT: Taub
DELAWARE: Britton and Rohs
FLORIDA, 2ND ED.: Petrila and Otto
GEORGIA: Remar and Hubert
MASSACHUSETTS, 2ND ED.: Brant
MICHIGAN: Clark and Clark
MINNESOTA: Janus, Mickelsen, and Sanders
NEVADA: Johns and Dillehay
NEW JERSEY, 2ND ED.: Wulach
NEW YORK: Wulach
NORTH DAKOTA: O'Neill and Lochow
PENNSYLVANIA: Bersoff, Field, Anderer, and Zaplac
SOUTH CAROLINA: Follingstad and McCormick
SOUTH DAKOTA: Cichon
TEXAS, 2ND ED.: Shuman
VIRGINIA: Porfiri and Resnick
WASHINGTON: Benjamin, Rosenwald, Overcast, and Feldman
WISCONSIN: Kaplan and Miller
WYOMING: Blau

LAW & MENTAL HEALTH PROFESSIONALS

FLORIDA

SECOND EDITION

John Petrila, JD, LLM
Randy K. Otto, PhD

American Psychological Association
Washington, DC

Copyright © 2003 by the American Psychological Association. All rights reserved. Except as permitted under the United States Copyright Act of 1976, no part of this publication may be reproduced or distributed in any form or by any means, or stored in a database or retrieval system, without the prior written permission of the publisher.

Published by
American Psychological Association
750 First Street, NE
Washington, DC 20002
www.apa.org

To order
APA Order Department
P.O. Box 92984
Washington, DC 20090-2984

Tel: (800) 374-2721,
Direct: (202) 336-5510
Fax: (202) 336-5502,
TDD/TTY: (202) 336-6123
Online: www.apa.org/books/
E-mail: order@apa.org

In the U.K., Europe, Africa, and the Middle East, copies may be ordered from
American Psychological Association
3 Henrietta Street
Covent Garden, London
WC2E 8LU England

Typeset in Palatino by World Composition Services, Inc., Sterling, VA

Printer: Edwards Brothers, Inc., Ann Arbor, MI
Cover designer: Rubin Krassner, Silver Spring, MD
Project Manager: Debbie K. Hardin, Carlsbad, CA

The opinions and statements published are the responsibility of the authors, and such opinions and statements do not necessarily represent the policies of the American Psychological Association.

The information in this publication is intended for general guidance and is not meant to be a substitute for professional legal advice. The publisher, editors, and authors accept no responsibility for loss occasioned to any person or organization acting or refraining from action as a result of using any material in this publication. Readers are advised to seek the advice of a competent lawyer before making decisions based on their reading of this publication.

Library of Congress Cataloging-in-Publication Data
Petrila, John.
 Law & mental health professionals. Florida/John Petrila and Randy K. Otto.—2nd ed.
 p. cm—(Law & mental health professionals series)
 Includes bibliographical references and index.
 ISBN 1-55798-994-X
 1. Mental health personnel—Legal status, laws, etc.—Florida. 2. Mental health laws—Florida. 3. Forensic psychiatry—Florida. I. Otto, Randy K. II. Title. III. Series.
 KFF326.5.P73 P48 2003
 344.759'044—dc21   2002153098

Printed in the United States of America
First Edition

Contents

Editors' Preface		ix
Authors' Preface		xv

Section 1. Legal Credentialing — 1

1.1	Licensure and Regulation of Mental Health Professionals	3
1.2	Licensure and Regulation of Psychiatrists	4
1.3	Licensure and Regulation of Psychiatric Nurses	14
1.4	Licensure and Regulation of Psychologists	23
1.5	Subdoctoral and Unlicensed Psychologists	33
1.6	Licensure and Regulation of Social Workers	35
1.7	Certification and Regulation of School Psychologists	44
1.8	Certification of School Social Workers	48
1.9	Licensure and Regulation of Marriage and Family Counselors	53
1.10	Licensure of Other Types of Mental Health Professionals	61
1.11	Licensure and Regulation of Hypnotists	69
1.12	Licensure and Regulation of Polygraph Examiners	72
1.13	Regulation of Unlicensed Mental Health Professionals	73
1.14	Sunset of Credentialing Agencies	74
1.15	Licensure and Regulation of Sex Therapists	76

Section 2. Business Matters — 79

2.1	Sole Proprietorships	81
2.2	Professional Corporations	82
2.3	Partnerships	85
2.4	Health Maintenance Organizations	89
2.5	Preferred Provider Organizations	92
2.6	Individual Practice Associations	95
2.7	Hospital, Administrative, and Staff Privileges	97
2.8	Zoning for Community Homes	99
2.9	Insurance Reimbursement for Services	102
2.10	Mental Health Benefits in State Insurance Plans	104
2.11	Tax Deductions for Services	108

Section 3. Limitations on and Liability for Practice — 111

- 3.1 Informed Consent for Services — 113
- 3.2 Extensiveness, Ownership, Maintenance, and Access to Records — 117
- 3.3 Confidential Relations and Communications — 130
- 3.4 Privileged Communications — 141
- 3.5 Search, Seizure, and Subpoena of Records — 144
- 3.6 State Freedom of Information Act — 149
- 3.7 Right to Refuse Treatment — 150
- 3.8 Regulation of Aversive and Avoidance Conditioning — 152
- 3.9 Quality Assurance for Hospital Care — 153
- 3.10 Malpractice Liability — 155
- 3.11 Other Forms of Professional Liability — 159
- 3.12 Criminal Liability — 163
- 3.13 Liability of Credentialing Boards — 168
- 3.14 Antitrust Limitations to Practice — 169

Section 4. Families and Juveniles — 173

- 4.1 Competency to Marry — 175
- 4.2 Guardianship for Adults — 177
- 4.3 Conservatorship for Adults — 184
- 4.4 Annulment — 186
- 4.5 Divorce — 188
- 4.6 Child Custody After Marital Dissolution — 190
- 4.7 Reporting of Adult Abuse — 197
- 4.8 Reporting of Child Abuse — 202
- 4.9 Abused, Neglected, and Abandoned Children — 207
- 4.10 Termination of Parental Rights — 215
- 4.11 Guardianship for Minors — 219
- 4.12 Conservatorship for Minors — 221
- 4.13 Foster Care — 222
- 4.14 Adoption — 227
- 4.15 Delinquency and Persons in Need of Supervision — 233
- 4.16 Competency of Juveniles to Stand Trial — 243
- 4.17 Nonresponsibility Defense — 248
- 4.18 Transfer of Juveniles to Stand Trial as Adults — 252
- 4.19 Voluntary Admission and Civil Commitment of Minors — 259
- 4.20 Education for Gifted and Handicapped Children — 272
- 4.21 Consent, Confidentiality, and Services for Minors — 277
- 4.22 Consent for Abortion — 282

	4.23	Evaluation and Treatment of Children at the Request of a Noncustodial Parent	284

Section 5. Other Civil Matters — 287

5.1	Mental Status of Licensed or Certified Professionals	289
5.2	Workers' Compensation	295
5.3	Vocational Disability Determinations	299
5.4	Emotional Distress as a Basis for Civil Liability	303
5.5	Insanity of Wrongdoers and Civil Liability	306
5.6	Competency to Contract	308
5.7	Competency to Sign a Will	310
5.8	Competency to Vote	313
5.9	Competency to Obtain a Driver's License	315
5.10	Product Liability	316
5.11	Unfair Competition	318
5.12	Employment Discrimination	321

Section 6. Civil and Criminal Trial Matters — 325

6.1	Jury Selection	327
6.2	Expert Witnesses	331
6.3	Polygraph Evidence	335
6.4	Competency to Testify	337
6.5	Psychological/Psychiatric Autopsy	340
6.6	Battered Woman's Syndrome	342
6.7	Rape Trauma Syndrome	345
6.8	Hypnosis of Witnesses	347
6.9	Eyewitness Identification	349
6.10	Child Sexual Abuse Syndrome	351
6.11	Profiles or Propensity of Sexual Offenders	353

Section 7. Criminal Matters — 355

7.1	Screening of Police Officers	357
7.2	Competency to Waive the Rights to Silence, Counsel, and a Jury	358
7.3	Precharging and Pretrial Intervention Programs	361
7.4	Bail Determinations	363
7.5	Competency to Stand Trial	366
7.6	Provocation	374
7.7	Mens Rea	376
7.8	Diminished Capacity	378
7.9	Criminal Responsibility	380
7.10	Competency to Be Sentenced	386
7.11	Sentencing	388

	7.12	Probation	391
	7.13	Dangerous Offenders	393
	7.14	Habitual Offenders	394
	7.15	Competency to Serve a Sentence	395
	7.16	Mental Health Services in Jails and Prisons	396
	7.17	Transfer From Penal to Mental Health Facilities	401
	7.18	Parole Determinations	403
	7.19	Competency to Be Executed	406
	7.20	Pornography	409
	7.21	Services for Sex Offenders	411
	7.22	Services for Victims of Crimes	419

Section 8. Voluntary or Involuntary Receipt of State Services — 421

	8.1	Medicaid	423
	8.2	Health Care Cost Containment System	429
	8.3	Voluntary Admission of Mentally Ill Adults	431
	8.4	Involuntary Commitment of Mentally Ill Adults	433
	8.5	Voluntary Admission and Involuntary Commitment of People With Substance Problems	442
	8.6	Voluntary and Involuntary Commitment of Drug Addicts	452
	8.7	Services for People With Developmental Disabilities	453
	8.8	Hospice Care	461

Appendix — 465

Table of Cases	467
Table of Statutes	471
Table of Rules of Court	481
Table of Administrative Rules and Regulations	482
Table of References to Constitution	484

Index	485
About the Authors	493

Editors' Preface

The Need to Know the Law

For years, providers of mental health services (hereinafter mental health professionals or MHPs) have been directly affected by the law. At one end of the continuum, their practice has been controlled by laws covering such matters as licensure and certification, third-party reimbursement, and professional incorporation. At the other end, they have been courted by the legal system to aid in its administration, providing such services as evaluating the mental status of litigants, providing expert testimony in court, and engaging in therapy with court-referred juveniles and adults. Even when not directly affected, MHPs find themselves indirectly affected by the law because their clients sometimes become enmeshed in legal entanglements that involve mental status issues (e.g., divorce proceedings or termination of parental rights hearings).

Despite this pervasive influence, most professionals do not know about, much less understand, most of the laws that affect their practice, the services they render, and the clients they serve. This state of affairs is particularly troubling for several reasons. First, not knowing about the laws that affect one's practice typically results in the MHPs not gaining the benefits that the law may provide. Consider the law relating to the incorporation of professionals. It confers significant benefit, but only if it is known about and applied. The fact that it has been enacted by the state legislature does not help the MHP any more than an MHP will be of help to a distressed person who refuses to contact the MHP.

Second, not knowing about the laws that affect the services they render may result in incompetent performance of, and liability for, the MHP either through the civil law (e.g., malpractice law) or through criminal sanctions. A brief example may help underscore this point. When an MHP is asked to evaluate a party to a lawsuit and testify in court, the court (the law's term for the judge) is asking the professional to assess and testify about whether that litigant meets some legal standard. The court is often not concerned with the defendant's mental health per se, although this may be relevant to the MHP's evaluation of the person. Rather, the court wants to know whether the person meets the legal standard as it is set down by the law. Not knowing the legal standard means that the MHP is most likely evaluating the person for the wrong goal and providing the court with irrelevant information, at least from the court's point of view. Regretfully, there are too many cases in which this has occurred.

Third, not knowing the law that affects the clients that MHPs serve may significantly diminish their capability for handling their clients' distress. For example, a client who is undergoing a divorce and a child custody dispute may have distorted beliefs about what may happen during the legal proceedings. A basic understanding of the controlling law in this area will allow the therapist to be more sensitive in rendering therapy.

The Problem in Accessing Legal Information

Given the need for this information, why have MHPs not systematically sought it out? Part of the reason lies in the concern over their ability to understand legal doctrines. Indeed, this is a legitimate worry, especially if they had to read original legal materials that were not collected, organized, and described with an MHP audience in mind. This is of particular concern because laws are written in terms and phrases of "art" that do not always share the common law definition or usage, whereas some terms and phrases are left ambiguous and undefined or are used differently for different legal topics. Another part of the reason is that the law affecting MHPs and their clients is not readily available—even to lawyers. There are no compendiums that identify the topics that these laws cover or present an analysis of each topic for easy reference.

To compound the difficulty, the law does not treat the different mental health professional disciplines uniformly or always specify the particular disciplines as being covered by it. Nor does the law emanate from a single legal forum. Each state enacts its own rules and regulations, often resulting in wide variations in the way a topic is handled across the United States. Multiply this confusion by the one hundred or so topics that relate to mental health practice. In addition, the law within a state does not come from one legal source. Rather, there are five primary ones: the state constitution; state legislative enactments (statutes); state agency administrative rules and regulations; rules of court promulgated by the state supreme court; and state and federal court cases that apply, interpret, and construe this existing state law. To know about one of these sources without knowing how its pronouncements on a given topic have been modified by these other sources may result in one's making erroneous conclusions about the operation of the law. Finally, mental health practice also comes under the purview of federal law (constitutional and statutory law, administrative rules and regulations, and case law). Federal law authorizes direct payments to MHPs for their services to some clients, sets standards for delivery of services in federal facilities (e.g., Veterans Administration hospitals), and articulates the law that guides cases that are tried in federal courts under federal law.

Purposes of This Series

What is needed, therefore, is a book for each state, the District of Columbia, and the federal jurisdictions that comprehensively and accurately reviews and integrates all of the law that affects MHPs in that jurisdiction (hereinafter state). These materials should be written so that they are completely understandable to MHPs as well as to lawyers. To accomplish these goals, the editors have tried to identify every legal topic that affects mental health practice, making each one the subject of a chapter. Each chapter, in turn, describes the legal standards that the MHP will be operating under and the relevant legal process that the MHP will be operating within. If a state does not have relevant law on an issue, then a brief explanation of how this law works in other states will be presented while noting the lack of regulation in this area within the state under consideration.

This type of coverage facilitates other purposes of the series. Although each chapter is written in order to state exactly what is the present state of the law and not argue for or against any particular approach, it is hoped that the comprehensiveness of the coverage will encourage MHPs to question the desirability of their states' approach to each topic. Such information and concern should provide the impetus for initiating legislation and litigation on the part of state mental health associations to ensure that the law reflects the scientific knowledge and professional values to the greatest extent possible.

In some measure, states will initially be hampered in this proactivity because they will not know what legal alternatives are available and how desirable each alternative actually is. When a significant number of books in this series is available, however, it will allow for nationally oriented policy studies to identify the variety of legal approaches that are currently in use and to assess the validity of the behavioral assumptions underlying each variant and, ultimately, lead to a conclusion as to the relative desirability of alternate approaches.[1] Thus, two other purposes of this book are to foster comprehensive analyses of the laws affecting MHPs across all states and of the validity of the behavioral assumptions

---

1. Sales, B. D. (1983). The legal regulation of psychology: Professional and scientific interactions. In C. J. Scheirer & B. L. Hammonds (Eds.), *The master lecture series: Vol. 2. Psychology and law* (pp. 5–36). Washington, DC: American Psychological Association.

underlying these laws, and to promote political, legislative, and legal action to change laws that are inappropriate and impede the effective delivery of services. Legal change may be required because of gaps in legal regulation, overregulation, and regulation based on invalid behavioral and social assumptions. We hope that this process will increase the rationality of future laws in this area and improve the effectiveness and quality of mental health service delivery nationally.

There are three remaining purposes for this series. First, although it will not replace the need for legal counsel, this series will make the MHP an intelligent consumer of legal services. This ability is gaining importance in an era of increasing professionalization and litigiousness. Second, it will ensure that MHPs are aware of the law's mandates when providing expert services (e.g., evaluation and testimony) within the legal system. Although chapters will not address how to assess clinically for the legal standard, provider competency will increase because providers now will be sure of the goals of their service (e.g., the legal standard that they are to assess for) as well as their roles and responsibilities within the legal system as to the particular topic in issue. Third and finally, each book will make clear that the legal standards that MHPs are asked to assess for by the law have typically not been translated into behavioral correlates. Nor are there discussions of tests, scales, and procedures for MHPs to use in assessing for the behavioral correlates of the legal standards in most cases. This series will provide the impetus for such research and writing.

Content and Organization of Volumes

Each book in this series is organized into eight sections. Section 1 addresses the legal credentialing of MHPs. Section 2 deals with the different business forms for conducting one's practice, insurance reimbursement, and tax deductions that clients may receive for using mental health services. With the business matters covered, the book then turns to the law directly affecting service delivery. Section 3 covers the law that affects the maintenance and privacy of professional information and discusses the law that limits service delivery and sets liability for unethical and illegal behavior as a service provider. Sections 4 through 8 consider each area of law that may require the services of MHPs: adults, minors, and families; other civil matters; topics that apply similarly in both civil and criminal cases; criminal matters; and voluntary and involuntary receipt of state services by the clients of mental health services.

Collectively, the chapters in these sections represent all topics pertaining to the law as it affects MHPs in their practices. Two caveats are in order, however. First, the law changes slowly over time. Thus, this volume will be updated on a regular basis. As MHPs become more involved in the legal system, new opportunities for involvement are likely to arise. To be responsive to these developments, revisions will also contain additional chapters reflecting these new roles and responsibilities.

Some final points about the content of this book are in order. The exact terms that the law chooses are used in the book even if they are a poor choice from an MHP's point of view. Where terms are defined by the law, that information is presented. The reader will often be frustrated, however, because as has already been noted, the law does not always define terms or provide detailed guidance. This does not mean that legal words and phrases can be taken lightly. The law sets the rules by which MHPs and their clients must operate; thus, the chapters must be read carefully. This should not be too arduous a task because chapters are relatively short. However, such brevity will leave some readers frustrated because chapters may appear not to go far enough in answering their questions. Note that all of the law is covered. If there is no law, however, there is no coverage. If a question is not answered in the text, it is because Florida law has not addressed the issue. Relatedly, if an obligation or benefit is created by a professional regulation (i.e., a rule of a professional organization) but is not directly recognized by the law, it is not covered. Thus, for example, professional credentials are not addressed in these volumes.

Finally, we want to point out that in some instances, the pronoun "he" is used generically to refer to both genders. Most notably, the pronoun is used when quoting directly from the law. Legal language is generally consistent in its preference for using the masculine form of the pronoun; it is not always feasible to attempt a rewording.

Bruce D. Sales
Michael Owen Miller
Series Editors

Authors' Preface

This book is a treatment of Florida law applicable to mental health professionals (MHPs). A comprehensive treatment of federal law, which is also applicable to the actions of MHPs, is beyond the scope of this work because it would require either a separate volume or limited treatment within a single volume. In describing Florida law, this work includes the state constitution, state statutes, state administrative rules, state judicial decisions, and state judicial rules.

This is the second edition of a book first published in 1996. Since that time, there have been major changes in Florida law. For example, Florida has significantly changed its juvenile law framework, established a statute authorizing the indefinite confinement of individuals adjudicated as sexually violent predators, and made significant changes to the civil commitment law. In addition, Florida courts have made additional rulings on privilege and confidentiality. These changes, relevant to the practice of MHPs, are covered in this edition. The book also has been comprehensively updated in all other areas where change has occurred since the first edition.

It is worth noting briefly the organization of Florida law and the manner in which it is codified in statute and reported in judicial opinions. The Florida Constitution establishes the framework for state government and describes the discrete individual rights afforded the highest degree of importance in Florida. Reference citations for the Florida Constitution appear in the following form: FLA. CONST. art. I, § 1. This reference indicates that the citation refers to the first section (§) of the first article (art. I) in the Florida Constitution.

Citations to state statutes, which result from legislation passed by the Florida Senate and House, appear in the following form: 1 FLA. STAT. ANN. § 1 (West 2000). This particular citation is a reference to the bound volumes of statutes published by West Publishing Company, titled *West's Florida Statutes Annotated*. The laws are cited by volume number, series title, and then by section number. The year in which the particular volume was published is given in parentheses. Some references include the phrase "Supp." (e.g., West Supp. 2000). This indicates that the reference is found in a softback supplement inserted in the back of the main volume. The supplement provides annual updates on legislation enacted in the previous legislative session.

The Florida Constitution and the annotated Florida statutes contain additional material. The compilers attempt to include a citation and a one-sentence summary of any reported cases that have discussed the statute or constitutional provision in question. A researcher may use these case annotations to begin research on how the statute or constitutional provision has been interpreted by the courts. The compilations also contain references to previous statutes that have been repealed. A review of these repealed statutes may be necessary to understand an earlier judicial opinion interpreting them or to resolve an ambiguity in the intent of the legislature in changing the statute.

State administrative rules are created by state agencies operating under the authority delegated to them by the legislature to conduct specific agency functions. These rules do not appear in the volumes of statutes but are published as the Florida administrative code. They are noted in the following manner: FLA. ADMIN. CODE ANN. r. 5-28 (2000). In this example, the regulation cited is rule 5, section 28, and the volume in which it appears was published in 2000.

State judicial decisions are the product of judge-made law. Decisions that appear in printed volumes are typically those of appellate courts. They consist of decisions of the Florida district courts of appeals, to which decisions of trial courts typically are appealed, and the Florida supreme court, which is the highest court in Florida. A citation to a Florida supreme court decision would appear in the following format: *Mahan v. Mahan,* 88 So. 2d 363 (Fla. 1956). This citation tells the reader that the case involved two parties named Mahan and that the report of the decision appears in volume 88 of the *Southern Reporter,* second series, beginning on page 363, and that this Florida supreme court case was decided in 1956. A reference to a state appellate decision (e.g., Fifth District Court of Appeals) would appear in the following manner: *Younger v. State,* 433 So. 2d 636 (Fla. 5th D.C.A. 1983).

State judicial rules, as contrasted with judicial decisions, are the product of judges acting in a legislative rather than a judicial capacity. In this role, judges make rules of general application in the courts, not usually in the context of deciding cases. The supreme court of Florida is responsible for the administration of the Florida court system and promulgates court rules that relate to civil procedure, criminal procedure, civil appellate procedure, and practice in other courts. Most rules can be found in *West's Florida Statutes, Annotated,* in the volumes titled "Rules." They appear in the following form: 33 FLA. R. CRIM. P. 3.216(a) (West 1999). In this example, the reference would be to rule 3.216(a) of the rules of criminal procedure. *Rules of Civil Procedure* would be abbreviated as FLA. R. CIV. P.

There are 20 judicial circuit courts in the state of Florida. Most circuits comprise three or more counties. The first judicial circuit includes Escambia, Okaloosa, Santa Rosa, and Walton Counties. The second judicial circuit includes Franklin, Gadsden, Jefferson, Leon, Liberty, and Wakulla Counties. The third judicial circuit includes Columbia, Dixie, Hamilton, Lafayette, Madison, Suwannee, and Taylor Counties. The fourth judicial circuit includes Clay, Duval, and Nassau Counties. The fifth judicial circuit includes Citrus, Hernando, Lake, Marion, and Sumter counties. The sixth judicial circuit includes Pasco and Pinellas Counties. The seventh judicial circuit includes Flagler, Putnam, St. Johns, and Volusia Counties. The eighth judicial circuit includes Alachua, Baker, Bradford, Gilchrist, Levy, and Union Counties. The ninth judicial circuit includes Orange and Osceola Counties. The tenth judicial circuit includes Hardee, Highlands, and Polk Counties. The eleventh judicial circuit includes Dade County. The twelfth judicial circuit includes DeSoto, Manatee, and Sarasota Counties. The thirteenth judicial circuit includes Hillsborough County. The fourteenth judicial circuit includes Bay, Calhoun, Gulf, Holmes, Jackson, and Washington Counties. The fifteenth judicial circuit includes Palm Beach County. The sixteenth judicial circuit includes Monroe County. The seventeenth judicial circuit includes Broward County. The eighteenth judicial circuit includes Brevard and Seminole Counties. The nineteenth judicial circuit includes Indian River, Martin, Okeechobee, and St. Lucie Counties. The twentieth judicial circuit includes Charlotte, Collier, Glades, Hendry, and Lee Counties.

In addition to the 20 judicial circuit courts, there are five state appellate courts. The first appellate district includes the first, second, fourth, eighth, and fourteenth circuits. The second appellate district includes the sixth, tenth, twelfth, thirteenth, and twentieth circuits. The third appellate district includes the eleventh and sixteenth circuits. The fourth appellate district includes the fifteenth, seventeenth, and nineteenth circuits. The fifth appellate district includes the fifth, seventh, ninth, and eighteenth circuits.

Although the focus of this work is on state rather than federal law applicable to MHPs in Florida, occasional reference is made, of necessity, to federal decisions interpreting or limiting state law. The citations to these decisions are from the U.S. District Court, reported in the *Federal Supplement* (F. Supp.); the United States Court of Appeals, reported in the *Federal Reporter* (F. or F.2d); and the U.S. Supreme Court, reported in the *United States Reports, Supreme Court Reporter,* or *Lawyer's Edition* (U.S., S. Ct., or L. Ed). As is the case with the reporters for state decisions, the number preceding the reporter title is the volume number and the number following is the first page number. References to federal legislation appear in the form of 26 U.S.C. § 213(a) (1987). This particular citation to the *United States Code*—the repository for federal legislation—is from title 26, section 213(a), current as of 1987. Also included are citations to relevant treatises and law review articles. These references may provide a fuller background on issues of interest to MHPs.

Finally, although some chapters were updated until the manuscript went to press, the reader should consider the entire volume current as of June 2002.

Section 1

Legal Credentialing

1.1
Licensure and Regulation of Mental Health Professionals

Florida law provides for the licensing and regulation of health care professionals, including mental health professionals (MHPs). In general, the licensing and regulation of MHPs is under the jurisdiction of the Florida Department of Health (DOH), which exercises its authority through various boards that have the day-to-day responsibility for licensure decisions. Specific licensing laws for each MHP are covered in the remainder of this section.

1.2

Licensure and Regulation of Psychiatrists

The DOH governs the licensure and practice of physicians in Florida.[1] The DOH discharges its responsibilities through the Florida Board of Medicine.[2] In general, psychiatrists are regulated as physicians.[3] The Board's responsibilities include establishing qualifications for physician licensure, overseeing the conduct of physicians, and regulating the disciplinary process for physicians.

(A) Florida Board of Medicine

The Board has 15 members appointed by the governor, subject to Senate confirmation.[4] Twelve board members must be licensed physicians and Florida residents who either have at least four years of experience in active practice or who were teaching medicine immediately before their appointments to the Board.[5] One of the Board members must serve as a faculty member of a medical school located within the state; one must be a full-time staff member of a Florida teaching hospital; and one must be a foreign medical school graduate.[6] The three nonphysician Board members cannot ever have been licensed health care practitioners.[7] One member of the Board must be a certified hospital-risk manager,

---

1. 15 Fla. Stat. Ann. § 458.305 (West 2001).
2. 15 Fla. Stat. Ann. § 458.307 (West 2001).
3. An exception is the granting of a public psychiatry certificate, 15 Fla. Stat. Ann. § 458.3165 (West 2001), which is described in "Public Psychiatry Certificates" later in the chapter.
4. 15 Fla. Stat. Ann. § 458.307 (West 2001).
5. 15 Fla. Stat. Ann. § 458.307(2) (West 2001).
6. Id.
7. Id.

and at least one member must be 60 years of age or older.[8] Members serve four-year terms.[9]

The Board has general authority to make the rules necessary to carry out its duties and responsibilities, including those necessary to protect the health, safety, and welfare of the public.[10]

(A)(1) Practice of Medicine Defined

The *practice of medicine* is defined as "the diagnosis, treatment, operation, or prescription, for any human disease, pain, injury, deformity, or other physical or mental condition."[11]

(B) Licensure

(B)(1) Licensure by Examination

The DOH administers the licensure exam to applicants certified by the Board as meeting the following requirements.[12] The applicant must

1. Be at least 21 years of age;
2. Be of good moral character;
3. Have not committed any act or offense that would be a basis for disciplining a physician under Florida law;
4. If graduated after October 1, 1992, have completed the equivalent of two academic years of preprofessional, postsecondary education before entering medical school that, at a minimum, include courses in such fields as anatomy, biology, and chemistry;
5. Graduate from an accredited medical school;
6. Demonstrate competency in English if the medical school's language of instruction was not English;
7. Complete an approved residency of at least one year; or be a graduate of an allopathic foreign medical school registered with the World Health Organization, be proficient in English, and complete an approved residency of one year; or be a graduate of an allopathic foreign medical school not certified as meeting U.S. or comparable standards with demonstrated competency in English and a two-year residency in a specialty area;
8. Have submitted a complete set of fingerprints; and

---

8. *Id.*
9. 15 FLA. STAT. ANN. § 458.307(3) (West 2001).
10. 15 FLA. STAT. ANN. § 458.309(1) (West 2001).
11. 15 FLA. STAT. ANN. § 458.305(3) (West 2001).
12. 15 FLA. STAT. ANN. § 458.311(1) (West 2001).

9. Have a passing score on a national licensing examination as established by the Board.

The applicant must also submit a variety of information at the initial application and at subsequent renewals, including among other things a list of medical schools attended, hospitals at which privileges are held, specialty certificates, addresses of practice, any criminal offenses for which the applicant has been found guilty, and any final disciplinary action in the previous 10 years.[13]

(B)(2) Licensure by Endorsement

The DOH may issue a license by endorsement to an applicant who meets the age, character, and educational requirements of the general licensure statute and who has passed the U.S. Medical Licensing Examination. The examination must have been taken within 10 years of applying for licensure, and the applicant must have engaged in the active licensed practice of medicine in another state for two of the preceding four years or completed Board-approved postgraduate training within two years preceding the filing of the application, or passed a Board-approved competency examination within the year preceding filing for licensure.[14]

(B)(3) Restricted Licenses

The Board of Medicine is authorized legislatively to grant restricted licenses annually to as many as 100 persons meeting legislative and regulatory requirements.[15] The applicant must meet licensure requirements; show evidence of the active licensed practice of medicine in another jurisdiction for at least two of the immediately preceding four years or completion of Board-approved postgraduate training within the year preceding the filing of an application; and contract to practice for 24 months solely in the employ of the state or a federally funded community health center or migrant health center; and complete the licensure examination before the expiration of the 24-month period.[16] The legislature has also established criteria to permit graduates of foreign medical schools to obtain restricted licenses in some circumstances.[17]

(B)(4) Limited Licenses

The Board may issue limited licenses to practice medicine to applicants who have been licensed elsewhere in the United States

---

13. 15 FLA. STAT. ANN. § 455.565(1) (West 2001).
14. 15 FLA. STAT. ANN. § 458.313(1) (West Supp. 2000).
15. 15 FLA. STAT. ANN. § 458.310 (West 2001).
16. 15 FLA. STAT. ANN. § 458.310(2)-(3) (West 2001).
17. 15 FLA. STAT. ANN. §§ 458.3115 and 458.3124 (West 2001).

for at least 10 years and who are retired from the practice of medicine. The applicant has to meet the age, educational, and character requirements of the general licensure statute. He or she may only practice with public agencies or institutions or nonprofit agencies or institutions located in areas of critical medical need.[18]

(B)(5) Temporary Certificates for Locales in Critical Need

A physician licensed in another state may be issued a temporary certificate to practice in Florida communities that are determined by the Board of Medicine to have a critical need for physicians. The physician holding a temporary certificate may practice only in areas designated by the Board.[19]

(B)(6) Public Psychiatry Certificates

The Board may also issue public psychiatry certificates to applicants licensed to practice in another state and board-certified in psychiatry. The certificate, renewable biennially, permits the holder to practice only in a public mental health facility or program funded in whole or in part by state funds.[20]

(B)(7) Financial Issues

As a condition of licensure, a physician must demonstrate the financial capacity to pay claims arising from malpractice. The physician may do so by establishing an escrow account, obtaining a letter of credit for amounts fixed by statute, or by obtaining at least the minimum level ($100,000 per claim and not less than $300,000 aggregate at the time of writing) of professional liability coverage.[21] Similar provisions exist for physicians as a condition of maintaining hospital staff privileges.

When providing professional services, the physician, if requested, must submit itemized statements of the services rendered and the charge for each.[22]

(B)(8) Licensure Renewal

Licenses are renewed on a biennial basis. Renewal will be granted on receipt of a renewal application, payment of the applicable fee, and evidence that the applicant either has actively practiced medicine or has been an active teaching faculty member in an accredited medical school within the previous four years.[23]

---

18. 15 Fla. Stat. Ann. § 458.317 (West 2001).
19. 15 Fla. Stat. Ann. § 458.315 (West Supp. 2002).
20. 15 Fla. Stat. Ann. § 458.3165 (West 2001).
21. 15 Fla. Stat. Ann. § 458.320 (West 2001).
22. 15 Fla. Stat. Ann. § 458.323 (West 1991).
23. 15 Fla. Stat. Ann. §§ 458.319(1) and (2) (West Supp. 2002).

(C) Regulation

(C)(1) Unlawful and Prohibited Practices

The following actions are punishable as a felony of the third degree:[24]

1. Practicing medicine or attempting to practice medicine without a license;

2. Using or attempting to use a suspended or revoked license to practice;

3. Obtaining or attempting to obtain a license to practice medicine by knowingly using misrepresentation; and

4. Obtaining or attempting to obtain a position as a practitioner or resident in a clinic or hospital by knowingly misrepresenting education, training, or experience.

Other actions are misdemeanors of the first degree:[25]

1. Knowingly concealing information relevant to violations of the licensing statute;

2. Making a false oath or affirmation when an oath or affirmation is required as part of the licensing process;

3. Referring, with some exceptions, a patient to a partnership or other business entity in which the physician or the physician's employer has an equity interest of 10% or more unless, before the referral, the physician discloses the relationship to the patient; and

4. Leading the public to believe that one is licensed as a medical doctor without holding a valid license.

A wide variety of grounds exist for disciplinary action of physicians. These include the following:[26]

1. Attempting to obtain, obtaining, or renewing a license to practice medicine by bribery or fraudulent misrepresentations;

2. Having a license revoked, suspended, or otherwise acted against by any jurisdiction within the United States;

---

24. 15 FLA. STAT. ANN. § 458.327(1) (West 2001). A felony in the third degree is a crime punishable by a term of imprisonment not to exceed five years. 22 FLA. STAT. ANN. § 775.082 (West 2001).
25. 15 FLA. STAT. ANN. § 458.327(2) (West 2001). A misdemeanor of the first degree is a crime punishable by a definite term of imprisonment not to exceed one year. 22 FLA. STAT. ANN. § 775.082(4)(a) (West 2001).
26. 15 FLA. STAT. ANN. § 458.331(1) (West Supp. 2002).

3. Being convicted or found guilty of, or entering a plea of *nolo contendere* to, a crime in any jurisdiction that directly relates to the practice of medicine or the ability to practice medicine;[27]
4. Practicing false, deceptive, or misleading advertising;
5. Failing to report to the DOH any person whom the license holder knows has violated the licensing and regulatory provisions of state law;
6. Aiding or assisting an unlicensed person in the practice of medicine;
7. Failing to perform any statutory or legal obligation held by physicians;
8. Making or filing false reports or records required by state or federal law;
9. Paying or receiving any commission, bonus, kickback, or rebate, or engaging in split-fee arrangements with other practitioners or providers;
10. Attempting to influence a patient to engage in or engaging in sexual activity (patients are presumed to be incapable of giving informed consent to sexual activity with a physician);
11. Making deceptive, untrue, or fraudulent representations related to the practice of medicine;
12. Soliciting patients through fraud, intimidation, undue influence, or other forms of overreaching;
13. Failing to keep written medical records that justify the course of treatment of the patient, including patient history, examination results, test results, records of the use of prescribed drugs, and reports of consultations and hospitalizations;
14. Influencing a patient for financial gain;
15. Promoting or advertising a pharmacy on a prescription form unless the form states that the prescription may be filled at any pharmacy of the patient's choice;
16. Performing professional services not authorized by the patient or legal representative;
17. Prescribing or otherwise dispensing any drug other than in the course of professional practice;
18. Being unable to practice medicine with reasonable skill and safety because of illness, or the use of alcohol or drugs, or because of a mental or physical condition;

---

27. A plea of *nolo contendere* is used when the accused is unwilling to confess guilt but does not wish to go to trial; therefore he or she wants the court to impose sentence immediately. This plea is equal to a guilty plea. Vinton v. State, 515 So. 2d 711 (Fla. 1977).

19. Engaging in gross or repeated malpractice or failing to practice in accordance with professional standards;

20. Engaging in practices that are experimental in nature without full, written, and informed consent from the client;

21. Practicing or offering to practice beyond the scope of practice permitted by law or exceeding the physician's level of competence;

22. Delegating professional responsibilities to a person the physician knows or has reason to know is unqualified to assume them;

23. Violating any provisions of Florida's licensure laws or an order entered by the Board of Medicine or the DOH;

24. Conspiring with another person to coerce another licensee from lawfully advertising his or her services;

25. Being involved in the unlawful termination of a pregnancy;

26. Presigning blank prescription forms;

27. Prescribing or otherwise dispensing or administering any Schedule II amphetamine or Schedule II sympathomimetic amine drug, except for narcolepsy, hyperkinesis, appropriate behavioral syndromes in children, drug-induced brain dysfunction, the treatment of depression, or the clinical investigation of such drugs under appropriate protocols;

28. Failing to supervise adequately physicians' assistants, paramedics, emergency medical technicians, or nurse practitioners under the physician's supervision;

29. Prescribing or otherwise dispensing growth hormones or similar substances for the purpose of muscle building or enhancing athletic performance;

30. Prescribing or otherwise dispensing laetrile;

31. Referring any patient for health goods or services to an entity in which the physician's employer has an equity interest of 10% or more without full disclosure to the patient;

32. Misrepresenting or concealing a material fact during a licensure investigation or disciplinary process;

33. Interfering with an investigation;

34. Failing to report to the DOH any licensee whom the physician knows has violated grounds for disciplinary action;

35. Being found by a court to have provided expert opinion to a notice of claim in a malpractice case or response to a claim without reasonable investigation;

36. Failing to report to the Board of Medicine, in writing within 30 days, of action being taken by another jurisdiction against the physician's license;
37. Advertising oneself as a board-certified specialist when not qualified; and
38. Failing to provide patients with information about their rights.

(C)(2) Disciplinary Procedures

Disciplinary procedures are administered through the DOH by the Board of Medicine. Florida statutory and regulatory provisions provide a general outline of the procedures that the Board and the DOH are to follow in investigating a complaint and pursuing disciplinary action against a physician.

(C)(3) Investigatory Process

The DOH must investigate any signed, written complaint it receives that describes facts that would constitute a violation of the licensing and practice acts.[28] Anonymous, written complaints are investigated if the DOH concludes, after a preliminary inquiry, that the allegations in the complaint are true. The physician who is the subject of the complaint receives a copy of the complaint and has 20 days to respond in writing. Once the investigation is completed, a report containing the investigative findings and recommendations is submitted to a "probable cause" panel established by the Board, which determines by majority vote whether there is probable cause to believe that the complaint is true.[29] The panel is to reach a decision regarding probable cause within 30 days of its receipt of the final investigative report, though this period may be extended.[30]

In lieu of a finding of probable cause, the panel may issue a "letter of guidance" to the subject of the investigation.[31] In addition, in the case of violations that do not endanger the public health, safety, and welfare and that do not constitute a serious inability to practice the profession, the DOH, rather than pursuing a probable cause hearing, may provide the licensee with a notice of noncompliance for an initial offense or a minor violation. In such a case, the licensee has 15 days to take corrective action or the formal probable cause process will be initiated.[32]

---

28. 15 FLA. STAT. ANN. § 455.225 (West 2001).
29. 15 FLA. STAT. ANN. §§ 455.225(2) and 455.225(4) (West 2001).
30. 15 FLA. STAT. ANN. § 455.225(4) (West 2001).
31. Id.
32. 15 FLA. STAT. ANN. § 455.225(3) (West 2001).

(C)(4) Formal Hearing Process

If the panel finds that probable cause exists, a formal complaint may be initiated. The subject of the probable cause finding is entitled to a hearing "in all proceedings in which the substantial interests of a party" are at issue before the DOH and where there is a "disputed issue of material fact."[33] A party must request a hearing within 21 days of notice of the probable cause finding or the right to a hearing will be waived.[34] The hearing is conducted before a hearing officer from the state's Division of Administrative Hearings of the State Department of Management Services.

Hearings are conducted according to the same rules governing disciplinary proceedings involving other licensed professions. Notice of the hearing of not less than 14 days is to be provided the parties,[35] and the hearing officer may direct the parties to engage in a prehearing conference for the purpose of simplifying and clarifying issues, discussing settlement, examining documents, exchanging information regarding witnesses, resolving other procedural matters, and entering into a prehearing stipulation.[36] Discovery (the process by which parties to a lawsuit acquire information regarding the other party's case) according to the *Florida Rules of Civil Procedure* is available,[37] and the parties may subpoena witnesses.[38] At the hearing, all parties may present evidence, cross-examine witnesses, submit rebuttal evidence, submit proposed findings of facts and orders, file exceptions to any order or proposed order of the hearing officer, and be represented by counsel, if they so choose.[39] The hearing officer, within 30 days of the hearing or receipt of the hearing transcript (whichever is later) is to file a recommended order that is to include a caption (that is, the title of the case, which lists the parties to the case), time and place of the hearing, appearances entered by counsel or parties to the hearing, a statement of the issues, findings of fact and conclusions of law, and a recommendation for final agency action.[40] A party may file exceptions to the findings of fact and conclusions of law within 15 days of their entry, and each party within 10 days of service of the exceptions may file a response to those exceptions.[41] After this the DOH head may adopt, reject, or modify the hearing officer's conclusions of law or findings of

---

33. 7 FLA. STAT. ANN. § 120.569 (West Supp. 2002).
34. FLA. ADMIN. CODE ANN. r. 28-5.111 (2002).
35. FLA. ADMIN. CODE ANN. r. 28-106.208 (2002).
36. FLA. ADMIN. CODE ANN. r. 28-106.209 (2002).
37. FLA. ADMIN. CODE ANN. r. 28-106.206 (2002).
38. FLA. ADMIN. CODE ANN. r. 28-106.212 (2002).
39. 7 FLA. STAT. ANN. § 120.57(1)(b) (West Supp. 2002).
40. FLA. ADMIN. CODE ANN. r. 28-106.216 (2002).
41. FLA. ADMIN. CODE ANN. r. 28-106.217 (2002).

fact.[42] However, modification or rejection of the hearing officer's conclusions can occur only after a complete review of the record and a statement explaining particularly why the hearing officer's conclusions have been rejected and why the DOH's conclusions are more reasonable.[43] In addition, the penalty proposed may be reduced or increased only after review of the complete record and a statement with particularity as to why the penalty was changed.[44] Judicial review is available to a party adversely affected by a final agency action to the appellate district in which the DOH maintains its headquarters.[45]

(C)(5) Penalties for Violations

The Florida legislature has established a general range of penalties that the Board of Medicine may impose. These include[46]

1. Revoking or suspending a physician's license;
2. Refusing to certify to the DOH the applicant's application for licensure, certification, or registration;
3. Restricting the individual's license;
4. Imposing administrative fines not to exceed $10,000 for each offense;
5. Issuing a reprimand;
6. Placing the physician on probation under conditions specified by the Board; the Board may direct the physician to submit to treatment, take continuing education courses, submit to reexamination, or work under another physician's supervision;
7. Issuing a letter of concern to the physician;
8. Ordering a refund of fees billed to and collected from the patient;
9. Imposing an administrative fine for violation of patient rights;
10. Requiring remedial education; and
11. Taking other corrective action.

The Board has also adopted regulations that establish a schedule of penalties for the specific offenses set forth in the statute.[47] The Board is to create a range of penalties and is to distinguish between minor violations for those endangering public health, safety, or welfare and minor offenses. Mitigating and aggravating circumstances are to be considered as well.

---

42. 7 Fla. Stat. Ann. § 120.57(1)(l) (West Supp. 2002).
43. Id.
44. Id.
45. 7 Fla. Stat. Ann. § 120.68(2)(a) (West Supp. 2002).
46. 15 Fla. Stat. Ann. § 456.072(2) (West Supp. 2002).
47. 15 Fla. Stat. Ann. § 455.2273 (West 2001).

1.3
Licensure and Regulation of Psychiatric Nurses

There are no specific provisions in Florida regulating the practice of psychiatric nurses. A licensure statute establishes the framework for the licensure and regulation of registered nurses and licensed practical nurses. That statute is the basis of this chapter.

The DOH governs the licensure and practice of nurses. The DOH discharges its responsibilities through the Board of Nursing.[1] The Board's responsibilities include establishing the qualifications for nursing licensure, overseeing the conduct of nurses, and regulating the disciplinary process for nurses.

(A) Florida Board of Nursing

The Board has 13 members who are appointed by the governor and confirmed by the Senate.[2] Seven members of the Board must be registered nurses who are residents of Florida and have practiced professional nursing for at least four years, including at least one advanced registered nurse practitioner, one nurse educator, and one nurse executive.[3] Three additional members must be licensed practical nurses who are state residents and have been engaged in practice for at least four years before their appointment, and the last three members must be state residents who have never been licensed as nurses. No person may be appointed as a lay member who is in any way connected with, or has any

---
1. 15 FLA. STAT. ANN. § 464.004 (West 2001).
2. 15 FLA. STAT. ANN. § 464.004(1) (West 2001).
3. 15 FLA. STAT. ANN. § 464.004(2) (West 2001).

financial interest in, any health care facility, agency, or insurer.[4] At least one member of the board must be 60 years of age or older.[5]

(A)(1) Practice of Nursing Defined

The practice of *professional nursing* is defined[6] as

the performance of those acts requiring substantial specialized knowledge, judgment, and nursing skill based upon applied principles of psychological, biological, physical, and social sciences which shall include, but not be limited to

1. the observation, assessment, nursing diagnosis, planning, intervention, and evaluation of career health teaching and counseling of the ill, injured, or infirm; and the promotion of wellness, maintenance of health, and prevention of illness of others;
2. the administration of medications and treatments as prescribed or authorized by a duly licensed practitioner authorized by law to prescribe such medications and treatments;
3. the supervision and teaching of other personnel in the theory and performance of any of the above acts.

The practice of *practical nursing* is defined as "the performance of selected acts, including the administration of treatments and medications, in the care of the ill, injured, or infirm and the promotion of wellness, maintenance of health, and prevention of illness of others under the direction of a registered nurse, a licensed physician, a licensed osteopathic physician, a licensed podiatrist, or a licensed dentist."[7]

The practice of *advanced or specialized nursing* practice is defined as including, "in addition to the practice of professional nursing, the performance of advanced-level nursing acts approved by the Board which, by virtue of postbasic specialized education, training, and experience, are proper to be performed by an advanced registered nurse practitioner. . . . [T]he advanced registered nurse practitioner may perform acts of nursing diagnosis and nursing treatment or alterations of the health status . . . (as well as) acts of medical diagnosis and treatment, prescription, and operation which are identified, and approved by a joint committee" appointed by the Board of Nursing.[8]

---

4. *Id.*
5. *Id.*
6. 15 FLA. STAT. ANN. § 464.003(3)(a) (West 2001).
7. 15 FLA. STAT. ANN. § 464.003(3)(b) (West 2001).
8. 15 FLA. STAT. ANN. § 464.003(3)(c) (West 2001).

(B) Licensure

(B)(1) Licensure by Examination

An individual may become licensed by passing the nursing licensure examination. An applicant for licensure by examination must submit an application and pay a fee, undergo a statewide criminal records check, and be in good mental and physical health.[9] The applicant also must be a high school graduate and have completed the requirements of an approved program for the preparation of registered or licensed practical nurses. Finally, the applicant must have the ability to communicate in the English language.[10]

(B)(2) Licensure by Endorsement

An individual may be licensed by endorsement on receipt of the appropriate application and payment of the required fee if the individual has a valid license to practice in another state, assuming the state has requirements at least as stringent as those of Florida.[11] In addition, the person must meet the qualifications for licensure established by Florida law; must have successfully completed a state, regional, or national examination at least as stringent as the Florida nursing examination; and must not be under investigation in another state for an act that would violate the Florida licensure law.[12]

(B)(3) Licensure Renewal

Licenses are to be renewed on a biennial basis[13] with the provision that an inactive license cannot be renewed until payment of the applicable renewal fee.[14]

(B)(4) Certification of Advanced Registered Nurse Practitioners

To be certified as an advanced registered nurse practitioner, nurses are required to apply to the DOH, submit proof of licensure, and demonstrate that they meet at least one of the following criteria:[15]

1. Satisfactory completion of a formal postbasic educational program of at least one academic year, which has as its purpose the preparation of nurses far advanced or specialized practice;
2. Certification by an appropriate specialty board; or

---

9. 15 FLA. STAT. ANN. § 464.008(1)(a)–(c) (West 2001).
10. 15 FLA. STAT. ANN. § 464.008(1)(c)–(d) (West Supp. 2002).
11. 15 FLA. STAT. ANN. § 464.009(1)(a) (West Supp. 2002).
12. 15 FLA. STAT. ANN. §§ 464.009(1)(b) and 464.009(3) (West Supp. 2002).
13. 15 FLA. STAT. ANN. § 464.013 (West 2001).
14. 15 FLA. STAT. ANN. § 464.014 (West 2001).
15. 15 FLA. STAT. ANN. § 464.012(1)(a)–(c) (West 2001).

3. Graduation from a program leading to a master's degree in a nursing clinical specialty area with preparation in specialized practitioner skills.

In addition, the Board has authority to establish special requirements for the certification of advanced registered nurse practitioners in the categories of nurse anesthetists, nurse midwives, and nurse practitioners.[16]

(B)(5) Use of the Nursing Title

Only persons licensed to practice professional nursing may use the title of registered nurse and the abbreviation RN.[17] Only persons licensed to practice as licensed practical nurses may use the title of licensed practical nurse and the abbreviation LPN.[18] Only persons who are graduates of approved programs or their equivalent may use the term "graduate nurse" and the abbreviation "GN"[19] or the term "graduate practical nurse" and the abbreviation "GPN."[20] Only persons holding valid certificates to practice as advanced registered nurse practitioners may use the title "advanced registered nurse practitioner" and the abbreviation "ARNP."[21] It is a misdemeanor, punishable by up to one year of incarceration, to use the title of registered nurse or one of the other nursing titles if the person using the title does not have the applicable license or certification.[22]

(C) Regulation

(C)(1) Unlawful and Prohibited Practice

There are a number of acts or omissions that may lead to disciplinary action against a registered or licensed practical nurse. These include the following:

1. Procuring, attempting to procure, or renewing a license by bribery, misrepresentation, or through an error of the Boards;
2. Having a nursing license suspended or revoked by the licensing authority of another state, territory, or country;
3. Being found guilty of a crime directly related to the practice of nursing or the ability to practice nursing;[23]

---

16. 15 Fla. Stat. Ann. § 464.012(2) (West 2001).
17. 15 Fla. Stat. Ann. § 464.015 (West 2001).
18. 15 Fla. Stat. Ann. § 464.015(2) (West 2001).
19. 15 Fla. Stat. Ann. § 464.015(3) (West 2001).
20. 15 Fla. Stat. Ann. § 464.015(4) (West 2001).
21. 15 Fla. Stat. Ann. § 464.015(5) (West 2001).
22. 15 Fla. Stat. Ann. § 464.015(7) (West 2001).
23. 15 Fla. Stat. Ann. § 464.018(1)(c) (West Supp. 2002).

4. Being found guilty of offenses related to a forcible felony; theft, robbery, or related crime; fraudulent practice; lewdness and indecent exposure; assault, battery, and culpable negligence; child abuse; or abuse, neglect, or exploitation of another individual;[24] and

5. Having been judicially determined to have committed child abuse or neglect or an act of domestic violence.[25]

The statute also makes the following conduct subject to disciplinary action:

1. Making or filing a false report or record known to be false by the licensee, or intentionally or negligently failing to file a report or record required by state or federal law;

2. Practicing false, misleading, or deceptive advertising;

3. Engaging in unprofessional conduct, defined as deviating from the minimal standards of acceptable and prevailing nursing practice;

4. Using controlled substances illegally;

5. Being unable because of illness or alcohol or substance abuse to practice nursing;

6. Failing to report to the DOH a person the licensee knows to be in violation of the nursing statute;

7. Violating any provision of the nursing statute or an order or rule issued by the DOH or the Board of Nursing;[26] and

8. Failing to report to the DOH any physician whom the nurse knows has violated the rules governing the conduct of physicians, including osteopaths.[27]

The statute also prohibits *sexual misconduct*, defined as a situation in which a nurse uses the professional relationship to induce or attempt to induce the patient to engage in sexual activity outside the scope of practice or the scope of generally accepted examination or treatment of the patient.[28]

In addition, certain conduct is defined as a third degree felony, punishable through disciplinary action as well as criminal prosecution. This includes[29] practicing nursing without an active license or certificate; using or attempting to use a suspended or revoked license or certificate; knowingly employing unlicensed persons in nursing positions; and obtaining or attempting to obtain a

---

24. 15 FLA. STAT. ANN. § 464.018(1)(d) (West Supp. 2002).
25. 15 FLA. STAT. ANN. § 464.018(1)(e) (West Supp. 2002).
26. 15 FLA. STAT. ANN. § 464.018(1)(f)–(l) (West Supp. 2002).
27. 15 FLA. STAT. ANN. § 464.018(1)(m) (West Supp. 2002).
28. 15 FLA. STAT. ANN. § 464.017 (West 2001).
29. 15 FLA. STAT. ANN. § 464.016(1)(a)–(d) (West 2001).

license or certificate by misleading statements or knowing misrepresentation.

Finally, the regulations of the Board of Nursing define *additional conduct* as subject to disciplinary proceedings, including[30]

1. Inaccurate recording, falsifying or altering of patient records, nursing progress records, or employment or time records;
2. Administering medications or treatments in a negligent manner;
3. Misappropriating supplies, equipment, or drugs;
4. Leaving an assignment before properly advising appropriate personnel;
5. Violating confidentiality;
6. Discriminating on the basis of race, creed, religion, sex, age, or national origin in rendering nursing services;
7. Engaging in fraud or misrepresentation in taking the licensing examination;
8. Aiding and abetting the practice of nursing by an unlicensed person;
9. Practicing without a current license;
10. Impersonating an applicant for a license or certificate;
11. Engaging in acts of negligence and gross negligence, either by omission or commission;
12. Failing to conform to minimal standards of acceptable prevailing nursing practice, regardless of whether a patient was injured;
13. Exploiting a patient for financial gain;
14. Practicing beyond the scope of a license, education, or experience;
15. Falsely reporting compliance with continuing education requirements;
16. Testing positive for a drug screen without a prescription or legitimate medical use for the drug in question;
17. Violating a Board order entered in a licensure proceeding; and
18. Providing false or incorrect information to an employer regarding the status of a license.

(C)(2) Disciplinary Procedures

Disciplinary procedures are administered through the DOH by the Board of Nursing. Florida statutory provisions provide a general

---

30. FLA. ADMIN. CODE r. 64B9-8.005 (2002).

outline of the procedures that the Board and the DOH are to follow in investigating a complaint and pursuing disciplinary action against a nurse.

(C)(3) Investigatory Process

The DOH must investigate any signed, written complaint it receives that describes facts that would constitute a violation of the licensing and practice acts.[31] Anonymous, written complaints are investigated if the DOH concludes, after a preliminary inquiry, that the allegations in the complaint are true. The nurse who is the subject of the complaint receives a copy of the complaint and has 20 days to respond in writing. Once the investigation is completed, a report containing the investigative findings and recommendations is submitted to a "probable cause" panel established by the Board, which determines by majority vote whether there is probable cause to believe that the complaint is true.[32] The panel is to reach a decision regarding probable cause within 30 days of its receipt of the final investigative report, though this period may be extended.[33]

In lieu of a finding of probable cause, the panel may issue a "letter of guidance" to the subject of the investigation.[34] In addition, in the case of violations that do not endanger the public health, safety, and welfare, and that do not constitute a serious inability to practice the profession, the DOH, rather than pursuing a probable cause hearing, may provide the licensee with a notice of noncompliance for an initial offense or a minor violation. In such a case, the licensee has 15 days to take corrective action or the formal probable cause process will be initiated.[35]

(C)(4) Formal Hearing Process

If the panel finds that probable cause exists, a formal complaint may be initiated. The subject of the probable cause finding is entitled to a hearing "in all proceedings in which the substantial interests of a party" are at issue before the DOH and where there is a "disputed issue of material fact."[36] A party must request a hearing within 21 days of notice of the probable cause finding or the right to a hearing will be waived.[37] The hearing is conducted before a hearing officer from the state's Division of Administrative Hearings of the State Department of Management Services.

---

31. 15 FLA. STAT. ANN. § 455.225 (West 2001).
32. 15 FLA. STAT. ANN. §§ 455.225(2) and 455.225(4) (West 2001).
33. 15 FLA. STAT. ANN. § 455.225(4) (West 2001).
34. Id.
35. 15 FLA. STAT. ANN. § 455.225(3) (West 2001).
36. 7 FLA. STAT. ANN. § 120.569 (West Supp. 2002).
37. FLA. ADMIN. CODE ANN. r. 28-5.111 (2002).

Hearings are conducted according to the same rules governing disciplinary proceedings involving other licensed professions. Notice of the hearing of not less than 14 days is to be provided the parties,[38] and the hearing officer may direct the parties to engage in a prehearing conference for the purpose of simplifying and clarifying issues, discussing settlement, examining documents, exchanging information regarding witnesses, resolving other procedural matters, and entering into a prehearing stipulation.[39] Discovery (the process by which parties to a lawsuit gain information regarding the other party's case) according to the *Florida Rules of Civil Procedure* is available[40] and the parties may subpoena witnesses.[41] At the hearing, all parties may present evidence, cross-examine witnesses, submit rebuttal evidence, submit proposed findings of facts and orders, file exceptions to any order or proposed order of the hearing officer, and can be represented by counsel.[42] The hearing officer, within 30 days of the hearing or receipt of the hearing transcript (whichever is later) is to file a recommended order that is to include a caption (the title of the case, including the names of the parties), time and place of the hearing, appearances entered by counsel or parties to the hearing, a statement of the issues, findings of fact and conclusions of law, and a recommendation for final action.[43] A party may file exceptions to the findings of fact and conclusions of law within 15 days of their entry, and each party within 10 days of service of the exceptions may file a response to those exceptions.[44] After this DOH may adopt, reject, or modify the hearing officer's conclusions of law or findings of fact.[45] However, modification or rejection of the hearing officer's conclusions can occur only after a complete review of the record and a statement stating particularly why the hearing officer's conclusions have been rejected and why the agency's conclusions are more reasonable.[46] In addition, the penalty proposed may be reduced or increased only after review of the complete record and a statement with particularity as to why the penalty was changed.[47] Judicial review is available to a party adversely affected by final DOH action to the appellate district in which the agency maintains its headquarters.[48]

---

38. FLA. ADMIN. CODE ANN. r. 28-106.208 (2002).
39. FLA. ADMIN. CODE ANN. r. 28-106.209 (2002).
40. FLA. ADMIN. CODE ANN. r. 28-106.206 (2002).
41. FLA. ADMIN. CODE ANN. r. 28-106.212 (2002).
42. 7 FLA. STAT. ANN. § 120.57(1)(b) (West 2001).
43. FLA. ADMIN. CODE ANN. r. 28-106.216 (2002).
44. FLA. ADMIN. CODE ANN. r. 28-106.217 (2002).
45. 7 FLA. STAT. ANN. § 120.57(1)(l) (West 2001).
46. *Id.*
47. *Id.*
48. 7 FLA. STAT. ANN. § 120.68(2)(a) (West Supp. 2002).

(C)(5) Penalties for Violations

If the Board of Nursing finds any party guilty of the conduct noted earlier, it may choose from a range of penalties, including the following:[49]

1. Revoking or suspending a nurse's license;
2. Refusing to certify to the DOH the applicant's application for licensure, certification, or registration;
3. Restricting the individual's license;
4. Imposing administrative fines not to exceed $10,000 for each offense;
5. Issuing a reprimand;
6. Placing the nurse on probation under conditions specified by the Board; the Board may direct the nurse to submit to treatment, take continuing education courses, submit to reexamination, or work under another nurse's supervision;
7. Issuing a letter of concern to the nurse;
8. Ordering a refund of fees billed to and collected from the patient;
9. Imposing an administrative fine for violation of patient rights;
10. Requiring remedial education; and
11. Other corrective action.

In addition, the Board, in regulation, has created a schedule of penalties for various offenses—for example, unlicensed practice is subject to penalties ranging from a reprimand to denial of license, and conviction of a felony for controlled substances is subject to emergency suspension. The Board's regulations also make clear that it can use a variety of other techniques to ensure public safety, including probation with a specified remedial education program; personal appearances before the Board to monitor compliance; and a variety of other steps.[50]

---

49. 15 FLA. STAT. ANN. § 456.072(2) (West Supp. 2002).
50. FLA. ADMIN. CODE ANN. r. 64B9-8.006 (2002).

1.4
Licensure and Regulation of Psychologists

The DOH governs the licensure and practice of psychologists in Florida. The DOH discharges its responsibilities through the Florida Board of Psychology.[1] The Board's responsibilities include establishing qualifications for psychologist licensure, overseeing the conduct of psychologists, and regulating the disciplinary process for psychologists.

(A) Florida Board of Psychology

The Board has seven members appointed by the governor and confirmed by the state Senate.[2] Five members of the Board must be licensed psychologists who are in good standing, and the other two must be Florida citizens who have no connection to the practice of psychology. At least one member of the board must be 60 years of age or older.[3]

(A)(1) Practice of Psychology Defined

The practice of *psychology* is defined as "observations, description, evaluation, interpretation, and modification of human behavior, by the use of scientific and applied psychological principles, methods, and procedures, for the purpose of describing, preventing, alleviating, or eliminating symptomatic, maladaptive, or undesired behavior and of enhancing interpersonal behavioral health and mental or psychological health."[4]

---

1. 15 FLA. STAT. ANN. § 490.004 (West 2001).
2. 15 FLA. STAT. ANN. § 490.004(1) (West 2001).
3. 15 FLA. STAT. ANN. § 490.004(2) (West 2001).
4. 15 FLA. STAT. ANN. § 490.003(4) (West 2001).

The statute notes a number of types of interventions that are representative of "the ethical practice of psychology," including psychological testing and assessment of intelligence, personality, abilities, interests, aptitudes, and neuropsychological functioning; counseling; psychoanalysis; psychotherapy; sex therapy; hypnosis; biofeedback; behavioral analysis; psychoeducational evaluation and treatment; and the use of psychological methods to diagnose and treat mental, emotional, marital, and substance abuse disorders.[5]

(B) Licensure

(B)(1) Licensure by Examination

A person who wishes to be licensed as a psychologist must apply and pay an application fee. The applicant will be licensed by the DOH on certification by the Board of Psychology that the applicant[6]

1. Received doctoral level psychological education[7] as indicated by
   (a) A doctoral degree (i.e., PhD, PsyD, or EdD) from an educational institution that, at the time the applicant was enrolled and graduated, had institutional accreditation from an agency recognized and approved by the U.S. Department of Education or was recognized as a member in good standing with the Association of Universities and Colleges of Canada, and a psychology program within the educational institution that, at the time the applicant was enrolled and graduated, had programmatic accreditation from an agency recognized and approached by the U.S. Department of Education;[8]
   (b) The equivalent of a doctoral-level psychological education, as in defined earlier, from a program of a school or university located outside the United States and Canada, which was officially recognized by the government of the country in which it is located as an institution or program to train students to practice professional psychology;[9]
   (c) Certification (before July 1, 1999) of an augmented doctoral-level psychological education from the program

---

5. 15 FLA. STAT. ANN. § 490.003(4) (West 2001).
6. 15 FLA. STAT. ANN. § 490.005 (West 2001).
7. *Also see* FLA. ADMIN. CODE 64B19-11.0035 (2000) for a discussion of substantive criteria to evaluate doctoral training programs.
8. 15 FLA. STAT. ANN. § 490.003(3)(b)(1) (West 2001).
9. 15 FLA. STAT. ANN. § 490.003(3)(b)(2) (West 2001).

director of a doctoral-level psychology program accredited by a programmatic agency recognized and approved by the U.S. Department of Education;[10] or

(d) Certification (before August 31, 2001) of completion of a doctoral-level program that at the time the applicant was training was comparable to the standard of training or programs accredited by a programmatic agency recognized and approved by the U.S. Department of Education.

2. Completed at least two years or 4,000 hours of experience in the field of psychology in association with or under the supervision of a licensed psychologist meeting experience requirements of the psychology licensure act or the equivalent as determined by the Board of Psychology;[11]

3. Completed the application form and paid appropriate fees; and

4. Passed the national (Examination for Professional Practice in Psychology) and state examinations for licensure.[12]

(B)(2) Licensure by Endorsement

An individual may be licensed after paying appropriate fees, passing the portions of the licensure examination on state laws and rules governing practice, and on proving to the Board that he or she[13]

1. Has a valid psychology license or certificate from another state with standards comparable to or more stringent than those of Florida;

2. Is a diplomate in good standing with the American Board of Professional Psychology; or

3. Possesses a doctoral degree in psychology and has at least 20 years of experience as a licensed psychologist in any jurisdiction or territory of the United States within 25 years preceding the date of licensure application.

The Board of Psychology will not issue a license by endorsement to any applicant who is under investigation in Florida or another jurisdiction for an act that would constitute a violation of the psychology practice act.[14]

---

10. 15 FLA. STAT. ANN. § 490.003(3)(b)(3) (West 2001).
11. *Also see* FLA. ADMIN. CODE 64B19-11.005 (2002) for additional discussion of supervisory requirements.
12. FLA. ADMIN. CODE 64B19-11.001 (2002).
13. 15 FLA. STAT. ANN. § 490.006 (West 2001).
14. 15 FLA. STAT. ANN. § 490.003 (West 2001).

(B)(3) Provisional Licensure

The DOH will issue a provisional psychology license to each applicant the Board of Psychology certifies has completed the application form and paid the application fee and earned a doctoral degree in psychology. The provisional licensee must work under the supervision of a licensed psychologist until licensed as a psychologist. A provisional license expires 24 months after the date it is issued and it may not be renewed or reissued.[15]

(B)(4) Inactive Licenses

A licensee with an active license may apply to the DOH for inactive licensure.[16] The licensee can reactivate the license and place the license on active status by making application, paying requisite fees, and verifying that he or she has completed 40 hours of approved continuing education for each biennium or part thereof of inactive licensure.[17]

(B)(5) Licensure Renewal and Completion of Continuing Education

Licenses are renewed on a biennial basis at a fee not to exceed $500.[18] At the time of renewal the licensee must sign a statement certifying that he or she has completed 40 hours of approved continuing education that was required during the preceding two years.[19] Three of these hours must be focused on professional ethics and legal issues, two of these hours must be devoted to "medical errors," and one hour must be devoted to domestic violence or end-of-life and palliative health care.[20]

(B)(6) Exemptions From Licensure

Certain individuals do not have to obtain licensure to practice as psychologists[21] as long as they are not held out to the public as a psychologist.[22] These persons include

1. Salaried employees of a variety of organizations, including governmental agencies; mental health, substance abuse, alcohol, and developmental disability programs licensed by the state; licensed day care centers; domestic violence centers; academic and research institutes;

2. Salaried employees of private, nonprofit counseling agencies;

---

15. 15 FLA. STAT. ANN. § 490.0051 (West 2001).
16. FLA. ADMIN. CODE 64B19-15.001 (2002).
17. FLA. ADMIN. CODE 64B19-15.003 (2002).
18. 15 FLA. STAT. ANN. § 490.007(1) (West 2001).
19. FLA. ADMIN. CODE 64B19-13.001 (2002).
20. FLA. ADMIN. CODE 64B19-13.003(3) (2002).
21. 15 FLA. STAT. ANN. § 490.014(2) (West 2001).
22. 2001 Fla. Laws ch. 277, § 125-126.

3. Students providing services in a training setting with certain supervisory restrictions;

4. An individual certified in school psychology; or

5. A nonresident who is licensed as a psychologist in another state, province, or country and who provides services in Florida no more than 5 days in a month or 15 days in a calendar year.

(B)(7) Use of the Psychologist Title

An individual who is not licensed as a psychologist is prohibited from using the title of psychologist; it is a misdemeanor in the first degree, punishable up to a year in jail, for violation.[23]

(C) Regulation

(C)(1) Unlawful and Prohibited Practices

There are a number of actions and omissions that may subject a psychologist to disciplinary action. These include[24]

1. Procuring, attempting to procure, or renewing a license by bribery, misrepresentation, or through an error of the Board of Psychology or the DOH;

2. Having a license suspended or revoked or otherwise acted against by the licensing authority of another state, territory, or country;

3. Being found guilty of a crime directly related to the practice of psychology or the ability to practice psychology;

4. Engaging in false, deceptive, or misleading advertising;

5. Advertising, practicing, or attempting to practice under an assumed name;

6. Maintaining a professional association with an individual known to be in violation of the provisions governing psychologists;

7. Knowingly aiding or otherwise assisting a nonlicensed person to falsely represent him- or herself as licensed as a psychologist;

8. Failing to perform any statutory or legal obligation imposed on a psychologist by Florida law;

---

23. 15 FLA. STAT. ANN. § 490.012(1)(a) (West 2001).
24. 15 FLA. STAT. ANN. § 490.009(2)(a)–(w) (West 2001).

9. Willfully making a false report or record, failing to file a report or record required by law, obstructing the filing of a report or record, or inducing another to make a false report or record;

10. Paying a kickback or other type of remuneration for referrals of patients or clients or otherwise seeking payment from other sources when payment is already being provided, entering into a reciprocal referral agreement;

11. Engaging in conduct that would constitute sexual battery or sexual misconduct (see chapter 3.12, Criminal Liability);

12. Making misleading or fraudulent representations in the course of practice;

13. Soliciting patients personally or by an agent through fraud or other forms of coercion;

14. Failing to make available on request to a patient or client reports prepared and paid for by the patient or client;

15. Failing to respond within 30 days to a written communication from the DOH regarding a departmental investigation, failing to make available any relevant records with respect to an investigation about the licensee's conduct or background;

16. Being unable because of physical or mental disability or alcohol or substance abuse to practice the profession (see also chapter 5.1, Mental Status of Licensed or Certified Professionals);

17. Violating statutory provisions applicable to the practice of psychology;

18. Performing or prescribing any experimental treatment or therapy without meeting informed consent requirements;

19. Failing to meet minimal professional standards, including practicing beyond the scope of one's competence;

20. Delegating professional responsibilities to an unqualified person;

21. Violating a rule regulating the profession or violating a lawful order that was entered in a previous disciplinary proceeding;

22. Failing to maintain confidences of a client or patient except as provided and allowed by law; and

23. Disclosing through public statements material that identifies or damages research participants or clients.

(C)(2) Formal Hearing Process

Hearings are conducted according to the same rules governing disciplinary proceedings involving other licensed professions.

Notice of the hearing of not less than 14 days is to be provided the parties,[25] and the hearing officer may direct the parties to engage in a prehearing conference for the purpose of simplifying and clarifying issues, discussing settlement, examining documents, exchanging information regarding witnesses, resolving other procedural matters, and entering into a prehearing stipulation.[26] Discovery (the process by which parties to a lawsuit gain information regarding the other party's case) according to the *Florida Rules of Civil Procedure* is available[27] and the parties may subpoena witnesses.[28] At the hearing, all parties may present evidence, cross-examine witnesses, submit rebuttal evidence, submit proposed findings of facts and orders, file exceptions to any order or proposed order of the hearing officer, and may be represented by counsel.[29] The hearing officer, within 30 days of the hearing or receipt of the hearing transcript (whichever is later) is to file a recommended order that is to include a caption (the title of the case, including the names of the parties), time and place of the hearing, appearances entered by counsel or parties to the hearing, a statement of the issues, findings of fact and conclusions of law, and a recommendation for final agency action.[30] A party may file exceptions to the findings of fact and conclusions of law within 15 days of their entry, and each party within 10 days of service of the exceptions may file a response to those exceptions.[31] After this the Board may adopt, reject, or modify the hearing officer's conclusions of law or findings of fact.[32] However, modification or rejection of the hearing officer's conclusions can occur only after a complete review of the record and a statement stating particularly why the hearing officer's conclusions have been rejected and why the DOH's conclusions are more reasonable.[33] In addition, the penalty proposed may be reduced or increased only after review of the complete record and a statement with particularity as to why the penalty was changed.[34] Judicial review is available to a party adversely affected by a final agency action to the appellate district in which the DOH agency maintains its headquarters.[35]

---

25. FLA. ADMIN. CODE ANN. r. 28-106.208 (2002).
26. FLA. ADMIN. CODE ANN. r. 28-106.209 (2002).
27. FLA. ADMIN. CODE ANN. r. 28-106.206 (2002).
28. FLA. ADMIN. CODE ANN. r. 28-106.212 (2002).
29. 7 FLA. STAT. ANN. § 120.569(1) (West Supp. 2002).
30. FLA. ADMIN. CODE ANN. r. 28-106.216 (2000).
31. FLA. ADMIN. CODE ANN. r. 28-106.217 (2000).
32. 7 FLA. STAT. ANN. § 120.57(1)(l) (West 2001).
33. *Id.*
34. *Id.*
35. 7 FLA. STAT. ANN. § 120.68(2)(a) (West Supp. 2002).

(C)(3) Penalties for Violations

If the Board finds a violation of the standards and rules governing the practice of psychology as set forth previously, it may impose a variety of penalties. The range of possible penalties includes[36]

1. Revoking or suspending a psychologist's license;
2. Refusing to certify to the DOH the applicant's application for licensure, certification, or registration;
3. Restricting the individual's license;
4. Imposing administrative fines not to exceed $10,000 for each offense;
5. Issuing a reprimand;
6. Placing the psychologist on probation under conditions specified by the Board; the Board may direct the psychologist to submit to treatment, take continuing education courses, submit to reexamination, or work under another psychologist's supervision;
7. Issuing a letter of concern to the psychologist;
8. Ordering a refund of fees billed to and collected from the patient;
9. Imposing an administrative fine for violation of patient rights;
10. Requiring remedial education; and
11. Taking other corrective action.

(D) Regulation

The Board of Psychology has also promulgated specific rules regarding select areas of psychological practice, as summarized next.

(D)(1) Provision of Sex Therapy and Sex Offender Therapy

Before holding oneself out as a sex therapist a psychologist must receive training on the provision of psychological health services and completed a minimum of 150 hours of continuing education in sex therapy and in the interactions between sex therapy and the general provision of psychological health services.[37]

With some exceptions, an individual representing oneself as a juvenile sex offender therapist must be a licensed psychologist. Juvenile sex offender therapists must have education, training,

---

36. 15 FLA. STAT. ANN. § 456.072(2) (West Supp. 2002).
37. FLA. ADMIN. CODE ANN. 64B19-18.002 (2002); 15 FLA. STAT. ANN. § 490.0143 (West 2001).

and experience that demonstrates competency and interest in this area of practice. The training of juvenile sex offender therapists must include at least nine hours of coursework with child behavior and development and in child psychopathology, integrated with juvenile assessment, diagnosis, and treatment.[38]

(D)(2) Practice of Hypnosis

A licensed psychologist is permitted to practice hypnosis for purposes of stress management, self-hypnosis, guided imagery, or relaxation provided that the psychologist has completed a minimum of 10 hours of continuing education in hypnosis.[39]

(D)(3) Use of Test Instruments

Psychologists who use test instruments must[40]

1. Consider whether research supports the underlying presumption that governs the interpretive statements that would be made by the test instrument (sic);
2. Be able to justify use of any particular test instrument for the particular client who completes the test;
3. Integrate and reconcile the interpretive statements made by the test instrument (sic) based on group norms, with the psychologist's independent professional knowledge, evaluation, and assessment of the individual who takes the test; and
4. Specify in the test report the name of each person who assisted the psychologist in administering the test and the role that person played in test administration.

(D)(4) Child Custody Matters

Psychologists who have treated a minor or any of the adults involved in a custody or visitation dispute are barred from performing a forensic evaluation for purposes of determining custody, residence, or visitation of the minor. This does not limit a treating psychologist from providing the court or a custody evaluator with information about the parties, providing that confidentiality is not violated.[41]

When conducting an evaluation for purposes of custody, residence, or visitation of a minor, the psychologist must, at a minimum, communicate with the parties seeking custody of the minor

---

38. FLA. ADMIN. CODE ANN. 64B19-18.0025 (2002); 15 FLA. STAT. ANN. § 490.0145 (West 2001).
39. FLA. ADMIN. CODE ANN. 64B19-18.003 (2002); 15 FLA. STAT. ANN. § 490.0141 (West 2001).
40. FLA. ADMIN. CODE ANN. 64B19-18.004(2) (2002).
41. FLA. ADMIN. CODE ANN. 64B19-18.006 (2002).

or their legal representatives and with the mental health professionals and primary medical physician, if any, who are treating the minor, unless excused from doing so by court order. If a party fails to participate in the evaluation process, the psychologist must advise the court.[42] To perform a psychological evaluation of a minor for the purpose of making a forensic recommendation regarding custody, visitation, or residence the psychologist must have training in child development, child psychopathology, family dynamics, and legal issues and guidelines regarding child custody.[43]

---

42. FLA. ADMIN. CODE ANN. 64B19-18.007(1) (2002).
43. FLA. ADMIN. CODE ANN. 64B19-18.007(2) (2002).

1.5
Subdoctoral and Unlicensed Psychologists

Florida law, in contrast to that of some other states, does not recognize a category of subdoctoral and unlicensed psychologists.

(A) Psychologists Exempted From Licensure

The use of the term "psychologist" or "psychological" in describing one's occupation is restricted to individuals licensed as psychologists.[1] As described in chapter 1.4 (Licensure and Regulation of Psychologists), however, certain individuals do not have to obtain licensure[2] as long as they are not held out to the public as psychologists.[3] These persons include

1. Salaried employees of a variety of organizations, including governmental agencies; mental health, substance abuse, alcohol, and developmental disability programs licensed by the state; licensed day care centers; domestic violence centers; and academic and research institutes;

2. Salaried employees of private, nonprofit counseling agencies;

3. Students providing services in a training setting with certain supervisory restrictions;

4. An individual certified in school psychology; and

---

1. 15 FLA. STAT. ANN. § 490.012(1)(a) (West Supp. 2002).
2. 15 FLA. STAT. ANN. § 490.014(2) (West Supp. 2002).
3. 2001 Fla. Laws ch. 277, § 125-126.

5. A nonresident who is licensed as a psychologist in another state, province, or country and who provides services in Florida no more than 5 days in a month or 15 days in a calendar year;

However, in all of these cases, the individual who is not licensed as a psychologist is prohibited from using the title "psychologist."

(B) Rights and Responsibilities of Subdoctoral and Unlicensed Psychologists

Those exempt from licensure have two primary obligations. The first is to not hold themselves out as psychologists. The second is to ensure that they are performing only those duties for which they were trained and hired solely within the confines of the agency, facility, or institution employing them.[4] There are no cases further discussing any duties or limitations on those who are unlicensed—the primary limitation is that they confine their work to that done for the entity for which they are employed.

---

4. 15 FLA. STAT. ANN. § 490.014(2)(a)–(e) (West Supp. 2002).

1.6

Licensure and Regulation of Social Workers

The DOH governs the licensure and practice of social work in Florida.[1] The DOH discharges its responsibilities through the Board of Clinical Social Work, Marriage and Family Therapy, and Mental Health Counseling.[2]

(A) Florida Board of Clinical Social Work, Marriage and Family Therapy, and Mental Health Counseling

The Board has nine members who are appointed by the governor and confirmed by the state Senate. Six members of the Board must be licensed professionals (two licensed practicing clinical social workers, two licensed practicing marriage and family therapists, and two licensed practicing mental health counselors). Three members are to be Florida citizens who are not and have never been licensed in a mental health-related profession and who are in no way connected with the practice of any such profession.[3]

(A)(1) Practice of Social Work Defined

The practice of *clinical social work* is defined[4] as the use of scientific and applied knowledge, theories, and methods for the purpose

---

1. 15 FLA. STAT. ANN. § 491.003 (West 2001).
2. 15 FLA. STAT. ANN. § 491.004(1) (West 2001).
3. 15 FLA. STAT. ANN. § 491.004 (West 2001).
4. 15 FLA. STAT. ANN. § 491.003(7) (West 2001).

of describing, preventing, evaluating, and treating individual, couple, marital, family, or group behavior based on the person-in-situation perspective of psychosocial development, normal and abnormal behavior, psychopathology, unconscious motivation, interpersonal relationships, environmental stress, differential assessment, differential planning, and data gathering.

Social work practice includes the use of methods of a psychological nature to evaluate, assess, diagnose, treat, and prevent emotional and mental disorders and dysfunctions, whether cognitive, affective, or behavioral; sexual dysfunction; behavioral disorders; alcoholism; and substance abuse. Clinical social work treatments include but are not limited to psychotherapy; hypnotherapy; and sex therapy; as well as counseling; behavior modification; consultation; client-centered advocacy; crisis intervention; and providing needed information and education to clients. The practice of social work may also include clinical research into more effective psychotherapeutic modalities for treatment and prevention.[5]

The statute specifies that the terms *diagnose* and *treat,* as used in the clinical social work, marriage and family therapy, and mental health counseling statute, do not include admitting individuals to hospitals, treating persons in hospitals without medical supervision, prescribing medications, or authorizing clinical laboratory procedures, radiological procedures, or electroconvulsive therapy. The definition is also not to be construed to permit a licensed social worker to label a test or report or procedure as "psychological."[6]

(B) Licensure

(B)(1) Licensure by Examination

A license may be issued to an applicant who pays the appropriate fee and who[7]

1. Has received a doctorate or master's degree in social work from an accredited graduate school, from which the graduate program must have emphasized direct clinical patient or client health care services, and also included a supervised field placement, 24 semester hours or 32 quarter hours in theory of human behavior and practice methods;

2. Has had at least two years of clinical social work experience, subsequent to completing the graduate degree;

---

5. 15 FLA. STET. ANN. § 491.003(7) (West 2001).
6. 15 FLA. STAT. ANN. § 491.003(7)(c) (West 2001).
7. 15 FLA. STAT. ANN. § 491.005(1) (West 2001).

3. Has passed the licensing examination; and

4. Has demonstrated knowledge of the laws and rules governing the practice of clinical social work, marriage and family therapy, and mental health counseling.

In addition, to obtain licensure an applicant making an initial application must demonstrate completion of an educational course acceptable to the Board on human immunodeficiency virus and acquired immune deficiency syndrome.[8]

(B)(2) Licensure by Endorsement

A license may be granted to an applicant with an active valid license from another state who has actively practiced for at least three of the previous five years. The applicant must also meet the Florida education and experience requirements and have passed an equivalent licensure examination in another state. The applicant must also not be under investigation for an act that would violate Florida licensure laws.[9]

(B)(3) Licensure Renewal

Renewal of licenses is on a biennial basis, and by statute, the fee for renewal may not exceed $250.[10]

(B)(4) Exemptions From Licensure

Certain individuals do not have to obtain licensure to practice as a social worker. These include[11]

1. Salaried employees of a variety of organizations, including governmental agencies; mental health, substance abuse, alcohol, and developmental disability programs licensed by the state; licensed day care centers; domestic violence centers; academic and research institutes;

2. Salaried employees of private, nonprofit counseling agencies providing services to children, youth, and families, if the services are provided for no charge and the person is trained to render the services provided;

3. Students providing services in a training setting with certain supervisory restrictions; and

4. A nonresident who provides services no more than 15 days in a calendar year.

---

8. 15 Fla. Stat. Ann. § 491.0065 (West 2001).
9. 15 Fla. Stat. Ann. § 491.006 (West 2001).
10. 15 Fla. Stat. Ann. § 491.007 (West 2001).
11. 15 Fla. Stat. Ann. § 491.014(4) (West 2001).

However, individuals falling into one of the exempt categories may not use the title of "social worker" in describing themselves.[12]

(B)(5) Certified Master Social Worker

An applicant may be certified by the DOH as a master social worker on[13]

1. Completing an application and payment of the fee;
2. Submitting proof that the applicant has a doctoral degree in social work or a masters degree with a major emphasis or specialty in clinical practice or administration;
3. Having at least three years of experience including but not limited to clinical services or administrative activities, two years of which must be at the postmaster's level under the supervision of a person meeting the requirements of a certified master social worker; and
4. Passing the relevant examination that is a written theory examination that includes content on human development and behavior; effects of culture, race, ethnicity, sexual orientation, and gender; assessment and diagnosis in social work practice; social work practice with individuals, families, and groups; interpersonal communications; professional social worker/client relationships; professional values and ethics; supervision in social work; practice evaluation and the use of research; policies and procedures governing service delivery; and social work administration.[14]

(B)(6) Use of the Social Worker Title

An individual who is not licensed as a social worker may not use the titles "licensed clinical social worker," "clinical social worker," "licensed social worker," "psychiatric social worker," or "psychosocial worker."[15] Violation of this prohibition is a first-degree misdemeanor punishable by up to one year of incarceration.[16]

(C) Regulation

(C)(1) Unlawful and Prohibited Practices

There are a number of actions that may subject a social worker to disciplinary action. These include[17]

---

12. 15 FLA. STAT. ANN. § 491.012(1)(a) (West Supp. 2002).
13. 15 FLA. STAT. ANN. § 491.0145 (West 2001).
14. FLA. ADMIN. CODE r. 64B25-28.015 (2002).
15. 15 FLA. STAT. ANN. § 491.012(1)(a) (West Supp. 2002).
16. 15 FLA, STAT. ANN. § 490.012(3) (West Supp. 2002).
17. 15 FLA. STAT. ANN. § 491.009(1)(a)–(w) (West Supp. 2002).

1. Obtaining or attempting to obtain a license by fraud or bribery;
2. Having a license revoked or otherwise acted on by another state;
3. Being convicted of a crime directly related to the practice of the profession or ability to practice the profession;
4. Using false, deceptive, or misleading advertising;
5. Advertising under an assumed name;
6. Maintaining a professional association with an individual who is known or should be known to have violated statutory provisions governing practice;
7. Aiding a nonlicensed, nonregistered, or noncertified person falsely representing him- or herself as licensed or certified;
8. Failing to perform statutory or legal obligations placed on a licensed social worker;
9. Making a false report;
10. Paying a kickback or other form of remuneration to obtain a client;
11. Engaging in conduct that would constitute sexual battery or sexual misconduct;
12. Making misleading, deceptive, untrue, or fraudulent representations in the course of practice;
13. Soliciting patients or clients personally, or through an agent, through fraud, intimidation, undue influence, or other forms of overreaching;
14. Failing to make available to a patient or client, on written request, tests or other reports prepared and paid for by the client or patient;
15. Failing to respond within 30 days to a complaint or request for information from the Board or the DOH;
16. Violating statutory provisions applicable to the practice of social work;
17. Being an impaired professional because of the use of alcohol, drugs, or other substances (see also chapter 5.1, Mental Status of Licensed or Certified Professionals);
18. Performing any treatment or prescribing any therapy that would constitute human experimentation without full, informed, and written consent;
19. Failing to perform according to generally prevailing professional standards;
20. Delegating professional responsibilities to a person known to be unqualified;

21. Violating a rule regulating the profession or an order from a previous disciplinary hearing;

22. Failing to maintain confidentiality unless waived by the client or party authorized to give consent, or when the MHP is a defendant in a civil, criminal, or disciplinary action filed by the patient or client, or when there is a clear and immediate probability of physical harm to the patient or client, to other individuals, or to society, and the information is conveyed only to the potential victim, appropriate family members, or law enforcement authorities (see also chapters 3.3, Confidential Relations and Communications, and 3.4, Privileged Communications); and

23. Making public statements derived from test data, client contacts, or research that identifies or damages research participants or clients.

In addition, disciplinary action may be taken for sexual misconduct.[18]

(C)(2) Disciplinary Procedures

Disciplinary procedures are administered through the DOH by the Board of Clinical Social Work, Marriage and Family Therapy, and Mental Health Counseling. Florida statutory provisions provide a general outline of the procedures that the Board and the DOH are to follow in investigating a complaint and pursuing disciplinary action against a social worker.

(C)(3) Investigatory Process

The DOH must investigate any signed, written complaint it receives that describes facts that would constitute a violation of the licensing and practice acts.[19] Anonymous, written complaints are investigated if the DOH concludes, after a preliminary inquiry, that the allegations in the complaint are true. The licensee who is the subject of the complaint receives a copy of the complaint and has 20 days to respond in writing. Once the investigation is completed, a report containing the investigative findings and recommendations is submitted to a "probable cause" panel established by the Board, which determines by majority vote whether there is probable cause to believe that the complaint is true.[20] The panel is to reach a decision regarding probable cause within 30

---

18. 15 FLA. STAT. ANN. § 491.0112 (West 2001).
19. 15 FLA. STAT. ANN. § 455.225 (West 2001).
20. 15 FLA. STAT. ANN. §§ 455.225(2) and 455.225(4) (West 2001).

days of its receipt of the final investigative report, though this period may be extended.[21]

In lieu of a finding of probable cause, the panel may issue a "letter of guidance" to the subject of the investigation.[22] In addition, in the case of violations that do not endanger the public health, safety, and welfare and that do not constitute a serious inability to practice the profession, the DOH, rather than pursuing a probable cause hearing, may provide the licensee with a notice of noncompliance for an initial offense or a minor violation. In such a case, the licensee has 15 days to take corrective action or the formal probable cause process will be initiated.[23]

(C)(4) Formal Hearing Process

If the panel finds that probable cause exists, a formal complaint may be initiated. The subject of the probable cause finding is entitled to a hearing "in all proceedings in which the substantial interests of a party" are at issue before the DOH and where there is a "disputed issue of material fact."[24] A party must request a hearing within 21 days of notice of the probable cause finding or the right to a hearing will be waived.[25] The hearing is conducted before a hearing officer from the state's Division of Administrative Hearings of the State Department of Management Services.

Hearings are conducted according to the same rules governing disciplinary proceedings involving other licensed professions. Notice of the hearing of not less than 14 days is to be provided the parties,[26] and the hearing officer may direct the parties to engage in a prehearing conference for the purpose of simplifying and clarifying issues, discussing settlement, examining documents, exchanging information regarding witnesses, resolving other procedural matters, and entering into a prehearing stipulation.[27] Discovery (the process by which the parties to a lawsuit obtain information regarding the other party's case) according to the *Florida Rules of Civil Procedure* is available[28] and the parties may subpoena witnesses.[29] At the hearing, all parties may present evidence, cross-examine witnesses, submit rebuttal evidence, submit proposed findings of facts and orders, file exceptions to any order or proposed order of the hearing officer, and be represented

---

21. 15 Fla. Stat. Ann. § 455.225(4) (West 2001).
22. 15 Fla. Stat. Ann. § 455.225(4) (West 2001).
23. 15 Fla. Stat. Ann. § 455.225(3) (West 2001).
24. 7 Fla. Stat. Ann. § 120.569(1) (West Supp. 2002).
25. Fla. Admin. Code Ann. r. 28-5.111 (2002).
26. Fla. Admin. Code Ann. r. 28-106.208 (2002).
27. Fla. Admin. Code Ann. r. 28-106.209 (2002).
28. Fla. Admin. Code Ann. r. 28-106.206 (2002).
29. Fla. Admin. Code Ann. r. 28-106.212 (2002).

by counsel.[30] The hearing officer, within 30 days of the hearing or receipt of the hearing transcript (whichever is later) is to file a recommended order that is to include a caption (title of the case, including identity of the parties), time and place of the hearing, appearances entered by counsel or parties to the hearing, a statement of the issues, findings of fact and conclusions of law, and a recommendation for final DOH action.[31] A party may file exceptions to the findings of fact and conclusions of law within 15 days of their entry, and each party within 10 days of service of the exceptions may file a response to those exceptions.[32] After this the DOH head may adopt, reject, or modify the hearing officer's conclusions of law or findings of fact.[33] However, modification or rejection of the hearing officer's conclusions can occur only after a complete review of the record and a statement explaining particularly why the hearing officer's conclusions have been rejected and why the DOH's conclusions are more reasonable.[34] In addition, the penalty proposed may be reduced or increased only after review of the complete record and a statement with particularity as to why the penalty was changed.[35] Judicial review is available to a party adversely affected by a final action to the appellate district in which the DOH maintains its headquarters.[36]

(C)(5) Penalties for Violations

If the Board, after a hearing, finds that one of the provisions detailed has been violated, it can impose one of a variety of penalties, including the following:[37]

1. Revoking or suspending a social worker's license;
2. Refusing to certify to the DOH the applicant's application for licensure, certification, or registration;
3. Restricting the individual's license;
4. Imposing administrative fines not to exceed $10,000 for each offense;
5. Issuing a reprimand;
6. Placing the social worker on probation under conditions specified by the Board; the Board may direct the social worker to submit to treatment, take continuing education courses, sub-

---

30. 7 FLA. STAT. ANN. § 120.57(1)(b) (West Supp. 2002).
31. FLA. ADMIN. CODE ANN. r. 28-106.216 (2002).
32. FLA. ADMIN. CODE ANN. r. 28-106.217 (2002).
33. 7 FLA. STAT. ANN. § 120.57(1)(l) (West Supp. 2002).
34. Id.
35. Id.
36. 7 FLA. STAT. ANN. § 120.68(2)(a) (West Supp. 2002).
37. 15 FLA. STAT. ANN. § 456.072(2) (West Supp. 2002).

mit to reexamination, or work under another social worker's supervision;
7. Issuing a letter of concern to the social worker;
8. Ordering a refund of fees billed to and collected from the patient;
9. Imposing an administrative fine for violation of patient rights;
10. Requiring remedial education; and
11. Taking other corrective action.

1.7
Certification and Regulation of School Psychologists

The law regulating school psychologists is contained within the law regulating psychologists, discussed in chapter 1.4 (Licensure and Regulation of Psychologists). In general, school psychologists are regulated in the same manner and are subject to the same requirements as psychologists. However, there are requirements particular to school psychologists that are discussed in this chapter. One particularly important distinction between psychologists and school psychologists is that an individual may be licensed as a school psychologist without a doctoral degree.

(A) Practice of School Psychology Defined

The practice of *school psychology* consists of[1]

1. Assessment, including psychoeducational, developmental, and vocational assessments; and evaluations and interpretations of intelligence, aptitudes, achievement, adjustment, and other attributes in individuals and groups relating to learning, educational, or adjustment needs;

2. Counseling with children and parents or other adults to ameliorate or prevent learning and adjustment problems;

3. Consultation to schools, agencies, organizations, families, or individuals related to learning and adjustment problems, in-

---

1. 15 FLA. STAT. ANN. § 490.003(5)(a)–(d) (West 2001).

cluding psychoeducational, developmental, and vocational assistance or direct educational services; and

4. Development of programs, including activities related to the creation of a sound learning environment, assisting teachers in adaptations and innovations, and facilitating the psychoeducational development of individual families or groups.

(B) Licensure

(B)(1) Licensure by Examination

A person who wishes to be licensed as a school psychologist must apply and pay an application fee. The applicant will be licensed by the DOH on certification by the Board of Psychology that the applicant has[2]

1. Received a doctorate, specialist, or equivalent degree from a program primarily psychological in nature and has completed 60 semester hours or 90 quarter hours in areas relevant to school psychology from a college or university that, at the time the applicant was enrolled and graduated, was accredited by an accrediting agency recognized and approved by the Commission on Recognition of Postsecondary Accreditation or an institution that is publicly recognized as a member in good standing with the Association of University and Colleges of Canada;[3]

2. Had a minimum of three years experience in school psychology, two years of which must be supervised by a person who is a licensed school psychologist or who has otherwise qualified as a school psychologist supervisor;[4]

3. Passed an examination in school psychology adopted by the DOH; and

4. Completed an application and paid requisite fees.

(B)(2) Licensure by Endorsement

An individual may be licensed by endorsement after paying appropriate fees, passing the portions of the licensure examination on state laws and rules governing practice, and on proving to the Board that he or she[5]

---

2. 15 FLA. STAT. ANN. § 490.005(2) (West 2001).
3. *See* FLA. ADMIN. CODE ANN. 64B21-500.009 (2002) for a summary of the educational and curriculum requirements.
4. *See* FLA. ADMIN. CODE ANN. 64B21-500.005 (2002) for a summary of the experience requirements.
5. FLA. ADMIN. CODE ANN. 64B21-500.13 (2002).

1. Has a valid license or certificate to practice school psychology from another state with standards comparable or more stringent to those of Florida; or

2. Is a Diplomate in School Psychology in good standing with the American Board of Professional Psychology.

A license by endorsement will not be issued to any applicant until all states in which the applicant has ever been licensed as a school psychologist report the status of all licenses and any disciplinary action involving those licenses.[6]

(B)(3) Licensure Renewal and Completion of Continuing Education

Licenses are renewed on a biennial basis at a fee of $100.[7] Licensees must complete 30 hours of approved continuing education during each two-year licensure period.[8]

(C) Private Practice

A licensed school psychologist employed by a school district may provide private sector services to students in that district only if[9]

1. Written notice is given to parents, guardians, and adult clients regarding the availability of free services within the district;

2. The client is not a student in a school in which the school psychologist is currently employed;

3. The parent, guardian, or adult client is informed that as a dual practitioner the psychologist may not function as an independent evaluator;

4. The psychologist does not engage in private practice during school hours or promise 24-hour coverage;

5. The school psychologist does not use his or her school employment to promote private practice; and

6. The school psychologist does not use materials belonging to the school district in his or her private practice.

---

6. FLA. ADMIN. CODE ANN. 64B21-500.013(6) (2002).
7. FLA. ADMIN. CODE ANN. 64B21-501.003 (2002).
8. FLA. ADMIN. CODE 64B21-502.001 (2002). *See* FLA. ADMIN. CODE ANN. 64B21-502.004 (2002) for criteria for continuing education program approval.
9. 15 FLA. STAT. ANN. § 490.0121 (West 2001).

(D) Regulation

The disciplining of school psychologists is governed by general statutory provisions applicable to psychologists. Actions warranting disciplinary action and a description of the disciplinary process are found in chapter 1.4, Licensure and Regulation of Psychologists.

1.8

Certification of School Social Workers

Florida does not license school counselors. The licensure of mental health counselors is discussed in chapter 1.10 (Licensure of Other Types of Mental Health Professionals). However, individuals employed as public school counselors (as well as school supervisors, principals, teachers, library media specialists, coaches, and individuals in other instructional positions) must be certified.[1]

(A) Certification

The Board of Education has established specialization requirements for certification in guidance and counseling, grades prekindergarten through 12th.[2] There are two plans for specialization. Plan one requires a master's degree or higher with a graduate major in guidance and counseling or counselor education including three semester hours in an elementary or secondary school. Plan two requires a master's degree or higher with 30 semester hours of graduate credit in guidance and counseling that includes three semester hours in each of the following: the principles, philosophy, organization and administration of guidance; student appraisal, including the administration and interpretation of standardized tests; education, and career development information practices and systems; learning, personality theory, and human development; counseling theories and individual counseling techniques; group counseling and guidance techniques; consultation skills and techniques for conferring with groups such as agencies,

---

1. 11 FLA. STAT. ANN. § 231.15(1) (West Supp. 2002).
2. FLA. ADMIN. CODE ANN. r. 6A-4.0181 (2002).

teachers, and parents; legal, ethical, and current issues affecting school counselors; specialized counseling techniques for use with elementary- or secondary-level special populations such as exceptional students, dropouts, and minorities; and a supervised counseling practicum in an elementary or secondary school.

In addition to these specialization requirements, each person certified by the Board of Education (whether as a school counselor, a teacher, etc.) must meet a number of other qualifications. In general, the applicant must[3]

1. Be at least 18 years of age;
2. Swear in writing that he or she will uphold the principles in the U.S. and Florida constitutions;
3. Document receipt of a bachelor's or higher degree;
4. Submit to a fingerprint check;
5. Be of good moral character;
6. Be competent and capable of performing the duties, functions, and responsibilities of a teacher;
7. Demonstrate mastery of general knowledge;
8. Demonstrate mastery of subject area knowledge; and
9. Demonstrate mastery of professional preparation and education competence.

(B) Regulation

(B)(1) Unlawful and Prohibited Practices

Practices that may result in action being taken against the certificate holder include the following:[4]

1. Obtaining a certificate by fraudulent means;
2. Engaging in conduct proving incompetence;
3. Being found guilty of gross immorality or an act of moral turpitude;
4. Having had a certificate revoked in another state;
5. Having been convicted of a crime, other than a traffic offense;
6. Having been found guilty of personal conduct seriously reducing his or her effectiveness as a school board employee;
7. Breaching a contract;
8. Being the subject of a court order for delinquent child support;

---

3. 11 FLA. STAT. ANN. § 231.17(2) (West Supp. 2002).
4. 11 FLA. STAT. ANN. § 231.2615 (West Supp. 2002).

9. Violating the Board of Education Principles of Professional Conduct for the Education Profession; and
10. Otherwise violating legal provisions warranting licensure revocation.

(B)(2) Disciplinary Procedures

The Department of Education investigates complaints against educational personnel, including school counselors.[5] The Department administers this process through the Education Practices Commission, a body appointed by the Board of Education from nominations submitted by the commissioner of education, subject to Senate confirmation.[6] The Commission has 17 members, including 7 teachers, 5 administrators, and 5 lay citizens of whom 2 are to be former school board members.[7]

The Department is to investigate expeditiously a complaint that if legally sufficient would show a violation of one or more of the provisions noted earlier. The Department may continue an investigation even if the initial complainant withdraws the complaint.[8] The certificate holder under investigation may inspect and copy the complaint and material assembled during the investigation after the investigation is completed but before the Commission's determination of probable cause.[9] After investigation, the Department staff is to advise the Commissioner concerning the findings, and the Commissioner determines whether probable cause exists or not. The Commissioner also has the discretion to enter into deferred prosecution agreements in lieu of a probable cause finding if in his or her judgment such an agreement is in the best interests of the parties, including the public.[10] When it is deemed necessary to protect the health, safety, and welfare of a minor student, the superintendent of the school district in which the certificate holder is employed may (and shall if the commissioner of education requests it) temporarily suspend and reassign the employee with pay so that direct contact with students is avoided pending completion of the investigation and proceedings.[11]

On a finding of probable cause, the commissioner files a formal complaint and prosecutes the complaint administratively before an administrative law judge assigned by the Division of Administrative Hearings of the Department of Management Ser-

---

5. 11 FLA. STAT. ANN. § 231.262 (West Supp. 2002).
6. 11 FLA. STAT. ANN. § 231.261(1) (West Supp. 2002).
7. Id.
8. 11 FLA. STAT. ANN. § 231.262(1) (West Supp. 2002).
9. 11 FLA. STAT. ANN. § 231.262(4) (West Supp. 2002).
10. 11 FLA. STAT. ANN. § 231.262(3) (West Supp. 2002).
11. 11 FLA. STAT. ANN. § 231.262(5) (West Supp. 2002).

vices.[12] The administrative law judge is to make recommendations to an Education Practices Commission panel, which in turn conducts a formal review of the recommendations and issues a final order.[13]

(B)(3) Formal Hearing Process

Hearings are conducted according to the same rules governing disciplinary proceedings involving other licensed professions. Notice of the hearing of not less than 14 days is to be provided the parties,[14] and the hearing officer may direct the parties to engage in a prehearing conference for the purpose of simplifying and clarifying issues, discussing settlement, examining documents, exchanging information regarding witnesses, resolving other procedural matters, and entering into a prehearing stipulation.[15] Discovery (the process by which parties to a lawsuit gain information regarding the other party's case) according to the *Florida Rules of Civil Procedure* is available[16] and the parties may subpoena witnesses.[17] At the hearing, all parties may present evidence, cross-examine witnesses, submit rebuttal evidence, submit proposed findings of facts and orders, file exceptions to any order or proposed order of the hearing officer, and can be represented by counsel.[18] The hearing officer, within 30 days of the hearing or receipt of the hearing transcript (whichever is later) is to file a recommended order that is to include a caption (title of the case, including identity of the parties), time and place of the hearing, appearances entered by counsel or parties to the hearing, a statement of the issues, findings of fact and conclusions of law, and a recommendation for final agency action.[19] A party may file exceptions to the findings of fact and conclusions of law within 15 days of their entry, and each party within 10 days of service of the exceptions may file a response to those exceptions.[20] After this the education commissioner may adopt, reject, or modify the hearing officer's conclusions of law or findings of fact.[21] However, modification or rejection of the hearing officer's conclusions can occur only after a complete review of the record and a statement explaining particularly why the hearing officer's conclusions have been rejected and why the Department's conclusions

---

12. *Id.*
13. *Id.*
14. FLA. ADMIN. CODE ANN. r. 28-106.208 (2002).
15. FLA. ADMIN. CODE ANN. r. 28-106.209 (2002).
16. FLA. ADMIN. CODE ANN. r. 28-106.206 (2002).
17. FLA. ADMIN. CODE ANN. r. 28-106.212 (2002).
18. 7 FLA. STAT. ANN. § 120.57(1)(b) (West Supp. 2002).
19. FLA. ADMIN. CODE ANN. r. 28-106.216 (2002).
20. FLA. ADMIN. CODE ANN. r. 28-106.217 (2002).
21. 7 FLA. STAT. ANN. § 120.57(1)(l) (West Supp. 2002).

are more reasonable.[22] In addition, the penalty proposed may be reduced or increased only after review of the complete record and a statement explaining why the penalty was changed.[23] Judicial review is available to a party adversely affected by a final agency action to the appellate district in which the Department maintains its headquarters.[24]

(B)(4) Penalties for Violations

If, after investigation and hearing, the Department concludes action against the certificate holder is warranted, it may impose one or more of the following penalties:[25]

1. Denial of an application for a certificate;

2. Revocation or suspension of a certificate;

3. Imposition of an administrative fine not to exceed $2,000 for each count or separate offense;

4. Placement of an individual on probation, subject to conditions imposed by the agency;

5. Restriction of the authorized scope of practice;

6. Written reprimand; or

7. Denial of application for a new certificate that prohibits the person from reapplying for 10 years, or less, or permanently.

---

22. Id.
23. Id.
24. 7 FLA. STAT. ANN. § 120.68(2)(a) (West Supp. 2002).
25. 11 FLA. STAT. ANN. § 231.262(7)(a)–(g) (West Supp. 2002).

1.9
Licensure and Regulation of Marriage and Family Counselors

The DOH governs the licensure and practice of marriage and family therapists in Florida.[1] The DOH discharges its responsibilities through the Florida Board of Clinical Social Work, Marriage and Family Therapy, and Mental Health Counseling.[2]

(A) Florida Board of Clinical Social Work, Marriage and Family Therapy, and Mental Health Counseling

The Board has nine members who are appointed by the governor and confirmed by the state Senate. Six members of the Board must be licensed professionals (two licensed practicing clinical social workers, two licensed practicing marriage and family therapists, and two licensed practicing mental health counselors). Three members are to be Florida citizens who are not and have never been licensed in a mental health related profession and are in no way connected with the practice of any such profession.[3]

---

1. 15 FLA. STAT. ANN. § 491.003 (West 2001).
2. 15 FLA. STAT. ANN. § 491.004(1) (West 2001).
3. 15 FLA. STAT. ANN. § 491.004 (West 2001).

(B) Practice of Marriage and Family Therapy Defined

The practice of *marriage and family therapy* is defined[4] as

the use of scientific and applied marriage and family theories, methods, and procedures for the purpose of describing, evaluation, and modifying marital, family, and individual behavior within the context of marital and family systems, including the context of marital formation and dissolution, and is based on marriage and family systems theory, marriage and family development, human development, normal and abnormal behavior, psychopathology, human sexuality, psychotherapeutic and marriage and family therapy theories and techniques.

It includes the use of methods of a psychological nature to evaluate, assess, diagnose, treat, and prevent emotional and mental disorders and dysfunctions, whether cognitive, affective, or behavioral; sexual dysfunction; behavioral disorders; alcoholism; and substance abuse. Practices permitted by statute include but are not limited to marriage and family therapy, counseling, psychotherapy, behavior modification, hypnotherapy, sex therapy, consultation, client advocacy, crisis intervention, and providing needed information and education to clients.

The statute specifies that the terms "diagnose" and "treat," as used in the clinical social work, marriage and family therapy, and mental health counseling statute, do not include prescribing medication, authorizing clinical laboratory or radiological procedures, or administering electroconvulsive therapy. The terms also do not permit a marriage and family therapist to describe or label any test, report, or procedure as "psychological."[5]

(C) Licensure

(C)(1) Licensure by Examination

A license may be issued to an applicant who pays the appropriate fee and who[6]

1. Has received a minimum of a master's degree with a major emphasis in or related to marriage or family therapy and has completed course requirements spelled out in the statute;

2. Has had not fewer than two years of clinical experience during which 50% of the applicant's clients were receiving marriage

---
4. 15 FLA. STAT. ANN. § 491.003(8) (West 2001).
5. *Id.*
6. 15 FLA. STAT. ANN. § 491.005(3) (West 2001).

and family therapy under the supervision of a licensed marriage and family therapist;
3. Has passed the licensing examination; and
4. Has demonstrated knowledge of the laws and rules governing the practice of clinical social work, marriage and family therapy, and mental health counseling.

(C)(2) Licensure by Endorsement

A license may be granted to an applicant with an active valid license from another state who has actively practiced for at least three of the previous five years. The applicant must also meet the Florida education and experience requirements and have passed an equivalent licensure examination in another state. The applicant must also not be under investigation for an act that would violate Florida licensure laws.[7]

(C)(3) Licensure Renewal

Renewal of licenses is on a biennial basis and, by statute, the fee for renewal may not exceed $250.[8]

(C)(4) Exemptions From Licensure

Certain individuals do not have to obtain licensure to practice as a marriage and family therapist. These include[9]

1. Salaried employees of a variety of organizations, including governmental agencies; mental health, substance abuse, alcohol, and developmental disability programs licensed by the state; licensed day care centers; domestic violence centers; academic and research institutes;
2. Salaried employees of private, nonprofit counseling agencies providing services to children, youth, and families, if the services are provided for no charge and the person is trained to render the services provided;
3. Students providing services in a training setting with certain supervisory restrictions; and
4. A nonresident who provides services no more than 15 days in a calendar year.

However, individuals falling into one of the exempt categories may not use the title of marriage and family therapist in describing themselves.[10]

---

7. 15 Fla. Stat. Ann. § 491.006 (West 2001).
8. 15 Fla. Stat. Ann. § 491.007 (West Supp. 2001).
9. 15 Fla. Stat. Ann. § 491.014(4) (West Supp. 2002).
10. 15 Fla. Stat. Ann. § 491.012(1)(a) (West Supp. 2002).

(C)(5) Use of the Marriage and Family Therapist Title

An individual who is not licensed as a marriage and family therapist may not use the titles "licensed marriage and family therapist," "marriage and family therapist," "marriage counselor," "marriage consultant," "family therapist," "family counselor," or "family consultant."[11] Violation of this prohibition is a first-degree misdemeanor punishable by up to one year of incarceration.[12]

(D) Regulation

(D)(1) Unlawful and Prohibited Practices

There are a number of actions that may subject a marriage and family therapist to disciplinary action. These include[13]

1. Obtaining or attempting to obtain a license by fraud or bribery;
2. Having a license revoked or otherwise acted on by another state;
3. Being convicted of a crime directly related to the practice of the profession or ability to practice the profession;
4. Using false, deceptive, or misleading advertising;
5. Advertising under an assumed name;
6. Maintaining a professional association with an individual who is known or should be known to have violated statutory provisions governing practice;
7. Aiding a nonlicensed, nonregistered, or noncertified person falsely representing him- or herself as licensed or certified;
8. Failing to perform statutory or legal obligations placed on a licensed marriage and family therapist;
9. Making a false report;
10. Paying a kickback or other form of remuneration to obtain a client;
11. Engaging in conduct that would constitute sexual battery or sexual misconduct;
12. Making misleading, deceptive, untrue, or fraudulent representations in the course of practice;

---

11. 15 FLA. STAT. ANN. § 491.012(1)(b) (West Supp. 2002).
12. 15 FLA. STAT. ANN. § 490.012(3) (West Supp. 2002).
13. 15 FLA. STAT. ANN. § 491.009(1)(a)–(w) (West Supp. 2002).

13. Soliciting patients or clients personally, or through an agent, through fraud, intimidation, undue influence or other forms of overreaching;

14. Failing to make available to a patient or client, on written request, tests or other reports prepared and paid for by the client or patient;

15. Failing to respond within 30 days to a complaint or request for information from the Board or the DOH;

16. Violating statutory provisions applicable to the practice of marriage and family therapy;

17. Being an impaired professional because of the use of alcohol, drugs, or other substances (see also chapter 5.1, Mental Status of Licensed or Certified Professionals);

18. Performing any treatment or prescribing any therapy that would constitute human experimentation without full, informed, and written consent;

19. Failing to perform according to generally prevailing professional standards;

20. Delegating professional responsibilities to a person known to be unqualified;

21. Violating a rule regulating the profession or an order from a previous disciplinary hearing;

22. Failing to maintain a professional confidence absent consent or when the licensee is a defendant in a civil, criminal, or disciplinary action filed by the patient or client, or when there is a clear and immediate probability of physical harm to the patient or client, to other individuals, or to society, and the information is conveyed only to the potential victim, appropriate family members, or law enforcement authorities (see also chapters 3.3, Confidential Relations and Communications, and 3.4, Privileged Communications); and

23. Making public statements derived from test data, client contacts, or research that identifies or damages research participants or clients.

In addition, disciplinary action may be taken for sexual misconduct.[14]

(D)(2) Disciplinary Procedures

Disciplinary procedures are administered through the DOH by the Board of Clinical Social Work, Marriage and Family Therapy, and Mental Health Counseling. Florida statutory provisions

---

14. 15 FLA. STAT. ANN. § 491.0112 (West 1991).

provide a general outline of the procedures that the Board and the DOH are to follow in investigating a complaint and pursuing disciplinary action against a marriage and family therapist.

(D)(3) Investigatory Process

The DOH must investigate any signed, written complaint it receives that describes facts that would constitute a violation of the licensing and practice acts.[15] Anonymous, written complaints are investigated if the DOH concludes, after a preliminary inquiry, that the allegations in the complaint are true. The licensee who is the subject of the complaint receives a copy of the complaint and has 20 days to respond in writing. Once the investigation is completed, a report containing the investigative findings and recommendations is submitted to a "probable cause" panel established by the Board, which determines by majority vote whether there is probable cause to believe that the complaint is true.[16] The panel is to reach a decision regarding probable cause within 30 days of its receipt of the final investigative report, though this period may be extended.[17]

In lieu of a finding of probable cause, the panel may issue a "letter of guidance" to the subject of the investigation.[18] In addition, in the case of violations that do not endanger the public health, safety, and welfare and that do not constitute a serious inability to practice the profession, the DOH, rather than pursuing a probable cause hearing, may provide the licensee with a notice of noncompliance for an initial offense or a minor violation. In such a case, the licensee has 15 days to take corrective action or the formal probable cause process will be initiated.[19]

(D)(4) Formal Hearing Process

If the panel finds that probable cause exists, a formal complaint may be initiated. The subject of the probable cause finding is entitled to a hearing "in all proceedings in which the substantial interests of a party" are at issue before the DOH and where there is a "disputed issue of material fact."[20] A party must request a hearing within 21 days of notice of the probable cause finding or the right to a hearing will be waived.[21] The hearing is conducted before a hearing officer from the state's Division of Administrative Hearings of the State Department of Management Services.

---

15. 15 FLA. STAT. ANN. § 455.225 (West 2001).
16. 15 FLA. STAT. ANN. §§ 455.225(2) and 455.225(4) (West 2001).
17. 15 FLA. STAT. ANN. § 455.225(4) (West 2001).
18. 15 FLA. STAT. ANN. § 455.225(4) (West 2001).
19. 15 FLA. STAT. ANN. § 455.225(3) (West 2001).
20. 7 FLA. STAT. ANN. § 120.569 (West Supp. 2002).
21. FLA. ADMIN. CODE ANN. r. 28-5.111 (2002).

Hearings are conducted according to the same rules governing disciplinary proceedings involving other licensed professions. Notice of the hearing of not less than 14 days is to be provided the parties,[22] and the hearing officer may direct the parties to engage in a prehearing conference for the purpose of simplifying and clarifying issues, discussing settlement, examining documents, exchanging information regarding witnesses, resolving other procedural matters, and entering into a prehearing stipulation.[23] Discovery (the process by which parties to a lawsuit gain information regarding the other party's case) according to the *Florida Rules of Civil Procedure* is available,[24] and the parties may subpoena witnesses.[25] At the hearing, all parties may present evidence, cross-examine witnesses, submit rebuttal evidence, submit proposed findings of facts and orders, file exceptions to any order or proposed order of the hearing officer, and can be represented by counsel.[26] The hearing officer, within 30 days of the hearing or receipt of the hearing transcript (whichever is later) is to file a recommended order that is to include a caption (title of the case, including identity of the parties), time and place of the hearing, appearances entered by counsel or parties to the hearing, a statement of the issues, findings of fact and conclusions of law, and a recommendation for final agency action.[27] A party may file exceptions to the findings of fact and conclusions of law within 15 days of their entry, and each party within 10 days of service of the exceptions may file a response to those exceptions.[28] After this the DOH head may adopt, reject, or modify the hearing officer's conclusions of law or findings of fact.[29] However, modification or rejection of the hearing officer's conclusions can occur only after a complete review of the record and a statement stating particularly why the hearing officer's conclusions have been rejected and why the DOH's conclusions are more reasonable.[30] In addition, the penalty proposed may be reduced or increased only after review of the complete record and a statement with particularity as to why the penalty was changed.[31] Judicial review is available to a party adversely affected by a final DOH action to the appellate district in which the DOH maintains its headquarters.[32]

---

22. FLA. ADMIN. CODE ANN. r. 28-106.208 (2002).
23. FLA. ADMIN. CODE ANN. r. 28-106.209 (2002).
24. FLA. ADMIN. CODE ANN. r. 28-106.206 (2002).
25. FLA. ADMIN. CODE ANN. r. 28-106.212 (2002).
26. 7 FLA. STAT. ANN. § 120.57(1)(b) (West Supp. 2002).
27. FLA. ADMIN. CODE ANN. r. 28-106.216 (2002).
28. FLA. ADMIN. CODE ANN. r. 28-106.217 (2002).
29. 7 FLA. STAT. ANN. § 120.57(1)(l) (West Supp. 2002).
30. *Id.*
31. *Id.*
32. 7 FLA. STAT. ANN. § 120.68(2)(a) (West Supp. 2002).

(D)(5) Penalties for Violations

If the Board, after a hearing, finds that one of the provisions detailed previously has been violated, it can impose one of a variety of penalties, including the following:[33]

1. Revoking or suspending a marriage and family therapist's license;
2. Refusing to certify to the DOH the applicant's application for licensure, certification, or registration;
3. Restricting the individual's license;
4. Imposing administrative fines not to exceed $10,000 for each offense;
5. Issuing a reprimand;
6. Placing the marriage and family therapist on probation under conditions specified by the Board; the Board may direct the marriage and family therapist to submit to treatment, take continuing education courses, submit to reexamination, or work under another therapist's supervision;
7. Issuing a letter of concern to the therapist;
8. Ordering a refund of fees billed to and collected from the patient;
9. Imposing an administrative fine for violation of patient rights;
10. Requiring remedial education; and
11. Other corrective action.

---

33. 15 FLA. STAT. ANN. § 456.072(2) (West Supp. 2002).

1.10

Licensure of Other Types of Mental Health Professionals

The DOH governs the licensure and practice of mental health counselors in Florida. The DOH discharges its responsibilities through the Board of Social Work, Marriage and Family Therapy and Mental Health Counseling.[1] The Board's responsibilities include establishing qualifications for licensure as a mental health counselor, overseeing the conduct of mental health counselors, and regulating the disciplinary process for mental health counselors.

(A) Florida Board of Clinical Social Work, Marriage and Family Therapy, and Mental Health Counseling

The Board has nine members who are appointed by the governor and confirmed by the state Senate. Six members of the Board are to be licensed professionals (two licensed practicing clinical social workers, two licensed practicing marriage and family therapists, and two licensed practicing mental health counselors) and three are laypersons who have never been licensed as mental health professionals and have no connection with the practice of any mental health profession.[2]

---

1. 15 FLA. STAT. ANN. § 491.004(1) (West 2001).
2. 15 FLA. STAT. ANN. § 491.004(2) (West 2001).

(B) Practice of Mental Health Counseling Defined

The practice of *mental health counseling* is defined[3] as "the use of scientific and applied behavioral science theories, methods, and techniques for the purpose of describing, preventing, and treating undesired behavior and enhancing mental health and human development." Mental health counseling practice includes the use of methods of a psychological nature to evaluate, assess, diagnose, treat, and prevent emotional and mental disorders and dysfunctions, whether cognitive, affective, or behavioral; behavioral disorders; interpersonal relationships; sexual dysfunction; alcoholism; and substance abuse. Practices permitted by statute include but are not limited to counseling, psychotherapy, behavior modification, hypnotherapy, sex therapy, consultation, client advocacy, crisis intervention, and providing needed information and education to clients.[4] Diagnosing and treating persons does not include prescribing medication, authorizing clinical laboratory or radiological procedures, or administering electroconvulsive therapy.[5]

(C) Licensure

(C)(1) Licensure by Examination

A license may be issued to an applicant who completes the application, pays the appropriate fee, and who[6]

1. Has received a minimum of a master's degree from a mental health counseling program accredited by the Council for Accreditation of Counseling and Related Educational Programs that consists of at least 60 semester hours or 80 quarter hours of clinical and didactic instruction, including a course in human sexuality and a course in substance abuse; or has received a minimum of a master's degree from a mental health counseling program that is not accredited by the Council for Accreditation of Counseling and Related Educational Programs consisting of at least 60 semester hours or 80 quarter hours, and which education consists of 33 semester hours or 44 quarter hours of graduate course work, including a minimum of three semester hours or four quarter hours in the following areas: counseling theories and practice; human growth and development; diag-

---

3. 15 FLA. STAT. ANN. § 491.003(9) (West 2001).
4. *Id.*
5. 15 FLA. STAT. ANN. § 491.003(9)(c) (West 2001).
6. 15 FLA. STAT. ANN. § 491.005(4) (West 2001).

nosis and treatment of psychopathology; human sexuality; group theories and practice; individual evaluation and assessment; career and lifestyle assessment; research and program evaluation; social and cultural foundations; counseling in community settings; substance abuse; and legal, ethical, and professional standards and issues in the practice of mental health counseling;

2. Has completed at least 1000 hours of university-sponsored clinical practicum, internship, or field experience as required in the accrediting standards of the Council for Accreditation of Counseling and Related Educational Programs for mental health counseling programs;

3. Has a minimum of two years of clinical experience in mental health counseling, which must be at the postmaster's level under the supervision of a licensed mental health counselor or the equivalent who is a qualified supervisor as determined by the Board; and

4. Has passed a theory and practice examination provided by the Board and has demonstrated knowledge of the laws and rules governing the practice of clinical social work, marriage, and family therapy, and mental health counseling.

(C)(2) Licensure by Endorsement

A license will be granted to an applicant with a valid license from another state, who has actively practiced for at least three of the previous five years. The applicant must also meet the education and experience requirements discussed earlier, have passed an equivalent licensure examination in another state, and demonstrated knowledge of Florida laws regulating practice in the state. The applicant must have a license in good standing and not be under investigation for an act that would violate Florida licensure laws.[7]

(C)(3) Provisional Licensure

Individuals applying for licensure by examination who have satisfied the clinical experience requirements and individuals applying for licensure by endorsement must be provisionally licensed before beginning practice. Persons holding a provisional license must work under the supervision of a licensed mental health professional.[8] The department will issue a provisional mental

---

7. 15 FLA. STAT. ANN. § 491.006 (West 2001).
8. 15 FLA. STAT. ANN. § 491.0046(3) (West 2001).

health counselor license, which expires after 24 months,[9] providing the applicant[10]

1. Completes the application form and pays the required application fee;
2. Earned a graduate degree in a major related to mental health counseling; and
3. Has completed a minimum of seven of the following courses: counseling theories and practice; human growth and development; diagnosis and treatment of psychopathology; human sexuality; group theories and practice; individual evaluation and assessment; career and lifestyle assessment; research and program evaluation; social and cultural foundations; counseling in community settings; substance abuse; and legal, ethical, and professional standards and issues in the practice of mental health counseling.

(C)(4) Licensure Renewal and Continuing Education

Renewal of licenses is on a biennial basis, and by statute the fee for renewal may not exceed $250.[11]

Licensees must complete 30 hours of approved continuing education credit, including one hour on domestic violence during the two-year period ending on the last day of the biennial renewal period. In lieu of the domestic violence course, a licensee may complete a course in end of life care and palliative health care if the licensee has completed a domestic violence course during the immediately preceding biennium.[12] A maximum of six hours can be earned by providing pro bono services to the indigent, underserved, or areas with critical need. Such services must be approved in advance by the Board and must be documented.[13] A maximum of six hours can be earned for credit by attending programs designed to enhance the licensee's administrative, office management, or nonclinical skills.[14] A maximum of six hours of continuing education can be completed via videocassette courses.[15]

(C)(5) Licensure Exemptions

Certain individuals do not have to obtain licensure to practice as a mental health counselor. These include[16]

---

9. 15 FLA. STAT. ANN. § 491.0046(4) (West 2001).
10. 15 FLA. STAT. ANN. § 491.0046 (West 2001).
11. 15 FLA. STAT. ANN. § 491.007 (West 2001).
12. FLA. ADMIN. CODE ANN. 64B-6.001(2)(a) (2002).
13. FLA. ADMIN. CODE ANN. 64B-6.001(2)(c) (2002).
14. FLA. ADMIN. CODE ANN. 64B-6.001(2)(b) (2002).
15. FLA. ADMIN. CODE ANN. 64B-6.001(3) (2002).
16. 15 FLA. STAT. ANN. § 491.014(4) (West Supp. 2002).

1. Salaried employees of a variety of organizations, including governmental agencies; mental health, substance abuse, alcohol, and developmental disability programs licensed by the state; licensed day care and child care centers; certified domestic violence centers; and research institutions;
2. Salaried employees of private, nonprofit counseling agencies or organizations providing counseling services to children, youth, and families at no charge;
3. Students providing services in a training setting with certain supervisory restrictions; and
4. Nonresidents of the state who are licensed in another jurisdiction and provide services for no more than 5 days in a month or 15 days in a calendar year.

Individuals qualifying for a categorical exemption are prohibited from using the title "mental health counselor" or related titles (also see the next section).[17]

(C)(6) Use of the Mental Health Counselor Title

Individuals who are not licensed as mental health counselors are prohibited from using the titles of "mental health counselor," "mental health therapist," or "mental health consultant."[18] Violation of this prohibition constitutes a first-degree misdemeanor punishable by up to a year of incarceration.[19]

(D) Regulation

(D)(1) Unlawful and Prohibited Practices

There are a number of actions that may subject a mental health counselor to disciplinary action. These include[20]

1. Obtaining or attempting to obtain a license by fraud or bribery;
2. Having a license revoked or otherwise acted on by another state;
3. Being convicted of a crime directly related to the practice of the profession or ability to practice the profession;
4. Engaging in false, deceptive, or misleading advertising;
5. Advertising under an assumed name;

---

17. 15 FLA. STAT. ANN. § 491.012(1)(c) (West Supp. 2002).
18. Id.
19. 15 FLA. STAT. ANN. § 491.012(3) (West Supp. 2002).
20. 15 FLA. STAT. ANN. § 491.009(1)(a)–(w) (West Supp. 2001).

6. Maintaining a professional association with an individual who is known or should be known to have violated statutory provisions governing practice;

7. Aiding a nonlicensed or noncertified person to falsely represent him- or herself as licensed or certified;

8. Failing to perform statutory or legal obligations placed on a licensed mental health counselor;

9. Making a false report or record or failing to file a report or record required by law;

10. Paying a kickback or other form of remuneration to obtain clients;

11. Committing sexual battery or misconduct on a patient;

12. Making misleading, deceptive, untrue, or fraudulent representations in the course of practice;

13. Soliciting patients or clients personally, or through an agent, through fraud, intimidation, undue influence, or ether forms of overreaching;

14. Failing to make available to a patient or client, on written request, tests or other reports or documents prepared and paid for by the client;

15. Failing to respond within 30 days to a complaint or request for information from the Board or Department;

16. Violating statutory provisions applicable to the practice of mental health counseling;

17. Being an impaired professional because of alcohol, drug, or other substance abuse (see also chapter 5.1, Mental Status of Licensed or Certified Professionals);

18. Performing any treatment or prescribing any therapy that would constitute human experimentation, without first obtaining full, informed, and written consent;

19. Failing to perform according to generally prevailing professional standards;

20. Delegating professional responsibilities to a person known to be unqualified;

21. Violating a rule or order from a previous disciplinary hearing;

22. Failing to maintain a professional confidence absent consent or the clear and immediate probability of bodily harm to the patient or another;[21] and

---

21. *Also see* chapters 3.3, Confidential Relations and Communications, and 3.4, Privileged Communications.

23. Making public statements derived from test data, client contacts, or research that identifies or damages research participants or clients.

(D)(2) Formal Hearing Process

Hearings are conducted according to the same rules governing disciplinary proceedings involving other licensed professions. Notice of the hearing of not less than 14 days is to be provided the parties,[22] and the hearing officer may direct the parties to engage in a prehearing conference for the purpose of simplifying and clarifying issues, discussing settlement, examining documents, exchanging information regarding witnesses, resolving other procedural matters, and entering into a prehearing stipulation.[23] Discovery (the process by which parties to a lawsuit gain information regarding the other party's case) according to the *Florida Rules of Civil Procedure* is available[24] and the parties may subpoena witnesses.[25] At the hearing, all parties may present evidence, cross-examine witnesses, submit rebuttal evidence, submit proposed findings of facts and orders, file exceptions to any order or proposed order of the hearing officer, and may be represented by counsel.[26] The hearing officer, within 30 days of the hearing or receipt of the hearing transcript (whichever is later) is to file a recommended order that is to include a caption (title of the case, including identity of the parties), time and place of the hearing, appearances entered by counsel or parties to the hearing, a statement of the issues, findings of fact and conclusions of law, and a recommendation for final agency action.[27] A party may file exceptions to the findings of fact and conclusions of law within 15 days of their entry, and each party within 10 days of service of the exceptions may file a response to those exceptions.[28] After this the Board may adopt, reject, or modify the hearing officer's conclusions of law or findings of fact.[29] However, modification or rejection of the hearing officer's conclusions can occur only after a complete review of the record and a statement stating particularly why the hearing officer's conclusions have been rejected and why the agency's conclusions are more reasonable.[30] In addition, the penalty proposed may be reduced or increased only after review

---

22. FLA. ADMIN. CODE ANN. r. 28-106.208 (2002).
23. FLA. ADMIN. CODE ANN. r. 28-106.209 (2002).
24. FLA. ADMIN. CODE ANN. r. 28-106.206 (2002).
25. FLA. ADMIN. CODE ANN. r. 28-106.212 (2002).
26. 7 FLA. STAT. ANN. § 120.57(1)(b) (West Supp. 2002).
27. FLA. ADMIN. CODE ANN. r. 28-106.216 (2002).
28. FLA. ADMIN. CODE ANN. r. 28-106.217 (2002).
29. 7 FLA. STAT. ANN. § 120.57(1)(l) (West Supp. 2002).
30. *Id.*

of the complete record and a statement that explains why the penalty was changed.[31] Judicial review is available to a party adversely affected by a final agency action to the appellate district in which the agency maintains its headquarters.[32]

(D)(3) Penalties for Violation

If the Board, after a hearing, finds that one of the provisions detailed earlier has been violated, it can impose one of a variety of penalties, including the following:[33]

1. Revoking or suspending a mental health counselor's license;
2. Refusing to certify to the DOH the applicant's application for licensure, certification, or registration;
3. Restricting the individual's license;
4. Imposing administrative fines not to exceed $10,000 for each offense;
5. Issuing a reprimand;
6. Placing the mental health counselor on probation under conditions specified by the Board; the Board may direct the professional to submit to treatment, take continuing education courses, submit to reexamination, or work under another mental health counselor's supervision;
7. Issuing a letter of concern to the nurse;
8. Ordering a refund of fees billed to and collected from the patient;
9. Imposing an administrative fine for violation of patient rights;
10. Requiring remedial education; and
11. Taking other corrective action.

---

31. *Id.*
32. 7 FLA. STAT. ANN. § 120.68(2)(a) (West Supp. 2002).
33. 15 FLA. STAT. ANN. §. 456.072(2) (West Supp. 2002).

1.11
Licensure and Regulation of Hypnotists

Some MHPs practice hypnosis as part of their psychotherapeutic work. In addition, other kinds of health care professionals (e.g., nonpsychiatric physicians, dentists, osteopaths) may use hypnosis to induce relaxation and allay anxiety during medical procedures. Florida law does not recognize a discipline of "hypnotists," but the legislature has regulated its practice by health care professionals.

(A) Practice of Hypnosis: General Principles

The legislature permits the use of hypnosis for therapeutic purposes "only by certain practitioners of the healing arts within the limits and framework of their own particular field of competence" or by "qualified persons" to whom a patient may be referred. In the event of a referral the health care professional making the referral is jointly liable for any damages suffered as a result of the use of hypnosis.[1]

Hypnosis is defined as "hypnosis, hypnotism, mesmerism, posthypnotic suggestion, or any similar act or process which produces or is intended to produce in any person any form of induced sleep or trance in which the susceptibility of the person's mind to suggestion or direction is increased or is intended to be increased, where such a condition is used or intended to be used in the treatment of any human ill, disease, injury, or for any other therapeutic purpose."[2]

---

1. 15 FLA. STAT. ANN. § 485.002(3) (West 2002).
2. 15 FLA. STAT. ANN. § 485.003(1) (West 2002).

The use of hypnosis for therapeutic purposes by health care professionals is limited to "practitioners of the healing arts," defined in the statute as people licensed in Florida to practice medicine, surgery, psychiatry, dentistry, osteopathic medicine, chiropractic medicine, naturopathy, podiatric medicine, chiropody, psychology, clinical social work, marriage and family therapy, mental health counseling, or optometry within the scope of his or her professional training.[3] Such practitioners may also refer a patient to a person deemed competent by the practitioner to use hypnosis for therapeutic purposes,[4] though dentists, optometrists, podiatric physicians, chiropractic physicians, osteopathic physicians, and other physicians are explicitly prohibited from referring a patient for hypnosis "for the treatment of neurotic difficulties of a patient."[5]

(B) Practice of Hypnosis by Specific Professions

(B)(1) Psychologists

Psychologists can practice basic hypnosis if they complete at least 10 clock hours of education in basic hypnosis, which is defined as "the use of hypnotic approaches for the purpose of stress management, self-hypnosis, guided imagery, or relaxation."[6]

(B)(2) Psychiatrists

There are no specific provisions governing the use of hypnosis by psychiatrists. The statute noted earlier governs the use of hypnosis for therapeutic purposes by psychiatrists and other physicians.

(B)(3) Clinical Social Workers, Marriage and Family Therapists, and Mental Health Counselors

Professionals licensed under these categories can practice hypnosis for therapeutic purposes, other than for stress management, self-hypnosis, guided imagery, or relaxation, only after completing at least 50 hours of instruction in the concepts and misconceptions of hypnotic induction techniques, contraindications to

---

3. 15 FLA. STAT. ANN. § 485.003)(3) (West 2002).
4. 15 FLA. STAT. ANN. § 485.003(4) (West 2002).
5. 15 FLA. STAT. ANN. § 485.002(2) (West 2002).
6. FLA. ADMIN. CODE ANN. r. 64B19-18.003 (2002).

hypnosis, and the relationships of personality dynamics, psychopathology, and ethical issues in hypnosis.[7]

A person cannot qualify as a teacher of hypnosis absent documentation of a minimum of 200 hours of graduate- or postgraduate-level hypnosis training and a minimum of three years of practical experience in the use of hypnosis, or be a practitioner of the healing arts as defined by statute.[8]

---

7. FLA. ADMIN. CODE ANN. r. 64B4-7.002 (2002).
8. *Id.*

1.12
Licensure and Regulation of Polygraph Examiners

Florida does not license or regulate polygraph examiners.[1] However, the law does require individuals convicted of specific sexual offenses[2] when on conditional release to undergo at a minimum one annual polygraph examination as part of a treatment program. The polygraph examination must be conducted by a polygrapher trained specifically in the use of the polygraph for the monitoring of sex offenders, where available, and must be paid for by the offender. The purpose of the polygraph examination is to obtain information necessary for risk management and treatment and "to reduce the sex offender's denial mechanisms."[3]

---

1. For a discussion of the admissibility of polygraph evidence, see chapter 6.3, Polygraph Evidence.
2. Sexual battery, indecent assault on or in the presence of a child, offenses involving sexual performance by a child, or selling a child for the purposes of sex.
3. 24 FLA. STAT. ANN. § 947.1405(7)(b)(1) (West Supp. 2002).

1.13
Regulation of Unlicensed Mental Health Professionals

Florida does not recognize, and therefore generally does not regulate unlicensed MHPs. However the boards for each profession may discipline those who practice without a license. The DOH which has responsibilities for licensing health care professionals, including MHPs, may through its boards pursue a variety of penalties for unauthorized practice. These include administrative penalties as well as civil penalties through the courts, including financial penalties of $500 to $5000 per offense. In addition, criminal penalties for unlicensed practice may be imposed.[1]

---

1. *See, generally*, FLA. STAT. ANN. § 456.065 (West).

1.14
Sunset of Credentialing Agencies

Florida has a sunshine act that creates a process for the legislature to follow in considering proposals to regulate professions or occupations not already expressly subject to regulation by a state licensing board or agency.[1]

(A) Sunrise Act

In making this decision, the legislature is to consider whether the practice or profession in question if unregulated will substantially endanger the public; whether it requires specialized skill or training and if so whether examinations of that skill or training are possible; whether the public can be protected by other means; and whether the overall cost-effectiveness and economic impact of regulation is favorable.[2]

Proponents of legislation to regulate a profession or occupation must provide information to the appropriate legislative committees, as well as the state agency that would oversee regulation, including the number of individuals that would be subject to regulation; other states' policies regarding the profession or occupation; any federal legislation mandating regulation; and why current laws are inadequate to protect the public.[3]

---

1. 1 FLA. STAT. ANN. § 11.62 (West Supp. 2002).
2. 1 FLA. STAT. ANN. § 11.62(3)(a)–(d) (West Supp. 2002).
3. 1 FLA. STAT. ANN. § 11.62(4)(a)–(k) (West Supp. 2002).

(B) Sunset Act

Some states provide for the periodic review of agencies, boards, and laws (typically licensure laws) that regulate the practice of professions and occupations. Florida had provisions for such a process but repealed it in the early 1990s.[4] The legislature, of course, remains free to review, revise, or abolish any statute regulating a profession or occupation and to make changes in licensure laws and requirements.

---

4. 1 FLA. STAT. ANN. § 11.61 (West Supp. 2002).

1.15
Licensure and Regulation of Sex Therapists

Florida does not license sex therapists separately. However, Florida law does regulate the conditions under which an MHP may hold him- or herself out as a sex therapist. Thus, in Florida, sex therapy is best conceptualized as a substantive area of practice rather than a profession.

(A) Psychologists

Psychologists can identify themselves as sex therapists if they hold a license as a psychologist under Florida law and if they meet standards established by the Board of Psychology.[1] The Board of Psychology has specified that a psychologist must receive 150 hours of education in the specific area of sex therapy and in the interaction between sex therapy and the general provision of psychological health services.[2]

(B) Psychiatrists

There are no specific statutes or rules establishing requirements that physicians must meet to identify themselves as sex therapists or perform sex therapy.

---

1. 15 FLA. STAT. ANN. § 490.0143 (West 2001).
2. FLA. ADMIN. CODE ANN. r. 64B19-18.002 (2002).

(C) Licensed Social Workers, Licensed Mental Health Counselors, and Licensed Marriage and Family Therapists

Clinical social workers, marriage and family therapists, and mental health counselors can identify themselves as sex therapists only if licensed under Florida law and meeting the requirements of the Board of Clinical Social Work, Marriage and Family Therapy and Mental Health Counseling.[3] The Board's requirements are more detailed than those of the Board of Psychology for psychologists. Use of the title "sex therapist" requires a minimum of 120 hours of approved education credit from 12 of the following areas with a minimum of 10 hours in each area taken:[4]

1. Sexual and reproductive anatomy and physiology;
2. Developmental sexuality;
3. Gender-identity issues;
4. Sociocultural factors in sexual values and behavior;
5. Medical factors related to sexuality and sexual functioning;
6. Interaction between sexuality and dynamics of interpersonal and family relationships;
7. Sexual offender treatment;
8. Diagnosis of sexual dysfunctions, disorders, and deviancy;
9. Treatment of sexual dysfunctions, disorders, and deviancy;
10. Legal, ethical, and forensic issues in sex therapy;
11. Sexually transmitted diseases;
12. Risk assessment with sex offenders;
13. Psychopharmacological therapy with sexual dysfunctions, disorders, and deviancy;
14. Research on sexual dysfunctions, disorders, and deviancy;
15. Sexual abuse treatment;
16. Victimology/victim therapy; and
17. Group therapy in sexual dysfunctions, disorders, and deviancy.

---

3. 15 FLA. STAT. ANN. § 491.0143 (West 2001).
4. FLA. ADMIN. CODE ANN. r. 64b4-7.004 (2002).

In addition, the practitioner must have a minimum of 40 contact hours in the clinical practice of sex therapy within a six-month period, as well as a minimum of 20 hours of supervision with each supervisory session lasting no more than 1½ hours within a six-month period.

A therapist who held him- or herself out as a sex therapist under the educational requirements in effect between February 25, 1990, and December 31, 1996, is permitted to continue to use the title "sex therapist."

Section 2

Business Matters

2.1
Sole Proprietorships

The *sole proprietorship* is the oldest and most frequently used form of business enterprise. Many mental health professionals (MHPs) are sole proprietorships. In this form of enterprise, the individual is self-employed and hires other employees or agents as he or she sees fit.

There are several responsibilities borne by the person conducting business in this manner. For example, the individual is personally liable for torts he or she commits in the course of business. In contrast, there are few circumstances in which personal liability may be imposed when a business is organized as a corporation. In addition, the sole proprietor pays income tax on income created by the proprietorship. The sole proprietor may take advantage of some savings on contributions to qualified retirement plans, although taxes are still paid at the personal, rather than the lower corporate, level.

Florida law does not impose rules for conducting business exclusively applicable to sole proprietorships, nor does Florida define the characteristics of a sole proprietorship in statute. An MHP conducting business as a sole proprietorship must meet applicable licensure requirements. If a sole proprietorship is sold to another party, Florida adopts the rule followed by most states that the buyer of the proprietorship will not become liable for the legal liabilities of the seller, absent a contractual agreement to do so.[1]

---

1. Bernard v. Kee Mfg. Co., 409 So. 2d 1047 (1982).

2.2
Professional Corporations

A *corporation* is one of a variety of forms of business organizations by which MHPs may choose to conduct their business. Other types of organizations are discussed throughout this section. When MHPs incorporate, they generally must do so under a special statute known as the Professional Service Corporation and Limited Liability Company Act (hereinafter, Liability Act).[1]

(A) Benefits of Incorporation

MHPs may choose to conduct business as a corporation for a number of reasons. Some favor this structure for tax reasons: A corporation may deduct certain expenses (for example, health insurance). In addition, personal liability under the Liability Act is limited, and there are limitations on the amount of corporate liability as well (liability is discussed in more detail later). Furthermore, incorporating may create a greater capacity for attracting capital to the business than might be available under other forms of organization, such as a sole proprietorship.

---

1. 18 FLA. STAT. ANN. § 621.02 (West 2001).

(B) Incorporation and Operations Procedures

A professional service corporation[2] may exist only for the purpose of providing professional services.[3] Professional service is defined as "any type of personal service to the public which requires as a condition ... to the rendering of such service ... a license or other legal authorization."[4] Examples of professional services enumerated by statute include but are not limited to services provided by physicians and surgeons.[5] Therefore, anyone providing services on behalf of the corporation, with the exception of clerks, secretaries, and other support staff,[6] must be licensed, and shareholders either must be a licensed professional, a professional corporation, or a professional limited liability company.[7] (A professional limited liability company is a company organized for the sole and specific purpose of rendering professional service and that has as its members only other professional limited liability companies, professional corporations, or individuals who themselves are duly licensed or otherwise legally authorized to render the same professional service as the limited liability company. For purposes of this discussion, there is no practical difference between a professional services corporation and a professional limited liability company.)[8]

To incorporate and operate legally, the corporation must file articles of incorporation and other documents with the Florida Department of State.[9] There are statutory rules that govern the name of the corporation. For example, the corporation may contain the last name or names of the shareholders. The name must contain the word "chartered" or the words "professional association" or the abbreviation "PA" in the case of a professional

---

2. Although the term *corporation* is used throughout this discussion, Florida law also provides for the creation of *limited liability companies*. *See generally*, 18 FLA. STAT. ANN. §§ 608.401–514 (West 2001). There are some distinctions between such companies and other forms of organization not relevant here. For purposes of the professional service corporation statute, the terms *corporation* and *limited liability company*" are virtually indistinguishable, so the term *corporation* is used.
3. 18 FLA. STAT. ANN. § 621.03(2) (West 2001).
4. 18 FLA. STAT. ANN. § 621.03(1) (West 2001).
5. *Id.*
6. 18 FLA. STAT. ANN. § 621.06 (West 2001).
7. 18 FLA. STAT. ANN. § 621.03(2) and (3) (West 2001).
8. 18 FLA. STAT. ANN. § 621.03(3) (West 2001).
9. 18 FLA. STAT. ANN. § 607.0120 (West 2001).

corporation or the words "professional limited company" or the abbreviation "PL" in the case of a professional limited liability company.[10]

(C) Liability and Accountability

Incorporation limits liability in some respects. However, the nature of the individual clinical relationship between the MHP and patient or client does not change and continues to be governed by ordinary liability principles (see, for example, chapter 3.10, Malpractice Liability).

Personal liability accrues to an officer, agent, member, manager, or employee of a professional service corporation only for negligent or wrongful acts committed directly by that individual or by someone under his or her supervision.[11] There are also financial limits on liability. In contrast, all partners to a partnership may be liable for the actions of an individual partner.[12] Absent special circumstances, for example, criminal conduct or conduct resulting in improper personal gain, the directors of a corporation are not liable personally for the actions of corporate employees or agents or for their own breaches of their responsibilities as directors.[13] However, the corporation may be liable up to the full value of its property for any negligent or wrongful act of its employees, agents, managers, or officers while they are providing professional services on behalf of the corporation.[14]

(D) Termination of the Professional Corporation

A corporation may be terminated voluntarily by the directors, or if there are no directors, the incorporator or a majority of incorporators.[15] Documentation of the dissolution must be filed with the secretary of state.[16] The secretary of state may also administratively dissolve a corporation for noncompliance with statutory requirements mandating certain filings by the corporation with the secretary of state.[17]

---

10. 18 FLA. STAT. ANN. § 621.12 (West 2001).
11. 18 FLA. STAT. ANN. § 621.07 (West 2001).
12. *See* chapter 2.3, Partnerships.
13. 18 FLA. STAT. ANN. § 607.0831 (West 2001).
14. 18 FLA. STAT. ANN. § 621.07 (West 2001).
15. 18 FLA. STAT. ANN. § 617.1401 (West 2001).
16. 18 FLA. STAT. ANN. § 617.01201 (West 2001).
17. 18 FLA. STAT. ANN. § 617.1420 (West 2001).

2.3

Partnerships

A *partnership* is "an association of two or more persons to carry on a business for profit as co-owners."[1] A partnership, at its core, enables partners to pool their money, goods, labor, or skills to carry on a trade, profession, or business and, by doing so, to create a shared interest in the profits and losses of the enterprise.[2] As the discussion that follows suggests, a limited partnership limits the liability of the partners. Partnerships are popular forms of doing business because they permit individuals to aggregate resources. At the same time, partners share liability for each other's actions, a fact that should be considered when deciding whether or not to enter a partnership.

(A) Formation of a Partnership/Types of Partners

A partnership is formed when two or more persons agree to carry on a business as partners. There are two types of partnerships: general and limited. The distinction is important primarily because a limited partner has less exposure to liability. A *limited partner* is defined as a person who has been admitted to a limited partnership as a limited partner in accord with the partnership agreement.[3] The reason for permitting limited partners is to encourage individuals to invest capital into a business without incurring liability for all of the obligations of the partnership. In contrast

---

1. 18 FLA. STAT. ANN. § 620.8101(7) (West 2001).
2. Mauldin v. C.I.R., 155 F.2d 666 (4th Cir. 1946).
3. 18 FLA. STAT. ANN. § 620.102(6) (West 2001).

to a *general partnership*, which may be formed without the filing of any certificate with the state (though the partnership may register if it wishes with the secretary of state),[4] a limited partnership can be formed only by filing a certificate of limited partnership with the secretary of state.[5] The distinctions in the liability of general and limited partners are discussed in (B), Rights, Duties, and Liabilities of Partners, of this chapter.

There are certain actions that people take in the course of business that do not result automatically in the creation of a partnership. These include joint tenancy and other arrangements regarding property, in which profits from the use of the property are not shared; the sharing of gross returns (as distinct from profits) from a business; and the sharing of profits where the payment was for the purpose of repaying a debt, paying wages, paying an annuity to the representative or spouse of a deceased partner, or payment of interest on a loan or related transaction or the sale of the goodwill of a business.[6] Note that the core concept that defines and distinguishes partnerships from other types of business arrangements is that of profit sharing. If an MHP enters an arrangement in which profits from his or her practice are shared with others, the MHP should be aware that the arrangement could be construed as a general partnership (though not a limited partnership, absent the necessary filing with the secretary of state). This is potentially important because of the liability issues that exist in a partnership.

The profits from a partnership are generally split equally in the absence of an express agreement distributing them in some other fashion. In a limited partnership, the statute requires that profits be distributed according to the written partnership agreement. As a general rule, profits in a limited partnership are to be distributed according to the value of the contributions made to the partnership by each partner if the distribution is not specified in the partnership agreement.[7]

(B) Rights, Duties, and Liabilities of Partners

The core obligation owed by each partner to the others is to act as a fiduciary. This means that each partner must account to the

---

4. 18 FLA. STAT. ANN. § 620.8105 (West 2001).
5. 18 FLA. STAT. ANN. § 620.108 (West 2001).
6. 18 FLA. STAT. ANN. § 620.8202(3) (West Supp. 2000).
7. 18 FLA. STAT. ANN. § 620.137 (West 1993).

partnership for any benefit or profit realized as a partner with or without the earlier consent of other partners.[8] Partners may modify by agreement their duties to each other. However, in the absence of such modification by agreement, partners have several statutorily established rights and duties.[9] These include a right to an account crediting the partner with an amount equal to the contributions of the partner to the partnership, and profits, minus liabilities, as well as a duty to be charged with losses in the same fashion. Partners also have rights to reimbursement for payments made in the ordinary course of business and to be indemnified for liabilities incurred in the ordinary course of business, and equal rights to the management and conduct of the partnership business. A new partner may be accepted only with the consent of all other partners, and decisions to be made in the ordinary course of business may be decided by a majority of partners, whereas decisions outside the ordinary course of business require unanimity.

As a general rule, each partner is liable not only for his or her actions but also for those of the other partners, though new partners are not liable for actions committed before their joining the partnership.[10] The partnership must make whole the losses caused by the misappropriation of money or property by one partner.[11] However, limited partners, as a general rule, are not liable for the obligations of the partnership unless they take part in the control of the business of the partnership, in which case their liability is restricted to those who dealt with the partnership believing that the limited partner in fact was a general partner.[12]

(C) Dissolution of a Partnership

A partnership may end in several ways, either through actions taken by the partners or, in some cases, through the courts. For example, a limited partnership will terminate[13]

1. At a time specified in the certificate of limited partnership;

2. At the happening of an event specified in writing in the partnership agreement;

3. When all partners have given their written consent; and

---

8. 18 Fla. Stat. Ann. § 620.8404 (West Supp. 2000).
9. 18 Fla. Stat. Ann. § 620.8401 (West 2001).
10. 18 Fla. Stat. Ann. § 620.8306 (West 2001).
11. 18 Fla. Stat. Ann. § 620.8305 (West 2001).
12. 18 Fla. Stat. Ann. § 620.129 (West 2001).
13. 18 Fla. Stat. Ann. § 620.157 (West 2001).

4. When a general partner withdraws, unless there is at least one other general partner and the written partnership agreement permits the partnership to continue, or in the absence of another general partner, all limited partners agree in writing within 90 days to continue the partnership and appoint another general partner.

In addition, a circuit court may order dissolution of a limited partnership on application of a partner if it is no longer reasonably practicable to carry on the business of the partnership in conformity with the partnership agreement.[14]

A general partnership is dissolved by[15]

1. The withdrawal of a partner;
2. A partnership created for a definite period of time or for a definite purpose on the death or disassociation of a partner followed by a decision by at least half of the remaining partners to end the partnership business;
3. Occurrence of an event specified in the written partnership agreement as resulting in the winding up of the partnership business;
4. Events that makes it unlawful for the partnership business to continue; and
5. Judicial determination, on the application of a partner, that
    (a) The economic purpose of the partnership is likely to be unreasonably frustrated (that is, very difficult to achieve);
    (b) Another partner has engaged in conduct that makes it not reasonably practicable to carry on the partnership business with that partner;
    (c) It is not otherwise practicable to carry on the business in conformity with the partnership agreement; or
    (d) On application of a transferee of a partner's transferable interest that it is equitable to wind up the partnership business.

The fact that a partnership is dissolved does not end the existing liability of any partner.[16] In addition, the partnership is not formally terminated at the time of dissolution but continues in existence until the affairs and obligations of the partnership are completed.[17]

---

14. 18 FLA. STAT. ANN. § 620.158 (West 1993).
15. 18 FLA. STAT. ANN. § 620.8801 (West 2001).
16. 18 FLA. STAT. ANN. § 620.8806 (West 2001).
17. 18 FLA. STAT. ANN. § 620.8803 (West 2001).

2.4

Health Maintenance Organizations

Health maintenance organizations (HMOs) are health care provider organizations that provide services to enrollees (rather than to the general public) and that usually are compensated on a prepaid basis (rather than retrospectively, as typically was the case in a traditional, fee-for-service reimbursement system). Florida law defines an HMO as any organization meeting statutory requirements and that[1]

1. Provides emergency care, inpatient hospital services, physician care, ambulatory diagnostic treatment, and preventive health care services;

2. Provides, either directly or through arrangements with other persons, health care services to persons enrolled with the organization on a prepaid per capita or prepaid aggregate fixed-sum basis;

3. Provides either directly or through arrangements with other persons comprehensive health care services that subscribers are entitled to receive pursuant to a contract;

4. Provides physician services directly through physicians who are employees or partners of the HMO or under arrangements with a physician or physician group; and

5. If the HMO provides services through a managed care system, must be a managed care system in which a licensed physician is designated to manage the care of each subscriber of services.

HMOs, although they may set rates for services provided, are distinct from insurance companies. However, to operate,

---

1. 18 FLA. STAT. ANN. § 641.19(13) (West Supp. 2002).

HMOs must meet certain state requirements, particularly regarding fiscal soundness.[2] In addition, there are extensive legislative requirements governing the content of contracts HMOs enter with subscribers, including provisions for notifying subscribers of their rights under the contract, mandates for the offering of certain benefits (e.g., in care of a mother after the birth of a child), and rules on copayments.[3] In addition, certain marketing activities—for example, those directed at Medicare recipients—are regulated by statute.[4]

(A) Benefits for Mental Health Services

Like other insurers and providers, HMOs are required to offer mental health benefits as optional coverage to subscribers. These benefits must be made available for an "appropriate additional premium" and must consist at least of the following:[5]

1. 30 days of inpatient benefits per benefit year;

2. At least $1000 of outpatient benefits for consultation with a licensed physician, psychologist, mental health counselor, marriage and family therapist, or social worker; and

3. Partial hospitalization benefits under a physician's direction, provided that the cost of 30 days of partial hospitalization or a combination of partial hospitalization and inpatient care does not exceed the cost of 30 days of inpatient hospitalization in the community in which the partial hospitalization is provided.

If an HMO offers mental health benefits in excess of these statutorily mandated minimums, the durational limits, dollar amounts, and coinsurance factors do not have to be the same as applicable to physical illness generally.[6]

(B) Provider Contracts

All contracts between an HMO and a health care provider must be in writing and provide that the individual who receives services

---

2. 18 FLA. STAT. ANN. § 641.225 (West Supp. 2002).
3. 18 FLA. STAT. ANN. § 641.31 (West Supp. 2002).
4. 18 FLA. STAT. ANN. § 641.309 (West Supp. 2002).
5. 18 FLA. STAT. ANN. § 627.668(2)(a) (West Supp. 2002).
6. 18 FLA. STAT. ANN. § 627.668(2) (West Supp. 2002).

is not liable financially for services for which the HMO is liable.[7] The provider must give the HMO 60 days notice for cancellation of the contract. In addition, the HMO must provide 60 days notice to the provider and the state before canceling a contract with a provider, unless a patient is in imminent danger or the physician's ability to practice medicine is deemed *impaired* by the Board of Medicine.[8]

A contract between an HMO and a health care provider also shall not contain any provision restricting the provider's ability to communicate information to a patient regarding medical care or treatment options the provider believes are in the best interests of the patient.[9]

The HMO is also to ensure that[10]

1. Services rendered meet a reasonable standard of care consistent with prevailing standards of care within the community;
2. Services are available from a broad panel of providers;
3. The HMO is accredited by a national review organization and is financially secure;
4. Continuity of health care is available;
5. The subscriber to the HMO receives timely and concise information regarding reimbursement practices and coverage;
6. The subscriber can transfer to another HMO regardless of health status;
7. The subscriber is not discriminated against based on health status in the provision of services;
8. Preexisting conditions must be covered subject to statutory limitations;
9. Timely grievance and appeals procedures are available to the subscriber;
10. The subscriber should receive at least 30 days written notice of a proposed change in rates; and
11. A handbook is made available summarizing this information.

(C) Liability

HMOs are subject to the same rules of liability in negligence and malpractice actions as other health care providers (see generally chapters 3.10, Malpractice Liability, and 3.11, Other Forms of Professional Liability).

---

7. 18 FLA. STAT. ANN. § 641.315(1) (West Supp. 2002).
8. 18 FLA. STAT. ANN. § 641.315(2)(a)(2)–(2)(b) (West Supp. 2002).
9. 18 FLA. STAT. ANN. § 641.315(5) (West Supp. 2002).
10. 18 FLA. STAT. ANN. § 641.185 (West Supp. 2002).

2.5
Preferred Provider Organizations

Florida law defines a *preferred provider* as "any licensed health care provider with which the insurer has directly or indirectly contracted for an alternative or reduced rate of payment."[1] A *preferred provider network* is a group of preferred providers. Its distinguishing characteristic is that an insurer has directly or indirectly contracted for alternative or reduced rates of payment.[2] This arrangement provides advantages to both parties—the insurer's overall payments for health care services are reduced, and the providers are ensured patient volume. If an insurer uses preferred providers, it must make available to each policy holder a current list of preferred providers and post the list for public inspection during regular business hours at its principal place of business.[3]

There are other statutory rules governing the use of preferred providers, particularly regarding payments and deductibles. For example, if payment schedules differ for services provided by preferred and nonpreferred providers, a number of limitations apply:[4]

1. The amount of an annual deductible for treatment in a facility that is not a preferred provider cannot exceed four times the amount of a deductible for a similar, preferred provider;

2. If there is no deductible for treatment in a preferred provider facility, the deductible for treatment in a nonpreferred facility cannot exceed $500 per covered person per visit;

---
1. 18 FLA. STAT. ANN. § 627.6471(1)(b) (West Supp. 2002).
2. 18 FLA. STAT. ANN. § 627.6471(1)(c) (West Supp. 2002).
3. 18 FLA. STAT. ANN. § 627.6471(2) (West Supp. 2002).
4. 18 FLA. STAT. ANN. § 627.6471(4)(a)–(h) (West Supp. 2002).

3. The amount of any deductible, other than for inpatient treatment, cannot exceed four times the amount for a nonpreferred provider of that for a preferred provider;

4. If the policy for a preferred provider (not a facility) has no deductible, the annual deductible for a nonpreferred provider cannot exceed $500 per covered person;

5. The percentage amount of coinsurance to be paid by the insured to a nonpreferred provider may not be more than 50 percentage points greater than the percentage amount of any coinsurance payment to be paid by a preferred provider;

6. The amount of any deductible and payment of coinsurance paid by an insured must be applied to the reduced charge negotiated between the insurer and the preferred provider;

7. An insurer may still require payment of a reasonable copayment for inpatient or outpatient care; and

8. If a service or treatment is not within the scope of services provided by the network of preferred providers but is within the scope of services or treatment covered by the policy, the service or treatment has to be reimbursed at a rate not less than 10 percentage points lower than the percentage rate paid to preferred providers.

Florida law also permits the formation of *exclusive provider organizations* in which an insurer contracts with a provider or providers to become the exclusive provider of specified services or treatment.[5] An insurer cannot use an exclusive provider arrangement until it receives approval of a plan filed with the Agency for Health Care Administration.[6] The plan must contain a variety of information about the network, as well as assurances that emergency care is available 24 hours per day, 7 days per week, as well as a grievance process for plan enrollees.[7] If the insurer relies on an exclusive provider arrangement, it must offer to a policyholder at the time of initial enrollment the opportunity to purchase a policy offered by the insurer that is not subject to an exclusive provider network.[8]

If an insurer covers psychotherapeutic services, in either a preferred or exclusive provider arrangement, it must provide criteria for those licensed professions eligible to provide psychotherapeutic services within the scope of their practice. The insurer

---

5. 18 FLA. STAT. ANN. § 627.6472 (West Supp. 2002).
6. 18 FLA. STAT. ANN. § 627.6472(4) (West Supp. 2002).
7. 18 FLA. STAT. ANN. § 627.6472(4)–(5) (West Supp. 2002).
8. 18 FLA. STAT. ANN. § 627.6472(13) (West Supp. 2002).

may not exclude a practitioner from its provider network because of that practitioner's license.[9] In other words, a social worker may not be excluded from participating in a provider network simply because he or she holds a social work license rather than a psychologist (or other MHP) license.

---

9. 18 FLA. STAT. ANN. § 627.6471(5) (West Supp. 2002); 18 FLA. STAT. ANN. § 627.6472(15) (West Supp. 2002).

2.6
Individual Practice Associations

Individual practice associations (IPAs) are an increasingly popular type of provider organization developing in response to changes in the financing of health care. An IPA typically comprises individual practitioners (usually physicians) who contract with a payer or provider of services to provide certain types of services to an enrolled group of patients. Payment to the IPA members may be made in a variety of ways, from fee-for-service to capitation.[1] The members of the IPA retain their individual businesses or practices but agree to act as a group for contracting purposes to enhance their market position.

Florida has no statute addressing IPAs. However, the regulations governing the operation of HMOs do provide for HMOs based on an IPA model. It defines an IPA model of providing services through an HMO as a model in which the HMO contracts with individual physicians, a medical group, or physician organization that, in turn, may contract with other individual physicians or groups. The regulations note that the physicians may practice in their own offices and continue to treat their fee-for-service patients, in addition to the care they provide through their HMO contract.[2]

The state also requires staff model HMOs and combination IPA and staff model HMOs with an annual premium volume of

---

1. In a capitated reimbursement system, a fixed amount of money is made available to a provider to provide all contracted-for-services to a group of plan enrollees. If the provider's expenditures exceed the amount of reimbursement made available under the contract, the provider usually must bear all or a significant portion of the excess costs. If the provider's expenditures are below the contracted amount, the provider may retain all or a significant portion of the money left in the contract.
2. FLA. ADMIN. CODE r. 4-191.024(12) (2002).

$10,000,000 or more to employ or contract with a licensed risk manager who is responsible for establishing and administering the organization's internal risk management program. If the premium volume is less than $10,000,000, then the organization must designate an officer or employee to serve as risk manager.[3]

---

3. FLA. ADMIN. CODE r. 59A-12.012(2) (2002).

2.7
Hospital, Administrative, and Staff Privileges

In general, Florida law does not require particular qualifications of individuals in administrative positions beyond that required for licensure.

(A) Agency and Administrative Positions

Individuals holding positions, for example, as medical directors, do not have to meet additional statutory requirements for such positions. In some instances, when mental illness issues are involved—for example, in addressing civil commitment issues—the law does define physicians as individuals who are licensed and who have "experience in the diagnosis and treatment of mental and nervous disorders."[1]

(B) Hospital Staff Privileges

An individual who wishes to practice in a hospital setting must obtain privileges from the hospital to do so. Administration of this process generally is under the control and supervision of the medical staff, operating under standards and procedures set by the facility's governing board.[2]

---

1. 14 Fla. Stat. Ann. § 394.455(21) (West 2002).
2. 14 Fla. Stat. Ann. § 395.0191(4) (West Supp. 2002).

In determining whether an individual will receive privileges, applications from physicians, nurse practitioners, and psychologists are to be considered according to the licensing criteria for their respective professions.[3] In addition, the applicant's eligibility for clinical records or staff membership is to be determined by the applicant's background, experience, health, training, and demonstrated competency, as well as his or her adherence to professional ethical standards and his or her ability to work with others.[4]

Licensed facilities must also establish peer review processes for physicians and other staff members delivering health care services at the facility.[5] Disciplinary action, including suspension, denial, revocation or curtailment of privileges; reprimands; mandatory counseling; or a requirement for additional professional training and education may be taken after a determination that the physician or staff member is incompetent, a habitual user of intoxicants or drugs to the point that he or she endangers others or self, has a mental or physical impairment that may adversely affect patient care, has been found liable for medical malpractice or negligence, has had one or more settlements exceeding $10,000 for medical negligence or malpractice involving negligence, or has been found guilty of other types of medical negligence or has failed to comply with risk management policies, procedures, or directives.[6]

The legislature, in an effort to encourage staff members to participate in the peer review and disciplinary processes, has provided that participants acting in good faith generally will be immune from tort suits and antitrust actions.[7]

---

3. *Id.*
4. *Id.*
5. 14 FLA. STAT. ANN. § 395.0193(2) (West Supp. 2002).
6. 14 FLA. STAT. ANN. § 395.0193(3) (West Supp. 2002).
7. 14 FLA. STAT. ANN. § 395.0193(1) (West Supp. 2002).

2.8
Zoning for Community Homes

The creation of housing for people with mental disabilities is often affected by zoning laws. Municipalities use zoning laws to regulate the purposes for which land may be used. Zoning ordinances define geographically where residential and business use may occur, and may create rules regarding the design of buildings as well. In residential areas, there may be restrictions on occupancy, for example, by limiting the number of unrelated persons who may reside in a single residence.

Often, it has been difficult to create housing for people with mental disabilities, in part because of discrimination and in part because of neighborhood concerns that property values may decline if such housing is established. In response, many states, including Florida, have enacted legislation that creates special rules to govern the siting of housing for people with mental disabilities.

(A) Definition of Community Homes

Florida law creates specific requirements for the creation of *community residential homes*, defined in statute as dwelling units licensed to serve clients of the Department of Children and Families (DCF) and that provide a living environment for 7 to 14 unrelated residents who, in turn, operate as the functional equivalent of a family, including such supervision and care by supportive staff as is necessary to meet the residents' physical, emotional, and social needs.[1]

---

1. 14 FLA. STAT. ANN. § 419.001(1)(a) (West Supp. 2002).

(B) Applications for Community Homes

The law requires that, on identification of a potential site for a community home, the home's sponsoring agency must provide written notice to the chief executive officer of the local government. The notice must include information regarding the site's address, the residential licensing category into which the home falls, the number of proposed residents, and the kind of community support the home will require.[2] The notice must also provide information regarding the need for the home and how the home will meet that need. Information regarding other residential sites within the DCF district must also be provided.[3]

The local government then may review the submission. After review, the local government has several choices. It may determine that the proposed home meets local zoning requirements and approve the site; fail to respond within 60 days, after which time the home may be established; or deny approval of the site.[4] The local government may deny the application for siting only if the government shows that placement of the home at the proposed site does not conform to existing zoning regulations applicable to other multifamily uses in the area; does not meet licensing criteria established by the DCF; or would result in a concentration of residential homes such that the nature and character of the area in question would be substantially affected. If a home is located within a radius of 1200 feet from an existing community residential home, overconcentration is presumed if the area is zoned for multifamily use. If a community residential home is located within a radius of 500 feet of an area of single-family zoning, the statute provides that the nature and character of the area has been substantially altered.[5] If the local government and sponsoring agency disagree regarding the siting decision, informal mediation may be used with the consent of both parties; however, resorting to mediation does not restrict either party's right to appeal to the courts for resolution of issues within the court's jurisdiction.[6]

If an agency does not follow these statutory procedures, the DCF is not to issue a license for the home's operation.[7] Local laws and ordinances applicable to residential family units in the same

---

2. 14 Fla. Stat. Ann. § 419.001(3)(a) (West Supp. 2002).
3. Id.
4. 14 Fla. Stat. Ann. § 419.001(3)(b) (West Supp. 2002).
5. 14 Fla. Stat. Ann. § 419.001(3)(c)(1)–(3) (West Supp. 2002).
6. 14 Fla. Stat. Ann. § 419.001(5) (West Supp. 2002).
7. 14 Fla. Stat. Ann. § 419.001(6) (West Supp. 2002).

area apply to the community residence.[8] In addition, individuals who would constitute a direct threat to the health and safety of others or whose residency would result in substantial physical damage to the property of others may be prohibited from living in such residences.[9]

This statute does not apply to homes of six or fewer residents that would otherwise meet the statutory definition of a community residential home.[10] Rather, such homes can be established in areas zoned for single-family use without resorting to the process described earlier. However, homes of six or fewer residents may not be established within a radius of 1000 feet of a similar home, and the operator must notify the local government of the licensed status of the home at the time of occupancy.

---

8. 14 FLA. STAT. ANN. § 419.001(7) (West Supp. 2002).
9. 14 FLA. STAT. ANN. § 419.001(9) (West Supp. 2002).
10. 14 FLA. STAT. ANN. § 419.001(2) (West Supp. 2002).

2.9

Insurance Reimbursement for Services

This chapter describes briefly the statutory and regulatory structure governing the issuance of insurance policies in Florida. Insurance coverage for mental health and substance abuse services is described in chapter 2.10, Mental Health Benefits in State Insurance Plans.

The Department of Insurance regulates the insurance industry. The Department is charged with adopting rules to establish minimum benefits for individual and family accident and health insurance policies in the following categories:[1]

1. Basic hospital expense insurance;
2. Basic medical expense insurance;
3. Basic surgical expense insurance;
4. Hospital confinement indemnity insurance;
5. Major medical expense insurance;
6. Disability income protection insurance;
7. Accident-only insurance;
8. Limited benefit insurance;
9. Supplemental insurance;
10. Home health care coverage; and
11. Nonconventional coverage.

Insurers are prohibited from discriminating in providing coverage solely on the basis of a mental or physical handicap, though insurers do not have to insure against a preexisting condition.[2]

---

1. 18 FLA. STAT. ANN. § 627.643(2) (West Supp. 2002).
2. 18 FLA. STAT. ANN. § 627.644 (West Supp. 2002).

The Department of Insurance has created administrative regulations defining the terms used in statutes and establishing criteria for each type of policy.[3] For example, a basic medical expense insurance policy is defined as[4]

> a policy of accident and health insurance which provides coverage for each person insured under the policy for the expense incurred for the necessary services and treatment of an injury or sickness for at least the following: in-hospital medical services, consisting of physician services rendered to a person who is a bed patient in a hospital for treatment of sickness or injury other than that for which surgical care is required, in an amount not less than $5.00 per call, one call per day, for at least 21 such calls during "one period of confinement" or similar benefit acceptable to the Department.

In contrast, rules for the group health plan covering state employees are set by the Division of State Group Insurance within the Department of Management Services.[5] For a discussion of the Medicaid program, which is essentially insurance for indigent people, see chapters 8.1, Medicaid, and 8.2, Medical Care Cost Containment.

---

3. FLA. ADMIN. CODE ANN. r. 4-154.106 (2002).
4. FLA. ADMIN. CODE ANN. r. 4-154.106(2) (2002).
5. 2001 Fla. Laws ch. 192, § 1.

2.10
Mental Health Benefits in State Insurance Plans

A major goal for mental health providers, consumers, and advocates in recent years has been to achieve parity in insurance coverage for mental health benefits. To date, the Florida legislature has not approved parity legislation, although the legislature has created statutory rules to ensure that individuals have the option of obtaining coverage for mental health treatment.

(A) Types of Insurance Affected

It is illegal to discriminate when providing insurance to someone or to charge discriminatory rates for health insurance coverage simply because a person has a physical or mental handicap.[1] A minimum package of services provided by an HMO is to include physician services; inpatient and outpatient hospital services, including out-of-area emergency coverage; diagnostic laboratory and diagnostic and therapeutic radiologic services; mental health, alcohol, and chemical dependency treatment services that meet the minimum requirements of state and federal law; skilled nursing facilities and services; prescription drugs; and other services prescribed by the Division of State Group Insurance.[2]

---

1. 18 FLA. STAT. ANN. § 627.644 (West Supp. 2002) (prohibiting discrimination in individual policies); 18 FLA. STAT. ANN. § 627.65625 (West Supp. 2002).
2. 7 FLA. STAT. ANN. § 110.123(3)(h)(2)(a) (West Supp. 2002).

(B) Required Coverage of Psychiatric Services

All group plans or health insurance coverage offered in connection with such a plan, which provides both medical and surgical benefits and mental health benefits, have certain rules applicable to them.[3] If the plan does not have an aggregate lifetime limit on substantially all medical and surgical benefits, then the plan cannot impose an aggregate lifetime limit on mental health benefits (however, substance abuse and chemical dependency are not included in the statutory definition of mental health benefits). If an aggregate lifetime limit is included on medical and surgical benefits, then the aggregate limit on mental health benefits cannot be less.

In addition, all insurers, HMOs, and nonprofit hospital and medical service plan corporations transacting group health insurance or providing prepaid health care must, for an appropriate additional premium, offer mental health benefits for the necessary care and treatment of "mental and nervous disorders" as defined by the standard diagnostic nomenclature of the American Psychiatric Association.[4] The coverage made available under this section is not to be less favorable than that offered for physical illness, with the following exceptions:[5]

1. Inpatient benefits may be limited to not less than 30 days per benefit year as defined in the policy or contract, and if inpatient hospital benefits are provided beyond 30 days per benefit year the durational limits, dollar amounts, and coinsurance may differ from those applicable to physical illnesses;

2. Outpatient benefits may be limited to $1000 for consultations with a licensed physician, psychologist, mental health counselor, marriage and family therapist, or clinical social worker. If the benefits are beyond the $1000 per year for consultations, then the durational limits, dollar amounts, and coinsurance may differ from those applicable to physical illnesses; and

3. Partial hospitalization benefits must be provided under the direction of a licensed physician, and meet the standards of the Joint Commission on Accreditation of Health Care Organizations (JCAHO) or equivalent standards. The total benefits in a given year paid for partial hospitalization or a combination

---

3. 18 FLA. STAT. ANN. § 627.6685 (West Supp. 2002).
4. 18 FLA. STAT. ANN. § 627.668(1) (West Supp. 2002).
5. 18 FLA. STAT. ANN. § 627.668(2) (West Supp. 2002).

of inpatient and partial hospitalization shall not exceed the cost of 30 days of hospitalization for inpatient psychiatric services, including physician fees, which prevail in the community in which partial hospitalization services are provided. If the partial hospitalization benefit exceeds this limitation, then the durational limits, dollar amounts, and coinsurance may differ from those applicable to physical illnesses.

Insurers and other health care payers are also required to offer optional coverage of substance abuse services for individuals who are "substance abuse impaired."[6] The basic benefit that must be offered is an intensive substance abuse treatment program. However, the benefit is only available to covered individuals in a group health plan; there is a minimum lifetime benefit of $2000; there is a maximum of 44 outpatient visits, with a maximum benefit payable for an outpatient visit not to exceed $35; and detoxification is not considered a benefit under an outpatient program. Finally, the services must be offered by or under the supervision of a licensed physician or psychologist and meet JCAHO standards or be approved by the state.

(C) Prohibiting Denial of Reimbursement for Psychological Services

There is no Florida law directly on point prohibiting the denial of reimbursement for services simply because they are provided by a psychologist. However, at least one Florida appellate case suggests implicitly that there is no reason to differentiate between the services provided by a psychiatrist and those provided by a psychologist, at least in the context of a workers' compensation claim.[7]

(D) Prohibiting Denial of Reimbursement for Social Work Service

There is no law in Florida specifically addressing the issue of denial of reimbursement for services provided by a social worker.

---

6. 18 FLA. STAT. ANN. § 627.669 (West Supp. 2002).
7. Robinson v. Shands Teaching Hospital, 625 So. 2d 21 (1st D.C.A. 1993).

One may infer that the mental health benefits discussed in the statute discussed earlier would be available from a licensed social worker practicing within the scope of practice as defined by his or her license.

(E) Effect of Federal ERISA Legislation

The Employee Retirement Income Security Act of 1974 (ERISA)[8] is a federal statute that was designed to provide protection for employee pension and health insurance benefits while giving employers that met ERISA statutory requirements tax breaks and a general exemption from state regulatory requirements governing insurance. In general, it preempts (that is, displaces) state laws that address topics covered by ERISA. This has meant, as a practical matter, that litigation against ERISA-qualified health plans that went to the administration of the plan (for example, whether a plan provided coverage for a particular treatment or procedure) had to proceed in federal rather than state court.[9] However, a recent decision by the U.S. Supreme Court appears to presage an expansion of state authority to exercise jurisdiction in some types of cases that involve ERISA-qualified plans. In this case, the Supreme Court upheld an Illinois statute requiring review by an independent panel of claims denied by an HMO that argued that ERISA invalidated the statutory requirement.[10]

---

8. ERISA is codified at 29 U.S.C. § 1001-1461 (West 2002).
9. Bradshaw v. Ultra-Tech Enter., Inc. 747 So. 2d 1008 (2d D.C.A. 2000); Villazon v. Prudential Health Care Plan, 794 So. 2d 625 (3d D.C.A. 2001).
10. Rush Prudential HMO v. Moran, 122 S. Ct. 2251 (2002).

2.11
Tax Deductions for Services

Florida has no state income tax, so deductibility of medical expenses is not an issue. However, the federal tax codes permit deduction of medical expenses, including expenses incurred in obtaining mental health treatment, if certain conditions are met.

(A) Mental Health Services as a Medical Deduction

Individuals may deduct medical expenses for medical care for themselves, spouses, or dependents if the expenses paid in the taxable year are not compensated by insurance or otherwise, to the extent that the expenses exceed 7.5% of the taxpayer's adjusted gross income.[1] *Medical care* is defined as the amounts paid for diagnosis, care, mitigation, treatment, or prevention of disease, or for the purpose of affecting any structure or function of the body; transportation primarily for and essential to medical care; qualified long-term services; or for insurance covering medical care or qualified long-term services.[2] The term includes hospital care provided under the care of a physician where there is no significant element of personal pleasure or vacation in the travel associated with being away from home and the amount considered for tax purposes does not exceed $50 per night.[3]

---

1. 26 U.S.C.A. § 213(a) (West 2002).
2. 26 U.S.C.A. § 213(d)(1) (West 2002).
3. 26 U.S.C.A. § 213(d)(2)(A)(B) (West 2002).

Services provided by psychiatrists, psychologists, and other providers may be deducted as well.[4] However, the Internal Revenue Service (IRS) has rejected efforts by taxpayers to deduct as medical expenses other types of expenses incurred as the result of advice from an MHP. For example, a taxpayer was not permitted to deduct, as a medical expense, money paid to his spouse as part of a property settlement in a divorce action. Nor was he permitted to deduct attorney's fees paid to his own or his spouse's attorney for expenses in connection with the divorce, even though the taxpayer insisted that he had initiated the divorce on the advice of his psychiatrist. In the view of the IRS, there was no proof that the taxpayer would not have taken the same action absent the illness and subsequent advice of his psychiatrist.[5]

(B) Mental Health Services as a Business Deduction

The use of mental health services by a business is deductible as a business expense. Federal law states that "there shall be allowed as a deduction all the ordinary and necessary expenses paid or incurred during the taxable year in carrying on any trade or business."[6] The use of the words "ordinary" and "necessary" have been defined as "common and accepted" and "appropriate and helpful."[7] Therefore, the use of mental health services would be deductible if it met these standards.

(C) Other Deductions Received by MHPs

Basic education costs—for example, costs incurred in obtaining a degree—may not be deducted as a business expense. However, professional education expenses are deductible if the MHP is employed or self-employed; the courses meet the minimum requirements of his or her job or profession; and the course maintains or improves job skills or is required by his or her employer

---

4. Rev. Rul. 53-143, 1953-2 C.B. 129; Rev. Rul. 63-91, 1963-1, C.B. 54.
5. Doody v. C.I.R., 32 T.C.M. (CCH) 547 (1973).
6. 26 U.S.C.A. § 162(a) (West 2002).
7. Welch v. Helvering, 290 U.S. 111, 113–114 (1933).

or the law to maintain a present position or salary.[8] Although the law is not completely settled, at least some rulings have permitted personal psychotherapy costs to be deducted if the experience improves the MHP's job skills.[9]

---

8. Treas. Reg. § 1.162-5(a) (2002).
9. Voigt v. Commissioner, 74 T.C. 82 (1980), *nonacq.*, 1981-033; Porter v. Commissioner, T.C. Memo. 1986-70.

Section 3

Limitations on and Liability for Practice

3.1
Informed Consent for Services

Informed consent is a legal and ethical doctrine that requires health care professionals to inform their clients about their assessment of the client's problems and the risks and benefits of various treatment options. Assessment or treatment of individuals without informed consent constitutes malpractice except where the law presumes consent (e.g., in an emergency).

The doctrine of informed consent emphasizes the client's participation in the assessment and treatment decision-making process. As such, it requires that an interaction take place between the health care professional and the client. Thus, the legal or ethical requirements of informed consent are not met simply by obtaining a signature on a consent form.

(A) Elements of Informed Consent

Informed consent must be voluntary, knowledgeable, and competent. Clients must voluntarily agree to the assessment or treatment procedure, and they cannot be subject to duress or coercion. They must be informed about the mental health professional's (MHP's) conceptualization of their problems, the risks and benefits of the various treatments (including no intervention), and likely and possible outcomes of treatment. Clients must have some ability to weigh and manipulate information they are provided to reach a decision about the treatment process.

(B) Informed Consent in Outpatient Contexts

MHPs must obtain informed consent from clients or their guardians when providing outpatient assessment or treatment services. Psychologists are required to obtain informed consent in writing for all assessment and treatment services.[1] Social workers, marriage and family therapists, and mental health counselors are required to document informed consent for all services in the clinical record, but there is not a requirement that the consent be documented in writing.[2]

(C) Informed Consent Requirements Specific to Inpatient Mental Health Treatment

Clients entering any kind of inpatient mental health treatment facility in the state must provide express and informed consent for admission and treatment in writing after an adequate explanation about the admission. The client (or guardian, if the client is incapacitated) must be informed about the reason for the admission, the purpose of the treatment to be provided, the common side effects of treatment and alternative treatments, approximate length of stay, and that any consent for treatment can be revoked orally or in writing.[3]

For minors, a parent or guardian must provide consent for hospitalization, and informed consent need not be obtained from the minor. Informed consent need not be obtained from the parent or guardian of a minor when the minor is being hospitalized for purposes of involuntary examination or involuntary placement (see also chapters 4.19, Voluntary Admission and Civil Commitment of Minors, and 4.21, Consent, Confidentiality, and Services for Minors).

The administrator of a receiving or treatment facility may, on the recommendation of the client's attending physician, authorize emergency medical treatment, including a surgical procedure, if such treatment is deemed life-saving, or if the situation threatens serious bodily harm to the patient and permission of the client

---

1. FLA. ADMIN. CODE ANN. r. 64B19-19.0025(2) (2002).
2. FLA. ADMIN. CODE ANN. r. 64B4-9.002(2) (2002).
3. 14 FLA. STAT. ANN. § 394.459(3)(a) (West 2002).

or the client's guardian or guardian advocate cannot be obtained.[4] This provision allows for treatment over the objection of, or without the consent of, the client.

(D) Provisions for Persons in Forensic Facilities

Persons entering state forensic hospitals (as incompetent to proceed with the criminal process or not guilty by reason of insanity) also enjoy the right to express and informed written consent to treatment. However, if a client in a forensic facility refuses treatment and the recommended treatment is considered necessary by the client's treatment team for the appropriate care of the client and the safety of the client and others, such treatment may be provided under the following circumstances:[5]

1. In an emergency situation in which there is an immediate danger to the safety of the client or others, such treatment may proceed on the written order of a physician for a period not to exceed 48 hours, excluding weekends and holidays. If, after 48 hours, the client continues to refuse treatment, the facility administrator must petition the court for an order authorizing treatment, and involuntary treatment can be continued on the written order of a physician providing that the emergency situation continues; and

2. In nonemergency situations the facility administrator can petition the court for an order authorizing treatment. The order can allow treatment for a period not to exceed 90 days, but the order can be renewed for additional 90-day periods as necessary.

(E) Informed Consent for Electroconvulsive and Psychosurgical Procedures

Florida law requires special consent procedures for use of electroconvulsive therapy (ECT) and psychosurgery.[6] Previous written

---

4. 14 FLA. STAT. ANN. § 394.459(3)(c) (West 2002). *See also* chapter 4.2, Guardianship for Adults, for a discussion of guardians and guardian advocates.
5. 23 FLA. STAT. ANN. § 916.107(3)(c) (West 2001); Dinardo v. State, 742 So. 2d 287 (Fla. 1st D.C.A. 1998).
6. 14 FLA. STAT. ANN. § 394.459(3)(b) (West 2002); 14 FLA. STAT. ANN. § 458.325 (West 2002); 14 FLA. STAT. ANN. § 916.107(3)(b) (West 2001).

consent must be obtained after disclosure of the purpose of the procedure, common side effects of the proposed treatment, alternative treatments, and the approximate number of procedures considered necessary. Consent is to be obtained from the client or, if he or she is incompetent or a minor, the client's guardian.

In addition, before ECT or psychosurgery procedures are initiated a second physician, who is not directly involved with the client's treatment, must review the record, agree that the treatment is appropriate, and document such agreement in the client's treatment record.[7]

---

7. 14 FLA. STAT. ANN. § 458.325(2) (West 2001).

3.2

Extensiveness, Ownership, Maintenance, and Access to Records

The clinical record is an important document that chronicles the client's assessment and treatment. Professional ethics and practice guidelines dictate that client records be accurate and complete. In addition, Florida law specifies what must be included within the clinical record, how records are to be maintained, and conditions under which records can and must be released.

Florida MHPs gain direction regarding record keeping and access from several sections of the law. The records of all health care practitioners are regulated by a general statute that identifies which professionals are obligated and permitted to keep independent patient/client records and under what conditions information contained in the records may or must be released.[1] In addition, the record-keeping practices and requirements of specific professionals are dictated by the provisions of Florida law and administrative code that are devoted to each profession or discipline. Unfortunately, these provisions of law are sometimes not consistent, leaving it unclear as to what the MHP may do or must do. In such cases, the prudent course of action is for the MHP to act in a way that is most protective of the client and the client's privacy, confidentiality, and privilege.

(A) General Provisions

Health care professionals who conduct physical or mental examinations or who provide treatment are required to maintain a

---

1. 15 FLA. STAT. ANN. § 456.057 (West Supp. 2002).

clinical record,[2] and health care professionals must develop and implement policies, procedures, and standards to protect the confidentiality and security of the record, including training of staff in handling such records.[3] Records must be furnished to the patient, on the request of the patient or the patient's legal representative. However, psychiatrists, psychologists, social workers, marriage and family therapists, and mental health counselors are allowed to provide a report of the examination or treatment in lieu of a copy of the record (although psychiatrists who have treated a patient's nonpsychiatric medical conditions must release this information).[4] On a patient's written request, however, complete copies of the patient's psychiatric record must be provided to a subsequent treating psychiatrist. Provision of reports or record copies cannot be contingent on payment of a fee for services rendered,[5] and costs charged for reproducing records are limited to actual copying costs, including staff time.[6] The professional must keep a record of all disclosures of information to third parties, including the purpose of the disclosure. The third party to whom information is disclosed is prohibited from further disclosure of any information contained in the released record without the expressed written consent of the patient or the patient's legal representative.[7]

Release of records or information contained in them to third parties requires the written authorization of the patient, but the records can be released to or discussed with the patient's legal representative or other health care practitioners and providers involved in the care of treatment of the patient.[8] In addition, records can be released without the written authorization of the patient[9]

1. To any person, firm, or corporation that has procured or furnished such examination or treatment with the patient's consent;
2. When compulsory physical examination is made pursuant to *Florida Rules of Civil Procedure*,[10] in which case copies of the medical records shall be furnished to both the defendant and the plaintiff;

---

2. 15 FLA. STAT. ANN. § 456.057(5) (West Supp. 2002); 15 FLA. STAT. ANN. § 456.057(6) (West Supp. 2000).
3. 15 FLA. STAT. ANN. § 456.057(9) (West Supp. 2002);
4. 15 FLA. STAT. ANN. § 456.057(7)(b) (West Supp. 2002).
5. 15 FLA. STAT. ANN. § 456.057(4) (West Supp. 2002).
6. 15 FLA. STAT. ANN. § 456.057(6) (West Supp. 2002).
7. 15 FLA. STAT. ANN. § 456.057(10) (West Supp. 2002).
8. 15 FLA. STAT. ANN. §§ 456.057(5) and 456.057(17) (West Supp. 2002).
9. *Id.*
10. FLA. R. CIV. P. 1.360.

3. In any civil or criminal action, unless otherwise prohibited by law, on issuance of a subpoena from a court of competent jurisdiction and proper notice to the patient and the patient's legal representative by the part seeking such records (see chapter 3.4, Privileged Communications, for discussion of psychotherapeutic privilege);

4. For statistical or research purposes, providing the information is abstracted in such a way as to protect the identity of the patient or provided written permission from the patient or the patient's legal representative; and

5. When the provider is named in a medical negligence action or administrative proceeding or when a health care practitioner reasonably expects to be named as defendant.

In addition, the Department of Health (DOH) may obtain patient records without written authorization from the patient (providing reasonable attempts to obtain the release were made) under the following circumstances:[11]

1. Pursuant to a subpoena and if the DOH and a probable cause panel of the relevant board find reasonable cause to believe that a health care practitioner has prescribed medication excessively or has practiced below the standard of care;

2. Pursuant to a subpoena if the DOH and a probable cause panel of the relevant board find reasonable cause to believe that a health care practitioner has provided inadequate medical care based on termination of insurance; and

3. Pursuant to a subpoena and if the DOH and a probable cause panel of the relevant board find reasonable cause to believe that a health care practitioner has engaged in fraudulent or wrongful billing practice.

(B) Psychologists

(B)(1) General Confidentiality Concerns

For purposes of considering confidentiality and its limitations, it is the person receiving the services from the psychologist rather than the entity paying the psychologist's fee who is considered to be the client who has an expectation of confidentiality of communications.[12]

---

11. 15 FLA. STAT. ANN. § 456.057(7) (West Supp. 2002).
12. FLA. ADMIN. CODE ANN. r. 64B19-19.002 (2002).

Florida law recognizes that communications made by clients to their psychologists are confidential.[13] This applies to verbal communications as well as written records. Disclosure of verbal communications or aspects of the record can occur only with the written consent of the client (unless otherwise provided for by law) or under other exceptions noted by law, such as when the psychologist is a defendant in a civil, criminal, or disciplinary action arising from a complaint filed by the client (in which case the waiver is limited to that action), or when there is a "clear and immediate probability of physical harm to the patient or client, to other individuals, or to society and the [psychologist] communicates the information only to the potential victim, appropriate family member, or law enforcement or other appropriate authorities" (see also chapter 3.3, Confidential Relations and Communications).[14] In cases where more than one person in a family is receiving therapy, each family member in family therapy must agree to the waiver, in writing, unless otherwise provided for by law.[15] Psychologists are also responsible for insuring that persons working for them in any capacity do not violate the client's confidentiality.[16]

The psychologist has an affirmative obligation to inform the client about third parties who may have access to records (e.g., clinical supervisors, other hospital or clinic personnel, other school personnel, military officials, insurers/third-party payers, clinical supervisors). This will vary according to the setting in which the psychologist works. The client must sign a form indicating that he or she has been informed about others' access to the clinical records.[17]

In cases where the psychologist performs an evaluation of someone for use by a third party (e.g., the Florida Department of Children and Families, a disability insurer, court, employer) the psychologist must explain to the person being evaluated the limits of confidentiality in that specific situation, document that such information was explained and understood by the person being evaluated, and obtain written informed consent to all aspects of the testing and evaluative procedures.[18]

Psychologists are responsible for developing and implementing policies, standards, and procedures to protect the confidenti-

---

13. 15 FLA. STAT. ANN. § 490.0147 (West 2001); FLA. ADMIN. CODE ANN. r. 64B19-19.006(1) (2002).
14. 15 FLA. STAT. ANN. § 490.0147 (West 2001); FLA. ADMIN. CODE ANN. r. 64B19-19.006(1) (2002).
15. 15 FLA. STAT. ANN. § 490.0147 (2) (West 2001); FLA. ADMIN. CODE ANN. r. 64B19-19.006(1) (2002).
16. FLA. ADMIN. CODE ANN. r. 64B19-19.006(5) (2002).
17. FLA. ADMIN. CODE ANN. r. 64B19-19.006(1) (2002).
18. FLA. ADMIN. CODE ANN. r. 64B19-19.006(2) (2002).

ality and security of client records. Employees of psychologists must be trained regarding these policies, standards, and procedures.[19]

(B)(2) Confidentiality With Minors and Incapacitated Persons

The rights of minors and incapacitated persons with respect to the confidentiality of their communications with psychologists is unclear. Although the Board of Psychology recognizes that minors and legally incapacitated individuals cannot provide informed consent under the law (presumably for purposes of assessment and treatment, as well as for release of confidential information), psychologists are nonetheless considered to owe a duty of confidentiality to minor and legally incapacitated service users "consistent with [the general duty of confidentiality]."[20] The rule goes on to direct, however, that this does not mean that the psychologist cannot provide the psychologist's own evaluation, assessment, analysis, diagnosis, or recommendations regarding the minor or legally incapacitated person to the client's guardian or any court of law.

As a general matter of law, parents are assumed to have access to their minor children's medical records.[21] A minor or incapacitated person may make communications to the psychologist in the course of treatment that, in the psychologist's opinion, should be kept confidential and private. In such circumstances, the MHP may choose to restrict parental access to some parts of the record, but whether the parent can ultimately gain access to the record is unclear.

(B)(3) Extensiveness of Records

Thorough and descriptive client records are a requirement of good psychological practice and the law.[22] Regulations issued by the Board of Psychology require that records include basic identifying information (i.e., name, address, phone number, age, sex), relevant history, clear statements summarizing the client's presenting symptoms, documentation of informed consent for assessment or treatment services, what transpired in treatment, concerns about sensitive issues such as risk to self or others, treatment progress or lack thereof, relevant correspondence and communications about the patient, and accounting matters or financial records. Entries in the record must be made within 10 days following each consultation or rendering of services. Entries that are made after

---

19. 15 FLA. STAT. ANN. § 456.057(9) (West Supp. 2002).
20. FLA. ADMIN. CODE ANN. r. 64B19-19.006(3) (2002).
21. 15 FLA. STAT. ANN. § 395.3025 (West Supp. 2002).
22. 15 FLA. STAT. ANN. § 490.0148 (West 2001).

the date of service should indicate both when the entries are made as well as when the entry was recorded.[23]

(B)(4) Maintenance of Records

Psychologists are required to maintain complete records for a minimum of three years after the completion of services or the date of last contact with the client. Thereafter, summaries of the records or the records themselves must be maintained for an additional four years (making a total of seven years). Psychologists are not required to maintain records if a business entity, which agrees to maintain confidentiality of the records, assigned the client to the psychologist.[24]

(B)(5) Access to Psychological Records

Psychologists who agree to provide copies of psychological records to a client, service user, service user's designee, or service user's legal representative are permitted a reasonable amount of time, not to exceed 30 days, to make final entries and copy the records. Release of the records can be conditioned on reasonable payment for copying costs.[25] Psychologists are permitted to provide a report or summary of assessment or treatment, however, in lieu of providing the actual record.[26] Psychologists who decide to issue a report or summary rather than a copy of the record must provide it within 30 days of the request and may charge a reasonable fee for preparation of the report. Release of the report can be conditioned on payment of a reasonable fee.[27]

(B)(6) Access to and Release of Test Data

A psychologist who uses test instruments may not release test data (such as test protocols, test questions, or written answer sheets, except (a) to a licensed psychologist, or (b) after complying with general requirements for the release of confidential information (see section (B)(1), General Confidentiality Concerns), and obtaining an order from a court or other tribunal of competent jurisdiction, or (c) when the release of the material is otherwise required by law. When raw test data is released pursuant to this paragraph, the psychologist must verify to the service user or the services user's designees that all raw test data from those test instruments have been provided. Psychologists are also expected

---

23. FLA. ADMIN. CODE ANN. r. 64B19-19.0025 (2002).
24. FLA. ADMIN. CODE ANN. r. 64B19-19.003 (2002).
25. FLA. ADMIN. CODE ANN. r. 64B19-19.005(1) (2002).
26. 15 FLA. STAT. ANN. 455.667(4) (West Supp. 2002).
27. FLA. ADMIN. CODE ANN. r. 64B19-19.005(2) (2002).

to make all reasonable efforts to maintain the integrity of test protocols, modalities, and instruments when releasing information and test data.[28]

The release of test data to nonpsychologists has received considerable attention in the professional literature, and the Board of Psychology rules, as written, leave a number of unanswered questions. First, "test scores" or "test profile sheets" are not identified as examples of test data for which release is governed by the above described rule. This rule therefore might be interpreted as allowing the release of some test results or data (e.g., MMPI–2 profile sheet, WAIS–III profile sheet). Furthermore, the Board of Psychology's direction that release of test data is permitted "when otherwise required by law" raises a number of questions. For example, *Florida Rules of Evidence* might be interpreted as granting attorneys access to test data when it forms, in part, the basis for an opinion offered by a psychologist in court. The *Rule of Evidence*, then could be interpreted to mean that psychologists would be permitted to release any and all test data to an attorney when they form, in part, the basis of an opinion that psychologists are prepared to offer in court.

(B)(7) Disposition of Records on Termination or Relocation of Practice

Psychologists who are terminating or relocating practices and are no longer available to service users/clients must publish notice of their intent to do so for four consecutive weeks in the newspaper with the greatest circulation within the county(ies) in which they practiced. The details of their relocation and termination, including where records will be available and where they will be stored, must be identified.[29]

The representative or survivor of a deceased psychologist must ensure the retention of psychological records on the death of the psychologist for at least 26 months after the psychologist's death. Within one month of the psychologist's death, a notice announcing the psychologist's death and where such records will be maintained must be published for four consecutive weeks in the newspaper with the greatest circulation within the county(ies) in which the psychologist practiced. After the 26-month period elapses, another notice is to be published for four consecutive weeks indicating that records will be destroyed no sooner than one month from the last publication of the notice. Records can then be destroyed.[30]

---

28. FLA. ADMIN. CODE ANN. r. 64B19-18.004(3) (2002).
29. FLA. ADMIN. CODE ANN. r. 64B19-19.004(1) (2002).
30. FLA. ADMIN. CODE ANN. r. 64B19-19.004(2) (2002).

(C) Psychiatrists

(C)(1) General Confidentiality Concerns

Florida law recognizes that communications made by clients to their psychiatrists are confidential and are not to be disclosed except on the request of the client or the client's legal representative.[31] This applies to verbal communications as well as to written records. Psychiatrists are responsible for developing and implementing policies, standards, and procedures to protect the confidentiality and security of client records. Employees of psychiatrists must be trained regarding these policies, standards, and procedures.[32]

There are a number of exceptions to the general rule of confidentiality noted earlier, however. Records of assessment and treatment can be provided, without any written authorization, to any person, firm, or corporation that has procured or furnished such examination or treatment with the client's consent;[33] when compulsory physical examination is made pursuant to the *Florida Rules of Civil Procedure*;[34] in a civil or criminal action, unless otherwise prohibited by law, on issuance of a subpoena from a court of competence jurisdiction and proper notice to the client or the client's legal representative seeking such records (see chapter 3.4, Privileged Communications, for a discussion of privilege, which may limit disclosure);[35] for statistical and scientific research, providing the information is abstracted in such a way as to protect the identity of the client, or when written permission is received from the client or the client's legal representative;[36] and when the psychiatrist is named or expects to be named in a medical negligence action or administrative proceeding.[37]

In addition, where a psychiatrist is involved in a treatment relationship with a client, the client makes an actual threat to physically harm an identifiable victim or victims, and the psychiatrist makes a clinical judgment that the client has the apparent capability of committing such an act and it is more likely than not that in the near future the client will carry out the threat, the psychiatrist may disclose client communications to the extent necessary to warn any potential victim or to communicate the threat to a law enforcement agency. No civil or criminal action can be instituted, and there is no liability because of disclosure

---

31. 15 FLA. STAT. ANN. § 455.671(1) (West Supp. 2002).
32. 15 FLA. STAT. ANN. § 456.057(9) (West Supp. 2002).
33. 15 FLA. STAT. ANN. § 456.057(5)(a) (West Supp. 2002).
34. 15 FLA. STAT. ANN. § 456.057(5)(b) (West Supp. 2002).
35. 15 FLA. STAT. ANN. § 456.057(5)(c) (West Supp. 2002).
36. 15 FLA. STAT. ANN. § 456.057(5)(d) (West Supp. 2002).
37. 15 FLA. STAT. ANN. § 456.057(5)(6) (West Supp. 2002).

of otherwise confidential communications by a psychiatrist in disclosing such threats.[38]

(C)(2) Extensiveness/Maintenance of Records

Maintaining thorough and descriptive client records is a requirement of good psychiatric practice and the law.[39] Physicians are required to keep written medical records that document the physician responsible for care, patient history, examination and test results, medication records, treatment history, and reports of consultations and hospitalizations.[40]

(C)(3) Access to Psychiatric Records

Physicians are required to provide clients or their legal representatives with a copy of their medical record in a timely manner. However, psychiatrists can provide a report or summary of examination or treatment in lieu of a copy of the record.[41] On a client's written request, however, complete copies of the client's psychiatric record must be provided directly to a subsequent treating psychiatrist.[42] Medical doctors and osteopathic physicians are permitted to condition release of records on payment of reasonable costs for photocopying (no more than $1.00 per page for the first 25 pages and $.25 per page for all pages thereafter).[43]

However, there is some legal authority stating that persons who undergo independent medical examinations by an adverse party in a legal proceedings may, in some cases, not be entitled to copies of their records.[44]

(C)(4) Disposition of Records on Termination or Relocation of Practice

Physicians are required to maintain complete records for a minimum of five years after the date of the last contact with their patients.[45] When a medical doctor terminates a practice or relocates and is no longer available, clients must be notified by

---

38. 15 FLA. STAT. ANN. § 456.057 (West Supp. 2002); *see also* chapter 3.3, Confidential Relations and Communications, for a more detailed discussion.
39. 15 FLA. STAT. ANN. § 458.331(1)(m) (West 2001); 15 FLA. STAT. ANN. § 459.015(1)(o) (West Supp. 2002).
40. 15 FLA. STAT. ANN. § 458.331(1)(m) (West 2001); 15 FLA. STAT. ANN. § 459.015(1)(o) (West Supp. 2002); FLA. ADMIN. CODE r. 64B8-10.002(3) (2002); FLA. ADMIN. CODE r. 64B15-15.004(1) (2002).
41. 15 FLA. STAT. ANN. § 455.667(4) (West Supp. 2002).
42. *Id.*
43. FLA. ADMIN. CODE ANN. r. 64B8-10.003(2002); FLA. ADMIN. CODE ANN. r. 64B15-15.003 (2002).
44. West v. Branham, 576 So. 2d 381 (Fla. 4th D.C.A. 1991).
45. 15 FLA. STAT. ANN. § 458.331(1)(m) (West 2001); 15 FLA. STAT. ANN. § 459.015(1)(o) (West Supp. 2002). FLA. ADMIN. CODE r. 64B15-15.004(3) (2002).

publishing a notice for four consecutive weeks in the newspaper with the greatest circulation within the county(ies) in which the physician practiced. This notice must contain information about the date of termination, sale, or relocation and an address at which the records may be obtained within one month from the termination, date, or sale.[46] When an osteopathic physician terminates a practice or relocates and is no longer available, clients must be notified by publishing a notice for four consecutive weeks in the newspaper with the greatest circulation within the county(ies) in which the physician practiced. This notice must contain information about the date of termination, sale, or relocation and an address at which the records may be obtained.[47] A sign notifying clients must also be posted in the osteopathic physician's office.[48]

The executor, administrator, personal representative, or survivor of a medical doctor or osteopathic physician must maintain client records for a period of at least two years after the death of the physician. Within one month of the physician's death, the representative must publish in the newspaper of greatest circulation within the county(ies) in which the physician practiced, information indicating that the physician's records are available to clients or their representatives from a specific person at a specific location.[49]

(D) Clinical Social Workers, Marriage and Family Therapists, and Mental Health Counselors

(D)(1) General Confidentiality Concerns

For purposes of considering confidentiality and its limitations, it is the person receiving the services from the social worker, marriage and family therapist, or mental health counselor, rather than the entity paying the therapist's fee, who is considered to be the client who has an expectation of confidentiality of communications.[50]

Florida law recognizes that communications made by clients to their social workers, marriage and family therapists, and mental

---

46. FLA. ADMIN. CODE ANN. r. 64B8-10.002(4) (2002); FLA. ADMIN. CODE 64B15-15.002 (2002).
47. FLA. ADMIN. CODE ANN. r. 64B15-15.002 (2002).
48. FLA. ADMIN. CODE ANN. r. 64B15-15.002(3) (2002).
49. FLA. ADMIN. CODE ANN. r. 64B8-10.001 (2002); FLA. ADMIN. CODE ANN. r. 64B15-15.001 (2002).
50. FLA. ADMIN. CODE ANN. r. 64B19-9.002(3) (2002).

health counselors are confidential.[51] This applies to verbal communications as well as to written records. Disclosure of verbal communications or aspects of the record can only occur with the written consent of the client or under other exceptions noted by law, such as when the therapist is a defendant in a legal proceeding arising from a complaint filed by the client or when there is "a clear and immediate probability of physical harm to the patient or client, to other individuals, or to society and the [therapist] communicates the information only to the potential victim, appropriate family members, or law enforcement or other appropriate officials" (see also chapter 3.3, Confidential Relations and Communications, on the duty to protect).[52]

Social workers, marriage and family therapists, and mental health counselors are responsible for developing and implementing policies, standards, and procedures to protect the confidentiality and security of client records. Employees must be trained regarding these policies, standards, and procedures.[53]

(D)(2) Extensiveness of Records

Maintaining thorough and descriptive client records is a requirement of good mental health practice and the law.[54] Regulations issued by the Board of Clinical Social Work, Marriage and Family Therapy, and Mental Health Counseling require that records include basic identifying information (e.g., name, address, telephone number) dates of therapy sessions, treatment plans and results achieved, diagnosis if applicable, notes or documentation of the client's consent to all aspects of treatment, copies of client authorizations for release of information, any legal forms pertaining to the client, documentation of any contact the therapist has with other professionals regarding the client, and fees assessed and collected.[55]

(D)(3) Maintenance of Records

Clinical social workers, marriage and family therapists, and mental health counselors are required to maintain complete records for a minimum of seven years after the date of the last contact with the client.[56]

---

51. 15 Fla. Stat. Ann. § 491.0141 (West 2001); Fla. Admin. Code Ann. r. 64B4-9.001(1) (2002).
52. 15 Fla. Stat. Ann. § 491.0147 (West 2001).
53. 15 Fla. Stat. Ann. § 456.057(9) (West Supp. 2002).
54. 15 Fla. Stat. Ann. § 491.0148 (West 2001).
55. Fla. Admin. Code Ann. r. 64B-9.002(2) (2002).
56. Fla. Admin. Code Ann. r. 64B-9.001(2) (2002).

(D)(4) Access to Records

Clinical social workers, marriage and family therapists, and mental health counselors are required to provide clients or their legal representatives with a copy of their clinical record on their request and in a timely manner.[57] However, a report or summary of examination or treatment may be sent in lieu of copies of the record.[58]

(D)(5) Disposition of Records on Termination or Relocation of Practice

Clinical social workers, marriage and family therapists, and mental health counselors who are terminating or relocating practices must publish notice of their intent in the newspaper with the greatest circulation within the county(ies) in which they practiced. The details of their relocation or termination, including where records will be available and where they will be stored, must be identified. Records must be maintained for at least two years after the termination or relocation of the practice.[59]

The representative or survivor of a deceased clinical social worker, marriage and family therapist, or mental health counselor must ensure the retention of client records for at least 24 months after the therapist's death. Twenty-two months after the death, the representative or survivor must publish a notice for four consecutive weeks in the newspaper of greatest general circulation in the county(ies) in which the therapist practiced, stating that the records will be destroyed four weeks or later from the last day of the final week of the publication of the notice.[60]

(E) Hospital Utilization Review

Hospitals are required to establish medical review committees with responsibilities to screen, evaluate, and review the professional and medical competence of staff. In addition, the Department of Business and Professional Regulation may enter letters of agreement with a professional society of physicians to review cases alleging a breach by a physician of a prevailing standard of care (see chapter 3.9, Quality Assurance for Hospital Care, for a discussion of medical review committees). The proceedings of such committees are immune from *discovery* (a legal process by which each party obtains information from the other after a lawsuit has been filed), though records otherwise available are not

---

57. 15 FLA. STAT. ANN. § 455.667(4) (West Supp. 2002).
58. 15 FLA. STAT. ANN. § 456.057(4) (West Supp. 2002).
59. FLA. ADMIN. CODE ANN. r. 64B4-9.001(3) (2002).
60. FLA. ADMIN. CODE ANN. r. 64B4-9.001(4) (2002).

shielded from discovery simply because they were presented to a medical review committee.[61]

(F) Liability for Violation

A breach of confidentiality, unless in accord with statutory exceptions, may result in disciplinary action against an MHP, including denial or revocation of a license.[62] In addition, a breach of confidentiality may lead to a civil lawsuit claiming damages for the breach.

---

61. 21 FLA. STAT. ANN. § 766.101(7)(c) (West Supp. 2002); Humana Medical Plan, Inc. v. Erdely, 773 So. 2d 1272 (Fla. 4th D.C.A. 2001).
62. See, e.g., 15 FLA. ANN. STAT. § 490.009(1) (West Supp. 2002), listing various actions, including failure to maintain a confidence, that may result in disciplinary action.

3.3
Confidential Relations and Communications

Confidentiality is best conceptualized as the MHP's ethical and legal obligation to the client with regard to privacy of communications. *Privilege* constitutes the law's recognition of confidentiality in legal proceedings in which the protected material otherwise would be subject to disclosure. Although privileged communications are protected from being revealed in the course of legal proceedings, nonprivileged communications have no legal protection in such proceedings (see chapter 3.4, Privileged Communications, for a discussion). Of course, professional ethics of all mental health disciplines require that communications made to MHPs in the course of evaluation or treatment be confidential absent exceptions created by law. The law may recognize and enforce the expectation of privacy of communications made in the course of psychotherapy by requiring MHPs to keep communications made to them confidential or by granting communications made to them privileged status in legal proceedings.

Confidentiality, the duty to protect it, and the law's recognition of it are not absolute. Ethics or the law may provide for instances in which the general guarantee of confidentiality may or must be breached. Because communications made by clients to MHPs may be relevant to legal proceedings, MHPs must be knowledgeable about the ethical and legal requirements regarding the confidentiality of communications. Whether this information can or must be revealed in court depends on whether the information is privileged.

Florida law regarding confidentiality is somewhat complicated because references to confidentiality are found in case law[1] and state statutes regulating the practice of various professions,[2] abuse reporting,[3] and the provision of mental health[4] and substance abuse[5] services.

(A) Confidentiality in Mental Health Treatment Facilities

Persons entering state-operated or state-funded inpatient or outpatient mental health treatment facilities are entitled to confidentiality of their mental health treatment record.[6] With some exceptions the clinical record must remain confidential. Of course, the record or information contained within it must be released when confidentiality is waived via express and informed consent by the client, the client's guardian, or guardian advocate (or if deceased, by the client's personal representative or family member who stands next in line for intestate succession).[7] The record must also be released, or information from it revealed, under the following conditions:[8]

1. When the patient is represented by counsel and the records are needed for adequate representation apply;

2. When the court orders such release, after the court has weighed the need for information against the possible harm of disclosure; and

3. When the patient is committed to, or is to be returned to, the Department of Corrections (DOC) from the Department of Children and Families (DCF), and the DOC requests such records.

Information from the clinical record can be released when:[9]

1. The patient has declared an intention to harm others. In such cases the facility administrator can authorize the release of

---

1. *See, e.g.,* Boynton v. Burglass, 590 So. 2d 446 (Fla. 3d D.C.A. 1991); *see* later sections for additional discussion of this case and others related to confidential communications.
2. 15 Fla. Stat. Ann. § 456.059 (West Supp. 2002); 15 Fla. Stat. Ann. § 490.0147 (West 2002).
3. 6 Fla. Stat. Ann. § 39.201 (West Supp. 2002).
4. 14 Fla. Stat. Ann. § 394.4615 (West 2002).
5. 14 Fla. Stat. Ann. § 397.501(7) (West 2002).
6. 14 Fla. Stat. Ann. § 394.4615(1) (West 2002).
7. *Id.*
8. 14 Fla. Stat. Ann. § 394.4615(2) (West 2002).
9. 14 Fla. Stat. Ann. § 394.4615(3) (West 2002).

sufficient information to provide adequate warning to the person threatened;

2. Requested by a qualified researcher for purposes of program evaluation;

3. Requested by an aftercare treatment provider or a DCF employee or agent when such information is necessary for patient treatment;

4. Used for statistical and research purposes providing information is abstracted so that patient identity is protected; and

5. Requested by the Agency for Health Care Administration, the DCF, or human rights advocacy committees for the purpose of monitoring facility activity and complaints;

Recipients of confidential patient information must maintain this information as confidential.[10] Any facility or private mental health practitioner who acts in good faith when releasing such information pursuant to these limitations is immune from civil or criminal liability.[11]

(A)(1) Special Regulations Regarding Confidentiality Relating to Substance Abuse Services

There are specific federal and state rules and regulations regarding confidentiality that apply only to substance abuse treatment records. Florida law is consistent with applicable federal law on this subject. The treatment records of persons receiving substance abuse services in any setting are confidential. Release of information may be made only with the written consent of the client. However, information can be released without written consent under the following circumstances:[12]

1. To medical personnel in a medical emergency;

2. To service provider personnel if those persons need to know the information to provide services to a client;

3. To DCF personnel (or their designees) for purposes of research provided that there is written agreement that the client's name and other identifying information is not disclosed;

4. To persons providing audits or evaluations on behalf of any government agency or third-party payer providing financial assistance or reimbursement to the service provider; and

5. On court order on the basis of application showing good cause for disclosure and after the court has considered whether the

---

10. 14 FLA. STAT. ANN. § 394.4615(6) (West 2002).
11. 14 FLA. STAT. ANN. § 394.4615(7) (West 2002).
12. 14 FLA. STAT. ANN. § 397.501(7) (West 2002).

public interest and need for disclosure outweighs the potential injury to the client, the service provider–client relationship, and the service provider.

A court may authorize the disclosure and use of client records for the purposes of conducting a criminal investigation or prosecution of a client only if the court finds that[13]

1. The crime involved is extremely serious, such as one that causes or directly threatens loss of life or serious bodily injury, including but not limited to homicide, sexual assault, sexual battery, kidnapping, armed robbery, assault with a deadly weapon, and child abuse and neglect;
2. There is a reasonable likelihood that the records will disclose information of substantial value in the investigation or prosecution;
3. Other ways of obtaining the information are not available or would be ineffective; and
4. The potential injury to the client, to the physician–client relationship, and to the ability of the program to provide services to other clients is outweighed by the public interest and the need for disclosure.

The general restriction against release of information does not apply to:[14]

1. Providers' communications to law enforcement about crimes committed or threatened by the client on the premises of the provider providing that the information revealed is limited to the circumstances of the incident, the client's name, address, and client status; and
2. Providers' reports of child abuse. However, confidentiality restrictions continue to apply to the original substance abuse treatment records maintained by the provider, including their disclosure and use for civil or criminal proceedings that may arise out of the abuse or neglect report.

Although it is not specifically identified as an exception in the statute, mandated reporting of abuse of elderly and disabled adults also presumably requires breach of confidentiality in the context of substance abuse treatment (see chapters 4.7, Reporting of Adult Abuse, and 4.8, Reporting of Child Abuse).

In addition, Florida law provides that the records of a minor who has voluntarily sought substance abuse treatment can be released only on the written consent of the minor client. This

---

13. 14 FLA. STAT. ANN. § 397.501(7)(j) (West 2002).
14. 14 FLA. STAT. ANN. § 397.501(7)(b) (West 2002).

restriction covers disclosure of client-identifying information to the parent, legal guardian, or custodian for the purpose of obtaining financial reimbursement.[15]

(B) Confidentiality as Related to Mental Health Professionals

Statutes regulating each of the major professions[16] provide for confidentiality of communications made to the practitioners by patients in the course of treatment.[17] Health care professionals can also be held responsible for maintaining the confidentiality of records of clients whom they have not treated or with whom they have not had a professional relationship, and they can be sanctioned for violating confidence.[18]

Legislation describing the nature and limitations of confidentiality for specific professions[19] offers similar provisions with the addition that confidentiality can be breached by the professional when the client poses a threat to self or others (see later discussion).

In addition, Florida statutes requiring the reporting of abuse and neglect of children and of elderly and disabled persons also constitute exceptions to the general guarantee of confidentiality (see chapters 4.7, Reporting of Adult Abuse, 4.8, Reporting of Child Abuse, and 4.13, Foster Care, on reporting adult and child abuse).

---

15. 14 FLA. STAT. ANN. § 397.501(7)(e)1 (West 2002).
16. That is, psychology, psychiatry (medicine, osteopathy), social work, marriage and family therapy, and mental health counseling, with the exception of nursing, which has no specific statutory provision governing confidentiality.
17. 15 FLA. STAT. ANN. § 490.0147 (West 2001); 15 FLA. STAT. ANN. § 456.059 (West Supp. 2002); 15 FLA. STAT. ANN. § 491.0147 (West 2001). In addition, Florida's generic psychotherapist–patient privilege statute (6 FLA. STAT. ANN. § 90.503 (West Supp. 2002), *see also* chapter 3.4, Privileged Communications) directs that, except under limited circumstances, communications made by a client to an MHP in the course of assessment or treatment are to remain confidential and cannot be revealed in court. This applies essentially to all practicing licensed MHPs (i.e., psychologists, psychiatrists, social workers, marriage and family therapists, mental health counselors, and other treatment providers working in DCF-licensed facilities).
18. Sanifel v. Department of Health, 749 So. 2d 525 (Fla. 5th D.C.A. 1999).
19. 15 FLA. STAT ANN. § 491.0147 (West 2001); 15 FLA. STAT. ANN. § 491.0147 (West 2001).

(B)(1) Psychologists

(B)(1)(a) Scope of the Duty

Communications made by a client to a psychologist in the course of treatment are required, by law, to remain confidential[20] absent waiver by the client or certain exceptions, including when the psychologist is a defendant in a civil, criminal, or disciplinary action arising from a complaint filed by the client; or when there is a clear and immediate probability of physical harm to the patient or client, to other individuals, or to society and (the psychologist) communicates the information only to the potential victim, appropriate family member, or law enforcement or other appropriate authorities.

Other exceptions to the general guarantee of confidentiality include cases in which the psychologist suspects abuse or neglect of children, elderly persons, or disabled adults, insofar as psychologists who suspect abuse or neglect must make a report to the DCF.

(B)(1)(b) Liability for Violation of Confidentiality

There is no penalty specified for breaching confidentiality, but penalties that can be imposed by the Board of Psychology for violation of any statutes or rules range from revocation of licensure and fines to a public reprimand.[21]

(B)(2) Psychiatrists

(B)(2)(a) Scope of the Duty

Communications between psychiatrists and their clients are confidential and are not to be disclosed unless authorized by the client or under other exceptions noted by law, such as when the client has made an actual threat to physically harm an identifiable victim or victims and the psychiatrist determines that the client is capable of committing such an act and is more likely than not to carry out the threat in the near future.[22] In such cases the psychiatrist can disclose patient communications to the extent necessary to warn a potential victim or to communicate the threat to a law enforcement agency. Other exceptions to the general guarantee of confidentiality are cases in which the psychiatrist suspects abuse or neglect of children, elderly persons, or disabled adults, insofar as psychiatrists who suspect abuse or neglect must make a report to the DCF.

---

20. Fla. Stat. Ann. § 490.0147 (West 2001); Fla. Admin. Code Ann. § 64B19-19.006 (2002).
21. Fla. Admin. Code Ann. § 64B19-17.002 (2002).
22. 15 Fla. Stat. Ann. § 456.073 (West Supp. 2002).

(B)(2)(b) Liability for Violation of Confidentiality

Psychiatrists who breach confidentiality while disclosing a threat as described earlier cannot be held liable for the disclosure.[23] There is no penalty specified for breaching confidentiality inappropriately, but penalties that can be imposed by the Board of Medicine for violation of any statutes or rules range from suspension or revocation of licensure to fines.[24]

(B)(3) Clinical Social Workers, Marriage and Family Therapists, and Mental Health Counselors

(B)(3)(a) Scope of the Duty

Communications between clinical social workers, marriage and family therapists, and mental health counselors and their clients are confidential and are not to be disclosed unless authorized by the client or under other exceptions noted by law, such as when the therapist is a defendant in a legal proceeding arising from a complaint filed by the client or when there is a clear and immediate probability of physical harm to the patient or client, to other individuals, or to society and the [therapist] communicates the information only to the potential victim, appropriate family members, or law enforcement or other appropriate officials.[25]

Other exceptions to the general guarantee of confidentiality include cases in which the clinical social worker, marriage and family therapist, or mental health counselor suspects abuse or neglect of children, elderly persons, or disabled adults, insofar as therapists who suspect abuse or neglect must make a report to the DCF (see chapters 4.7, Reporting of Adult Abuse, 4.8, Reporting of Child Abuse, and 4.13, Foster Care, on reporting abuse).

(B)(3)(b) Liability for Violation of Confidentiality

There is no penalty specified for breaching confidentiality, but penalties that can be imposed by the Board for violation of any statutes or rules range from revocation of licensure and fines of to a public reprimand.[26]

---

23. 15 FLA. STAT. ANN. § 456.059 (West Supp. 2002).
24. FLA. ADMIN. CODE ANN. § 61F66-2101 (2002).
25. 15 FLA. STAT. ANN. § 491.0147 (West 2001).
26. FLA. ADMIN. CODE ANN. § 64B4-5 (2002).

(C) Confidentiality and the Duty to Protect or Warn: "Tarasoff Issues"

MHPs in most jurisdictions have some knowledge of *Tarasoff v. the Regents of the University of California*,[27] a 1976 case in which the supreme court of California ruled that MHPs are obligated to protect third parties from the dangerous acts of their clients. *Tarasoff* situations are relevant to the issues of confidentiality (and privilege; see chapter 3.4, Privileged Communications) because this duty to protect might require the MHP to breach confidentiality either by acknowledging that a psychotherapeutic relationship exists or by relaying communications that were made by the client in the course of assessment or treatment to third parties (e.g., law enforcement agencies, potential victims).

Tarasoff-like situations have occurred in a number of jurisdictions, and some states have adopted laws regarding the general duty to protect third parties. Other states have rejected this principle, either by case law or by statute. There is a general trend in Florida case law that specifically rejects the reasoning and obligations imposed by *Tarasoff* and its progeny, both with regard to MHPs' duty to protect third parties from the acts of their clients and MHPs' duty to protect clients from their own acts.[28]

With regard to an MHP's duty to protect third parties from the acts of his or her clients, the authoritative Florida case to date is *Boynton v. Burglass*,[29] which was decided by the Third District court of appeals. Lawrence Blaylock, an outpatient of Dr. Milton Burglass, killed Wayne Boynton. Boynton's parents alleged that Dr. Burglass knew or should have known that Blaylock presented a serious risk to their son. They sued Dr. Burglass for his failure to warn or otherwise protect their son. The trial court dismissed the suit and found in favor of Dr. Burglass. On appeal, the Third District court of appeals reviewed relevant case and statutory law from Florida and other states and rejected the reasoning offered in *Tarasoff* and similar decisions. The court gave considerable latitude to MHPs, ruling that they were permitted, but not obligated, to breach confidentiality and take steps to warn or otherwise protect third parties from the potentially violent actions of their clients. In reaching this decision, the court implicitly gave permission to MHPs to take steps to notify or otherwise protect third parties without becoming liable for a breach of confidentiality by its citation to the Florida statute that permits psychiatrists to

---

27. 551 P.2d 1334 (Cal. 1976).
28. *See* Greenberg, A.C. (1992). Florida rejects a *Tarasoff* duty to protect. *Stetson Law Review*, 22, 239.
29. 590 So. 2d 446 (Fla. 3d D.C.A. 1991).

breach confidentiality in cases of perceived threat to third parties.[30] Although this statute, by its terms, applies only to physicians, the court noted that the reasoning of the case applied to all MHPs,[31] not just to psychiatrists, indicating that nonphysician MHPs will be treated similarly. When presented with a similar fact situation involving a licensed mental health counselor, the Second District court of appeals also rejected the claim that mental health professionals have a duty to protect third parties from the potentially harmful acts of their outpatient clients (see *Green v. Ross*).[32]

Together, these cases suggest that MHPs are permitted, but not obligated, to take steps (including breaching confidentiality) to protect identifiable third parties from the potentially violent actions of their outpatient clients. It is emphasized that the supreme court of Florida has yet to respond to the court of appeals' request that it hear the case because of its significance, and it is unclear whether the Florida supreme court (or other Florida appellate courts) would follow the reasoning of the appellate courts. However, reasoning consistent with and supportive of the general thrust of *Boynton* and *Green* can be found in other Florida appellate decisions.

In *Santa Cruz v. Northwest Dade Community Health Center*,[33] victims who were injured by a person receiving outpatient mental health services sued the treating mental health center alleging that it was negligent for not controlling the patient's behavior via hospitalization or detention. On appeal, the Third District court of appeals ruled that the defendant mental health center did not owe a duty to the plaintiffs to control the perpetrator's/outpatient's behavior via detention or involuntary hospitalization.

Regarding the issue of the duty to protect clients from their own acts, at least one Florida appellate court has ruled that MHPs have no such duty. In *Paddock v. Chacko*,[34] a patient alleged that her psychiatrist was negligent and liable for self-inflicted injuries because of his failure to involuntarily hospitalize her after learning that she was experiencing symptoms of psychosis. The Fifth District court of appeals upheld the trial court's decision and ruled that the psychiatrist was under no obligation to detain the plaintiff or compel the plaintiff's hospitalization. The court noted that the statute outlining involuntary hospitalization was permissive and

---

30. The statute the court cited—Florida Statute 455.2425, which has been renumbered as Florida Statute 455.671—is applicable only to physicians and allows psychiatrists to divulge confidential communications to warn or protect identifiable victims in some circumstances.
31. Boynton v. Burglass, 590 So. 2d 446, at 448 (Fla. 3d D.C.A. 1991).
32. 691 So. 2d 542 (Fla. 2d D.C.A. 1997).
33. 590 So. 2d 444 (Fla. 3d D.C.A. 1991), *review denied*, 599 So. 2d 1278 (Fla. 1992).
34. 524 So. 410 (Fla. 5th D.C.A. 1998), *review denied*, 553 So. 2d 168 (Fla. 1989).

imposed no obligation on MHPs to compel hospitalization of their clients.

There are two Florida cases that suggest that mental health professionals have some duty to protect third parties from the potentially harmful actions of their clients. In *Nova University v. Wagner*, the issue was whether a residential treatment program had a duty to protect the general public from its residents.[35] The supreme court of Florida ruled that "a [residential] facility in the business of taking charge of persons likely to harm others has an ordinary duty to exercise reasonable care in its operation to avoid foreseeable attacks."[36] In *O'Keefe v. Orea*, the First District court of appeals emphasized that the psychiatrist who treated and released a teenager who ultimately killed his father knew or should have known of his patient's deteriorating condition and thus had a duty to disclose this and information related to his hospitalization to his parents and family, who were already aware of their son's violent tendencies.[37]

(D) Notification of Partner of HIV-Positive/AIDS Status

Professionals regulated by the Division of Medical Quality Assurance are permitted to notify identifiable sexual partners or needle-sharing partners of the status of an HIV-positive client, provided that[38]

1. The patient notifies the practitioner of the identity of the partner(s);

2. The practitioner recommends that the patient notify the partner(s) of his or her positive status and refrain from engaging in activities that are likely to transmit the virus and the patient refuses to do so;

3. The practitioner informs the patient of his or her intent to notify the partner(s); and

4. The practitioner perceives him- or herself as required to inform the partner of the patient's status as a result of a perceived civil duty or ethical guidelines.

---

35. Nova University v. Wagner, 491 So. 2d 1116 (Fla. 1986).
36. *Id.* at 1118.
37. O'Keefe v. Orea, 731 So. 2d 680 (Fla. 1st D.C.A. 1998).
38. 15 FLA. STAT. ANN. § 456.061 (West Supp. 2002).

Like the *Tarasoff* duties described earlier, however, this law is permissive in that, in some circumstances, MHPs are permitted to notify partners but are not required to do so. Moreover, MHPs may not be held civilly or criminally liable for failure to notify their clients' partner(s).[39]

---

39. *Id.*

3.4

Privileged Communications

The courts may seek access to information that has been revealed in confidence by a client to an MHP in the course of evaluation or treatment when the information may be relevant to a legal proceeding. All information, even confidential information, is discoverable in the course of legal proceedings unless it is privileged.

(A) Psychotherapist–Patient Privilege

With the exception of the circumstances noted next, communications that are intended to be confidential and are made to an MHP in the course of treatment are privileged and cannot be revealed in a legal proceeding without the patient's[1] consent.[2]

(A)(1) Definition of Psychotherapist

For purposes of the psychotherapist–patient privilege statute, *psychotherapist is* defined broadly and includes licensed psychologists, psychiatrists (and other physicians who treat mental disorders), licensed or certified social workers, marriage and family therapists, mental health counselors, or treatment providers working in mental health, mental retardation, or substance abuse treatment facilities that are licensed by the DCF.[3]

---

1. In this chapter, the term *patient* is used instead of *client*, given the title and language of the statute.
2. 6 FLA. STAT. ANN. § 90.503(2) (West Supp. 2002); 15 FLA. STAT. ANN. § 456.059 (West Supp. 2002); 15 FLA. STAT. ANN. § 490.0147 (West 2001); 15 FLA. STAT. ANN. § 491.047 (West 2001).
3. 6 FLA. STAT. ANN. § 90.50 3(1)(a) (West Supp. 2002).

(A)(2) Assertion and Waiver of the Privilege

Patients can refuse to disclose and can prevent others from disclosing, in a legal proceeding, communications or records made for the purpose of diagnosis or treatment of mental disorders, including drug and alcohol addiction. Patients themselves can claim the privilege, or the privilege can be claimed on their behalf by an attorney, psychotherapist, or guardian. (It should be noted that patients may also waive the privilege explicitly and that, in some circumstances, particularly those in which the patient has placed his or her mental state at issue in a legal proceeding, the patient may waive the privilege effectively.) The privilege may also be claimed on behalf of a deceased patient by a personal representative.[4] Minors may be able to assert the psychotherapist–patient independently and over the objective of their parents in some circumstances.[5]

(A)(3) Limitations and Scope of the Privilege

The psychotherapist–patient privilege is not absolute, and the Florida statute recognizes the following exceptions:[6]

1. Communications relevant to an issue in proceedings to compel hospitalization of a patient for mental illness if the psychotherapist, in the course of treatment, determines that the patient is in need of hospitalization. Thus, a person cannot prevent an MHP who has evaluated or treated him or her from testifying at an involuntary examination or involuntary placement hearing by invoking the privilege;

2. Communications made in the course of a court-ordered examination of the mental or emotional condition of the patient. Accordingly, a person who has been examined by an MHP as the result of a court order cannot prevent the MHP from disclosing information obtained in the evaluation in the subsequent legal proceedings; and

3. Communications relevant to an issue of the mental or emotional condition of the patient in any proceeding in which the patient relies on the condition as an element of his or her claim or defense. Therefore a person who makes his or her mental state an issue in a legal proceeding cannot prevent records or accounts of previous treatment that are relevant to the proceedings from being admitted by invoking the privilege.[7] It is impor-

---

4. 6 FLA. STAT. ANN. § 90.503(3) (West Supp. 2002).
5. D.K. v. Parents of D.K., 780 So. 2d 301 (Fla. 5th D.C.A. 2001).
6. 6 FLA. STAT. ANN. § 90.503 (West Supp. 2002).
7. Nelson v. Womble, 657 So. 2d 1221 (Fla. 5th D.C.A. 1995); Arzola v Reigosa, 534 So. 2d 883 (Fla. 3d D.C.A. 1988); Russell v. Stardust Cruisers 690 So. 2d 743 (Fla. 5th D.C.A. 1997).

tant to note that simple involvement in a legal proceeding in which the litigant's mental state may be relevant (e.g., child custody) is not necessarily interpreted by the court as raising one's mental state as an issue and result in automatic waiver of the privilege under this statutory exception.[8]

In addition to these described statutory exceptions, Florida's child abuse reporting laws (see chapter 4.7, Reporting of Adult Abuse, and 4.8, Reporting of Child Abuse) also appear to limit the scope of the privilege insofar as psychotherapeutic communications that are otherwise privileged may no longer be when the patient is the subject of a mandated child abuse or neglect report.[9]

Even when the privilege does not apply patients can seek to limit what communications or information from the clinical record are divulged. For example, the patient litigant can seek to have the judge review the clinical record and release only those sections that are pertinent to the legal proceeding and issue.[10]

(B) Sexual Assault Counselor–Victim Privilege

Florida also provides for a sexual assault counselor–victim privilege. This privilege provides for the confidentiality and privilege of communications made to a "sexual assault counselor" or "trained volunteer" associated with a rape crisis center when the communications were made "for purposes of securing advice, counseling or assistance concerning a mental, physical, or emotional condition caused by a sexual assault or sexual battery, an alleged sexual assault or sexual battery, or an attempted sexual assault or sexual battery.[11] The privilege may be claimed by the victim or, on behalf of the victim, by the victim's attorney, guardian, conservator, sexual assault counselor, trained volunteer, or in the case of a deceased victim, by the victim's personal representative.[12]

---

8. Leonard v. Leonard, 673 So. 2d 97 (Fla. 1st D.C.A. 1996); Freshwater v. Freshwater, 659 So. 2d 1206 (Fla. 3d D.C.A. 1995); Palm Beach County School Board v. Morrison, 621 So. 2d 464 (Fla. 4th D.C.A. 1993).
9. State v. Jett, 626 So. 2d 691 (Fla. 1993).
10. Boyle v. Thebaut, 645 So. 2d 64 (Fla. 4th D.C.A. 1994); Russell v. Stardust Cruisers, 690 So. 2d 743 (Fla. 5th D.C.A. 1997).
11. 6 FLA. STAT. ANN. § 90.503 (West Supp. 2000).
12. 6 FLA. STAT. ANN. § 90.503(3) (West Supp. 2000).

3.5
Search, Seizure, and Subpoena of Records

There are a variety of ways in which records and other materials may become available to another party. In a criminal case, a court may issue a search warrant permitting the seizure of identified materials. In either a criminal or civil case, records may be subpoenaed. MHPs must be aware of the basic principles governing these methods of discovery because each represents an exception to the ordinary rules of confidentiality and privilege.

(A) Search and Seizure

The U.S. Constitution, through the Fourth Amendment, protects citizens from unreasonable searches and seizures. The Florida constitution provides similar protection, requiring that "the right of the people to be secure in their persons, houses, papers and effects against unreasonable searches and seizures and against the unreasonable interception of private communications by any means, shall not be violated."[1] The Florida constitution also provides that no warrant shall be issued except on probable cause, and that probable cause must be established by an affidavit that particularly describes the place or places to be searched, the individual or individuals, thing or things to be seized, the communication to be intercepted, and the nature of the evidence to be obtained.[2] Interpretation of the Florida constitutional protection against unreasonable searches and seizures is governed by inter-

---

1. FLA. CONST. art. I, § 12.
2. *Id.*

pretation and application of the Fourth Amendment to the U.S. Constitution.

Under Florida law, a search warrant may be issued by any judge or magistrate with jurisdiction over the subject of the search.[3] A search warrant may be issued for the seizure of property when there is probable cause to believe that the property[4]

1. Has been stolen or embezzled;
2. Has been used to commit a crime, in connection with gambling, or in violation of laws governing obscenity;
3. Is relevant to proving the commission of a felony;
4. Is being held in violation of liquor laws, in violation of fish and game laws, or in violation of food and drug laws; or
5. Is relevant to violation of animal cruelty laws.

A search warrant may also be issued to provide for the search of a private dwelling in certain circumstances. These include situations in which[5]

1. The private dwelling is being used in violation of liquor laws;
2. Stolen property is being held there;
3. Gambling is being conducted;
4. The dwelling is used for fraudulent activities;
5. Narcotics laws are being violated;
6. A weapon used in a felony is in the dwelling;
7. Specified misdemeanor child abuse offenses are being committed there;
8. It is being used for illegal business purposes;
9. Unlawful sales or possession of wildlife or fish are occurring there; or
10. Animal cruelty laws are being violated.

(A)(1) Grounds for Obtaining a Search Warrant

In obtaining a search warrant, the applicant must create an affidavit under oath that provides the basis for the court's determination of whether there is probable cause to issue the warrant.[6] Although Florida statutory law provides little definition of what constitutes an adequate affidavit, the courts have articulated the general principle that the affidavit must identify facts, not simply

---

3. 23 FLA. STAT. ANN. § 933.01 (West 2001).
4. 23 FLA. STAT. ANN. § 933.02 (West 2001).
5. 23 FLA. STAT. ANN. § 933.18 (West 2001).
6. 23 FLA. STAT. ANN. § 933.04 (West 2001).

conclusions, and that the recitation of facts must provide the basis for the warrant's issue.[7]

(A)(2) Searches of Physicians' Offices

There are special provisions governing searches of physicians' offices. If the DOH has reason to believe that the statutory provisions governing the prescription and administration of medications are being violated, it may obtain a search warrant from a judge, on a showing of probable cause, to obtain evidence necessary to prosecute such violations.[8] However, in such cases, the medical records of patients may not be seized absent patient consent, and if patient consent is obtained, the records are not to be made available to any other agency.[9]

If patient records are obtained, the psychotherapist–patient privilege is *not* waived as a result. In addition, although records cannot be obtained without patient consent under this provision, they may be obtained through a judicial subpoena, as noted next.

(B) Subpoenas

(B)(1) Overview of Confidentiality and Privilege

Mental health records are confidential absent specific exceptions. One exception is that a record shall be released to persons authorized by a court order, after consideration by the court of the need for disclosure against the possible harm of disclosure to the person to whom the information in the record pertains.[10] This illustrates the interrelationship of several principles that may cause confusion for the MHP in this area. These principles may be stated in the following manner:

1. Mental health records generally are confidential, absent application of a specific, statutorily authorized exception (see also chapter 3.3, Confidential Relations and Communications);

2. One of those exceptions is a court order directing the production of the record; and

3. Even when the material is ordered to be made available, production of the material in the record in a legal proceeding, and the MHP's testimony about the record and treatment may be

---

7. Younger v. State, 433 So. 2d 636 (Fla. 5th D.C.A. 1983); *review denied*, 440 So. 2d 354 (1983).
8. 15 FLA. STAT. ANN. § 458.341 (West 2001).
9. *Id.*
10. 14 FLA. STAT. ANN. § 394.4615 (West 2002).

curtailed by the application of the psychotherapist–patient privilege (see also chapter 3.4, Privileged Communications).

When uncertain about the relationship of these principles, the MHP should seek guidance, either from counsel or, if appearing as a witness unrepresented by counsel, from the court.

(B)(2) The Subpoena Process

A court order directing a person to appear as a witness or to produce records is known as a subpoena. There are two general types of subpoenas. The first (generally referred to simply as a *subpoena*) is a written document directing a person to appear as a witness in a judicial or administrative proceeding.[11] The second, often known as a *subpoena duces tecum*, directs the production of records. As a general rule, subpoenas are served in person—for example, by the sheriff's department in a criminal case.

The subpoena of medical records in Florida is permitted "in any civil or criminal action, unless otherwise prohibited by law, upon the issuance of a subpoena from a court of competent jurisdiction and proper notice to the patient or his legal representative by the party seeking such records."[12] However, the information in the records continues to be confidential unless the patient consents to the disclosure or the testimony or disclosure is compelled and the privilege is held to be no longer applicable.

In addition, the DOH, in investigating the conduct of a physician against whom a complaint has been filed, may issue a *subpoena duces tecum* requiring the production of the names and addresses of the physician's patients.[13] The DOH may also obtain patient records pursuant to a subpoena without the patients' consent if the DOH finds reasonable cause to believe that a practitioner has violated prescription practices established by the Florida statute or has practiced the profession below the customary level of care and skill.[14] However, the psychotherapist–patient privilege continues to apply when treatment for mental illness has been provided by a practitioner who has been engaged primarily in the diagnosis and treatment of mental and nervous disorders for a period of not less than three years, inclusive of psychiatric residence.[15] If mental health treatment is at issue and

---

11. A subpoena may command an appearance as a witness before a court, or a person may be subpoenaed to appear for a deposition—for example, in an attorney's office. In addition, subpoenas may be issued by administrative bodies, for example the Department of Business and Professional Regulation, directing an appearance in an administrative proceeding.
12. 15 FLA. STAT. ANN. § 456.057(5)(c) (West Supp. 2002).
13. 15 FLA. STAT. ANN. § 458.343 (West 2001).
14. 15 FLA. STAT. ANN. § 456.057(7)(a) (West Supp. 2002).
15. 15 FLA. STAT. ANN. § 456.057(7)(b) (West Supp. 2002).

the privilege applies, the DOH may ask a court to appoint experts to review the records to determine whether the privilege should be waived.[16] In all cases in which patient records are obtained by the DOH, the records may only be used in disciplinary proceedings brought against the practitioner.

Finally, although not a matter governed by the laws relevant to subpoenas, the MHP should be aware that, in criminal cases, Florida law provides for discovery that may result in the production of records of examinations into the defendant's mental state. A defendant is given the option to participate in discovery under the *Florida Rules of Criminal Procedure*.[17] If the defendant elects to participate, the prosecution, within 15 days of being served with the defendant's notice of intent to participate, must disclose to defense counsel and permit the inspection and copying of a variety of materials, including results of physical or mental examinations and the names of witnesses.[18] The defendant has a reciprocal obligation to make certain materials available to the prosecution as well.[19]

Whenever an MHP receives a subpoena, the MHP should first review the principles articulated in this and other chapters on confidentiality and privilege. Although it will be necessary generally to ultimately produce the records or testimony sought, there are occasions in which material is sought that is privileged under Florida law and does not have to be revealed. Therefore, the distinctions noted throughout these chapters between confidentiality and privilege are important to note. The MHP, before complying, should take the time to learn the source of the subpoena and the type of proceeding in which the subpoena has been issued. The MHP should also seek counsel in cases in which he or she has doubts regarding whether the subpoenaed material should be disclosed or, in the absence of counsel, should consider raising those doubts with the court or attorneys representing the parties to the proceeding.

---

16. *Id.*
17. 33 FLA. R. CRIM. P. 3.220(a) (West Supp. 2002).
18. 33 FLA. R. CRIM. P. 3.220(b) (West Supp. 2002).
19. 33 FLA. R. CRIM. P. 3.220(c) (West Supp. 2002).

3.6

State Freedom of Information Act

The Florida constitution provides that every person has the right to inspect or copy any public record made or received in connection with the official business of any public body, officer, or employee of the state, or persons acting on their behalf, unless other provisions of law specifically exempt the records from disclosure.[1] The Florida constitution also provides that meetings of any public body of the executive or legislative branches of state, county, or municipal government are open to the public when official acts are to be taken or public business is to be transacted or discussed.[2] These constitutional provisions are also applied through statutory provisions that articulate a state policy that all state, county, and municipal records at all times are to be open to inspection by any person.[3]

Although these laws contemplate very broad public access, they recognize by their terms that exemptions from disclosure will be available. For example, medical information pertaining to public employees or former or future employees that would identify that person, if disclosed, are exempt from disclosure, absent court order or consent by the individual.[4] In addition, mental health records are subject to disclosure only according to rules established specifically in other parts of Florida law—for example, the provisions on subpoenas discussed in chapter 3.5, Search, Seizure, and Subpoena of Records. Therefore, as a general rule, state law mandating that all government records be open to inspection does not apply to mental health records maintained by an MHP or government agency.

---

1. FLA. CONST. art. I, § 24.
2. Id.
3. 7 FLA. STAT. ANN. § 119.01 (West 1995).
4. 7 FLA. STAT. ANN. § 119.07(v) (West 1995).

3.7
Right to Refuse Treatment

The doctrine of informed consent supports the general right of people with mental illness to refuse treatment. In general, treatment cannot be administered without the individual's consent. (Chapter 3.1, Informed Consent for Services, provides a discussion of informed consent.)

In addition, individuals treated either voluntarily or involuntarily in civil[1] and forensic[2] mental health facilities must be allowed the opportunity to provide "express and informed consent" for admission and treatment. Consent must also be obtained before the use of general anesthetic or electroconvulsive treatment.[3]

Treatment may be administered in an emergency situation, overriding the right to refuse psychotropic medication, when the physician determines that the individual is not capable of exercising voluntary control over his or her behavior and that these uncontrolled symptoms or behaviors present an imminent danger to the patient or others in the facility. Emergency treatment orders are valid for 24 hours. If such orders are issued twice in the same week for a patient, the facility must take steps to ensure the appointment of a guardian advocate to provide consent to additional treatment.[4]

In cases where persons are hospitalized in state forensic facilities (as incompetent to proceed with the criminal process or not guilty by reason of insanity) and refuse treatment that is consid-

---

1. 14 FLA. STAT. ANN. § 394.459(3)(a) (West 2002).
2. 23 FLA. STAT. ANN. § 916.107(3) (West 2001).
3. 14 FLA. STAT. ANN. § 394.459(3)(b) (West 2002); 23 FLA. STAT. ANN. § 916.107(3)(b) (West Supp. 2000).
4. FLA. ADMIN. CODE ANN. r. 65E-5.1703 (2002).

ered necessary by the client's treatment team for the appropriate care of the client and the safety of the client and others, such treatment may be provided under the following circumstances:[5]

1. In an emergency situation in which there is an immediate danger to the safety of the client or others, such treatment may proceed on the written order of a physician for a period not to exceed 48 hours, excluding weekends and holidays. If, after 48 hours, the client continues to refuse treatment, the facility administrator must petition the court for an order authorizing such, and involuntary treatment can be continued on the written order of a physician providing that the emergency situation continues; and

2. In nonemergency situations the facility administrator can petition the court for an order authorizing treatment. The order can allow treatment for a period not to exceed 90 days, but the order can be renewed for additional 90-day periods as necessary.

---

5. 23 FLA. STAT. ANN. § 916.107(3)(c) (West Supp. 2000); Dinardo v. State, 742 So. 2d 287 (Fla. 1st D.C.A. 1998).

3.8
Regulation of Aversive and Avoidance Conditioning

Use of aversive conditioning is regulated in a number of ways in Florida. For example, persons with mental illness (or their surrogates—for example, guardians or guardian advocates) have the right to consent to and refuse treatment, which limits the use of aversive and other behavioral techniques to those approved of by the clients or their lawful designees.[1]

(A) Developmental Disabilities and Aversive Stimuli

Use of "noxious or painful" stimuli for persons with developmental disabilities is prohibited.[2] The DCF has regulatory authority to create rules for treating persons with developmental disabilities with nonaversive behavioral programs.[3] The DCF's rules require behavioral programs to be documented to include, among other things, measurable definitions of the behaviors to be changed and precise descriptions of the various methods used to change behavior.[4] Individuals with developmental disabilities (if competent) or their guardians or guardian advocates also have the right to consent to and refuse treatment, which presumably also should limit use of behavioral techniques to those approved by clients or their designees.[5]

---

1. 14 FLA. STAT. ANN. § 394.459(3) (West 2002).
2. 14 FLA. STAT. ANN. § 393.13(4)(g)(1) (West 2002).
3. 14 FLA. STAT. ANN. § 393.13(4)(g)(3) (West 2002).
4. FLA. ADMIN. CODE r. 65B-6.013(5)(d) (2002).
5. 14 FLA. STAT. ANN. § 393.13(3)(h) (West 2002).

3.9
Quality Assurance for Hospital Care

All health care facilities in Florida are required to ensure comprehensive risk management and the competence of their medical staff and personnel through careful selection and review and are liable for a failure to exercise due care in fulfilling these duties.[1]

(A) Quality Assurance Programs

Such duties include but are not limited to[2]

1. Adoption of written procedures for the selection of staff members and periodic review of the medical care and treatment rendered to patients by each member of the medical staff;

2. Adoption of a comprehensive risk management program; and

3. Initiation and administration of medical review and risk-management processes.

In addition to these state requirements, federal law[3] and various accrediting standards ensure the adoption of quality assurance programs by Florida's health care facilities.

---

1. 21 FLA. STAT. ANN. § 766.110(1) (West Supp. 2002).
2. 21 FLA. STAT. ANN. § 766.110(1)(a)–(c) (West Supp. 2002).
3. 5 U.S.C. S. 11101 et seq.

(B) Medical Review Committees

(B)(1) Nature and Purpose of Medical Review Committees

Medical review committees are to be established in health care facilities to screen, evaluate, and review the professional and medical competence of applicants to, and members of, the medical staff.[4] Medical review committees may also be established by state or local professional societies of health care providers.[5] In addition, quality assurance committees operated by mental health and substance abuse treatment providers may function as medical review committees if they operate in accordance with guidelines established by the governing board of the agency in question.[6]

The DOH has statutory authority to enter into letters of agreement with a professional society of physicians, pursuant to which the medical review committee or peer review committee of the professional society is to conduct reviews of complaints or cases referred to the committee by the DOH in which there is a question regarding whether a physician breached the prevailing standard of care.[7] The committee, after review, is to submit a nonbinding advisory report to the DOH, which is to include a statement of relevant factual findings, as well as the committee's judgment as to whether the physician's actions breached the prevailing standard of care.[8] The DOH may use the committee's report as background in pursuing disciplinary action, but must prepare an independent case for its use in such actions.[9]

(B)(2) Confidentiality of Committee Findings

Investigations, proceedings, and the records of medical review committees associated with health care facilities or professional societies of health care providers are confidential, are not subject to discovery, and cannot be introduced into evidence in any civil or administrative action against a health care provider. Documents or evidence that are otherwise available, however, are not immune from discovery or introduction into evidence simply because they were presented during the proceedings of a medical review committee.[10] In addition, members of medical review committees are exempt from liability for actions taken as part of the committee's work, absent intentional fraud.[11]

---

4. 21 FLA. STAT. ANN. § 766.101(2) (West Supp. 2002).
5. 21 FLA. STAT. ANN. § 766.101(a)(1)(c) (West Supp. 2002).
6. 21 FLA. STAT. ANN. § 766.101(g)–(h) (West Supp. 2002).
7. 21 FLA. STAT. ANN. § 766.101(7)(a) (West Supp. 2002).
8. 21 FLA. STAT. ANN. § 766.101(7)(a)1–2 (West Supp. 2002).
9. 21 FLA. STAT. ANN. § 766.101(7)(c) (West Supp. 2002).
10. 21 FLA. STAT. ANN. § 766.101(5) (West Supp. 2002).
11. 21 FLA. STAT. ANN. § 766.101(3)(a) (West Supp. 2002).

3.10
Malpractice Liability

Malpractice actions are tort or personal injury claims in which the plaintiff (the party bringing suit) claims that a health care professional caused harm by an action or omission that deviates from the prevailing standard of care within the particular profession. Plaintiffs may allege malpractice and seek compensation for the losses allegedly suffered as a result of the malpractice. MHPs, like other health care professionals, owe a duty to their clients based on the fiduciary responsibilities that arise in the course of a treatment relationship. It is the treatment relationship that gives rise to these duties; in general, an MHP does not owe a duty to someone who is not a client or patient.

(A) Malpractice Law

MHPs may be involved in malpractice suits either as defendants or through providing consultation and testimony as expert witnesses for the plaintiff or defendant. As an expert witness, an MHP may testify about one or more of the following issues:

1. The appropriate standard of care in a particular case;
2. Whether the defendant MHP breached or met the professional standard of care;
3. The nature and extent, if any, of injuries suffered by the plaintiff;
4. The relationship between the defendant MHP's actions and the plaintiff's injuries; and
5. Prospective treatment that may be necessary to treat the plaintiff's injuries.

(A)(1) Who May Be Sued

In general, MHPs are sued for malpractice less than most physician specialties. However, because of professional concerns regarding malpractice, it is useful for the MHP to understand the elements of a malpractice claim.

(A)(2) Elements of a Malpractice Claim

A plaintiff, in bringing a malpractice action, must show that

1. The MHP owed a duty of care to the plaintiff as a result of a professional relationship;

2. The MHP breached this duty of care by failing to act consistently with prevailing professional norms;

3. The plaintiff suffered some kind of damages as a result of the MHP's failure to act appropriately; and

4. The MHP's actions were the proximate cause of the injuries suffered by the plaintiff.

Although Florida statutes concerned with malpractice claims against health care professionals do not specifically include nonmedical practitioners, malpractice cases can still be brought against MHPs based on the criteria enumerated earlier.

It is also worth noting that the Florida legislature has taken a number of steps in an effort to reduce the overall number of malpractice claims, as well as the size of some of the monetary awards received by plaintiffs as a result of such cases. These include requiring that plaintiff's counsel certify that he or she has reviewed the claim before it is filed and believes it to be meritorious;[1] establishing provisions for attempting to settle the case before trial;[2] and limiting some types of damages.

(A)(3) Standards of Care

The plaintiff must prove, by a preponderance of evidence, that the MHP breached the prevailing standard of care and that the breach was the proximate cause of the damage claimed. The prevailing professional standard of care for a given health care provider is that level of care, skill, and treatment that, in light of relevant circumstances, is recognized as acceptable and appropriate by reasonably prudent health care professionals like the

---

1. 21 Fla. Stat. Ann. § 766.104 (West Supp. 2002).
2. 21 Fla. Stat. Ann. § 766.106 (West Supp. 2002).

defendant (in this case, the reasonably prudent MHP).[3] The existence of an injury, in and of itself, cannot create an inference or presumption of negligence against the MHP.[4]

(A)(4) Expert Testimony

Although malpractice testimony addressing some of the elements of the malpractice action is typically offered, and is usually required, expert testimony need not be offered in cases in which common sense or ordinary judgment suggest the breach of a standard of care.[5]

(A)(5) Statute of Limitations

A lawsuit alleging medical malpractice[6] must be brought within two years from the occurrence of the incident giving rise to the action or within two years from the time at which the incident should have been discovered or was discovered. In no case, however, can a lawsuit be initiated later than four years after the date of the incident, unless it can be shown that the incident went undiscovered because of fraud, concealment, or intentional misrepresentation.[7]

Because malpractice by nonmedical MHPs is considered professional malpractice and not medical malpractice, the action must be brought within two years of when the incident was or should have been discovered.[8]

(B) Avoiding Malpractice

The most important consideration in avoiding malpractice lawsuits is to practice in accordance with prevailing professional standards. There are a variety of sources for such standards, including rules and regulations promulgated by the state and ethical

---

3. 21 FLA. STAT. ANN. § 766.102(1) (West Supp. 2002).
4. 21 FLA. STAT. ANN. § 766.102(4) (West Supp. 2002).
5. Stepien v. Bay Memorial Medical Center, 397 So. 2d 333 (Fla. 1st D.C.A. 1981); Brooks v. Serrano, 209 So. 2d 279 (Fla. 4th D.C.A. 1968).
6. For purposes of the Medical Reform Malpractice Act, psychologists are not considered to be health care providers because they are not mentioned in the definition of "health care providers" within the statute; therefore the special provisions of the statute, permitting cases to be brought in some circumstances up to four years after the event, do not apply; Weinstock v. Groth, 629 So. 2d 835 (1993). The same interpretation presumably applies to other nonmedical MHPs (i.e., social workers, marriage and family therapists, mental health counselors), none of whom fall within the definition of health care providers in the malpractice statute.
7. 7 FLA. STAT. ANN. § 95.11(4)(b) (West Supp. 2002).
8. 7 FLA. STAT. ANN. § 95.11(4)(a) (West Supp. 2002).

and practice standards established by professional associations. These sources vary in their effect on legal standards. For example, a rule established by a licensing board constitutes a standard of care that must be followed, whereas ethical principles of a profession may be useful in ascertaining a standard of care but will not bind a court to follow such rules. In addition, the MHP should be aware of the coverage and limitations on coverage provided within any malpractice insurance policy he or she carries. Such policies now routinely exclude coverage for intentional misconduct—for example, sexual misconduct with a client.

(C) Malpractice Review Committees

Florida does not have a formal malpractice review committee. However, after a plaintiff files notice of intent to bring a lawsuit with the defendant, the suit itself may not be filed for 90 days. During this period, the prospective defendant's insurer is to conduct a review to determine whether the defendant may be liable. The review is to include one or more of the following:[9]

1. An internal review by a qualified insurance claims adjuster;

2. A panel comprising an attorney knowledgeable about malpractice claims, a health care provider trained in the same or similar specialty as the defendant, and a qualified claims adjuster;

3. Use of a contractual agreement with a state or local professional society of health care providers that has a medical review committee; and

4. Any other similar procedure that provides a fair and prompt evaluation of the claim.

At the end of this review, but no later than 90 days from receipt of the notice of intent to file, the defendant's insurer is to provide the claimant with a response that either rejects the claim, makes a settlement offer, or admits liability and asks for arbitration on the issue of damages. The claimant then has 30 days to respond. If the case cannot be resolved at this point, the claimant may bring a lawsuit.

---

9. 21 FLA. STAT. ANN. § 766.106(3)(a)1–4 (West Supp. 2002).

3.11
Other Forms of Professional Liability

MHPs may be liable to patients and clients for damages resulting from malpractice. At the same time, MHPs may engage in other types of conduct that may result in criminal charges or lawsuits for civil damages. It is the latter type of conduct that may result in tort litigation that is the subject of this chapter.

(A) Intentional Torts

An individual may be found liable for negligence if he or she engages in conduct or fails to act in circumstances that expose another individual to a foreseeable risk and that result in injury to that individual. Malpractice litigation generally uses a negligence standard (see chapter 3.10, Malpractice Liability). Other types of conduct may constitute an intentional tort. A plaintiff pursuing damages for an intentional tort must demonstrate that the defendant had some degree of knowledge that the conduct in question would result in injury. For example, in the case of defamation, discussed next, the plaintiff must show that the defendant knew or should have known that the material that was disseminated to others by the defendant was false.

(A)(1) Criminal-Related Acts

A violation of criminal law (see chapter 3.12, Criminal Liability) may also result in civil liability. The state, through its prosecutorial arm, may pursue criminal liability. The injured party may also seek monetary damages through a civil lawsuit. However, it should be noted that not all intentional torts are criminal in nature.

(A)(2) Defamation of Character

Defamation is an intentional tort and involves either written or verbal statements by a defendant that are false and injure another person's professional or personal reputation. If the false statements are written, it is libel; if verbal, they may constitute slander.[1]

Some statements that otherwise would be defamatory may be *privileged*, which means that the party claiming injury may not bring a lawsuit. One form of privilege applies to statements made in the context of a court proceeding.[2] Therefore, if an MHP testifies that an individual has a mental illness and should be declared incompetent, this testimony, although it may harm the individual in some fashion, cannot be the basis for a defamation suit, as long as it is made in good faith. Other types of material cannot be discovered in a defamation suit. For example, materials reflecting the deliberations of professional peer review committees are not discoverable in a defamation action.[3]

(A)(3) Invasion of Privacy

The tort of *invasion of privacy* encompasses actions that intrude on an individual's right to be left alone and to live without unwarranted intrusion into his or her privacy.[4] To prove an invasion of privacy, the act causing injury must be of such a nature that a reasonable person could foresee that it would probably cause mental injury and distress to anyone possessed of ordinary feelings and intelligence and in similar circumstances.[5] The MHP may possess information regarding an individual that ethically and legally should be kept confidential. In addition to these legal and ethical principles, the MHP who makes information about a patient or client available to others without consent or legal authorization may risk a lawsuit for invasion of privacy.

(A)(4) Malicious Prosecution, False Imprisonment, and Abuse of Process

Malicious prosecution involves the initiation of civil or criminal proceedings against an individual without a reasonable factual or legal basis. *False imprisonment* is the illegal detention of an individual and the deprivation of his or her liberty against his or her will, absent legitimate legal proceedings. The tort requires that a person be unable to exercise freedom or reasonably believe

---

1. 19 FLA. JUR. 2d, Defamation and Privacy, §§ 1–3 (2000).
2. 19 FLA. JUR. 2d, Defamation and Privacy, §§ 76–86 (2000).
3. Parkway General Hospital v. Allinson, 453 So. 2d 123 (Fla. 3d D.C.A. 1984).
4. 19 FLA. JUR. 2d, Defamation and Privacy, § 195 (2000).
5. 19 FLA. JUR. 2d, Defamation and Privacy, § 198 (2000).

the exercise of freedom is not possible. The use of force is not an essential element of this tort.[6]

Although lawsuits alleging false imprisonment are occasionally brought against an MHP who participates in the civil commitment process, the statute prohibits the imposition of liability for wrongful detention as long as the MHP acts in good faith:

> any person who acts in good faith in compliance with the provisions of this part is immune from civil or criminal liability for his actions in connection with the admission, diagnosis, treatment, or discharge of a patient to or from a facility. However, this chapter does not relieve any person from liability if such person is guilty of negligence.[7]

Abuse of process is the malicious misuse or misapplication of a legal process (e.g., civil commitment) for a purpose other than that for which the process is established.[8]

(B) Other Types of Civil Liability

(B)(1) Fiduciary Duty

An MHP has a fiduciary duty to clients—that is, an obligation to act in the client's interests and to avoid exploitation of the client. The underlying assumption of a fiduciary relationship is that the two parties involved are not on equal terms or capacities. One party (here, the client of the MHP) has placed trust and confidence in the MHP, and the MHP because of his or her position is able to exercise influence and power over the client. As a result of this imbalance in power, the MHP must act in the interests of the client and must exercise duties of loyalty, reasonable care, and impartiality in interactions with the client.

(B)(2) Breach of Contract

A *contract* is a promise or set of promises that, if breached, will give rise to a legal action. An MHP may enter a variety of contracts, including contracts for office space, employment, or provision of professional services. As a general rule, contracts must be in writing to be enforceable. MHPs entering complex contracts, in particular, should seek legal counsel in the negotiation of such contracts.

In addition, contract principles provide the basis for the therapist–client relationship. MHPs and other health care professionals typically are not required to provide services to any individuals seeking services (an exception exists for emergency rooms

---

6. 24 FLA. JUR. 2d, False Imprisonment, §§ 1–2 (2000).
7. 14 FLA. STAT. ANN. § 394.459(10) (West 2002).
8. 41 FLA. JUR. 2d, § 7 (2000).

because of federal laws not covered in this volume). However, once an MHP decides to provide services and a treatment relationship is formed, the MHP becomes obligated to provide treatment within the MHP's area of professional competence. If the MHP wishes to terminate the relationship, in most circumstances, the MHP must provide a referral to another service provider if the individual continues to be in need of services. Failure to do so, in the context of a unilateral termination of the treatment relationship by the MHP, may lead to a tort lawsuit alleging abandonment of the client.

3.12
Criminal Liability

There are a number of ethical and legal principles designed to ensure that MHPs and other health care professionals do not violate the privacy or physical integrity of people they treat. However, there may be circumstances in which MHPs ignore those principles. In some instances, criminal conduct may occur. Of course, any conduct that qualifies as a criminal offense generally would classify as a criminal offense if committed against a client. However, there are two classes of offenses that are particularly relevant to mental health professionals: (a) those against persons whose mental state or functioning is considered to be impaired, and (b) those that specifically involve interactions between the MHP professional and client.

(A) Sexual Offenses

There are a number of different sexual offenses, most of which involve nonconsensual sexual acts. A number of sexual offenses involve acts with persons who are considered to be nonconsenting as a result of some kind of mental impairment.

Engaging in sexual activity (i.e., oral, anal, or vaginal penetration, or union with, the sexual organ of another, or the anal or vaginal penetration of another by any object) with a person after administering to the victim, or having knowledge that the victim was administered, any narcotic, anesthetic, or other intoxicating substance that mentally or physically incapacitates the victim constitutes sexual battery.[1] Similarly, engaging in sexual activity

---

1. 22 FLA. STAT. ANN. § 794.011(4)(d) (West 2000).

with another who is incapable of consenting to sexual activity as a function of being "mentally defective" (i.e., who has a mental disease or defect that renders the person temporarily or permanently incapable of appraising the nature of his or her conduct)[2] constitutes sexual battery.[3]

(A)(1) Sexual Contact With Clients

There are specific statutory prohibitions against sexual relations between MHPs and clients. For example, "any psychotherapist (i.e., any licensed psychologist, social worker, marriage and family therapist, physician or other person who provides or purports to provide treatment, diagnosis, assessment, evaluation, or counseling of mental or emotional illness, symptom or condition) who commits sexual misconduct [this includes oral, anal, or vaginal penetration; intercourse; kissing, and fondling][4] with a client, or former client when the professional relationship was terminated primarily for the purpose of engaging in sexual contact, commits a felony."[5] Psychiatrists are also prohibited from sexual contact with current clients via Florida law, which bars sexual misconduct in the practice of medicine and directs that current clients are presumed incompetent to consent to sexual activity with their physicians.[6] Nurses are also prohibited from sexual contact with current clients via Florida law, which bars sexual misconduct in the practice of nursing.[7]

In addition, social workers, marriage and family therapists, and mental health counselors are barred from engaging in sexual contact with immediate family members of clients (i.e., spouse, child, parents, parents-in-law, siblings, grandchild, grandparents, and other household members)[8] while services are being provided.[9] Physicians and nurses are also prohibited from sexual involvement with immediate family members, guardians, or representatives of the client.[10]

(A)(2) Sexual Contact With Ex-Clients

It is essentially universally agreed that sexual involvement of any type between an MHP and a current client is inappropriate. There

---

2. 22 FLA. STAT. ANN. § 794.011(1)(b) (West 2000).
3. 22 FLA. STAT. ANN. § 794.011(4)(e) (West 2000).
4. FLA. ADMIN. CODE ANN. r. 64-10.002 (2002).
5. 15 FLA. STAT. ANN. § 491.0112(1) (West 2001).
6. 15 FLA. STAT. ANN. § 458.331(j) (West Supp. 2002); 15 FLA. STAT. ANN. § 459.015(l) (West Supp. 2002).
7. 15 FLA. STAT. ANN. § 464.017 (West 2001).
8. FLA. ADMIN. CODE ANN. r. 64B19-10.004(3) (2002).
9. FLA. ADMIN. CODE ANN. r. 64B19-10.004 (2002).
10. 15 FLA. STAT. ANN. § 456.063 (West Supp. 2002).

is less agreement regarding sexual involvement between MHPs and former clients, and Florida law does not offer absolute prohibition of such involvement.

(A)(2)(a) Psychologists

Historically, the *Florida Administrative Code* regulating the practice of psychology directed that the psychologist–client relationship, for purposes of sexual involvement, was considered to continue in perpetuity.[11] Thus, psychologists were prohibited from sexual involvement with current *or* past clients. This rule, however, was struck down as unconstitutional by the First District court of appeal in *Caddy v. State*.[12] In this case, a psychologist challenged sanctions imposed against him by the Board of Psychology for engaging in an extended sexual relationship with a woman whom he had previously evaluated in the context of a child custody case. The appellate court ruled that the Board of Psychology rule directing that the psychologist–client relationship continue in perpetuity was overly broad because it failed to meet the least intrusive means tests and violated clients' and psychologists' privacy rights as guaranteed by the Florida Privacy Amendment. Sexual contact between a psychologist and a current client, however, remains a felony.[13]

The Board of Psychology revised its rules in response to this appellate court ruling so that there is not a per se bar against sexual involvement with ex-clients. Determining whether a psychologist–client relationship has been terminated is not determined simply by the passage of time but is also affected by various considerations, including formal termination procedures, transfer of the case to another psychologist, the length of time since the client's last visit to the psychologist, the nature and duration of the professional relationship, the extent to which the client confided personal or private information to the psychologist, the nature of the client's personal history, the degree of emotional dependence that the client has on the psychologist, the circumstances of termination of the professional relationship, the client's current mental status, the likelihood of adverse impact on the client and others, and any statements or actions by the psychologist during the provision of psychological services suggesting or inviting the possibility of a posttermination sexual or romantic relationship with the client.[14]

---

11. FLA. ADMIN. CODE ANN. r. 64B19-16.003 (2002).
12. 764 So. 2d 625 (Fla. 1st D.C.A. 2000).
13. 15 FLA. STAT. ANN. § 491.0112(1) (West 2001).
14. FLA. ADMIN. CODE ANN. r. 64B19-16.003 (2002).

(A)(2)(b) Psychiatrists

Sexual behavior or involvement with a patient not actively receiving treatment from the physician, including verbal or physical behavior, is considered to constitute sexual misconduct when it results from exploitation of trust, knowledge, influence, or emotions derived from the professional relationship, misuses privileged information or access to privileged information to meet the physician's personal or sexual needs, or reasonably appears to be an abuse of authority or power.[15]

The determination of when a person is a patient is made on a case-by-case basis, with consideration given to the nature, extent, and context of the professional relationship between the physician and the patient. The fact that a person is not actively receiving treatment or professional services from a physician is not determinative of the issue of whether the person is a patient, and a person is presumed to remain a patient until the physician–patient relationship is terminated.[16] Nor is the mere passage of time since the patient's last visit to the physician solely determinative of whether or not the physician–patient relationship has been terminated. Factors that are considered by the Board of Medicine in determining whether physician–patient relationships have been terminated include, but are not limited to, formal termination procedures, transfer of the patient to another physician, the length of time since the patient's last visit to the physician, the nature and duration of the professional relationship, the extent to which the patient has confided personal or private information to the physician, the nature of the patient's medical problem, and the degree of emotional dependence that the patient has on the physician.[17]

(A)(2)(c) Social Workers, Marriage and Family Therapists, and Mental Health Counselors

As noted, social workers, marriage and family therapists, and mental health counselors (and psychiatrists and psychologists) are prohibited from engaging in any sexual activity with a current client or an ex-client when the therapeutic relationship was terminated "primarily for the purpose of engaging in sexual contact."[18] Sexual contact under either of these circumstances constitutes a felony.[19]

In the case of social workers, marriage and family therapists, and mental health counselors, for purposes of determining the

---

15. FLA. ADMIN. CODE ANN. r. 64B8-9.008(2) (2002).
16. FLA. ADMIN. CODE ANN. r. 64B19-9.008(4) (2002).
17. FLA. ADMIN. CODE ANN. r. 64B8-9.008(5) (2002).
18. 15 FLA. STAT. ANN. § 491.0112(1) (West 2001).
19. Id.

existence of sexual misconduct the psychotherapist–client relationship, once established, is deemed to continue for a minimum of two years after termination of psychotherapy or the date of the last professional contact with the client.[20] And under no circumstances are social workers, marriage and family therapists, or mental health counselors permitted to engage in any sexual contact with an ex-client if such contact would be exploitive, abusive, or detrimental to the client's welfare.[21]

(B) Assault

An *assault* is defined as "an intentional, unlawful threat by word or act to do violence to the person of another, coupled with an apparent ability to do so, and doing some act which creates a well-founded fear in such other person that such violence is imminent."[22]

There may be circumstances in which an MHP is justified in touching a client, for example, if the client has become agitated and appears to present a threat of harm to self or others. In such cases, the force that may be used is only that degree of force necessary to ameliorate the potential danger. However, the general rule is that all unconsented touching is impermissible. Therefore, the MHP should be wary of touching a client in any but the most socially permissible manner (for example, a handshake at the beginning or end of a session).

(C) Manslaughter

Manslaughter is defined as the killing of another human being without justification or excuse.[23] A person who kills another individual is guilty of manslaughter when he or she lacks the necessary intent for the offense to rise to the level of first- or second-degree homicide. Assisting another person in committing suicide constitutes manslaughter.[24]

---

20. FLA. ADMIN. CODE ANN. r. 64B10.003(2) (2002).
21. FLA. ADMIN. CODE ANN. r. 64B10.003(3)–16.003 (2002).
22. 22 FLA. STAT. ANN. § 784.011(1) (West 2000).
23. FLA. STAT. ANN. § 782.07 (West 2000).
24. FLA. STAT. ANN. § 782.08 (West 2000).

3.13
Liability of Credentialing Boards

The boards that license practitioners and regulate practice comprise licensed professionals from the various disciplines subject to discipline, as well as individuals who are not members of the regulated profession. Section 1, Legal Credentialing, discusses the various boards relevant to MHPs. The issue of potential liability for board members may be of interest to MHPs and others who might serve on these boards.

Individuals who serve or who have served on the "probable cause" panels that determine whether there is sufficient evidence to proceed with disciplinary action against a licensed professional are exempt from liability for any actions taken while acting in their official capacity.[1] If suit is brought against a board member acting in an official capacity, the state provides for the legal defense and its costs. Thus, providing that board members do not engage in conduct that clearly lies outside of their statutory charge (for example, deciding that disciplinary action is warranted because of the race or gender of an individual) or engage in other conduct that is clearly impermissible (for example, using membership on the board to further one's own business interests), liability will not be incurred.

---

1. 15 FLA. STAT. ANN. § 455.209(2) (West 2001).

3.14
Antitrust Limitations to Practice

Antitrust law is the body of law by which federal and state government, as well as private parties, attempt to create a competitive economic environment by prohibiting practices that illegally reduce competition in the marketplace. The underlying principle of antitrust law is that competition among businesses benefits the consumer by widening available choice (because competitors will attempt to expand their market share) and by making the cost of goods lower than it might otherwise be (because competitors will compete with each other on the basis of price).

(A) Prohibited Activities

The Florida antitrust statutes[1] generally mirror federal antitrust law. Florida law, like federal law, bars "every contract, combination, or conspiracy in restraint of trade or commerce"[2] and also makes it illegal for any person to "monopolize, or combine or conspire with any other person to monopolize any part of trade or commerce" in Florida.[3]

Although the statutes prohibit "every" contract in restraint of trade, the courts in applying the antitrust laws generally seek to prohibit only those restraints that are unreasonable. The first issue is whether parties or individuals who are in competition are taking the actions that are subject of the antitrust inquiry. For example, psychologists practicing in the same community will be

---
1. 16 FLA. STAT. ANN. § 542.15 *et seq.* (West 1997).
2. 16 FLA. STAT. ANN. § 542.18 (West 1997).
3. 16 FLA. STAT. ANN. § 542.19 (West 1997).

considered competitors for purposes of antitrust analysis. A second core issue is whether the activities in question violate the law. The courts use two types of analysis in making this determination. The first is called the per se rule. This rule is applied to activities deemed so harmful in their impact on a competitive marketplace that they are always illegal. In such cases, a simple showing of the prohibited activity will be sufficient to make out an antitrust claim. One type of activity historically judged a per se violation of the antitrust laws was price-fixing: If competitors agreed to set a price that they would charge for a good or service then they automatically violated antitrust laws. Consumers may bring lawsuits challenging price-fixing activities in Florida.[4] However, in health care, the courts in recent years, as well as federal regulatory agencies, have begun to loosen their analysis of such activities in certain circumstances to accommodate the manner in which health care has evolved in the managed care era. For example, when health care competitors band together to create a provider network and assume financial risk under a capitated contract, then restrictions on setting prices are relaxed.

The second type of analysis is called the rule of reason. This analysis focuses on the share of the market held by the party whose actions are being scrutinized and seeks to determine whether the party can influence the market by its anticompetitive behavior in a way that warrants intervention under the antitrust laws. Perhaps the most prominent example in modern American antitrust law was the trial of the Microsoft corporation, in which the federal government alleged that Microsoft had engaged in predatory behaviors in creating and maintaining a monopoly.

Historically, the health care professions (and the legal profession) were exempt from antitrust laws on the grounds that they were "learned professions," not businesses. However, the U.S. Supreme Court ultimately rejected this view[5] and, as a result, certain prohibitions on professional activity enforced by professional associations (for example, the ban on advertising that used to exist in the health care and legal professions) are no longer legal. As a result, there has been an increase in antitrust scrutiny and litigation in the health care industry. At the same time, certain defenses to such actions still exist. For example, the Florida legislature, in an effort to insulate staff privileging decisions (see chapter 2.7, Hospital, Administrative, and Staff Privileges) from antitrust challenges by health care professionals denied privileges, generally exempts such decisions from antitrust challenge.[6] In addition,

---

4. Mack v. Bristol-Myer Squibb Co., 673 So. 2d 100 (Fla. 1st D.C.A. 1997).
5. *See, e.g.*, Goldfarb v. Virginia State Bar, 421 U.S. 773 (1975).
6. 14 FLA. STAT. ANN. § 395.0193 (West 2002).

actions that might reduce competition in the health care system but that are taken by government (for example, state certificate-of-need decisions that grant one health care applicant a license to engage in a business that other health care competitors may thereby be unable to pursue) are exempted from antitrust challenge on the basis of the state action defense.[7]

(B) Enforcement of the Law

There are a number of ways that antitrust laws are enforced. A person or party alleging injury from a violation of antitrust laws may bring a lawsuit in circuit court. Damages three times actual damages may be awarded, as well as attorney's fees.[8] Antitrust laws generally contain a provision permitting the award of damages three times the actual damages to act as a deterrent to antitrust violations.

In addition, the Florida attorney general or a state attorney with written permission of the attorney general may bring a civil action in the name of the state, to recover damages in an amount three times the actual damages.[9] Both the attorney general and a private party also may seek an injunction against future behavior violating the antitrust laws.

Finally, the U.S. attorney general and the Federal Trade Commission have authority to enforce federal antitrust laws.

Antitrust law continues to play a significant role in the health care environment because of the continued evolution in the ways in which health care entities are organized and financed, the growing role of profit in the provision of health care, and the public and political ambivalence regarding whether health care is a product like other products (which therefore should be subject to the ordinary rules governing business) or whether it is sufficiently different from other businesses that it warrants the application of different rules in at least some circumstances.

---

7. Central Florida Clinic for Rehabilitation, Inc. v. Citrus County Hosp. Board, 738 F. Supp. 459 (M.D. Fla. 1989), aff'd, 888 F.2d 1396 (11th Cir. 1989), cert. denied, 110 S. Ct. 2207 (1990); FTC v. Hospital Board of Directors of Lee County, 38 F.3d 1184 (11th Cir. 1994).
8. 16 FLA. STAT. ANN. § 544.22(1) (West).
9. 16 FLA. STAT. ANN. § 544.22(2) (West).

Section 4

Families and Juveniles

4.1
Competency to Marry

Individuals who marry must be competent to do so. Mental health professionals (MHPs) maybe called on to assess a person's capacity or competency to make a decision about marriage under the guardianship statute, which specifically addresses competency to marry (see chapter 4.2, Guardianship for Adults). Evaluations of competency to marry that are conducted after a marriage has occurred are most likely to be conducted in the course of annulment proceedings (see chapter 4.4, Annulment).

(A) Eligibility for Marriage

People wishing to marry must be single, at least 18 years of age, and of opposite sexes.[1] Persons who are 16 or 17 years of age may marry with the written consent of their parents or guardians. A person who is 17 years of age or younger may marry without the consent of a parent or guardian if he or she and the intended spouse are expectant or current parents.[2] A woman under the age of 18 may marry a man over the age of 18 without parental consent if she is pregnant.[3]

---

1. 21 FLA. STAT. ANN. § 741.04 (West Supp. 2002).
2. 21 FLA. STAT. ANN. § 741.0405 (West Supp. 2002).
3. Id.

(B) Competency/Capacity to Marry

A person may be considered to be incompetent to marry because of mental disorder or disability,[4] intoxication or other drug-induced impairment,[5] or, presumably, other altered mental states. The relevant legal test in considering whether a person lacks or lacked capacity to marry is whether the individual suffered from some kind of impaired mental state that rendered him or her incapable of understanding the nature, duties, and requirements of marriage.

(C) Standard for Voiding a Marriage

A court may issue an order dissolving a marriage if[6]

1. The marriage is irretrievably broken; or
2. One of the parties has been adjudicated as mentally incompetent for at least three years preceding the petition for divorce.

---

4. *In re* Estate of Shadow, 356 So. 2d 845 (Fla. 4th D.C.A. 1978).
5. Mahan v. Mahan, 88 So. 2d 545 (Fla. 1956); Martin v. Martin, 26 So. 2d 901 (Fla. 1946).
6. FLA. STAT. ANN. § 61.052 (West Supp. 2002).

4.2
Guardianship for Adults

Florida law allows for appointment of guardians for people who, as a function of a physical or mental disability, are unable to make decisions about their personal affairs, financial affairs, legal affairs, and health care affairs. Florida law is designed to encourage the least restrictive form of guardianship possible (i.e., a preference for limited versus plenary—total or complete—guardianship) so that the ward retains as many rights as possible.[1]

MHPs may be called on to assess persons who are allegedly incapacitated as a result of some kind of mental disorder or disability. The court may ask MHPs to identify the mental disorder responsible for the alleged incapacities, describe the alleged incapacitated person's functional abilities and limitations, and make recommendations for treatment or interventions that may rectify or minimize any observed incapacities.

(A) Scope of Guardianship/Delegation of Rights

To appoint a guardian, the court must find that the potential ward is incapacitated with respect to decision making in one or more of the following areas:[2]

1. Marriage (discussed in chapter 4.1, Competency to Marry);
2. Voting (discussed in chapter 5.8, Competency to Vote);

---

1. 22 FLA. STAT. ANN. § 744.1012 (West Supp. 2002); 21 FLA. STAT. ANN. § 744.3215 (West Supp. 2002).
2. 21 FLA. STAT. ANN. § 744.3215(2) and (3) (West Supp. 2002).

3. Applying for government benefits;

4. Having a driver's license (discussed in chapter 5.9, Competency to Obtain a Driver's License);

5. Traveling;

6. Seeking and retaining employment;

7. Entering into contracts (discussed in chapter 5.6, Competency to Contract);

8. Responding to or initiating lawsuits (discussed in chapter 5.5, Insanity of Wrongdoers and Civil Liability);

9. Managing or making a gift of property or possessions (discussed in chapters 5.6, Competency to Contract, and 5.7, Competency to Sign a Will);

10. Making decisions about one's residence;

11. Consenting to medical and mental health treatment (discussed in chapter 3.1, Informed Consent for Services); and

12. Making decisions about one's social environment and social life.

The rights to contract, respond to or initiate lawsuits, apply for government benefits, manage or make a gift of property or possessions, make decisions about one's residence, consent to medical treatment, travel and make decisions about one's social environment and social life can be removed from an individual on a finding of incapacity and delegated to the appointed guardian, who can exercise them on behalf of the ward.[3]

The rights to marry, vote, drive an automobile, and seek and retain employment can be removed from a person on a finding of incapacity but cannot be delegated to the guardian.[4]

(B) The Petitioning and Examination Process

Any adult can petition the circuit court to consider guardianship of a proposed ward. Among other things, the petitioner must identify the alleged incapacity(ies) of the proposed ward and the factual basis for his or her claims.[5]

---

3. 21 FLA. STAT. ANN. § 744.3215(3) (West Supp. 2002).
4. 21 FLA. STAT. ANN. § 744.3215(2) (West Supp. 2002).
5. 21 FLA. STAT. ANN. § 744.3201 (West Supp. 2002); *see* earlier discussion for the abilities and behaviors that the petitioner can allege are impaired as the result of some kind of disability.

On receiving a petition for determination of incapacity, the circuit court appoints a three-member committee, one of whom must be a physician. The other two committee members can be a psychologist, gerontologist, another physician, a registered nurse, nurse practitioner, a licensed social worker; or a person who is otherwise qualified by knowledge, skill, training, experience, or education.[6]

The court must appoint an attorney for the alleged incapacitated individual if he or she does not have one.[7] Before being examined, the proposed ward, his or her attorney, and next of kin must be served with the guardianship petition, and his or her attorney must receive a copy of the petition.[8]

All members of the examining committee must examine the individual with regard to the alleged incapacities. The proposed ward's treating physician must be contacted if available. The committee is to submit a report summarizing its findings to the court within 15 days of being appointed.[9]

The guardianship examination must include a physical examination, a mental health examination, and a functional assessment of the proposed ward's abilities.[10] In its report to the court the examining committee must offer a diagnosis, prognosis, and recommended treatments, if any; and an evaluation and description of the proposed ward's ability or capacity to make decisions with regard to the areas identified by the petitioner.[11]

(C) The Guardianship Hearing

The adjudicatory hearing must be set no later than 14 days after the report from the examining committee is filed, unless cause is shown. The proposed ward must be present at the hearing unless this is waived by the proposed ward's attorney or a reason can be shown for exclusion.[12]

If the court finds, by clear and convincing evidence, that the proposed ward is incapacitated in one or more areas and that no alternatives to guardianship are acceptable, then the person is declared to be incapacitated in the specific areas identified, and

---

6. 21 FLA. STAT. ANN. § 744.331(3)(a) (West Supp. 2002).
7. 21 FLA. STAT. ANN. § 744.331(2)(a) (West Supp. 2002).
8. 21 FLA. STAT. ANN. § 744.331(1) (West Supp. 2002).
9. 21 FLA. STAT. ANN. § 744.331(3)(b) (West Supp. 2002).
10. 21 FLA. STAT. ANN. § 744.331(3)(r) (West Supp. 2002).
11. 21 FLA. STAT. ANN. § 744.331(3)(d) (West Supp. 2002).
12. 21 FLA. STAT. ANN. § 744.331(5)(a) and (5)(b) (West Supp. 2002).

a guardian is appointed. The guardian can be removed on petition of the ward.[13]

(D) Types of Guardianships and Guardians

(D)(1) Permanent Guardianship

This is the most common type of guardianship. It authorizes the guardian to act on behalf of the ward for an undetermined period of time or until the court finds that the ward is no longer incapacitated.[14]

(D)(2) Preneed Guardianship

Before becoming incapacitated, an individual may name a preneed guardian who will serve as guardian in the event that he or she becomes incapacitated. If the individual is eventually adjudicated as incapacitated, the preneed guardian assumes the duties of the guardian.[15]

(D)(3) Emergency Temporary Guardianship

Subsequent to the filing of a petition for determination of incapacity but before appointment of a guardian, the court may appoint an emergency temporary guardian for an alleged incapacitated person if it determines that the subject of the petition is in imminent danger, that his or her physical or mental health is at risk, or that his or her property is at risk of being wasted, misappropriated, or lost. The initial appointment lasts no longer than 60 days but can be extended an additional 30 days. The court must specifically identify the powers and duties of the temporary emergency guardian. The alleged incapacitated person must have an attorney appointed during these proceedings.[16]

(D)(4) Voluntary Guardianship

Without adjudication of incapacity, the court may appoint a guardian for the property of an individual who, although mentally competent, is unable to care for or manage his or her assets by reason of age or physical infirmity and who has voluntarily peti-

---
13. 21 FLA. STAT. ANN. § 744.331(6) (West Supp. 2002).
14. 21 FLA. STAT. ANN. § 744.361 (West Supp. 2002).
15. 21 FLA. STAT. ANN. § 744.3045(3) (West 1997).
16. 21 FLA. STAT. ANN. § 744.3031 (West Supp. 2002).

tioned for appointment of a voluntary guardian (see chapter 8.7, Services for People With Developmental Disabilities).[17]

(D)(5) Standby Guardianship

On petition of the permanent guardian, the court may appoint a standby guardian of the person or property of a minor or an incapacitated person. The standby guardian assumes responsibility for the incapacitated person on the death, removal, or resignation of the permanent guardian. The standby guardian must then petition the court to be appointed as the incapacitated person's permanent guardian.[18]

(E) Appointment of a Guardian

In considering appointment of a guardian, the court must give preference to a person who[19]

1. Is related by blood or marriage to the ward;

2. Has educational, professional, or business experiences relevant to the nature of the services that need to be provided to the ward;

3. Has the capacity to manage the financial resources involved; and

4. Has the ability to meet the requirements of the law and unique needs of the individual case.

In considering appointment of a guardian, the court must also consider[20]

1. The wishes expressed by the incapacitated adult person regarding who should serve as his or her guardian;

2. The preference of a minor age 14 years or older regarding who should serve as guardian; and

3. Any person designated as guardian in any will in which the ward is a beneficiary.

---

17. 21 FLA. STAT. ANN. § 744.341 (West Supp. 2002); *see also* 14 FLA. STAT. ANN. § 393.12 (West 1993) regarding guardian advocates for developmentally disabled persons.
18. 21 FLA. STAT. ANN. § 744.304 (West Supp. 2002).
19. 21 FLA. STAT. ANN. § 744.312(2)(d) (West 1997).
20. 21 FLA. STAT. ANN. § 744.312(3)(c) (West 1997).

(F) Duties and Powers of the Guardian

The guardian is authorized to act on behalf of the ward in those areas or pursuits in which the ward has been determined to be incapacitated. However, without first obtaining specific authority from the court the guardian cannot[21]

1. Admit the ward to any type of mental health, mental retardation, substance abuse, or forensic treatment facility without a formal placement proceeding;
2. Consent on behalf of the ward to performance of any experimental biomedical or behavioral procedure or experiments;
3. Initiate a petition for dissolution of marriage for the ward;
4. Consent on behalf of the ward to the termination of the ward's parental rights; or
5. Consent on behalf of the ward to the performance of a sterilization or abortion procedure.

In reviewing requests for these items, the court must

1. Appoint an attorney to represent the ward and act in his or her behalf;
2. Consider expert evidence and opinions regarding the ward;
3. Personally meet with the ward to determine his or her capacity and preferences;
4. Find by clear and convincing evidence that the ward lacks the capacity to make the relevant decision and this will not change in the near future;
5. Determine by clear and convincing evidence that the intervention being requested is in the ward's best interests; and
6. In the case of dissolution of marriage, determine that the ward's spouse has consented to the dissolution.[22]

(G) Restoration to Capacity/Termination of Guardianship

Any interested person, including the ward, can file a suggestion of capacity with the court identifying rights that can be exercised

---

21. 21 FLA. STAT. ANN. § 744.3215(4) (West Supp. 2002); 21 FLA. STAT. ANN. § 744.3725 (West Supp. 2002).
22. 21 FLA. STAT. ANN. § 744.3725 (West Supp. 2002).

by the ward and should therefore be restored.[23] The ward, the guardian, and other interested persons identified by the court must be notified of such a filing.[24] In response to this filing the court appoints a physician who must examine the ward and inform the court of his or her findings within 20 days of the appointment.[25] If the court is satisfied with the physician's report, which indicates that the ward has regained partial or full capacity, and there is no objection filed, the court enters an order of restoration for all or some of the rights that were originally removed from the ward.[26]

---

23. 21 FLA. STAT. ANN. § 744.464(2)(a) (West Supp. 2002).
24. 21 FLA. STAT. ANN. § 744.464(2)(c) (West Supp. 2002).
25. 21 FLA. STAT. ANN. § 744.464(2)(l) (West Supp. 2002).
26. 21 FLA. STAT. ANN. § 744.464(3) (West Supp. 2002).

4.3

Conservatorship for Adults

A "conservator" is appointed to manage the property of an individual who is no longer able to manage his or her own property or financial affairs. In those states with discrete conservatorship laws, a mental or physical impairment that causes a person to become incapable of managing his or her property is often the reason a court appoints a conservator.

Florida law is somewhat different. The guardianship laws contain provisions that allow a guardian to be appointed to manage the property and finances of people who are incapable of doing so for themselves as a result of some kind of mental or physical disability (see chapter 4.2, Guardianship for Adults). Another statute provides for the appointment of a conservator if an individual is an "absentee." A person is considered an absentee in several circumstances, including being in the Armed Forces or Red Cross during a state of hostilities involving the United States and one year after, if the person is reported as missing in action or captured by the enemy.[1] A person may also be an absentee if he or she disappears under circumstances indicating that he or she may have died, naturally, accidentally, or at another's hand, or if the person may have disappeared as the result of "mental derangement, amnesia or other mental cause."[2]

Florida law provides for a judicial process for the appointment, duties, and termination of a conservator.[3] The conservator has the powers of a guardian appointed to handle property and financial affairs under the guardianship law.[4]

---

1. 21 FLA. STAT. ANN. § 747.01 (West Supp. 2002).
2. *Id.*
3. 21 FLA. STAT. ANN. §§ 747.031–747.052 (West Supp. 2002).
4. 21 FLA. STAT. ANN. § 747.035 (West Supp. 2002).

It is unlikely that an MHP would be involved in a proceeding under this statute, because the statute turns on whether the person is an "absentee" as defined in the law. One exception would be a proceeding seeking to establish that a person may have disappeared as a result of mental illness. In such a case, an MHP could be asked to provide evidence regarding an underlying mental illness and its impact on the person's behavior. The ultimate legal question of whether the person has disappeared as a result of the mental illness is for the court to decide.

4.4
Annulment

An annulment is a judicial termination of a voidable marriage. Marriages may be annulled for a number of reasons, including when the married person is determined to have been incapable or incompetent to marry at the time of the marriage. Mental health professionals may be asked to offer opinions about the mental state of a person at the time he or she married to assist the court in determining whether he or she had the capacity to do so. Similar to the issue of competency to marry (see chapter 4.1, Competency to Marry) the issue in annulment is whether the person understood the nature, duties, and responsibilities of the contract he or she entered (i.e., the marriage). If the court determines that the person did not have the capacity to do so, then the contract is void and the marriage is annulled.

(A) Grounds for Annulment

Although there is no Florida statute that addresses the grounds for annulment, a number of Florida statutes recognize annulment,[1] and there is considerable case law in this area.[2] In Florida, marriages may be annulled or voided on a number of grounds, including lack of mental capacity of one of the parties

---

1. *See, e.g.*, 21 FLA. STAT. ANN. § 765.104(2) (West Supp. 2002).
2. *See also* chapter 4.1, Competency to Marry, for a discussion and accompanying case law.

involved as the result of mental disorder, intoxication, or duress and coercion.[3]

As described, the relevant legal test is whether the person suffered from an impaired mental state of some kind that rendered him or her incapable of understanding the nature, duties, and requirements of marriage.

---

3. Feller v. Kisiel, 161 So. 2d 575 (Fla. 3d D.C.A. 1964); Crews v. Norris, 13 Fla. Supp. 151 (Nassau County Ct. 1958); Kuehmsted v. Turnwall, 138 So. 775 (Fla. 1932); Savage v. Olson, 9 So. 2d 363 (Fla. 1942); Mahan v. Mahan, 88 So. 2d 545 (Fla. 1956); Martin v. Martin, So. 2d 901 (Fla. 1946); Courtney v. Courtney, 150 So. 137 (Fla. 1933).

4.5
Divorce

Mental health professionals may become involved in divorce proceedings in a number of ways. A court may ask an MHP to assess or counsel spouses considering or in the process of obtaining a divorce. An MHP also may provide an evaluation on the issue of child custody before or after a divorce.

An MHP also may be asked to testify about the details of individual or family psychotherapy that took place with the parents or child/children if it is determined that such information is relevant to a child custody decision. Florida courts have been very protective about privilege in such cases, because of the privacy interests of people seeking treatment for mental illness.[1]

(A) Divorce Procedure

One of the parties to a divorce action must have resided in the state of Florida for at least six months.[2] Florida, like most states, has a no-fault divorce law that does not require either spouse to be "at fault" for a divorce to be granted.

A Florida court must find one of the following acts before a divorce is granted

1. If the court finds that a marriage is "irretrievably broken," it must grant a divorce.[3] When there are minor children in the marriage or when the party not filing for divorce denies that

---
1. Attorney ad litem for D. K. v. Parents of D. K., 780 So. 2d 301 (4th D.C.A. 2001); Leonard v. Leonard, 673 So. 2d 97 (1st D.C.A. 1996).
2. 5 FLA. STAT. ANN. § 61.021 (West 1997).
3. 5 FLA. STAT. ANN. § 61.052(2) (West Supp. 2002).

the marriage is "irretrievably broken," the court may order one or both spouses to meet with a marriage counselor, psychologist, psychiatrist, minister, priest, rabbi, or any other person deemed qualified by the court to offer assistance with regard to determining the condition of the marriage.[4] The court may also continue the proceeding for up to three months to enable the parties themselves to attempt to reach a reconciliation;[5] or

2. If one of the parties has been adjudicated by a court in a guardianship proceeding as having a mental incapacity for at least three years before the divorce proceeding.[6] If no formal adjudication of incompetency has occurred, then a divorce may not be obtained on the grounds of incapacity of the spouse.[7] Notice of the proceedings must be provided to a blood relative of the incapacitated spouse, who has a right to appear and be heard at the divorce proceedings. If the incapacitated spouse's guardian is someone other than the spouse seeking the divorce, the guardian must also be notified. If the divorcing spouse is the guardian, the court must appoint a guardian ad litem (a guardian appointed to represent an individual's interests during a legal proceeding). The guardian is responsible for protecting the interests of the incapacitated spouse in the divorce proceedings.[8]

A guardian may also file for divorce on behalf of the ward.[9] In such a case, the guardianship court also must hold an evidentiary hearing, if requested by the spouse against whom the guardian wishes to file for divorce, to determine whether the action is in the ward's best interest.[10] If the court determines that it is in the ward's best interest and permits the guardian to proceed with a divorce petition, the court hearing the divorce petition is to consider only the statutory requirements for divorce, not whether the divorce is in the ward's best interest.[11]

---

4. 5 FLA. STAT. ANN. § 61.052(2)(b)1 (West Supp. 2002).
5. 5 FLA. STAT. ANN. § 61.052(2)(b)2 (West Supp. 2002).
6. 5 FLA. STAT. ANN. § 61.052(2) (West Supp. 2002).
7. Goldberg v. Goldberg, 643 So. 2d 656 (Fla. 4th D.C.A. 1994).
8. 5 FLA. STAT. ANN. § 61.052(1)(b) (West Supp. 2002).
9. 21 FLA. STAT. ANN. § 744.3215 (West Supp. 2002).
10. Vaughan v. Guardianship of Vaughan, 648 So. 2d 193 (Fla 5th D.C.A. 1995).
11. Id.

4.6
Child Custody After Marital Dissolution

When divorce occurs, the spouses must decide who will have physical custody of the minor child or children (where the children will live) and who will have legal custody of the children (i.e., who will be responsible for making important decisions about them; this is also referred to as parental responsibility in the Florida statutes). If the parents are unable to reach an agreement between themselves regarding physical custody and parental responsibility, the court must decide with whom and under what conditions the child or children should live.

MHPs can be involved in child custody proceedings in a variety of ways. They may conduct evaluations of the parents and children if there is a dispute about the physical and legal custody of the children. They may also be asked to testify about parents' or children's involvement in psychotherapy with them, although this information may be privileged (see chapter 3.4, Privileged Communications). The court may also order parents and the family into treatment if there are difficulties related to the custody arrangement.

(A) Presumptions of Law and Standards for Decision Making

In Florida, when making decisions about the custody of children, the court is obligated to act "in the best interests of the child" and in accordance with the Uniform Marriage Child Custody Jurisdiction Act.[1] There is no presumption regarding which parent

---

1. 5 FLA. STAT. ANN. § 61.1302 (West Supp. 2002).

(the mother or father) is better suited to provide the child with primary residence/custody.[2] The court may order rotating residential placement (i.e., physical custody) if the court considers that this will be in the best interests of the child,[3] but case law suggests the existence of a presumption that rotating or alternating residence/custody is not in the best interest of the child.[4] Although Florida law allows for the court to award visitation rights to grandparents[5] and for grandparents to have standing in and be considered for custody in instances in which they have established an ongoing relationship with their grandchildren,[6] recent court cases have described such provisions as constituting unconstitutional interference with parental decision making.[7]

The court may direct divorcing parents to attend a parenting course approved by the judicial circuit.[8]

(B) Shared Parental Responsibility

Florida law seeks to ensure that both parents have frequent contact with the child and that both parents share in child-rearing rights and responsibilities, regardless of with which parent the child lives.[9] The court must order that parental responsibility be shared by both parents unless there is evidence that this would be detrimental to the child.[10] Shared parental responsibility requires both parents to confer so that major decisions affecting the child are determined jointly.[11] Thus, in those cases in which shared responsibility is awarded, both parents retain the right to be involved in decision making about the child, even though the child will typically be in the physical custody of one of the parents (i.e., the child will reside with one parent the majority of the time). The court may order that "sole parental responsibility" be awarded

---

2. *Id.*
3. 5 FLA. STAT. ANN. § 61.121 (West Supp. 2002).
4. Martin v. Martin, 582 So. 2d 734 (Fla. 5th D.C.A. 1991); Wilking v. Reiford, 582 So. 2d 727 (Fla. 5th D.C.A. 1991); Parker v. Parker, 553 So. 2d 3119 (Fla. 1st D.C.A. 1989); Chaifair v. Chaifair, 552 So. 2d 248 (Fla. 1st D.C.A. 1989); Caraballo v. Hernandez, 623 So. 563 (Fla. 4th D.C.A. 1993).
5. Fla. Stat. § 752.01(1)(a) (West Supp. 2002).
6. 5 FLA. STAT. ANN. § 61.13(2)(b)2.c (West Supp. 2002).
7. Von Eiff v. Azicri, 720 So. 2d 510 (Fla. 1998); Belair v. Belair, 776 So. 2d 1105 (Fla 5th D.C.A. 2001); Richardson v. Richardson, 766 So. 2d 1036 (Fla. 1st D.C.A. 2000); Smith v. Koolidge, 780 So. 2d 1025 (Fla. 4th D.C.A. 2001); Alderman v. Winn, 804 So. 2d 542 (Fla. 5th D.C.A. 2002).
8. 5 FLA. STAT. ANN. § 61.13(4)(c)2 (West Supp. 2002).
9. 5 FLA. STAT. ANN. § 61.13(2)(b) (West Supp. 2002); Kuharcik v. Kuharcik, 629 So. 2d 224 (Fla. 4th D.C.A. 1993).
10. 5 FLA. STAT. ANN. § 61.13(2)(b)2 (West Supp. 2002).
11. 5 FLA. STAT. ANN. § 62.13(2)(b)2.a (West Supp. 2002).

to one parent, and the court can also bar visitation if it determines that this is "in the best interests of the child."[12] Evidence of spousal abuse or domestic violence can be considered as evidence of detriment to the child and conviction of a felony of the third degree or higher involving domestic violence constitutes a rebuttable presumption of detriment to the child for purposes of custody and visitation decision making.[13]

(C) Considerations in Determining Placement

In determining parental responsibility (i.e., legal custody) and primary residence (i.e., physical custody) of the child, the court must consider all factors that affect the best interests of the child, including, but not limited to[14]

1. The parent who is more likely to allow that child frequent and continuing contact with the nonresidential parent;

2. The love, affection, and other emotional ties existing between the parents and the child;

3. The capacity and disposition of the parents to provide the child with food, clothing, medical care, and other material needs;

4. The length of time that the child has lived in a stable, satisfactory environment and the desirability of maintaining continuity;

5. The permanence, as a family unit, of the existing and proposed custodial homes;

6. The moral fitness of the parents;

7. The mental and physical health of the parents;

8. The home, school, and community record of the child;

9. The reasonable preference of the child, if the court considers the child to be of sufficient intelligence, understanding, and experience to express a preference;

10. The willingness and ability of each parent to encourage a close and continuing parent–child relationship between the child and the other parent;

---

12. 5 FLA. STAT. ANN. § 61.13(2)(b)2.b (West Supp. 2002).
13. 5 FLA. STAT. ANN. § 61.13(2)(b)2 (West Supp. 2002).
14. 5 FLA. STAT. ANN. § 61.13(3) (West Supp. 2002).

11. Evidence that a party has provided false information to the court regarding a domestic violence proceeding;
12. Evidence of domestic violence or child abuse; and
13. Other factors that may be relevant.

(D) Considerations in Determining Requests for Parental Relocation

There is no presumption in favor of or against a request to relocate after the primary residential parent seeks to move the child and the move will significantly affect the nonresidential parent's access to and contact with the child.[15] When determining whether the primary residential parent can relocate with the child the court must consider[16]

1. Whether the move is likely to improve the general quality of life for both the residential parent and the child;
2. The extent to which visitation rights have been allowed and exercised;
3. Whether the primary residential parent will comply with the new visitation arrangement;
4. Whether the new visitation arrangement will be adequate to foster a continuing meaningful relationship between the child and the nonresidential parent;
5. Whether transportation costs are affordable to one or both parents; and
6. Whether the move is in the best interests of the child.

(E) Considerations in Considering Requests for Modification of Custody

In considering cases of modification (e.g., when the parent not granted residential or physical custody subsequently seeks residential custody), the courts employ a two-prong test.[17] A parent

---

15. 5 FLA. STAT. ANN. § 61.13(2)(d) (West Supp. 2002); Flint v. Fortson, 744 So. 2d 1217 (Fla. 4th D.C.A. 1999).
16. 5 FLA. STAT. ANN. § 61.20 (West Supp. 2002).
17. Blosser v. Blosser, 707 So. 2d 778 (Fla. 2d D.C.A. 1998); Perez v. Perez, 767 So. 2d 513 (Fla. 3d D.C.A. 2000).

seeking to modify a previous custody award bears a heavy burden[18] and must demonstrate (a) a substantial change in circumstances since the entry of the initial custody decree and (b) that the child's best interests or welfare will be promoted by the proposed change.[19] With respect to demonstrating a substantial change in circumstances, courts have typically required a showing that continuing the existing custody arrangement would have a detrimental or adverse impact on the child.[20] A showing that the child may simply be better off with the proposed custody arrangement is not enough.[21]

(F) Rights of Custodial and Noncustodial Parents

The parent who is not the primary residential parent still retains the right to access the child's relevant records such as medical records, dental records, and school records.[22] This presumably also applies to mental health records. The noncustodial parent also retains the right to be involved in making important decisions about the child, unless the custodial parent has been awarded "sole parental responsibility" (see earlier and chapter 4.2, Guardianship for Adults).[23]

If the noncustodial parent is ordered to pay child support and fails to do so, the custodial parent cannot deny visitation. Similarly, if the custodial parent denies visitation to a noncustodial parent who is paying child support, the noncustodial parent cannot withhold child support payments.[24]

---

18. Zediker v. Zediker, 444 So. 2d 1034 (Fla. 1st D.C.A. 1984); McGregor v. McGregor, 418 So. 2d 1073 (Fla. 5th D.C.A. 1982).
19. Sullivan v. Sullivan, 736 So. 2d 103 (Fla. 4th D.C.A. 1999); Perez v. Perez, 767 So. 2d 513 (Fla. 3d D.C.A. 2000); Young v. Young, 732 So. 2d 1133 (Fla. 1st D.C.A. 1999); Chant v. Chant, 725 So. 2d 445 (Fla. 2d D.C.A. 1999); Schweinberg v. Click, 627 So. 2d 548 (Fla. 5th D.C.A. 1993).
20. Kilgore v. Kilgore, 729 So. 2d 402 (Fla. 1st D.C.A. 1998); Enyeart v. Stull, 715 So. 2d 320 (Fla. 2d D.C.A. 1998); Metcalfe v. Metcalfe, 655 So. 2d 1251 (Fla. 3d D.C.A. 1995).
21. Young v. Young, 732 So. 2d 1133 (Fla. 1st D.C.A. 1999); Chant v. Chant, 725 So. 2d 445 (Fla. 2d D.C.A. 1999); Gibbs v. Gibbs, 686 So. 2d 639 (Fla. 2d D.C.A. 1996).
22. 5 FLA. STAT. ANN. § 61.13(2)(b)3 (West Supp. 2002).
23. 5 FLA. STAT. ANN. § 61.13(2)(b)2.b (West Supp. 2002).
24. 5 FLA. STAT. ANN. § 61.13(4)(a) and (b) (West Supp. 2002).

(G) Child Custody Evaluations

Evaluations relating to the custody issue can be initiated by either parent, or the court can order such an evaluation if it deems it necessary.[25] A social investigation and study, when ordered by the court, shall be conducted by qualified staff of the court, a licensed child-placing agency, a licensed psychologist, or a licensed clinical social worker, marriage and family therapist, or mental health counselor.[26] Except in cases where the parties are indigent, the parties disputing custody are responsible for the cost of the evaluation.[27]

Psychologists who conduct child custody evaluations are required by rule to attempt to make contact with all parties (i.e., both parents and perhaps others) who are seeking custody of the child or children. Psychologists must also attempt to make contact with the medical or mental health professionals who are treating the child or children.[28] Although this requirement does not apply to other MHPs, professional practice dictates that all parties with information relevant to making decisions about custody or placement of a child (including but not limited to both parents and the treating medical and mental health professionals) be contacted in the course of conducting a child custody evaluation.

Because it is considered to be a conflict of interest, psychologists are prohibited from performing custody evaluations in cases where they have treated the child or any of the adults involved in the disputed custody issue.[29] Psychologists who conduct custody evaluations must have training in child development and child psychopathology, family dynamics, and legal issues and guidelines regarding child custody.[30]

Mental health counselors, marriage and family therapists, and social workers who conduct child custody evaluations must attempt to make contact with all parties (i.e., both parents and perhaps others) who are seeking custody of the child or children. These professionals must also attempt to make contact with the medical or mental health professionals who are treating the child

---

25. 5 Fla. Stat. Ann. § 61.20 (West Supp. 2002).
26. 5 Fla. Stat. Ann. § 61.20(2) (West Supp. 2002).
27. 5 Fla. Stat. Ann. § 61.20(3) (West Supp. 2002).
28. Fla. Admin. Code Ann. § 64B19-18.007 (2002).
29. Fla. Admin. Code Ann. § 64B19-18.006 (2002).
30. Fla. Admin. Code Ann. § 64B19-18.007 (2002).

or children.[31] Mental health counselors, marriage and family therapists, and social workers who conduct child custody evaluations are required to be impartial, avoid conflicts of interest, act in the child's best interests, and not have treated any parties involved in the custody evaluation.[32] Mental health counselors, marriage and family therapists, and social workers who conduct child custody evaluations must be competent in evaluating children and families; they must have education and training in the areas of child and family development, psychopathology, and the impact of divorce on children and families; and they must be knowledgeable about the legal standards and procedures governing divorce and child custody.[33]

---

31. FLA. ADMIN. CODE ANN. § 64B4-7.006 (2002).
32. Id.
33. Id.

4.7

Reporting of Adult Abuse

To protect adult persons who may be unable to protect themselves, Florida requires MHPs and other kinds of professionals to report known or suspected abuse, neglect, or exploitation of certain classes of adults.

(A) Definitions

To understand the law concerning the reporting of abuse and neglect, MHPs should be familiar with the following terms and their legal meanings. *Abuse* is defined as

> the non-accidental infliction of physical or psychological injury, or sexual abuse upon a disabled adult or an elderly person by a relative, caregiver, or household member, or an action by any of these persons which could reasonably be expected to result in physical or psychological injury, or sexual abuse of a disabled adult or elderly person by another person. "Abuse" also means the active encouragement of any person by a relative, caregiver, or household member to commit an act that inflicts or could reasonably be expected to result in physical or psychological injury of a disabled adult or elderly person.[1]

Neglect is defined as

> the failure or omission on the part of the caregiver for the disabled adult or elderly person to provide the care, supervision, and services necessary to maintain the physical and mental health of the disabled adult or elderly person, including, but not limited to food, clothing, medicine, shelter, supervision, and medical services that a prudent person would consider essential

---

1. 14 FLA. STAT. ANN. § 415.102(1) (West 2002).

for the well-being of a disabled adult or an elderly person. The term "neglect" also means the failure of a caregiver to make a reasonable effort to protect a disabled adult or an elderly person from abuse, neglect, or exploitation by others. "Neglect" is repeated conduct or a single incident of carelessness which produces or could reasonably be expected to result in serious physical or psychological injury or risk of death.[2]

Exploitation is committed by a person who

stands in a position of trust and confidence with a disabled adult or elderly person and knowingly or by deception or intimidation, obtains or uses, or endeavors to obtain or use, a disabled adult's or elderly person's funds, assets, or property with the intent to temporarily or permanently deprive a disabled adult or elderly person of the use, benefit, or possession of the funds, assets, or property for the benefit of someone other than the disabled or elderly person; or knows or should know that the disabled adult or elderly person lacks the capacity to consent, and obtains or uses, or endeavors to obtain or use, the disabled adult's or elderly person's funds, assets or property with the intent to temporarily or permanently deprive the disabled adult or elderly person of the use, benefit, or possession of the funds, assets, or property for the benefit of someone other than the disabled adult.[3]

Elderly person is defined as someone 60 years of age or older who

is suffering from the infirmities of aging as manifested by advanced age or organic brain damage, or other physical, mental or emotional dysfunctioning [sic] to the extent that the ability of the person to provide adequately for his or her own care or protection is impaired.[4]

Disabled adult is defined as a person 18 years of age or older who

suffers from a condition of physical or mental incapacitation due to a developmental disability, organic brain damage, or mental illness, or who has one or more physical or mental limitations that substantially restrict the ability to perform the normal activities of daily living.[5]

(B) Who Must Report

Florida law requires that all MHPs (including psychologists, psychiatrists, social workers, marriage and family therapists, and mental health counselors—and a variety of other professionals)

---

2. 14 FLA. STAT. ANN. § 415.102(22) (West 2002).
3. 14 FLA. STAT. ANN. § 415.102(14a) (West 2002).
4. 14 FLA. STAT. ANN. § 415.102(12) (West 2002).
5. 14 FLA. STAT. ANN. § 415.102(10) West 2002).

immediately report suspected or known abuse, neglect, or exploitation of any disabled adult or elderly person.[6]

(B)(1) Abrogation of Confidentiality and Privilege

This reporting requirement supersedes any guarantee of confidentiality or privilege that is granted by Florida law.[7] Thus, confidentiality and privilege do not apply and cannot prevent an MHP from reporting suspected or known abuse, neglect, or exploitation. Confidentiality and privilege are discussed in more detail in chapters 3.3, Confidential Relations and Communications, and 3.4, Privileged Communications.

(C) When Must a Report Be Made?

As noted earlier, the statute requires that reports of suspected abuse are to be reported "immediately."[8] Neither statute nor case law provides additional definition of the term *immediately*.

(D) How a Report Must Be Made

The report must be made to the Department of Children and Families (DCF) via the central abuse registry.[9] This registry compiles all abuse reports made to the DCF; the DCF must maintain a statewide toll-free number for reporting of abuse.[10] To the extent possible, the report must include[11]

1. Name, age, race, sex, physical description, and location of each disabled adult or elderly person alleged to have been abused, neglected, or exploited;

2. Names, addresses, and telephone numbers of family members of the alleged victim;

3. Name, address, and telephone number of each alleged perpetrator of abuse;

4. Name, address, and telephone number of the caregiver of the alleged victim, if different from the alleged perpetrator;

5. Name, address, and telephone number of the reporter of alleged abuse;

---

6. 14 FLA. STAT. ANN. § 415.1034 (West 2002).
7. 14 FLA. STAT. ANN. § 415.1045(5) (West 2002).
8. 14 FLA. STAT. ANN. § 415.1034 (West 2002).
9. 14 FLA. STAT. ANN. § 415.1034(1)(b)7 (West 2002).
10. 14 FLA. STAT. ANN. § 415.103(1) (West 2002).
11. 14 FLA. STAT. ANN. § 415.1034(1)(b)1–8 (West 2002).

6. Descriptions of injuries sustained; and
7. Any other information that might assist in establishing the cause of abuse, neglect, or exploitation.

If the individuals staffing the abuse registry believe a report requires an immediate onsite investigation, staff at a district level are to be notified immediately; otherwise notice to protective investigators is to be given in sufficient time to allow an investigation to be begun within 24 hours of receipt of the report.[12]

(E) Immunity From Liability

Anyone who makes an abuse or neglect report or testifies about such a report in any kind of legal proceeding is presumed to be acting "in good faith." Unless a lack of good faith is proven by clear and convincing evidence, the reporter is immune from any criminal liability for making the report.[13]

(F) Confidentiality of Record

All records concerning reports of abuse, neglect, or exploitation of disabled adults or elderly persons are confidential, with some exceptions (e.g., criminal justice agencies investigating reports of abuse, neglect or exploitation; a court on issuance of a subpoena and a finding that the information is needed to determine an issue before the court; program auditors; professionals assessing or treating the abused, neglected, or exploited disabled adult or elderly person if it is necessary for purposes of assessment or treatment).[14] Persons accused of abusing, neglecting, or exploiting disabled adults or elderly persons are entitled to some limited information from the record.[15]

(G) Failure to Report

Failure to report known or suspected abuse, neglect, or exploitation, or preventing someone else from reporting known or suspected abuse, neglect, or exploitation constitutes a second-degree

---

12. 14 FLA. STAT. ANN. § 415.103(2) (West 2002).
13. 14 FLA. STAT. ANN. § 415.111(5)(b) (West 1998).
14. 14 FLA. STAT. ANN. § 415.107 (West 2002).
15. 14 FLA. STAT. ANN. § 415.1055 (West 2002).

misdemeanor,[16] which is punishable by no more than 60 days in jail.[17]

(H) Protective Services

The DCF must take steps to ensure the provision of protective services if it determines that the subject of the investigation is in need of such services.[18]

---

16. 14 FLA. STAT. ANN. § 415.111(1) (West 1998).
17. 22 FLA. STAT. ANN. § 775.082(4)(b) (West Supp. 2002).
18. 14 FLA. STAT. ANN. § 415.105(1) (West 2002); 14 FLA. STAT. ANN. § 415.104(e) (West 2002).

4.8

Reporting of Child Abuse

To protect children who may be unable to protect themselves, Florida requires MHPs and many other professionals to report known or suspected abuse, neglect, or abandonment of children under the age of 18 years.

(A) Definitions

To understand the law concerning the reporting of child abuse, neglect and abandonment, MHPs should be familiar with the following terms and their legal meanings. *Child* is defined as "any unmarried person under the age of 18 years who has not been emancipated by order of the court."[1] *Abuse* is defined as

> Any willful act or threatened act that results in any physical, mental, or sexual injury or harm that causes or is likely to cause the child's physical, mental, or emotional health to be significantly impaired. Abuse of a child includes acts or omissions. Bodily punishment of a child by a parent or legal custodian for disciplinary purposes does not in itself constitute abuse when it does not result in harm to the child.[2]

Sexual abuse is defined as

1. Any penetration, however slight, of the vagina or anal opening of one person by the penis of another person, whether or not there is emission of semen;
2. Any sexual contact between the genitals or anal opening of one person and the mouth or tongue of another person;

---

1. 1 FLA. STAT. ANN. § 39.01(12) (West Supp. 2002).
2. 1 FLA. STAT. ANN. § 39.01(2) (West Supp. 2002).

3. Any intrusion by one person into the genital or anal opening of another person, including the use of any object for this purpose, except that this does not include any act intended for a valid medical purpose;
4. The intentional touching of the genital or intimate parts, including the breasts, genital area, groin, inner thighs, and buttocks, or the clothing covering them, either by the child or the perpetrator, except that this does not include any act which may be reasonably construed to be a normal caregiver responsibility, any interaction with or affection for a child, or any act intended for valid medical purposes;
5. The intentional masturbation of the perpetrator's genitals in the presence of a child, or any other sexual act intentionally perpetrated in the presence of a child, if such exposure or sexual act is for the purpose of sexual arousal or gratification, aggression, degradation, or other similar purpose; or
6. The sexual exploitation of a child, which includes allowing, encouraging, or forcing a child to solicit or engage in prostitution or engage in sexual performance.[3]

Child on child sexual abuse, or *juvenile sexual abuse* is defined as

sexual acts committed on a child by a child which occur without consent, without equality, or as a result of coercion.[4]

This behavior can range from noncontact sexual behavior such as making obscene phone calls, exhibitionism, voyeurism, and the showing or taking of lewd photographs to varying degrees of direct sexual contact such as frottage, fondling, digital penetration, rape, fellatio, sodomy, and various other sexually aggressive acts.[5]

Neglect is defined as occurring when

a child is deprived of, or is allowed to be deprived of, necessary food, clothing, shelter or medical treatment or a child is permitted to live in an environment when such deprivation or environment causes the child's physical, mental or emotional health to be significantly impaired or to be in danger of being significantly impaired. The foregoing circumstances shall not be considered neglect if caused primarily by financial inability unless actual services for relief have been offered to and rejected by such person. A parent or legal custodian legitimately practicing religious beliefs in accordance with a recognized church or religious organization who thereby does not provide specific medical treatment for a child shall not, for that reason alone, be considered a negligent parent or legal custodian.[6]

---

3. 1 FLA. STAT. ANN. § 39.01(64) (West Supp. 2002).
4. 1 FLA. STAT. ANN. § 39.01(7)(b) (West Supp. 2002).
5. *Id.*
6. 1 FLA. STAT. ANN. § 39.01(46) (West Supp. 2002).

Abandonment is defined as occurring when

the parent or legal custodian of a child, or in the absence of a parent or legal custodian, the caregiver responsible for the child's welfare, while being able, makes no provision for the child's support and makes no effort to communicate with the child, which situation is sufficient enough to evince a willful rejection of parental obligations.[7]

Corporal punishment, in and of itself, does not constitute physical abuse,[8] whereas corporal punishment leaving bruises that last for several days is considered to constitute physical abuse.[9] Failure to provide a child with food, clothing, shelter, or medical treatment constitutes neglect.[10] The incarceration of a parent, legal custodian, or caregiver responsible for a child's welfare may support a finding of abandonment.[11]

(B) Who Must Report

Florida law requires all MHPs (including psychologists, psychiatrists, social workers, marriage and family therapists, and mental health counselors—and a variety of other professionals) to immediately report any suspected or known abuse, neglect, or abandonment of a child by a parent, legal custodian, or caregiver.[12] *Child* for the purposes of the statute is defined as "any unmarried person under the age of 18 years who has not been emancipated by order of the court."[13]

(B)(1) Abrogation of Confidentiality and Privilege

This reporting requirement supersedes any guarantee of confidentiality or privilege that is granted by Florida law (see chapters 3.3, Confidential Relations and Communications, and 3.4, Privileged Communications).[14] Thus, confidentiality and privilege do not apply and cannot prevent an MHP from reporting suspected or known abuse, neglect, or abandonment.

---

7. 1 FLA. STAT. ANN. § 39.01(1) (West Supp. 2002).
8. M.O. McC. v. Department of Health and Rehabilitative Services, 575 So. 2d 1352 (1991); D.J. v. Department of Health and Rehabilitative Services, 565 So. 2d 863 (1990).
9. BL v. Department of Health and Rehabilitative Services, 545 So. 2d 2139 (1989); *review denied*, 553 So. 2d 1164.
10. State v. Winters, 346 So. 2d 991 (1977).
11. 1 FLA. STAT. ANN. § 39.01(1) (West Supp. 2002).
12. 1 FLA. STAT. ANN. § 39.201(1) (West Supp. 2002).
13. 1 FLA. STAT. ANN. § 39.01(12) (West Supp. 2002).
14. 1 FLA. STAT. ANN. § 39.204 (West Supp. 2002).

(C) When Must a Report Be Made?

The statute requires that a report of abuse, abandonment, or neglect be made "immediately," but neither statute nor case-law define further what *immediately* means in this context.

(D) How a Report Must Be Made

The report is made to the DCF via the central abuse hotline on a statewide toll-free telephone number.[15] In contrast to the statute mandating reporting of abuse, neglect, and exploitation of elderly individuals or a disabled adult (see chapter 4.7, Reporting of Adult Abuse), the child abuse reporting statute does not specify the types of information that should be included in the report. The statute requires that the DCF install equipment to automatically record the telephone number from which a report to the hotline is being made, and calls are to be automatically recorded.[16]

(E) Immunity From Liability

Anyone who, in good faith, reports known or suspected abuse, neglect or abandonment of a child as required by Florida law is immune from any criminal or civil liability.[17]

(F) Confidentiality of Record

The abuse/neglect/abandonment record maintained by the DCF, including reports, is generally confidential.[18] However, a variety of persons and entities are entitled to access information contained in the abuse/neglect/abandonment record, including professionals responsible for providing services to the child;[19] DCF staff for purposes of training, education, and research;[20] the court on demonstrating that information in the record is necessary to determine an issue before it;[21] the child's parents or legal custodian;[22]

---

15. 1 FLA. STAT. ANN. § 39.201 (West Supp. 2002).
16. 1 FLA. STAT. ANN. § 39.201(g)–(h) (West Supp. 2002).
17. 1 FLA. STAT. ANN. § 39.203 (West Supp. 2002).
18. 1 FLA. STAT. ANN. § 39.202 (West Supp. 2002).
19. 1 FLA. STAT. ANN. § 39.202(2)(a) (West Supp. 2002).
20. 1 FLA. STAT. ANN. § 39.202(2)(h) (West Supp. 2002).
21. 1 FLA. STAT. ANN. § 39.202(2)(f) (West Supp. 2002).
22. 1 FLA. STAT. ANN. § 39.202(2)(d) (West Supp. 2002).

and subjects of an investigation (i.e., persons alleged to have abused, neglected or exploited the child).[23] However, information regarding the identity of the person reporting the suspected abuse, neglect, or abandonment may only be released to DCF staff and the state attorney.[24]

(G) Failure to Report

Knowing and willing failure to report known or suspected child abuse, abandonment, or neglect, or preventing another from making such a report is a first-degree misdemeanor punishable by up to a year of incarceration.[25] A person who is older than 18 years of age and lives with an abuser and knowingly and willingly fails to report or prevents another from reporting abuse is guilty of a felony in the third degree, punishable by a term of imprisonment of no more than five years.[26] However, if the person is found by a court to have been a victim of domestic violence or there are other mitigating circumstances, the person shall not be guilty for nonreporting.

(H) Child Protection Teams

The Division of Medical Services of the Department of Health must develop, maintain, and coordinate the services of one or more multidisciplinary child protection teams in each DCF service district. These teams are composed of educational, medical, mental health, social service, legal, and law enforcement professionals.[27] The teams are to supplement the assessment and protective supervision activities of the DCF via a variety of activities, including medical evaluations, psychological or psychiatric evaluations, expert testimony in proceedings, case staffings, in-service training, and education and awareness campaigns.[28]

---

23. 1 FLA. STAT. ANN. § 39.202(2)(e) (West Supp. 2002).
24. 1 FLA. STAT. ANN. § 39.202(4) (West Supp. 2002).
25. 1 FLA. STAT. ANN. § 39.205 (West Supp. 2002).
26. 1 FLA. STAT. ANN. § 39.205(2) (West Supp. 2002).
27. 1 FLA. STAT. ANN. § 39.202(3) (West Supp. 2002).
28. 1 FLA. STAT. ANN. § 39.303(1) (West Supp. 2002).

4.9
Abused, Neglected, and Abandoned Children

Florida law attempts to protect children who allegedly have been abused and neglected and, at the same time, protect the rights of parents and other caretakers who may be wrongfully accused of abuse or neglect. In Florida, children can be taken from the custody of their parents and other caretakers and interventions can be implemented only after an adequate showing that abuse, neglect, or abandonment has occurred.

MHPs may be called on to assess children or their caretakers and make recommendations regarding placement, treatment, and other kinds of interventions in these proceedings.

(A) Taking Children Into Custody

A child may be taken from the custody of his or her parents or guardians and placed in the custody of the DCF[1]

1. Pursuant to a court order after testimony is heard that details the need for such action;

2. By a law enforcement officer or DCF personnel who believes that the child has been abused, neglected, or abandoned, or is suffering from or is in imminent danger of illness or injury as a result of abuse, neglect, or abandonment;

3. By a law enforcement officer or DCF personnel when the parent or legal custodian of a child under protective supervision has violated a significant condition of placement imposed by the court; or

---

1. 1 FLA. STAT. ANN. § 39.401(1) (West Supp. 2002).

4. By a law enforcement officer or DCF personnel when the child has no parent, legal custodian, or responsible adult relative immediately known and available to provide supervision and care.

Law enforcement personnel who take the child into custody must release the child to the parent or legal custodian of the child, a responsible adult approved by the court when limited to temporary emergency situations, a responsible adult relative who shall be given priority consideration over nonrelative placement when this is in the best interests of the child, or a responsible adult approved by the DCF, or deliver the child to an authorized agent of the DCF.[2]

Any person in charge of a hospital or similar institution or any licensed health care professional treating a child may detain a child without consent of the parents, caregiver, or legal custodian, whether or not additional medical treatment is required, if the circumstances are such, or if the condition of the child is such that returning the child to the care or custody of the parents, caregiver, or legal custodian presents an imminent danger to the child's life or physical or mental health. On initiating this detention these persons must immediately notify the DCF, in response to which the DCF will initiate a child protective investigation.[3] If it appears that the child may require custody for more than 24 hours, the DCF is to petition the court within 24 hours for an order authorizing the lengthier period.

(A)(1) Shelter Placement

Unless ordered by the court, children taken into the custody of the DCF cannot be placed in a shelter before a court hearing unless[4]

1. The child has been abused, neglected, or abandoned or is in imminent danger of illness or injury as a result of abuse, neglect, or abandonment;

2. The parents or legal custodian of the child has materially violated a condition of placement imposed by the court; or

3. The child has no parent, legal custodian, or responsible adult relative who can provide necessary supervision.

A child taken into custody may be placed in a shelter only if, in addition to one of the requirements being met, the court also finds that removal of the child from the home is necessary and provision of available and appropriate services will not elimi-

---

2. 1 FLA. STAT. ANN. § 39.401(2) (West Supp. 2002).
3. 1 FLA. STAT. ANN. § 39.395 (West Supp. 2002).
4. 1 FLA. STAT. ANN. § 39.402(1) (West Supp. 2002).

nate the need for placement.[5] If the child has been removed from the home and the reasons for his or her removal have been remedied, the child may be returned to the home.[6]

Children cannot be placed in shelters for more than 24 hours without a court order.[7] A child may not be held in a shelter for more than 60 days without an adjudication of dependency. A child may not be held in a shelter for more than 30 days after the entry of an order of adjudication unless an order of disposition has been entered by the court.[8]

Subsequent to placing a child in a shelter, a hearing must occur. The parents or legal guardians have a right to counsel and to present evidence. If they cannot afford an attorney, counsel will be appointed. At the shelter hearing the court must[9]

1. Appoint a guardian ad litem (a guardian appointed to represent the interests of an individual in litigation) to represent the child;

2. Inform the parents or legal guardians of their right to counsel;

3. Provide the parents an opportunity to be heard and be present; and

4. Hear evidence from the DCF.

To continue the child's placement in shelter care the court must conclude that[10]

1. Placement in shelter care is necessary and in the best interests of the child;

2. Placement of the child in the home is contrary to the welfare of the child because the home situation presents a substantial and immediate danger to the child's physical, mental, or emotional health or safety that cannot be mitigated by the provision of preventive services;

3. Based on allegations of the petition for placement in shelter care, there is probable cause to believe that the child is dependent or that the court needs additional time (which may not exceed 72 hours) in which to obtain and review documents pertaining to the family to appropriately determine the risk to the child;

4. The DCF has made reasonable efforts to prevent or eliminate the need for removal of the child from the home; and

---

5. 1 FLA. STAT. ANN. § 39.402(2) (West Supp. 2002).
6. 1 FLA. STAT. ANN. § 39.402(7) (West Supp. 2002).
7. 1 FLA. STAT. ANN. § 39.402(8)(a) (West Supp. 2002).
8. 1 FLA. STAT. ANN. § 39.402(13)(a) (West Supp. 2002).
9. 1 FLA. STAT. ANN. § 39.402(8) (West Supp. 2002).
10. 1 FLA. STAT. ANN. § 39.402(8)(h) (West Supp. 2002).

5. The court notified the parents or legal custodians of their right to counsel at the hearing.

The appointed guardian ad litem is to act as a "next friend" of the child, investigator, or evaluator, and is a party to any legal proceedings from the date of the appointment until the child's involvement in the dependency process is terminated. The guardian ad litem is not to act as the child's attorney.[11]

(B) Adjudication of Alleged Child Abuse or Neglect

The express purpose of the dependency process is to protect children and not to punish persons creating the condition.[12] The dependency petition, which is filed in the circuit court, must contain[13]

1. The alleged acts or omissions that constitute abuse, neglect, or abandonment;
2. The names of persons alleged to have committed the acts or omissions; and
3. The names of all parents or legal custodians of the child.

If known, the petition must also include whether any parent or legal custodian named in the petition has[14]

1. Previously unsuccessfully participated in voluntary services offered by the DCF;
2. Participated in mediation and whether a mediation agreement exists;
3. Rejected voluntary services offered by the DCF; or
4. The DCF has determined that voluntary services are not appropriate for the parent or legal custodian and an explanation of the reasons for such determination are provided.

After a petition alleging dependency is filed, or if the court deems that reasonable cause has been shown, the court, before a hearing, may[15]

1. Order the alleged offender to obtain counseling or participate in a treatment program;

---

11. 5 FLA. STAT. ANN. § 61.401 (West Supp. 2002).
12. 1 FLA. STAT. ANN. § 39.501(2) (West Supp. 2002).
13. 1 FLA. STAT. ANN. § 39.501(3) (West Supp. 2002).
14. 1 FLA. STAT. ANN. § 39.201(3)(d) (West Supp. 2002).
15. 1 FLA. STAT. ANN. § 39.504 (West Supp. 2002).

2. Limit the alleged offender's communication or visitation with the child;

3. Order the alleged offender to refrain from having any contact with the child;

4. Order the alleged offender to leave the home in which the child lives; or

5. Order the alleged offender to pay for temporary child support.

The adjudicatory hearing is to be held as soon as practicable after the petition for dependency is filed but no later than 30 days after the arraignment. Adjudicatory hearings are held by a judge with no jury, and allegations of abuse, neglect or abandonment must be proven by a preponderance of the evidence.[16] If the court finds that the child is not dependent, then it must enter such an order and dismiss the case.[17]

(C) Placement of Abused, Neglected, and Abandoned Children

The court has a variety of options regarding the placement of children who are found to be abused, neglected, or abandoned, or whose parents or legal custodians have consented to a finding of dependency.

(C)(1) Predisposition Study

Before determining placement, the court must receive and consider a predisposition study that is completed by DCF personnel.[18] MHPs are unlikely to be involved in such a study, though mental health treatment records conceivably could be of interest to the individual preparing the study.

The predisposition study must address the following:[19]

1. The dangers and risks of returning the child home, including a description of the changes and resolutions to the initial risks;

2. A description of risks that are still present and what resources are available and will be provided for the protection and safety of the child;

3. A description of the benefits of returning the child home;

4. A description of all unresolved issues;

---

16. 1 FLA. STAT. ANN. § 39.507(1) (West Supp. 2002).
17. 1 FLA. STAT. ANN. § 39.507(4) (West Supp. 2002).
18. 1 FLA. STAT. ANN. § 39.521(1) (West Supp. 2002).
19. 1 FLA. STAT. ANN. § 39.521(2) (West Supp. 2002).

5. An abuse registry history and criminal records check for all caregivers, family members, and individuals residing within the household;

6. The complete report and recommendation of the Child Protection Team (a team of professionals providing services to child abuse investigators), if one exists;

7. All opinions or recommendations from other professionals or agencies that provide evaluative, social, reunification, or other services to the parent or child;

8. The availability of appropriate prevention and reunification services for the parent and child to prevent removal of the child from the home or to unify the family after removal;

9. The inappropriateness of any prevention or reunification service that are available;

10. The efforts by the DCF to prevent out-of-home placement or to reunify the parent and child, and their effects;

11. The need for continuing service if the child remains in the home or is placed outside of the home;

12. Whether dependency mediation was provided;

13. In cases where the child has been removed from the home and there is a parent or legal custodian who may be considered for custody, a recommendation as to whether placement of the child with that parent or custodian would be detrimental to the child;

14. In cases where the child has been removed from the home and will be remaining with a relative or other adult approved by the court, a home study report concerning the proposed placement; and

15. In cases where the child will be removed from the home, a determination of the amount of child support each parent will be required to pay.

(C)(2) Dispositional Alternatives

On finding a child to be abused, neglected, or abandoned the court can[20]

1. Require the parent or legal custodian, and the child when appropriate, to participate in treatment and services identified as necessary;

---

20. 1 FLA. STAT. ANN. § 39.521(9) (West Supp. 2002).

2. Require the parent or legal custodian and the children when appropriate, to participate in mediation if the parent or legal custodian refused to participate in mediation;

3. Place the child under the protective supervision of an agent of the DCF, either in the child's home or, the prospective custodian being willing, in the home of a relative of the child or of another adult approved by the court, or in other suitable places as the court determines. Protective supervision continues until terminated by the court or until the child reaches the age of 18;

4. Place the child in the temporary legal custody of an adult relative or other adult approved by the court who is willing to care for the child; or

5. Commit the child to the temporary legal custody of the DCF to be continued until terminated by the court or the child reaches the age of 18.

When the parents have failed to comply with a case plan and the court determines at a hearing that reunification, termination of parental rights, or adoption is in the best interests of the child, the court can place the child in the long-term custody of an adult relative or other adult approved by the court who is willing to care for the child.[21]

(D) Case Plans

The DCF must develop a case plan for all children who have been adjudicated dependent. A parent cannot be required or coerced through threat of loss of custody or parental rights to admit in the case plan to abusing, neglecting, or abandoning a child.[22]

The case plan must[23]

1. Be developed in conference with the parent and guardian ad litem and, where appropriate, the child;

2. Be written in the parents' principal language and in an understandable way;

3. Identify the minimum number of face to face meetings to be held each month between the parents and DCF caseworkers to review progress of the plan and remove impediments;

4. Be subject to modification based on changing circumstances;

---

21. 1 FLA. STAT. ANN. § 39.521(9)(5) (West Supp. 2002).
22. 1 FLA. STAT. ANN. § 39.601(1) (West Supp. 2002).
23. Id.

5. Be reasonable, accurate, and in compliance with requirements of existing court orders; and
6. Be signed by all parties.

When the child or parent is receiving services, the case plan must include, in addition to the previous points:[24]

1. A description of the problem being addressed that includes the behavior or act of a parent resulting in risk to the child and the reasons for intervention;
2. A description of the tasks with which the parent must comply and the services to be provided to the parent and child specifically addressing the problems, including the types of services or treatment, frequency of services and treatment, and the location of treatment;
3. A description of measurable objectives including timeframes for achieving objectives.

When a child is receiving services in an out-of-home placement the case plan must be filed with the court, for approval by the court, 72 hours before the disposition hearing, and it must include, in addition to the items listed previously, descriptions of[25]

1. The permanency goal for the child;
2. The type of home or institution in which the child is to be placed;
3. The parents' financial support obligations to the child;
4. The parents' visitation rights and obligations;
5. The safety and appropriateness of the child's placement;
6. Efforts to be undertaken to maintain the stability of the child's educational placement;
7. The DCF's plans to carry out the court's judicial determination;
8. The plan to ensure that services outlined in the case plan will be carried out;
9. Financial costs to be borne by the parent related to any required service provision; and
10. For those children for whom the permanency plan is adoption or placement in another permanent home, a description of the steps being taken to find such a placement.

In addition, the case plan must make clear in writing to the parents that failure to comply with the case plan may result in termination of parental rights.[26]

---

24. 1 FLA. STAT. ANN. § 39.601(2) (West Supp. 2002).
25. 1 FLA. STAT. ANN. § 39.601(3) (West Supp. 2002).
26. 1 FLA. STAT. ANN. § 39.601(3)(k) (West Supp. 2002).

4.10
Termination of Parental Rights

Parents can forfeit or lose their rights as parents in some cases. Parental rights may be terminated voluntarily by parents or they can be terminated involuntarily by the court.

MHPs may be asked by the courts to evaluate children or their parents to assist in decision making in these types of cases. MHPs may be asked to evaluate the children's needs or psychological functioning, or they may be asked to evaluate the parents' psychological functioning to assist the court in determining whether termination of parental rights is necessary or whether rights can be retained with intervention of some type.

(A) Filing the Termination Petition

The DCF, the guardian ad litem, a licensed child placement agency, or any persons with appropriate knowledge can petition the court for termination of parental rights in cases where[1]

1. The parent or parents voluntarily agree to give custody to the DCF or the child placement agency for purposes of adoption;
2. The identity or location of the parents cannot be determined after a diligent search for 60 days;
3. The parent or parents engage in conduct toward the child or other children that demonstrates that continuing the parent–

---

1. 1 FLA. STAT. ANN. § 39.806(1) (West Supp. 2002).

child relationship threatens the life, safety, well-being, or physical, mental, or emotional health of the child, regardless of provision of social or mental health services;

4. The parents are incarcerated in a state or federal correctional facility and the parent is expected to be incarcerated for a substantial period of time before the child will turn 18 and the court determines that continuing the parental relationship will be harmful to the child and terminating the parental rights is in the best interests of the child;

5. The parent has been determined to be a habitual violent felony offender or sexual predator, or has been convicted of first- or second-degree murder, or a sexual battery that constitutes a capital, life, or first-degree felony (generally punishable by up to 30 years in prison[2]); and the court determines that continuing the parental relationship will be harmful to the child and terminating the parental rights is in the best interests of the child;

6. The child has been adjudicated dependent and the child continues to be abused or neglected by the parents. Failure to comply with a DCF case plan for a period of 12 months is evidence of continued abuse, neglect, or abandonment when lack of compliance is not attributable to the financial limitations of the parents or the DCF's failure to make reasonable efforts to reunify the parents;

7. The parent or parents engage in egregious conduct (i.e., deplorable, flagrant, or outrageous conduct that might only need to occur on one occasion) that threatens the life, safety, physical, mental, or emotional health of the child or the child's siblings;

8. The parent or parents have subjected the child to aggravated child abuse, sexual battery, sexual abuse, or chronic abuse;

9. The parent or parents have committed or aided in the murder or voluntary manslaughter of another child or a felony assault that results in serious bodily injury of the child or another child; or

10. The parental rights of a sibling have been terminated involuntarily.

Parents who are unable to make contact with their children (e.g., because of imprisonment or hospitalization) cannot be assumed to have abandoned them.[3]

---

2. FLA. STAT. ANN. § 775.082(3)(a)3 (West Supp. 2002).
3. *In re* BW, 498 So. 2d 946 (1986); *In re* RH, 726 So. 2d 377 (Fla. 2d D.C.A. 1999).

(B) Grounds for Termination

Proof of any of the grounds for which the DCF may petition the court (noted earlier) may result in termination of custody. In addition, Florida courts have held that severe physical abuse,[4] failure to protect children from abuse by others,[5] a diagnosis of pedophilia with no prospects for special treatment,[6] and neglect of a child with special needs[7] also can constitute grounds for termination of parental rights.

(C) Termination Hearing and Decision

If the court determines by clear and convincing evidence that the grounds for terminating parental rights for both parents have been established it shall order such and place the child in the custody of the DCF or a licensed child placement agency for purposes of adoption.[8] The court retains jurisdiction over the child until the child is adopted.[9]

If the child is in the custody of one parent and the court determines by clear and convincing evidence that the grounds for terminating parental rights of the other parent have been established, it shall order such and place the child in the custody of the remaining parent and grant sole parental responsibility to that parent.[10]

(D) Effect of Termination

Termination of parental rights does not affect the rights of grandparents unless the court determines that continued visitation is not in the best interests of the child or would interfere with the permanency goals for the child.[11] If the court orders termination

---

4. *In re* DJ, 553 So. 2d 378 (1989).
5. TB v. Department of Children and Family Services, 718 So. 2d (Fla 4th D.C.A. 1998).
6. Palmer v. HRS, 547 So. 2d 981 (1989).
7. *In re* RDD, 518 So. 2d 412 (1988); Caso v. HRS, 569 So. 2d 466 (1990).
8. 1 FLA. STAT. ANN. § 39.811(2) (West Supp. 2002).
9. 1 FLA. STAT. ANN. § 39.811(9) (West Supp. 2002).
10. 1 FLA. STAT. ANN. § 39.811(3) (West Supp. 2002).
11. 1 FLA. STAT. ANN. § 39.811(7a) (West Supp. 2002).

of parental rights it may, as appropriate, order that the parents, siblings, or relatives of the parents whose rights are terminated be allowed to maintain some communication or contact with the child pending adoption if such is in the best interests of the child.[12]

---

12. 1 FLA. STAT. ANN. § 39.811(7b) (West Supp. 2002).

4.11
Guardianship for Minors

Parents are the natural guardians of their children. If one parent dies, the other continues as natural guardian, even in the case of remarriage. If the parents divorce and the court awards shared parental responsibility, then both continue to be legal and natural guardians.[1] MHPs may be asked to provide evaluations of the potential ward or guardian in guardianship proceedings.

(A) Petition for Guardianship

On petition of a parent, brother, sister, next of kin, or other person interested in the minor's welfare, the court may appoint a guardian for a minor.[2]

A standby guardian is a person empowered to assume the duties of guardianship on the death or adjudication of incapacity of the last surviving natural or appointed guardian.[3] A standby guardian may be appointed on the petition or consent of both parents, if living, or the surviving parent. The standby guardian becomes the guardian of the minor immediately on the death or adjudication of incapacity of the minor's parents(s), until the court makes a determination regarding appointment of a permanent guardian for the minor. The standby guardian, however, can only protect the ward's property, not dispose or manage it in other ways, until the court issues a permanent guardianship order.[4]

---

1. 21 FLA. STAT. ANN. § 744.301(1) (West Supp. 2002).
2. 21 FLA. STAT. ANN. § 744.3021 (West 1997).
3. 21 FLA. STAT. ANN. § 744.102 (West Supp. 2002).
4. 21 FLA. STAT. ANN. § 744.304 (West Supp. 2002).

(B) The Guardianship Hearing

The processes governing appointment of an adult guardian do not apply to the proceeding conducted subsequent to the filing of the petition, though the statute does not specify what if any processes are to be followed. The minor may, but is not required to, attend the hearing, and the court in its discretion may appoint an attorney to represent the interests of the minor.[5]

(C) Powers of the Guardian

A guardian appointed for a minor, whether appointed as a guardian of the person or of property, has the authority of a plenary guardian (i.e., the guardian is authorized to make any and all legal decisions on behalf of the child).[6]

(D) Termination of the Guardianship

Guardianship of a minor terminates when the minor becomes 18 years of age or is otherwise emancipated by the court or through marriage.

---

5. 21 FLA. STAT. ANN. § 744.3021 (West 1997).
6. *Id.*

# 4.12
Conservatorship for Minors

Many states allow for the judicial appointment of a conservator to manage the estate of minors, who are generally presumed incompetent based on age to manage their property or financial affairs. Florida does not have a separate conservatorship law for minors, and, as is generally true with adults, provides in the guardianship law for the management by the guardian of the minor's person and property.[1]

However, in situations in which a minor has a legal claim in a personal injury, property damage, or wrongful death case, the court may, and in some cases must appoint a guardian ad litem to protect the child's interest prior to approving a settlement of the claim. The court *may* appoint a guardian ad litem when the proposed settlement equals or exceeds $10,000. The court *must* appoint a guardian ad litem when the proposed settlement equals or exceeds $25,000.[2] However, if the child already has a guardian, a guardian ad litem may be appointed only if the court finds that the appointment is otherwise necessary.[3]

---

1. *See* 21 FLA. STAT. ANN. § 744.3021 (West 1997), providing for the appointment of a guardian for a minor discussed in chapter 4.11, Guardianship for Minors.
2. 21 FLA. STAT. ANN. § 744.301(4)(a) (West Supp. 2000).
3. *Id.*

4.13
Foster Care

Abused, neglected, or abandoned children, as well as children in need of services, may be placed in temporary, out-of-home placements that are also referred to as *foster care*. The DCF traditionally has been responsible for the supervision of foster care. However, the state has been transferring responsibility for the operation of foster care services, by contract, to community-based, not-for-profit entities. The state, however, continues to bear overall responsibility for protecting and caring for children in foster care. MHPs may be asked by the courts to evaluate abused, neglected, or abandoned children, delinquent children, or children in need of services to determine their needs and the appropriateness of various placements, one of which might be foster care.

Foster care is designed to provide for the care and safety of the children placed in it.[1] It is the intent of the legislature that no child remain in foster care for more than one year, in an effort to achieve reunification with the biological family or placement with the adoptive family as quickly as possible.[2] The statute also establishes a policy of attempting to place siblings in the same home, or if they are separated, to keep them in contact with each other.[3]

Children in Florida, including those placed in foster care, are supposed to be provided with the following protections:[4]

1. Protection from abuse, abandonment, neglect, and exploitation;

2. A permanent and stable home;

---
1. 1 FLA. STAT. ANN. § 39.001 (West Supp. 2002).
2. 1 FLA. STAT. ANN. § 39.001(1)(h) (West Supp. 2002).
3. 1 FLA. STAT. ANN. § 39.001(1)(j) (West Supp. 2002).
4. 1 FLA. STAT. ANN. § 39.001(3)(a)–(h) (West Supp. 2002).

3. A safe and nurturing environment that preserves a sense of personal dignity and integrity;
4. Adequate nutrition, shelter, and clothing;
5. Effective treatment for physical, social, and emotional needs, regardless of geographic location;
6. Equal opportunity and access to education;
7. Access to preventive services; and
8. An independent, trained advocate when intervention is necessary and a skilled guardian or caregiver in a safe environment when alternative placement is necessary.

A major initiative in Florida that is on-going at the time of writing is the implementation of a legislative policy to privatize foster care—that is, to contract with community groups who would assume the responsibility for providing services to individuals who might enter foster care.[5]

(A) Certification of Foster Parents/ Licensing Requirements

A person, family foster home, or residential child-caring agency may not receive a child for full-time care or custody unless a license is first obtained from the DCF.[6] The licensing requirement does not apply to boarding schools, recreation and summer camps, nursing homes, hospitals, or caregivers who have a child in their care for no more than 90 days.[7] By statute, licensing requirements for foster parents and providers must include rules for[8]

1. The operation, conduct, and maintenance of the facility or home;
2. The provision of food, clothing, education, and other services;
3. The appropriateness, safety, cleanliness, and general adequacy of the home, including fire prevention and health standards;
4. The ratio of staff to children;
5. The good moral character of the provider;
6. The provision of training for all foster parents;

---
5. FLA. STAT. ANN. § 409.1671 (West Supp. 2002).
6. FLA. STAT. ANN. § 409.175(3)(a) (West 1998).
7. FLA. STAT. ANN. § 409.175(3)(d) (West 1998).
8. FLA. STAT. ANN. § 409.175(4)(a) (West 1998).

7. Evidence of financial ability to care for children in compliance with licensing requirements;
8. The maintenance of records as required;
9. The provision of parental involvement;
10. The transportation of children served in the home;
11. The safeguarding of the child's cultural, religious, and ethnic values; and
12. The safeguarding of the child's legal rights.

Applications are to be made on forms provided by the DCF.[9] Background checks are to be performed on all personnel involved with the home, including fingerprint checks and criminal history.[10] A license is initially good for no more than one year,[11] although a license may be granted for up to three years to a provider who has been licensed for at least the three previous years, is in good standing with the DCF, and has not been the subject of a report of child abuse or neglect with a finding of maltreatment.[12] A license may be revoked, denied, or suspended if the home intentionally or negligently acts in a manner that adversely affects the health or safety of a child, violates DCF rules implementing the foster care statute, or does not comply with the good moral character requirements.[13]

(B) Placement of Children in Foster Homes

A hearing on whether a child should be placed in foster care, or whether there should be some other disposition, follows an application alleging that the child should be adjudicated a "dependent" child who requires protection. The petition is to be in writing and set forth the acts or omissions on which the petition is based, as well as the identity of the person or persons who committed the acts or omissions.[14]

At a hearing, conducted by a judge without a jury,[15] the court may reach a number of conclusions, including the following:

---

9. FLA. STAT. ANN. § 409.175(5)(a) (West 1998).
10. FLA. STAT. ANN. § 409.175(5)(c) (West 1998).
11. FLA. STAT. ANN. § 409.175(5)(i) (West 1998).
12. FLA. STAT. ANN. § 409.175(5)(j) (West 1998).
13. FLA. STAT. ANN. § 409.175(8)(b) (West 1998).
14. 1 FLA. STAT. ANN. § 39.501(1)–(3) (West Supp. 2002).
15. 1 FLA. STAT. ANN. § 39.507(1)(b) (West Supp. 2002).

1. The child is not dependent, in which case the case is dismissed;[16]
2. The child is dependent, but the appropriate remedy is supervision of the home—noncompliance with any conditions established in conjunction with home supervision may lead immediately to placement of the child outside the home;[17] and
3. The child is dependent, and a disposition hearing is scheduled within 30 days of the adjudicatory hearing.[18]

At the disposition hearing[19] a written case plan and predisposition study, prepared by an entity acting on behalf of the DCF, is submitted. The court may approve the case plan or set further hearing on it.[20] The court as one of its dispositional alternatives may place the child in foster care.[21] If the child is placed in foster care, the court must find in writing that the child cannot safely remain at home even with supportive services and that removal of the child from the home is necessary for the child's safety.[22] If the child is placed in protective supervision, which includes foster care, the status of protective supervision continues until the court terminates it or the child turns 18, whichever comes first. Termination comes when the court determines that permanency of placement has been achieved, whether with the parent or with a foster parent or other adult.[23]

(C) Placement Review

The court has continuing jurisdiction over the case involving the child. The court is to conduct a review of the status of the child at least every six months, or more frequently if deemed necessary by the court.[24] In addition, citizen review panels may review cases referred by the court for review.[25] Before each review, an investigation is to be made by the relevant social service agency into the child's condition, including the type of placement the child is in at that time; documentation of efforts to comply with placement of the child; services provided the foster family or legal custodian to address the child's needs; a statement regarding the

---

16. 1 FLA. STAT. ANN. § 39.507(4) (West Supp. 2002).
17. 1 FLA. STAT. ANN. § 39.507(5) (West Supp. 2002).
18. 1 FLA. STAT. ANN. § 39.507(7) (West Supp. 2002).
19. 1 FLA. STAT. ANN. § 39.521 (West Supp. 2002).
20. 1 FLA. STAT. ANN. § 39.521(b) (West Supp. 2002).
21. 1 FLA. STAT. ANN. § 39.521(b)(3) (West Supp. 2002).
22. 1 FLA. STAT. ANN. § 39.521(d)(9)(f) (West Supp. 2002).
23. 1 FLA. STAT. ANN. § 39.521(b)(3) (West Supp. 2002).
24. 1 FLA. STAT. ANN. § 39.701(1)(a) (West Supp. 2002).
25. 1 FLA. STAT. ANN. § 39.701(2)(b) (West Supp. 2002).

degree of compliance by the parents with the care plan; the number of parent–child visits; a statement from the foster parent regarding the potential return of the child to the parents; and copies of relevant medical and educational records.[26]

In reviewing the child's status, the court (or citizen review panel, if applicable) is to determine

1. Whether the parent was advised of his or her right to counsel at the hearing;
2. Whether the parent was advised of the right to assistance in preparing the case plan;
3. Whether a guardian ad litem should be appointed for the child;
4. The compliance or lack of compliance by all parties with the child's case plan, including the parents' compliance with support orders;
5. The compliance or lack of compliance with a visitation contract between the parents and social service agency;
6. The compliance or lack of compliance by the parents in meeting specified financial obligations to the child;
7. The appropriateness of the child's current placement;
8. A projected date for the child's return home or other permanent placement; and
9. As appropriate, the basis for the parents' unwillingness or inability to become a party to the case plan.[27]

The court is to make a determination regarding the child's status after considering these factors. The court's jurisdiction over the case continues until a permanent solution to the child's status is reached.

---

26. 1 FLA. STAT. ANN. § 39.701(6)(a) (West Supp. 2002).
27. 1 FLA. STAT. ANN. § 39.701(7) (West Supp. 2002).

4.14
Adoption

Adoption is the legal transfer of responsibility for the care and support of a child from a parent to another person. For a valid adoption, the child's potential parents are required to meet certain criteria, and the rights of the natural parents must be fulfilled. MHPs may become involved in adoptions by court order or a party's request to evaluate the child or prospective parents regarding the suitability of the parents and child for proposed adoption.

(A) Adoption Requirements

(A)(1) Birth Parents

Unless consent is excused by the court, consent to adopt must always be obtained from the adoptee's mother.[1] Consent must be obtained from the adoptee's father if the child was born while the parents were married, if the child was adopted by the father, if it has been established in a court proceeding that the child is the father's child, if the father has acknowledged that the child is his, or if the father has supported the child in a repetitive and customary manner.[2] If the child is 12 years of age or older, the child's consent to the adoption must be obtained, unless the court decides that it is in the child's best interest to dispense with consent.[3]

The court may excuse consent of the following individuals to an adoption: parents who have deserted their children, parents

---

1. 5 FLA. STAT. ANN. § 63.062(1)(a) (West Supp. 2002).
2. 5 FLA. STAT. ANN. § 63.062(1)(b) (West Supp. 2002).
3. 5 FLA. STAT. ANN. § 63.062(1)(c) (West Supp. 2002).

who have had their parental rights terminated, parents who have been declared incompetent by a court and are unlikely to be restored to competency, and the legal guardian or lawful custodian of the person to be adopted (other than a parent) if the guardian or custodian has failed to respond in writing to a request for consent or whose reasons for withholding consent are considered by the court to be unreasonable.[4]

(A)(2) Adoptive Parents

With some exceptions, any adult is eligible to adopt a child. Married persons may adopt with the consent of their spouses; unmarried persons also can adopt.[5] People with a homosexual orientation may not adopt children according to Florida law.[6]

The person or persons seeking to adopt a child must file a petition with the clerk of the circuit court.[7] The petition must include reasons why the petitioner is seeking to adopt; financial and legal information about the potential adoptive parents; basic financial and legal information about the person to be adopted; identification of the people from whom consent to adopt is required; the required consents; a favorable preliminary home study conducted by the DCF, qualified court staff, a licensed child placement agency, or a professional (i.e., a psychologist licensed under Florida law or a clinical social worker, marriage and family therapist, or mental health counselor licensed under Florida law).[8]

The home study must be made to determine the suitability of the intended adoptive parent(s) and may be completed before identifying a prospective adoptive child.[9] The home study must include, at a minimum, an interview with the intended adoptive parent(s); record checks on the adoptive parent(s) with DCF's central abuse registry; assessment of the physical environment of the home; a determination of the financial security of the adoptive parent(s); and documentation of counseling and education of the adoptive parent(s) on adoptive parenting, adoption, the adoption process, and availability of community resources.[10] If the preliminary home study is favorable, a minor may be placed in the home pending entry of the adoption judgment.[11] Unless ordered by the

---

4. 5 FLA. STAT. ANN. § 63.072 (West Supp. 2002).
5. 5 FLA. STAT. ANN. § 63.042(2) (West Supp. 2002).
6. 5 FLA. STAT. ANN. § 63.042(3) (West Supp. 2002); Department of Health and Rehabilitative Services v. Cox, 627 So. 2d 1210 (Fla. 2d D.C.A. 1993), *review granted*, 637 So. 2d 234, *decision approved in part, quashed in part*, 656 So. 2d 902, *reh'g denied*.
7. 5 FLA. STAT. ANN. § 63.102(1) (West Supp. 2002).
8. *Id.*; 5 FLA. STAT. ANN. § 61.20(5) (West Supp. 2002).
9. 5 FLA. STAT. ANN. § 63.092(2) (West Supp. 2002).
10. *Id.*
11. 5 FLA. STAT. ANN. § 63.092(2)(i) (West Supp. 2002).

court, no home study report is required when the adoptive parent is related to the child within the third degree or is a stepparent.[12]

(A)(3) Adoptive Child

A child who is subject to adoption has the right to have the court consider the appropriateness of postadoption communication or contact, including but not limited to visits, letters, cards, or telephone calls with his or her siblings, or on the agreement of the adoptive parents, other specified biological relatives. In making its decision the court is to act in the best interests of the child.[13]

(B) Complaint for Adoption

A petition to terminate parental rights (in the absence of consent) must be filed before a court may determine that a child is available for adoption.[14] The court may terminate parental rights only after a full hearing.[15] The court may terminate parental rights on a number of grounds, including a finding that the necessary consents have been given or based on a finding of abandonment by the parents.[16]

(C) Adoption From Authorized Agencies

An adoption entity (defined as the DCF, a child-placing agency, a child-caring agency, or an intermediary)[17] intending to place a minor for adoption with a nonrelative must report its intent to do so to the court before placing the child.[18] Before placement, a home study must be performed. The home study must include at a minimum:[19]

1. An interview with the intended adoptive parents;
2. Records checks of DCF's central abuse registry and criminal records checks on the adoptive parents;
3. An assessment of the home's physical environment;

---

12. 5 FLA. STAT. ANN. § 63.112(3) (West Supp. 2002).
13. 5 FLA. STAT. ANN. § 63.0427 (West Supp. 2002).
14. 5 FLA. STAT. ANN. § 63.088 (West Supp. 2002).
15. 5 FLA. STAT. ANN. § 63.089(2) (West Supp. 2002).
16. 5 FLA. STAT. ANN. § 63.089(3) (West Supp. 2002).
17. Id.
18. 5 FLA. STAT. ANN. § 63.092(1) (West Supp. 2002).
19. 5 FLA. STAT. ANN. § 63.092(3) (West Supp. 2002).

4. A determination of the intended adoptive parents' financial security;
5. Documentation of counseling of the adoptive parents on adoptive parenting;
6. Documentation that the adoptive parents have received information on adoption and the adoption process; and
7. Documentation that the adoptive parents have received community support services.

If the home study is favorable, the child may be placed in the home pending entry of judgment by the court. If the report is unfavorable, the agency may ask the court to determine the fitness of the prospective adoptive parents.

A petition for adoption can be filed no sooner than 30 days after a judgment terminating parental rights.[20] The child remains under the supervision of the adoption entity until the adoption becomes final.[21] Before the adoption becomes final, a final home investigation must be conducted. The report of this investigation must include at least.[22]

1. Information from the preliminary home study;
2. After placement in the intended adoptive home, two scheduled visits with the minor and adoptive parents, at least one of which is in the home, to determine whether the placement is suitable;
3. Family social and medical history; and
4. Any other information relevant to the question of suitability.

After hearing, the court may enter a judgment of adoption.[23]

(D) Private-Placement Adoptions

There are no discrete provisions allowing for private adoptions in Florida without court orders terminating parental rights and approving adoption. A person may give consent to adoption with identified adoptive parents on release of the minor from the hospital after birth.[24] In such cases, the child is the responsibility of the adoptive entity until a court orders preliminary approval of the minor's placement according to the procedures outlined. Until the court terminates parental rights, the prospective adoptive

---

20. 5 FLA. STAT. ANN. § 63.102 (West Supp. 2002).
21. 5 FLA. STAT. ANN. § 63.122(1) (West Supp. 2002).
22. 5 FLA. STAT. ANN. § 63.125 (West Supp. 2002).
23. 5 FLA. STAT. ANN. § 63.142 (West Supp. 2002).
24. 5 FLA. STAT. ANN. § 63.082(4)(b) (West Supp. 2002).

parents serve as the child's guardian after preliminary placement pending finalization of adoption.[25]

(E) Adoption Subsidies

The legislature has provided for subsidies to facilitate the adoption of children with special needs.[26] A special needs child is defined as a child whose permanent custody has been awarded to the DCF or to a licensed child-placing agency and

1. Who has established significant emotional ties with his or her foster parents; and
2. Is not likely to be adopted because he or she is 8 years of age or older; mentally retarded; has a physical or emotional handicap; is of Black or racially mixed parentage; or is a member of a sibling group of any age, provided that two or more members of the sibling group remain together for adoption.

An adoption subsidy is available only when other alternatives for adoption are not available. Two types of subsidies are available.[27] One is for support and maintenance of a special needs child until he or she turns 18 year of age, and includes a monthly payment determined through agreement between the adoptive parents and the DCF. The second is for medical, surgical, hospital, or related services as a result of a physical or mental condition, the subsidy terminating no later than the child's 18th birthday. As a condition of receiving the subsidy, the adoptive parents must file an annual sworn statement with the DCF including any social or financial conditions that may have changed.

(F) Confidentiality of Adoption Records

All hearings pertaining to the adoption remain closed and confidential[28] and records of the adoption process are confidential and subject to inspection only on order of the court.[29] The name or identity of a natural parent, adoptive parent, or adopted person cannot be revealed unless[30]

---

25. 5 FLA. STAT. ANN. § 63.052(2) (West Supp. 2002).
26. 14 FLA. STAT. ANN. § 409.166 (West 1998).
27. 14 FLA. STAT. ANN. § 409.166(4) (West 1998).
28. 5 FLA. STAT. ANN. § 63.162(1) (West Supp. 2002).
29. 5 FLA. STAT. ANN. § 63.162(2) (West Supp. 2002).
30. 5 FLA. STAT. ANN. § 63.162(4) (West Supp. 2002).

1. The birth parent authorizes in writing release of his or her name;
2. The adoptee, if 18 years of age or older, authorizes release of his or her name, or, if under 18, consent to disclose his or her name is obtained from an adoptive parent;
3. The adoptive parent authorizes in writing release of his or her name; or
4. Good cause is shown to the court.

In determining whether good cause has been shown, the court must give primary consideration to the best interest of the adopted person, but must also consider the best interest of the adoptive and birth parents. Factors to be considered in determining whether "good cause" exists include but are not limited to[31]

1. The reason for which the information is sought;
2. Whether there are alternative means of disclosing the sought-after information without disclosing identities;
3. If known, the desires of the adopted person, the adoptive parents, and the birth parents;
4. The age, maturity, judgment, and expressed needs of the adopted person; and
5. The recommendations of the DCF, the licensed child placement agency, or professional who prepared the preliminary study and home investigation or the DCF if no such study was conducted.

---

31. 5 FLA. STAT. ANN. § 63.162(4)(d) (West Supp. 2002).

4.15
Delinquency and Persons in Need of Supervision

Historically, the primary role of the juvenile justice system, compared with the adult criminal justice system, has been to rehabilitate youth who engage in criminal activity. In recent years, however, there has been a legislative and judicial trend to adopt a more sanction- and punishment-oriented approach.

(A) Juvenile Delinquency

MHPs may be involved in delinquency proceedings in a number of ways. They may provide prehearing evaluations of the child's competency or criminal responsibility, much like their involvement in these matters in the adult criminal justice system.[1] They also may conduct evaluations to assist the court in determining appropriate disposition of children who are adjudicated delinquent, and they can offer treatment services to such children and their families.

(A)(1) Delinquent Behavior

The Florida Juvenile Justice Act[2] is designed both to rehabilitate and punish juveniles who are brought to the attention of the legal

---

1. *See, e.g.*, chapters 7.5, Competency to Stand Trial, and 7.9, Criminal Responsibility.
2. 24 FLA. STAT. ANN. § 985 (West 2001); *In re* D.B. & D.S., 385 So. 2d 3 (Fla. 1980).

system because of delinquent behavior.[3] *Delinquent behavior* is behavior that would otherwise constitute a violation of the law or contempt of court.[4]

Under common law, children under the age of 7 were presumed incapable of committing a crime insofar as it was believed that they lacked the capacity to form the requisite mental state; children between the ages of 7 and 14 were presumed incapable of committing a criminal offense given limitations in their cognitive capacities; and children over the age of 14 were presumed to have the requisite mental capacity.[5] The state supreme court, however, has ruled that the presumption of incapacity does not apply to delinquency proceedings, as distinguished from adult criminal proceedings.[6] Thus, in delinquency proceedings the state need not specifically prove that the minor had the ability to form the requisite mental state associated with the particular offense.

The circuit court has jurisdiction of proceedings in which a child is alleged to have committed a delinquent act.[7] Children who are alleged to have committed delinquent acts or who have been adjudicated as having committed delinquent acts also fall under the jurisdiction of the Department of Juvenile Justice (DJJ).[8]

(A)(2) Custody and Detention of Allegedly Delinquent Children

Any person who believes that a child has committed a delinquent act can file a report, affidavit, or complaint with sufficient facts supporting the allegation. On determining that the report, affidavit, or complaint is complete, the juvenile probation officer must, when indicated by the preliminary screening, provide for a comprehensive assessment of the child and family for substance abuse problems and mental health problems using community based agencies and professionals with the appropriate expertise.[9]

The state attorney can take action independent of the juvenile probation officer and determines the action that is in the best interests of the public and the child. In cases other than those in which the child is transferred to adult court, the state attorney can[10]

1. File a petition for dependency;

2. File a petition for delinquency;

---

3. 24 Fla. Stat. Ann. § 985.01(1)(c) (West 2001).
4. 24 Fla. Stat. Ann. § 985.03(9) (West 2001).
5. Clay v. State, 196 So. 462 (Fla. 1940); *also see* chapter 7.7, Mens Rea, for a discussion of the mental state requirement.
6. State v. Porter, 340 So. 2d 1163 (1976).
7. 24 Fla. Stat. Ann. § 985.201(1) (West 2001).
8. 24 Fla. Stat. Ann. § 985.03(15) (West 2001).
9. 24 Fla. Stat. Ann. § 985.21(4)(a) (West 2001).
10. 24 Fla. Stat. Ann. § 985.21(4)(d) (West 2001).

3. Refer the case to a grand jury;
4. Refer the child to a diversionary, pretrial intervention, arbitration, or mediation program, or to some other treatment or care program if such is voluntarily accepted by the child or the child's parents or legal guardians; or
5. Decline to file.

A child can be taken into custody:[11]

1. In response to a court order;
2. For a delinquent act or violation of law pursuant to arrest;
3. For failing to appear at a court hearing;
4. For violating conditions of probation, home detention, postcommitment community control; or
5. For absconding from commitment.

After a child is taken into custody, regular attempts must be made to contact the child's parent, guardian, or legal custodian.[12] The arresting authority must deliver the child with a juvenile probation officer who screens each child and:[13]

1. Determines the child's appropriateness for release, referral to a diversionary program, referral for community arbitration, or referral to some other program or agency for the purpose of nonjudicial handling;
2. Identifies any medical, psychiatric, psychological, substance abuse, educational, or vocational problems or other conditions that may have caused the child to come to the attention of law enforcement and the DJJ, and makes appropriate referrals;
3. Determines whether the child poses a danger to self or others in the community and the results of the screenings are made available to the court;
4. Conducts a risk assessment to establish the child's eligibility for detention and informs the court accordingly;
5. Assesses the child's understanding of his or her rights to counsel and against self-incrimination;
6. Coordinates the multidisciplinary assessment when required, which includes the classification and placement process that determines the child's priority needs, risk classification, and treatment plan; and
7. Makes recommendations for the delivery and provision of needed services.

---

11. 24 FLA. STAT. ANN. § 985.207(1) (West 2001).
12. 24 FLA. STAT. ANN. § 985.207(2) (West 2001).
13. 24 FLA. STAT. ANN. § 985.21 (West 2001).

The juvenile probation officer is responsible for making informed decisions and recommendations to other agencies, the state attorney, and the courts so that the child and family can receive the least intrusive services possible while both the needs of the child and family and public are met.[14]

A child taken into custody must be released from custody as soon as possible. Unless otherwise ordered by the court, the child can be released to[15]

1. The child's parent, guardian, or legal custodian or, if they are unavailable, any responsible adult;
2. A shelter;
3. A hospital in cases where the child is believed to be in need of medical care;
4. A crisis stabilization unit if the child is considered to be mentally ill and in need of inpatient treatment;
5. A hospital, addictions receiving facility, or other treatment facility if the child appears to be intoxicated and has threatened, attempted, or inflicted physical harm on self or others; or
6. If available, a Juvenile Assessment Center (JAC) for assessment.

Determinations regarding the use of secure, nonsecure, and home detention are to be based on whether the child[16]

1. Presents a substantial risk of not appearing at a subsequent hearing;
2. Presents a substantial risk of inflicting bodily harm on others as evidenced by recent behavior;
3. Presents a history of committing property offenses before adjudication, disposition, or placement;
4. Has committed contempt of court; or
5. Requests protection from imminent bodily harm.

A child alleged to have committed a delinquent act may not be placed into secure, nonsecure, or home detention care for any of the following reasons:[17]

1. To allow a parent to avoid legal responsibility;
2. To permit more convenient administrative access to the child;
3. To facilitate interrogation or investigation; or
4. Because of lack of more appropriate facilities.

---

14. 24 FLA. STAT. ANN. § 985.21(2) (West 2001).
15. 24 FLA. STAT. ANN. § 985.211 (West 2001).
16. 24 FLA. STAT. ANN. § 985.213 (West 2001).
17. 24 FLA. STAT. ANN. § 985.214 (West 2001).

Children cannot be detained in jails or other adult detention facilities unless they are wanted by another state for prosecution as an adult or they have been transferred to adult court.[18] Children housed in adult detention facilities must have no contact with adults.[19]

(A)(3) Petition

All proceedings seeking a finding that a child has committed a delinquent act are to be initiated by the state with the filing of a petition by the state attorney.[20]

(A)(4) Hearing Procedure and Rights of Children in Delinquency Proceedings

Adjudicatory hearings are to be held as soon as practicable after the delinquency petition has been filed.[21] The hearings are held without a jury, follow the rules of evidence used in criminal cases, and are to be conducted in language that is understandable to the child, to the extent possible.[22] The state must prove the allegations beyond a reasonable doubt.[23] In delinquency-juvenile justice proceedings, the child has the right to[24]

1. An attorney;
2. A hearing before the court;
3. An explanation of the nature and consequences of the proceeding;
4. Confront and present witnesses;
5. Avoid self-incrimination;
6. A transcript or record of the proceedings; and
7. Appeal the decision.

(A)(5) Fact-Finding Hearing

If the child is adjudicated delinquent, the court may order a predisposition report that is derived from the previous evaluations, assessments, and classification of the child. It should identify the child's needs and a plan for treatment and placement that

---

18. 1 FLA. STAT. ANN. § 39.044(4) (West Supp. 1995); *see also* chapter 4.18, Transfer of Juveniles to Stand Trial as Adults, for a discussion of transfer/waiver conditions.
19. 1 FLA. STAT. ANN. § 39.044(4) (West Supp. 1995).
20. 24 FLA. STAT. ANN. § 985.218 (West Supp. 2001).
21. 24 FLA. STAT. ANN. § 985.228(1) (West 2001).
22. 24 FLA. STAT. ANN. § 985.224(2) (West 2001).
23. 24 FLA. STAT. ANN. § 985.228(2)(a) (West 2001).
24. 24 FLA. STAT. ANN. § 985.228(2) (West 2001); 24 FLA. STAT. ANN. § 985.203 (West 2001).

considers the child's needs as well as the community's safety. Such reports, along with an evaluation of the child's physical health, mental health, substance abuse status, and educational and vocational needs must be ordered when a residential commitment is anticipated or recommended. These reports are not to be reviewed by the court without the consent of the child or counsel until the child has been found to have committed a delinquent act.[25]

The court must consider the child's assessment and predisposition report and review the records of earlier judicial proceedings before making a final disposition. The court may, by order, require additional evaluations and studies be performed by the DJJ; the county school system; or any social, psychological, or psychiatric agencies of the state.[26] All reports on which the court relies are to be made available before the hearing to the child, the child's parents or legal guardian, the child's attorney, and the state attorney.[27]

On an adjudication of delinquency, the court can[28]

1. Place the child in a probation program or postcommitment probation program;

2. Commit the child to a licensed child caring agency, but not a jail, detention center, or shelter;

3. Commit the child to the DJJ at a specified restrictiveness level;

4. Revoke or suspend the child's driver's license;

5. Require the child, or the child and the child's parent or guardian, to provide community service in a public service program or participate in a community work program for purposes of restitution;

6. Order the child to pay restitution;

7. Commit the child to the DJJ for placement in a program or facility for serious or habitual juvenile offenders; or

8. Commit a child with a history of sexual offending to the DJJ for placement in a program for juvenile sexual offenders.

Commitments to the DJJ are for an indeterminate period of time but cannot exceed the maximum term of imprisonment that an adult could serve for the same offense.[29] With some exceptions, children can only be retained under the juvenile court's jurisdic-

---

25. 24 FLA. STAT. ANN. § 985.229(1) (West 2001).
26. Id.
27. 24 FLA. STAT. ANN. § 985.229(2) and (3) (West 2001).
28. 24 FLA. STAT. ANN. § 985.231 (West 2001).
29. 24 FLA. STAT. ANN. § 985.231(1)(d) (West 2001).

tion until the age of 19. In no case does the juvenile court's jurisdiction hold once the child has reached the age of 22.[30]

(A)(6) Medical and Mental Health Examinations and Treatment

Necessary emergency mental health, substance abuse, and medical treatment can be provided without parental consent to children who have been taken into custody.[31] When a child is detained pending a hearing the facility administrator where a child is held can order appropriate triage examination as a preliminary screening device to determine if the child is in need of medical care or isolation, and the administrator can authorize the provision of services deemed necessary by a physician.[32] After a detention petition or petition for delinquency has been filed, the court can order the child to be examined by a psychologist, psychiatrist, physician, or other educational or health care professional.[33] Special provisions allow for evaluation and examination of children with a history of sexual offending.[34]

After a court hearing in which it is determined that a child committed a delinquent act, the judge may order the child to receive mental health, substance abuse, or developmental disabilities services from a psychologist, psychiatrist, or other health care professional.[35]

(B) Families and Children in Need of Services

Florida law has special provisions for children who fail to attend school, run away from home, or cannot be controlled by their parents. These children and families are described as being "in need of services." These kinds of behaviors, although they do not constitute abuse, neglect, or delinquency, are of enough concern for the state to intervene in some way. MHPs may be asked by the courts to evaluate children, their parents (or their guardians or custodians), or offer treatment in these cases.

(B)(1) Custody

A child may be taken into custody[36]

---

30. 24 FLA. STAT. ANN. § 985.201(4) (West 2001).
31. 24 FLA. STAT. ANN. § 985.224(5) (West 2001).
32. 24 FLA. STAT. ANN. § 985.224(3) (West 2001).
33. 24 FLA. STAT. ANN. § 985.224(1) (West 2001).
34. 24 FLA. STAT. ANN. § 985.231(3) (West 2001).
35. 24 FLA. STAT. ANN. § 985.224(2) (West 2001).
36. 24 FLA. STAT. ANN. § 984.13(1) (West 2001).

1. By a law enforcement officer when the officer believes that the child has run away from home;

2. By a law enforcement officer when the officer believes that the child is absent from school without authorization or is suspended or expelled and is not in the presence of a parent, guardian, or custodian. In such cases the child is to be delivered to the appropriate school site;

3. Pursuant to court order, based on sworn testimony; or

4. By a law enforcement officer when the child voluntarily agrees to such or requests placement in a shelter.

The person taking the child into custody must[37]

1. Release the child to the custody of a parent, guardian, custodian or the DCF provider if it is believed that the child has run away from home, is truant, or is beyond the control of the parent, guardian or custodian; or

2. Deliver the child to the DCF, identifying why the child was taken into custody and why the child and family is in need of services.

Before a court hearing, a child cannot be placed in a shelter unless such placement is ordered by the court or voluntarily agreed to by the child and the child's parent, guardian, or custodian; or it is determined that the provision of appropriate services will not eliminate the need for placement and such placement is required to provide the child and family with some time to agree on conditions for the child's return home; or because a parent, guardian, or custodian is unavailable to take custody of the child.[38] If the DCF determines that shelter placement is necessary, such placement can be authorized. A child who is involuntarily placed in a shelter must be provided a shelter hearing within 24 hours after being taken into custody to determine whether the placement is necessary. A child cannot be held involuntarily in a shelter for longer than 24 hours without a court order directing that the placement is necessary.

(B)(2) Intake and Service Provision

Reports that a child is from a family that is in need of services can be made by anyone to the DCF.[39] A DCF employee must review the complaint and determine if the best interests of the family, the child, and the public would be served by provision

---

37. 24 FLA. STAT. ANN. § 984.21(2) (West 2001).
38. 24 FLA. STAT. ANN. § 984.14(1) (West 2001).
39. 24 FLA. STAT. ANN. § 984.10(1) (West 2001).

of voluntary services and treatment, in which case appropriate referrals are to be made.[40]

Services that can be provided voluntarily or by order of the court include[41]

1. Homemaker or parent aide services;
2. Intensive crisis counseling;
3. Parent training;
4. Individual, group, or family counseling;
5. Community mental health services;
6. Prevention and diversion services;
7. Services provided by voluntary or community agencies;
8. Runaway service centers;
9. Housekeeper services;
10. Special educational, tutorial, or remedial services;
11. Vocational, job training, or employment services;
12. Recreational services; and
13. Assessment.

If the family or child will not accept services that the intake worker considers necessary, DCF staff must meet with the family during a DCF case staffing, in which the need for services and the most appropriate services will be determined.[42] If the family is unwilling to participate in services then the staffing committee can file a petition alleging that the child is a child in need of services.[43]

(B)(3) Hearing

Subsequent to a hearing, the court must dismiss the petition if it finds that the child is not in need of services, or if it finds that the child is in need of services the court can withhold adjudication and place the child under the supervision of the family and the DCF in the home, or order provision of services as necessary.[44] In ordering services, the court must identify the least intrusive and restrictive disposition. Dispositions that can be imposed by the court include[45]

1. Ordering the parent, guardian, or custodian and the child to participate in treatment services and other alternatives

---

40. 24 FLA. STAT. ANN. § 984.10(3) (West 2001).
41. 24 FLA. STAT. ANN. § 984.11 (West 2001).
42. 24 FLA. STAT. ANN. § 984.12(1) (West 2001).
43. 24 FLA. STAT. ANN. § 984.12(8) (West 2001).
44. 24 FLA. STAT. ANN. § 984.21 (West 2001).
45. 24 FLA. STAT. ANN. § 984.22 (West 2001).

identified as necessary (see earlier discussion for the range of services available);

2. Ordering the parent, guardian, or custodian to pay a fine or fee based on the DCF's recommendations;
3. Placing the child under the supervision of the DCF or one of its contractors;
4. Placing the child in the temporary legal custody of an adult willing to care for the child;
5. Committing the child to a licensed child caring agency;
6. Ordering the child, parent, guardian, or custodian of the child to render community services; or
7. Ordering the child, family, parent, guardian, or custodian of the child to participate in family counseling and other professional counseling activities or other alternatives as deemed necessary for the child's rehabilitation.

The participation and cooperation of the child, family, parent, guardian, or custodian with court-ordered services, treatment, or community service are mandatory. The court may enforce its order by holding a noncompliant individual in contempt of court.[46]

---

46. 24 FLA. STAT. ANN. § 984.22(6) (West 2001).

4.16
Competency of Juveniles to Stand Trial

Just as the law seeks to ensure that adults who are charged with crimes are competent to participate in the criminal justice process (see chapter 7.2, Competency to Waive the Rights to Silence, Counsel, and a Jury), the law seeks to ensure that juveniles charged with committing delinquent behaviors are competent to proceed in the delinquency process. MHPs may be asked by the court or counsel to assist in assessing a juvenile's ability to participate in the delinquency adjudication process.

(A) Legal Determination of Competency to Stand Trial

(A)(1) Test of Competency

Before the enactment of a statute codifying a competency standard in delinquency proceedings, Florida case law had implied that the standard for competency in juvenile proceedings was comparable to that used in assessing adult competency to stand trial.[1] Today, statutory law requires that children appearing in the juvenile justice system be competent to proceed. The statutory standard tracks the adult standard so that children are considered competent if they have sufficient present ability to consult with counsel with a reasonable degree of rational understanding and have a rational and factual understanding of the proceedings.[2]

---

1. *In re* W.W., J.R., v. State, 388 So. 2d 1317 (Fla. 5th D.C.A. 1980).
2. 24 FLA. STAT. ANN. § 985.223(1)(f) (West 2001).

An evaluation describing a child's competency must address the child's capacity to[3]

1. Appreciate the charges or allegations;
2. Appreciate the range and nature of the possible penalties that might be imposed;
3. Understand the adversarial nature of the legal process;
4. Disclose to counsel facts pertinent to the proceedings at issue;
5. Display appropriate courtroom behavior;
6. Testify relevantly; and
7. Engage in any other behaviors deemed relevant.

(A)(2) Raising the Competency Issue

If the court has reason to believe at any time before or during a delinquency proceeding that the child may be incompetent to proceed, the court on its own motion or on the motion of the child's attorney or the state attorney must stay all proceedings and order an evaluation.[4] The motion for a competency evaluation must be served on the child's attorney and state attorney, as well as attorneys representing the DJJ and the DCF.

(B) Competency Evaluation

The evaluation must be conducted by at least two but no more than three experts appointed by the court.[5] The DCF is to annually provide the courts with a list of MHPs who have completed the training program approved by the DCF to perform competency evaluations related to mental illness. For evaluations related to mental retardation, the court is to order the DCF to examine the child to determine if he or she meets the definition of retardation provided in the statutes,[6] and, if so, whether the child is competent.[7]

In addition to the elements of the report noted earlier, the report must include a recommendation about whether residential or nonresidential treatment or training is required in cases where the evaluator believes the child to be incompetent to proceed. The determination of competency is to be made at a hearing, with findings of fact based on the examiners' reports.[8]

---

3. 24 FLA. STAT. ANN. § 985.223(1)(f)1–6 (West 2001).
4. 24 FLA. STAT. ANN. § 985.223(1) (West 2001).
5. 24 FLA. STAT. ANN. § 985.223(1)(b) (West 2001).
6. 24 FLA. STAT. ANN. § 393.063 (West 2002).
7. 24 FLA. STAT. ANN. § 985.223(1)(d), (e) (West 2001).
8. 24 FLA. STAT. ANN. § 985.223(1)(b) (West 2001).

(C) Competency Hearing

The court is to make a determination of competency based on evidence presented at a hearing.[9] In addition to determining whether the child is competent or incompetent, the court is also to determine whether a child meets criteria for placement in a secure setting. In making this determination, the court must find by clear and convincing evidence that the child[10]

1. Is mentally ill or is mentally retarded and because of the mental illness or retardation, respectively:
   (a) Is manifestly incapable of surviving with the help of willing and responsible family or friends, including available alternative services, and without treatment or training the child is likely to suffer from neglect or refuse to care for him- or herself, and such neglect or refusal poses a real and present threat of substantial harm to the child's well-being; or
   (b) There is a substantial likelihood that in the near future the child will inflict serious bodily harm on him- or herself or others, as evidenced by recent behavior causing, attempting, or threatening such harm; and
2. All available less restrictive alternatives, including treatment or training in community residential facilities or community settings that would offer an opportunity for improvement of the child's condition are inappropriate.

(D) Confidentiality and Privileged Communications

There are no special rules governing privilege and confidentiality in juvenile competency hearings. Confidentiality and privilege are covered in chapters 3.3, Confidential Relations and Communications, and 3.4, Privileged Communications.

(E) Disposition of Juveniles Found Incompetent to Stand Trial

If the court finds a child incompetent, the DCF is to be notified. The DCF is to place the child in an appropriate setting, and

---

9. 24 FLA. STAT. ANN. § 985.223(1)(b) (West 2001).
10. 24 FLA. STAT. ANN. § 985.223(3) (West 2001).

within 30 days of placement, submit a treatment plan to the court addressing the child's restoration to competency.[11] If a child who is mentally ill or mentally retarded is adjudicated incompetent to proceed on charges that would constitute a felony if committed by an adult, the child must be committed to DCF for treatment or training. However, a child adjudicated incompetent because of age or immaturity, or for any reason other than mental illness or mental retardation, cannot be committed to the DCF, nor may a child who has committed an act that would be a misdemeanor if committed by an adult be committed to the DCF.[12]

If the child meets the criteria for placement in a secure setting, the DCF must place the child in a secure facility or program representing the least restrictive alternative consistent with public safety.[13] The child must not be placed in an adult forensic program. If the child does not meet the criteria for placement in a secure facility, the court is to commit the child to the DCF for restoration treatment within the community.[14] If the child regains competency, the child is to be transferred to the DJJ to continue the delinquency proceedings, but the court may order the DCF to provide continued treatment to maintain competency.[15]

The purpose of the treatment or training is to restore competency to proceed.[16] The competence restoration service provider is to file a written report with the court not later than six months after the date of commitment, or if the DCF determines the child has attained competency, or no longer meets the criteria for secure placement, or at shorter intervals ordered by the court.[17] If the court determines that the child is incompetent to proceed, the court is to retain jurisdiction of the child for up to two years from the date of adjudication, with reviews of competency status to occur at least every six months.[18] If the provider reports to the court that the child will never attain competency, the DCF is to develop a discharge plan for the child before a court hearing on competency. Services are to be provided to the child until the court determines that the child will never attain competency.[19]

If the court determines the child will never attain competency, the court may dismiss the delinquency petition. If at the end of

---

11. 24 FLA. STAT. ANN. § 985.223(1)(g), (h) (West 2001).
12. 24 FLA. STAT. ANN. § 985.223(2) (West 2001).
13. K.D. v. Department of Juvenile Justice, 694 So. 2d 817 (Fla. 4th D.C.A. 1997).
14. 24 FLA. STAT. ANN. § 985.223(6)(a) (West 2001).
15. 24 FLA. STAT. ANN. § 985.223(4) (West 2001).
16. 24 FLA. STAT. ANN. § 985.223(4)(d) (West 2001).
17. 24 FLA. STAT. ANN. § 985.223(4)(e) (West 2001).
18. 24 FLA. STAT. ANN. § 985.223(5)(a) (West 2001).
19. 24 FLA. STAT. ANN. § 985.223(5)(b) (West 2001).

the two-year period following the order of incompetency, the child has not attained competency and there is no evidence that he or she will do so within a year, the court must dismiss the delinquency petition, though the court may also order that involuntary commitment proceedings be initiated.[20]

---

20. 24 FLA. STAT. ANN. § 985.223(5)(c) (West 2001).

4.17
Nonresponsibility Defense

Florida permits an insanity defense that provides that juveniles not be held responsible for what would otherwise be criminal or delinquent actions when their mental state has impaired their reasoning abilities in specific ways. Thus, MHPs may be called on by the court if there is a question about a juvenile's mental state at the time of the alleged delinquent act. MHPs, as a function of their specialized expertise and knowledge, are considered by the court to be able to provide information about the juvenile's mental state at the time of the alleged offense, to which the court might not otherwise have access.

(A) Test of Insanity

The definition of insanity, for purposes of delinquency proceedings, is not defined. In the absence of a formal definition, reliance on the adult standard is appropriate. Florida's insanity test is a derivation of the *M'Naghten*[1] test. It directs that a defendant is insane if, at the time of the offense,[2]

1. The defendant had a mental infirmity, disease, or defect; and because of this condition, the defendant did not know what he or she was doing or its consequences; or

2. Although the defendant knew what he or she was doing and its consequences, he or she did not know that it was wrong.

---

1. 10 CL. & FIN. 200, 8 ENG. REP. 718 (1843).
2. *Fla. Standard Jury Instructions in Crim. Cases* § 3.04(b) (1985).

(B) Raising the Plea of Insanity

Minors charged with delinquent acts can plead not guilty by reason of insanity.[3] A child or representative must notify the court of his or her intent to plead insanity no less than 10 days before the delinquency hearing. The child must identify in a statement to the court, to the extent possible, a description of the nature of the alleged mental disorder and the witnesses expected to testify to this.[4]

(C) Mental Examination

In response to such a notice, the court may appoint up to three and no fewer than two experts to examine the child. The court may appoint these examiners on its own, and the court must appoint them at the request of either the child or the state. The state and child may also have additional expert witnesses examine the child and testify.[5] In cases where the child is determined to be indigent or partially indigent and represented by the public defender or a court appointed attorney and the attorney representing the child has concerns about the child's sanity/mental state at the time of the alleged delinquent act, the court shall appoint one expert to examine the child and assist in preparation of the defense.[6]

Attorneys for the child or state may be present at the examinations. In cases where evaluations are to be conducted both for competence to proceed as well as sanity/mental state at the time of the alleged delinquent act, both evaluations should take place at the same time.[7]

(D) Confidentiality and Privileged Communications

The Fifth Amendment privilege against self-incrimination requires that the defendant be informed of the risk that his or her statements may be used against him or her at trial. The attorney–client privilege protects communications between the defendant

---

3. 32 FLA. R. JUV. P. 8.095(b) (West Supp. 2001).
4. 32 FLA. R. JUV. P. 8.095(b)(1) (West Supp. 2001).
5. 32 FLA. R. JUV. P. 8.095(c)(1) (West Supp. 2001).
6. 32 FLA. R. JUV. P. 8.095(c)(3) (West Supp. 2001).
7. 32 FLA. R. JUV. P. 8.095(c)(1) (West Supp. 2001).

and individuals employed by the attorney (including a privately retained MHP conducting an insanity evaluation). Thus, if a defense attorney retains an MHP to evaluate a defendant but decides not to call the MHP as a witness, the attorney–client privilege prevents the prosecutor from calling the MHP as a witness without the defendant's consent.[8] Of course, this does not apply to evaluations conducted by court-retained evaluators.

(E) Commitment of Juveniles Found Not Guilty by Reason of Insanity

When the child is found not guilty of a delinquent act or violation of community control because of insanity, the court must conduct an inquiry to determine if the child meets statutory criteria for involuntary commitment to a residential psychiatric facility as governed by Florida law (see also chapters 4.19, Voluntary Admission and Civil Commitment of Minors, and 8.4, Involuntary Commitment of Mentally Ill Adults, on involuntary civil commitment).[9] If the court determines that these criteria are met, then it must order commitment to the DCF for immediate placement in a residential psychiatric facility, but the juvenile court maintains jurisdiction over the child and the commitment.[10] Any time during the commitment any party can request a hearing to determine the nature, quality, and need for continued treatment.[11] If the court determines that the child does not meet commitment criteria and is in not need of outpatient treatment, then the child is discharged from the court.[12]

If the court determines that the commitment criteria have not been met but that treatment is indicated, then the court must order that the child receive recommended and appropriate outpatient treatment.[13] If, during the course of outpatient treatment, it appears that the child has come to meet criteria for commitment, then a hearing is held to determine such. If it is determined that the child no longer needs treatment then the court enters an order discharging the child from treatment.[14] Any time during

---

8. 33 FLA. R. CRIM. P. 3.216(a) (West Supp. 2002); Lovette v. State, 635 So. 2d 1304 (Fla. 1994); Ursry v. State, 428 So. 2d 713 (Fla. 4th D.C.A. 1983); Pouncy v. State, 353 So. 2d 640 (Fla. 3d D.C.A. 1977).
9. 32 FLA. R. JUV. P. 8.095(e)(2) (West Supp. 2001).
10. 32 FLA. R. JUV. P. 8.095(e)(2)(A) (West Supp. 2001), 32 FLA. R. JUV. P. 8.095(e)(2)(D) (West Supp. 2000).
11. 32 FLA. R. JUV. P. 8.095(e)(2)(F) (West Supp. 2001).
12. 32 FLA. R. JUV. P. 8.095(e)(2)(C) (West Supp. 2001).
13. 32 FLA. R. JUV. P. 8.095(e)(2)(B) (West Supp. 2001).
14. 32 FLA. R. JUV. P. 8.095(e) (West Supp. 2001).

the outpatient treatment period any party can request a hearing to determine the nature, quality, and need for continued treatment.[15]

Children receiving court-ordered residential or outpatient treatment services subsequent to a finding of insanity must, no later than 30 days before reaching the age of 19 years, be provided a hearing to determine their need for continued hospitalization or treatment. If the court determines that continued residential treatment is necessary, then civil commitment proceedings must be initiated. Otherwise, the child will be discharged from the court's jurisdiction.[16]

---

15. 32 FLA. R. JUV. P. 8.095(e)(2)(F) (West Supp. 2001).
16. 32 FLA. R. JUV. P. 8.095(e)(2)(G) (West Supp. 2001).

4.18

Transfer of Juveniles to Stand Trial as Adults

Minors who are accused of committing delinquent/criminal acts typically fall under the jurisdiction of the juvenile court and the juvenile justice system. In some cases, however, minors who are accused of committing delinquent or criminal acts may be tried and sanctioned in the adult courts and adult criminal justice system. This occurs in one of two ways. In some cases, minors are transferred from the jurisdiction of the juvenile court to the jurisdiction of the adult criminal court. These transfers can be mandatory or discretionary. In other cases minors fall immediately under the jurisdiction of the adult court, and their charges are directly filed in the adult court by the state attorney (i.e., "direct files"). In some cases direct filing of the charges in adult court is mandatory on the state attorney's part, and in other cases whether the charges are filed in adult or juvenile court is left to the discretion of the state attorney.

(A) Definitions

A *child* or *juvenile* or *youth* means ". . . any married or unmarried person who is charged with a violation of law occurring prior to the time that person reached the age of 18 years."[1] *Violation of law* means a violation of any law of Florida, the United States, or any other state that is a misdemeanor or felony or a violation of a county or municipal ordinance that would be punishable by incarceration if the violation were committed by an adult.[2]

---

1. 24 FLA. STAT. ANN. § 985.03(6) (West Supp. 2002).
2. 24 FLA. STAT. ANN. § 985.03(57) (West Supp. 2002).

(B) Removal Procedures

A child can be transferred or waived to adult court in a variety of ways. The decision to transfer or waive a minor to adult court hinges on a variety of factors, and the courts sometimes request MHPs to evaluate minor defendants to assist them in making decisions about the appropriateness of transfer to adult court. Once a child has been transferred for criminal prosecution in adult court and has been found to have committed the alleged offense or a lesser included offense, the child is thereafter to be handled and treated in every aspect as an adult for any subsequent violation of state law, unless the court chooses to impose juvenile sanctions.[3] Once a child is transferred to adult court for one case, all pending delinquency cases are transferred to adult court.[4]

(B)(1) Voluntary Waiver

The court must transfer a child to adult court if the child is alleged to have committed a criminal act and, before the beginning of the delinquency hearing, the child, joined by a parent or, in the absence of a parent, a guardian or guardian ad litem (a guardian appointed to protect the interests of an incompetent individual during a legal proceeding), demands in writing to be tried as an adult. Subsequent to this transfer, the child shall be treated as an adult for any subsequent violations of the law.[5]

(B)(2) Mandatory Involuntary Waiver

The state attorney must request that the court transfer the child to adult court and certify him or her for prosecution as an adult or provide written reasons to the court for not making such a request in the following cases:

1. When a child who is 14 years of age and older is charged with a violent crime against a person and has previously been adjudicated delinquent for a specified felony (i.e., attempted murder, conspiracy to commit murder, sexual battery, armed or strong-armed robbery, carjacking, home-invasion robbery, aggravated battery, aggravated assault, or burglary with an assault or battery);[6] or

2. When a child is 14 years of age or older at the time of commission of a fourth or subsequent alleged felony offense and the

---

3. 24 FLA. STAT. ANN. § 985.226(4)(a) (West Supp. 2002).
4. 24 FLA. STAT. ANN. § 985.226(4)(b) (West Supp. 2002).
5. 24 FLA. STAT. ANN. § 985.226(1) (West Supp. 2002).
6. 24 FLA. STAT. ANN. § 985.226(2)(b)1. (West Supp. 2002).

child was previously adjudicated delinquent, had adjudication withheld for three or more offenses that are felony offenses if committed by an adult, and one or more of these offenses involved use or possession of a firearm or violence against a person.[7]

In those cases where the court does not issue an order granting transfer to adult court, the judge must identify the reasons for such in writing.[8]

(B)(3) Discretionary Involuntary Waivers

With the exception of the mandatory involuntary waiver noted, the state attorney may file a motion requesting the court to transfer any child who was 14 years of age or older at the time the alleged delinquent act was committed.[9]

(C) Factors in Removal Determination

The court must conduct a hearing on all transfer request motions to determine whether a child should be transferred. In making its decisions the court must consider[10]

1. The seriousness of the alleged offense(s) and whether protection of the community is best served by transfer for adult sanctions;

2. Whether the alleged offense was committed in an aggressive, violent, premeditated, or willful manner;

3. Whether the alleged offense was against persons or property, with greater consideration for transfer given to offenses against persons, particularly when injury results;

4. The probable cause for the alleged offense as contained in the report, affidavit, or complaint;

5. The desirability of trial and disposition of the entire offense in one court when the child's associates in the alleged crime are adults or children who are to be tried as adults;

6. The sophistication and maturity of the child;

7. The record and previous history of the child, including previous contact with the Department of Corrections, the DCF, other law enforcement agencies; before periods of probation; and before delinquency adjudications; and

---

7. 24 FLA. STAT. ANN. § 985.226(2)(b)2 (West Supp. 2002).
8. *Id.*
9. 24 FLA. STAT. ANN. § 985.226(2)(a) (West Supp. 2002).
10. 24 FLA. STAT. ANN. § 985.226(3) (West Supp. 2002).

8. The prospects for adequate protection of the public and the likelihood of reasonable rehabilitation of the child, if the child is found to have committed the alleged offense, by the use of procedures, services, and facilities available to the court.

(D) Direct Filing in Adult Court

In some cases charges against a child may be filed directly in the criminal division of the circuit court, rather than in the juvenile court. As is the case with mandatory and discretionary transfers, once a child has been transferred for criminal prosecution in adult court via direct filing and has been found to have committed the alleged offense or a lesser included offense, the child shall thereafter be handled and treated in every aspect as an adult for any subsequent violation of state law, unless the court chooses to impose juvenile sanctions.[11] Once a child is transferred to adult court for one case, all pending delinquency cases are transferred to adult court.[12]

(D)(1) Discretionary Direct File

In cases of children who were 14 or 15 years of age at time of the alleged offense, the state attorney may file a criminal information in adult court when, in his or her judgment, the public interest requires that adult sanctions be considered or imposed as a function of the child being charged with commission, attempt to commit, or conspiracy to commit arson; sexual battery; robbery; kidnapping; aggravated child abuse; aggravated assault; aggravated stalking; murder; manslaughter; unlawful throwing, placing, or discharging of a destructive device or bomb; armed burglary; burglary with an assault or battery; aggravated battery; any lewd or lascivious offense committed on or in the presence of a person under the age of 16 years; carrying, displaying, using, threatening, or attempting to use a weapon of firearm during the commission of a felony; grand theft; possession or discharging a weapon or firearm on school property; home invasion robbery; carjacking; or grand theft of a motor vehicle valued at more than $20,000 providing the child has a previous adjudication for grand theft of a motor vehicle.[13]

---

11. 24 FLA. STAT. ANN. § 985.227(3)(a) (West Supp 2002).
12. 24 FLA. STAT. ANN. § 985.226(3)(b) (West Supp. 2002).
13. 24 FLA. STAT. ANN. § 985.227(1)(a) (West Supp. 2002).

In cases of children who were 16 or 17 years of age at the time of the alleged offense, the state attorney may file a criminal information in adult court when, in his or her judgment, the public interest requires that adult sanctions be considered or imposed. However, the state attorney may not file a criminal information in adult court if the child is only charged with a misdemeanor unless the child has had at least two previous adjudications or adjudications withheld for delinquent acts, one of which involved an offense classified as a felony.[14] Felonies are punishable by terms ranging from up to five years in prison for a third-degree felony to death for a capital felony.[15]

(D)(2) Mandatory Direct File

In cases of children who were 16 or 17 years of age at the time of the alleged offense, the state attorney must file a criminal information in adult court if the child has previously been adjudicated delinquent for commission of, attempt to commit, or conspiracy to commit murder; sexual battery; armed or strong armed robbery; carjacking; home invasion robbery; aggravated battery; or aggravated assault, and the child is currently charged with a second or subsequent crime against a person.[16]

In cases of children who were 16 or 17 years of age at the time of the alleged offense that can be classified as a forcible felony, the state attorney must file a criminal information in adult court if the child has previously been adjudicated delinquent or had adjudication withheld for three acts classified as felonies, each of which occurred at least 45 days apart from each other. This rule, however, does not apply when the state attorney has good cause to believe that exceptional circumstances exist that preclude just prosecution of the child in adult court.[17]

Regardless of the child's age at the time of the alleged offense, the state attorney must file a criminal information in adult court in cases in which it is alleged that the child stole a motor vehicle and while the child was in possession of the stolen motor vehicle the child caused serious bodily injury or the death of a person who was not involved in the underlying offense.[18]

---

14. 24 FLA. STAT. ANN. § 985.227(1)(b) (West Supp. 2002).
15. 22 FLA. STAT. ANN. § 775.082 (West Supp. 2002).
16. 24 FLA. STAT. ANN. § 985.227(2)(a) (West Supp. 2002).
17. 24 FLA. STAT. ANN. § 985.227(2)(b) (West Supp. 2002).
18. 24 FLA. STAT. ANN. § 985.227(2)(c) (West Supp. 2002).

(E) Sanctions Imposed on Juveniles Transferred, Waived, or Direct Filed to Adult Court

In cases of children who have been prosecuted and convicted as adults, the court may impose juvenile or adult criminal sanctions.[19] If the state is *required* to file a motion to transfer the juvenile for prosecution as an adult via a transfer/waiver hearing[20] or direct filing,[21] the court must impose adult sanctions.[22] For the remaining juveniles who have been prosecuted as adults via a transfer/waiver hearing or direct filing, the court may impose juvenile or adult sanctions.[23] In determining whether to impose juvenile sanctions instead of adult sanctions, the court must consider[24]

1. The seriousness of the offense(s) and whether protection of the community is best served by juvenile or adult sanctions;

2. Whether the offense was committed in an aggressive, violent, premeditated, or willful manner;

3. Whether the offense was against persons or property, with greater consideration for transfer given to offenses against persons, particularly when injury results;

4. The sophistication and maturity of the juvenile;

5. The record and previous history of the juvenile including previous contact with the Department of Corrections, the DCF, other law enforcement agencies; previous periods of probation; and earlier delinquency adjudications;

6. The prospects for adequate protection of the public and the likelihood of deterrence and reasonable rehabilitation of the juvenile if assigned to services and facilities of the DJJ;

7. Whether the DJJ has appropriate programs, facilities, and services immediately available; and

8. Whether adult sanctions would provide more appropriate punishment and deterrence to additional violations of law than the imposition of juvenile sanctions.

At the sentencing hearing the court must receive and consider a presentence investigation report completed by Department of

---

19. 24 FLA. STAT. ANN. § 985.233(1)(a) (West Supp. 2002).
20. 24 FLA. STAT. ANN. § 985.226(2)(b) (West Supp. 2002).
21. 24 FLA. STAT. ANN. § 985.227(2)(a) (West Supp. 2002); 24 FLA. STAT. ANN. § 985.227(2)(b) (West Supp. 2002).
22. 24 FLA. STAT. ANN. § 985.233(3) (West Supp. 2002).
23. 24 FLA. STAT. ANN. § 985.233(5)(b) (West Supp. 2002).
24. 24 FLA. STAT. ANN. § 985.233(1)(b) (West Supp. 2002).

Corrections staff regarding the suitability of the offender for disposition as an adult or juvenile. The report must include a comments section prepared by the DJJ with its disposition recommendations. The offender may waive preparation of this report.

After considering the presentence investigation report the court must give all parties present an opportunity to comment on the issue of sentencing and any proposed rehabilitation plan. Persons who may comment include the offender, the offender's parent or guardian, staff from the Department of Corrections and the DJJ, the victim or victim's representative, representatives of the school system, and law enforcement officers involved in the case.[25] The court may also consider any other additional information it believes relevant.[26]

---

25. 24 FLA. STAT. ANN. § 985.233(3)(b) (West Supp. 2002).
26. 24 FLA. STAT. ANN. § 985.227(3)(c) (West Supp. 2002).

4.19
Voluntary Admission and Civil Commitment of Minors

(A) Voluntary Admission of Minors

For an individual 17 years of age or younger to be voluntarily admitted to an inpatient mental health facility, express and informed consent of a parent or guardian is required.[1] However, a hearing must first be held to verify the voluntariness of the minor's consent. This hearing need not be a legal proceeding and presumably can be an informal one, conducted by the admitting MHP with the minor.[2]

(A)(1) Voluntary Placement

If a minor is admitted to a state mental hospital and placed in the general population or in a specialized children or adolescent unit, the minor must have living quarters separate from adult patients. A minor who is not yet 14 admitted to a state mental hospital must have living quarters separate from minors 14 years of age or older.[3] An exception can occur if the patient's treatment

---

1. 24 FLA. STAT. ANN. § 394.4625(1)(a) (West 2002).
2. 14 FLA. STAT. ANN. § 394.4625(1)(a) (West 2002); in the case of medical emergencies, when parental consent cannot be obtained, emergency medical care can be administered by physicians and other medical personnel (e.g., paramedics and other emergency medical services personnel) when failure to administer treatment would risk the health or physical well-being of the minor. When the parent or legal guardian cannot be contacted by the treatment provider and the parent or guardian has not previously given notice not to consent to such treatment, a variety of other people can consent to treatment on behalf of the minor in the following order of priority: an individual with a power of attorney to provide consent for the minor, stepparents, grandparents, an adult sibling, or an adult aunt or uncle; see chapter 4.21, Consent, Confidentiality, and Services for Minors.
3. 14 FLA. STAT. ANN. § 394.4785(1)(a) (West 2002).

team determines that placement in the general population is necessary for reasons of safety.⁴ A minor not yet age 14 admitted to *any* licensed hospital also must have living quarters separate from adults, and a minor age 14 or older can be placed in a room or ward with an adult only if the admitting physician documents in the record that the placement is medically indicated or for reasons of safety.⁵

(B) Involuntary Civil Commitment

(B)(1) Definitions

To understand the law concerning involuntary commitment, MHPs should be familiar with the following terms and their legal meanings.⁶ **Mentally ill** means

> an impairment of the emotional processes that exercise conscious control of one's actions or of the ability to perceive or understand reality, which impairment substantially interferes with a person's ability to meet the ordinary demands of living, regardless of etiology [except that] this term does not include retardation or developmental disability, intoxication, or conditions manifested only by antisocial behavior or substance abuse impairment.⁷

> *Express and informed consent* means "consent voluntarily given in writing, by a competent person, after sufficient explanation and disclosure of the subject matter involved to enable the person to make a knowing and willful decision without any element of force, fraud, deceit, duress, or other form of constraint or coercion."⁸ *Clinical psychologist* is "a psychologist as defined by Florida law with 3 years of postdoctoral experience in the practice of clinical psychology, inclusive of the experience required for licensure, or a psychologist employed by a facility operated by the United States Department of Veterans affairs that qualifies as a receiving or treatment facility."⁹ *Psychiatrist* is a "medical practitioner licensed pursuant to [Florida law] who has primarily diagnosed and treated mental and nervous disorders for a period of not less than 3 years, inclusive of psychiatric residency."¹⁰ *Clinical social worker* is "A person licensed as a clinical social worker."¹¹

---

4. 14 FLA. STAT. ANN. § 394.4785(2) (West 2002).
5. 14 FLA. STAT. ANN. § 394.4785(1)(b) (West 2002).
6. 14 FLA. STAT. ANN. § 394.455 (West 2002).
7. 14 FLA. STAT. ANN. § 394.455(18) (West 2002).
8. 14 FLA. STAT. ANN. § 394.455(9) (West 2002).
9. 14 FLA. STAT. ANN. § 394.455(2) (West 2002).
10. 14 FLA. STAT. ANN. § 394.455(24) (West 2002).
11. 14 FLA. STAT. ANN. § 394.455(4) (West 2002).

Psychiatric nurse is "a registered nurse licensed under [Florida law] who has a masters degree or a doctorate in psychiatric nursing and 2 years of postmasters clinical experience under the supervision of a physician."[12] *Receiving facility* refers to "any public or private facility designated by the Department of Children and Families (DCF) to receive and hold involuntary patients under emergency conditions or for psychiatric evaluation and to provide short-term treatment. The term does not include a county jail."[13]

(B)(2) Distinction Between Examination and Placement

Civil commitment law in Florida distinguishes between the involuntary examination of allegedly mentally ill persons and involuntary placement of allegedly mentally ill persons. *Involuntary examination* refers to the process whereby a person who is believed to meet criteria for civil commitment is hospitalized for a short period of time in a community based facility so that he or she can be evaluated and observed more closely.[14] *Involuntary placement* refers to the involuntary admission and treatment of a person to an inpatient setting for a period not to exceed six months.[15] Whereas involuntary examinations can be initiated in a number of ways, involuntary placement can occur only after an evidentiary hearing (unless the hearing is waived by the individual) and in response to a judge's order.

The criteria for involuntary examination and placement are essentially the same. The general requirements are that the individual suffer from mental illness and, as a result of the mental illness, is likely to neglect or refuse to care for him- or herself or is likely to harm him- or herself or others.

(B)(3) Criteria for Involuntary Examination

An individual may be taken to a receiving facility for involuntary examination if there is reason to believe that[16]

1. He or she is mentally ill and, as a result of the mental illness,
   (a) Has refused voluntary examination after explanation and disclosure of the purpose of the examination, or
   (b) Is unable to determine whether examination is necessary;

2. Without care and treatment the person is likely to suffer from neglect or refuse to care for him- or herself, and this neglect or refusal poses a real and present threat of substantial harm

---

12. 14 FLA. STAT. ANN. § 394.455(23) (West 2002).
13. 14 FLA. STAT. ANN. § 394.455(26) (West 2002).
14. 14 FLA. STAT. ANN. § 399.463 (West 2002).
15. 14 FLA. STAT. ANN. § 394.467 (West 2002).
16. 14 FLA. STAT. ANN. § 394.463(1) (West 2002).

to his or her well-being, and it is not apparent that such harm can be avoided through the help of willing family or friends, or through the provision of services; or

3. There is a substantial likelihood that without care or treatment the person will cause serious bodily harm to him- or herself or others in the near future, as indicated by recent behavior.

(B)(4) **Initiating an Involuntary Examination**

An involuntary examination may be initiated in three ways:[17]

1. On hearing evidence in the form of sworn testimony, a court may enter an *ex parte* order (an order entered when only one party is before the court) directing that the individual appears to meet criteria for involuntary examination. This order becomes part of the clinical record. If other, less restrictive means are not available, such as voluntary appearance of the individual for outpatient evaluation, the court can direct a law enforcement officer or other designee to take the individual into custody and transport him or her to the nearest receiving facility for involuntary examination.

2. A law enforcement officer must take into custody an individual who appears to meet the criteria for involuntary examination and deliver him or her to a receiving facility for involuntary examination. The officer must submit a report that documents the circumstances under which the person was taken into custody, and this report becomes part of the clinical record.

3. Physicians, licensed psychologists, psychiatric nurses, and clinical social workers can complete a certificate indicating that they have examined the individual within the preceding 48 hours and believe that he or she meets the criteria for involuntary examination. The certificate, which must detail the observations on which the professional's conclusions are based, becomes part of the clinical record. If other, less restrictive means are not available, a law enforcement officer can take the individual into custody and transport him or her to the nearest receiving facility for involuntary examination.

(B)(5) **Involuntary Examination Process**

A patient admitted to a receiving facility for involuntary examination must be examined by a physician or clinical psychologist[18] without unnecessary delay and may, on order of a physician, be

---

17. 14 FLA. STAT. ANN. § 394.463(2)(a) (West 2002).
18. Note that the law identifies a "clinical psychologist" (*see* 14 FLA. STAT. ANN. § 394.455(2) (West 2002) and the earlier discussion for a definition) as opposed to a "licensed psychologist."

provided emergency treatment that is identified as necessary for the safety of the examinee or others. The examinee cannot be released without the documented approval of a psychiatrist or clinical psychologist.[19]

During the 72-hour examination period (excluding weekends and holidays), one of the following must happen:[20]

1. The examinee must be released, unless he or she is charged with a crime, in which case the examinee is returned to the custody of a law enforcement officer;
2. The examinee must be released for outpatient follow-up treatment;
3. The examinee must agree to placement or treatment as a voluntary patient; or
4. A petition for involuntary placement must be filed with the appropriate court.

(B)(6) Change of Status

An involuntary patient who requests transfer to voluntary status must be transferred to voluntary status unless charged with a crime or involuntarily placed for examination or treatment by a court and it is determined that he or she continues to meet criteria for involuntary placement.[21]

When a voluntary inpatient or his or her agent makes a request for discharge from the inpatient setting, the request for discharge must be communicated to a physician, clinical psychologist, or psychiatrist as quickly as possible, but no later than 12 hours after the request is made. If the professional believes that the patient meets criteria for involuntary placement, the facility administrator must file with the court a petition for involuntary placement within two court working days, or the patient must be discharged. Pending the filing of the petition, the patient can be held and emergency treatment rendered in the least restrictive manner on the written order of a physician, if it is determined that the treatment is necessary for the safety of the patient or others.[22]

(B)(7) Involuntary Placement Hearing and Process

A hearing must be held within five days after the court receives the petition for involuntary placement, unless a continuance is granted. The subject of the petition has the following rights with regard to the involuntary placement process and hearing:

---

19. 14 FLA. STAT. ANN. § 394.463(2)(f) (West 2002).
20. 14 FLA. STAT. ANN. § 394.463(2)(i) (West 2002).
21. 14 FLA. STAT. ANN. § 394.4625(4) (West 2002).
22. 14 FLA. STAT. ANN. § 394.4625(5) (West 2002).

1. The right to a copy of the petition for involuntary placement;[23]

2. The right to attend the hearing unless the court determines that attendance is not in the person's best interests and the person's attorney does not object;[24]

3. The right to an attorney (the court must appoint an attorney for the individual if he or she cannot afford one);[25]

4. The right to an independent expert examination that is confidential and not discoverable unless the expert is to be called as a witness at the hearing;[26]

5. The right to refuse to testify;[27] and

6. The right to review the medical or psychiatric record and have access to witnesses (via his or her attorney).[28]

At the hearing, the recommendation for involuntary placement must be supported by the opinion of two psychiatrists or a psychiatrist and clinical psychologist who have examined the individual within the preceding 72 hours. In counties of less than 50,000 people and in which a psychiatrist or a clinical psychologist is not available to provide the second opinion, a physician with psychiatric experience or a psychiatric nurse may provide such an opinion.[29]

At the involuntary placement hearing the court is to consider testimony regarding the person's competence to consent to treatment. If the court finds that the patient is incompetent to consent to treatment, it must appoint a guardian advocate.[30] The guardian advocate can consent to medical or mental health treatment on the person's behalf subsequent to commitment and placement, but the guardian advocate may not consent to abortion, sterilization, electroconvulsive treatment, psychosurgery, or experimental treatments without express and specific approval from the court in an independent hearing.[31] The guardian advocate is discharged when the patient is returned to the community, transferred to voluntary patient status, or determined to have had his or her competence to consent to treatment restored.[32]

---

23. 14 FLA. STAT. ANN. § 394.467(3) (West 2002).
24. 14 FLA. STAT. ANN. § 394.467(6)(a)1 (West 2002).
25. 14 FLA. STAT. ANN. § 394.467(4) (West 2002).
26. 14 FLA. STAT. ANN. § 394.467(6)(a)2 (West 2002).
27. Id.
28. 14 FLA. STAT. ANN. § 394.467(4) (West 2002).
29. 14 FLA. STAT. ANN. § 394.467(2) (West 2002).
30. 14 FLA. STAT. ANN. § 394.467(6)(d) (West 2002).
31. 14 FLA. STAT. ANN. § 394.4598(6) (West 2002).
32. 14 FLA. STAT. ANN. § 394.4598(7) (West 2002).

(B)(8) Criteria for Involuntary Placement

An individual may be involuntarily placed for treatment on a finding of the court, by clear and convincing evidence, that[33]

1. He or she is mentally ill and, because of the mental illness,
   (a) Has refused voluntary placement for treatment after sufficient and conscientious explanation and disclosure of the purpose for treatment; or
   (b) Is unable to determine whether placement is necessary;

2. Is manifestly incapable of surviving alone or with the help of willing and responsible family or friends, including available alternative services, and without treatment, is likely to suffer from neglect or refuse to care for him- or herself, and this neglect or refusal poses a real and present threat of substantial harm to his or her well-being; or

3. There is a substantial likelihood that in the near future the person will inflict serious bodily harm to him- or herself or others, as evidenced by recent behavior causing, attempting, or threatening such harm; and

4. All available, less restrictive treatment alternatives are inappropriate.

(B)(9) Disposition of Persons Who Meet Criteria for Involuntary Placement

If the court determines that the examinee meets the criteria for involuntary placement by clear and convincing evidence, then it must order that the person be transferred to a treatment facility for a period of up to six months. A patient must be released from the treatment facility or transferred to voluntary status whenever facility staff believe that the person no longer meets the criteria for involuntary placement.[34] If, after six months, it is believed that the client continues to meet criteria for involuntary placement, another hearing must be held to determine this issue. The request for continued commitment must be accompanied by a statement from the patient's physician or clinical psychologist justifying the request, a brief description of the patient's treatment during the period of involuntary placement, and an individualized treatment plan.[35] Subsequent placements are for six-month periods.[36] In those cases where the patient has previously been found incompetent

---

33. 14 Fla. Stat. Ann. § 394.467(1) (West 2002).
34. 14 Fla. Stat. Ann. § 394.467(6)(b) (West 2002).
35. 14 Fla. Stat. Ann. § 394.467(7)(b) (West 2002).
36. 14 Fla. Stat. Ann. § 394.467(7)(d) (West 2002).

to consent to treatment, the hearing officer will consider testimony and evidence regarding the patient's competence. If the hearing officer finds evidence that the patient is competent to consent to treatment, he or she may issue a recommended order to the court that found the patient incompetent to consent to treatment that the patient's competence be restored and that any previously appointed guardian advocate be discharged.[37]

(B)(10) Change of Status

An involuntary patient who requests transfer to voluntary status must be transferred to voluntary status unless charged with a crime or involuntarily placed for examination or treatment by a court and it is determined that he or she continues to meet criteria for involuntary placement.[38]

When a voluntary inpatient or his or her agent makes a request for discharge from the inpatient setting, the request for discharge must be communicated to a physician, clinical psychologist, or psychiatrist as quickly as possible, but no later than 12 hours after the request is made. If the professional believes that the patient meets criteria for involuntary placement, the facility administrator must file with the court a petition for involuntary placement within two court working days, or the patient must be discharged. Pending the filing of the petition, the patient can be held and emergency treatment rendered in the least restrictive manner on the written order of a physician, if it is determined that the treatment is necessary for the safety of the patient or others.[39]

(C) Voluntary Admissions of Minors for Substance Abuse Treatment

Individuals under the age of 18 years may consent to substance abuse treatment without the knowledge or consent of their parents, legal guardians, or legal custodians,[40] but their parents, legal guardians, or legal custodians are not responsible for payment for services unless they have voluntarily participated in such services or they have been ordered to participate in such services.[41]

---

37. 14 FLA. STAT. ANN. § 394.467(7)(f) (West 2002).
38. 14 FLA. STAT. ANN. § 394.4625(4) (West 2002).
39. 14 FLA. STAT. ANN. § 394.4625(5) (West 2002).
40. 14 FLA. STAT. ANN. § 397.601(4)(a) (West 2002).
41. 14 FLA. STAT. ANN. § 397.431(3) (West 2002).

(D) Involuntary Assessment, Stabilization, and Treatment

(D)(1) Definitions

To understand the law concerning involuntary assessment and treatment of substance abuse problems, MHPs should be familiar with the following terms and their legal meanings.[42] *Assessment* means

> the systematic evaluation of information gathered to determine the nature and severity of the client's need and motivation for services. Assessment entails the use of a psychosocial history supplemented, as required by rule, by medical examinations, laboratory testing, and psychometric measures.

A *habitual abuser* is "a person who is brought to the attention of law enforcement for being substance impaired, who meets the criteria for involuntary admission, and who has been taken into custody for such impairment three or more times during the preceding 12 months." *Stabilization* means "alleviation of a crisis condition or prevention of further deterioration, and connotes short-term emergency treatment." *Substance abuse impaired* refers to "a condition involving the use of alcoholic beverages or any psychoactive or mood-altering substance in such a manner as to induce mental, emotional, or physical problems and cause socially dysfunctional behavior."

(D)(2) Criteria for Involuntary Assessment and Stabilization

An individual meets the criteria for involuntary assessment/stabilization/protective custody if there is reason to believe that the individual is substance-abuse impaired and, as a result of that impairment[43]

1. Has lost the power of self-control with regard to substance abuse; and either

2. Has inflicted, threatened, or attempted to inflict, or unless admitted is likely to inflict physical harm on him- or herself or others; or

3. Is in need of substance abuse services and, as a result of the substance abuse impairment, his or her judgment is so impaired that the individual is incapable of appreciating the need for, or making a rational decision about, treatment. However, mere refusal of services does not constitute evidence of a lack of judgment.

---

42. 14 Fla. Stat. Ann. § 397.311 (West 2002).
43. 14 Fla. Stat. Ann. § 397.675 (West 2002).

(D)(3) Initiating Involuntary Assessment and Stabilization of Minors

A physician, the minor's parent, legal guardian, or legal custodian can request emergency admission to psychiatric hospitalization.[44] On such application a physician must complete a certificate for emergency admission that describes that the minor is substance-abuse impaired and meets criteria for emergency admission.[45] The physician's certificate for emergency admission must show how the minor meets the criteria for involuntary stabilization. This certificate becomes part of the clinical record.[46]

Within 72 hours after emergency admission to a hospital or residential facility, the minor must be assessed by the attending physician to determine the need for additional services. Within five days after admission to a nonresidential facility, the minor must be assessed by a qualified professional to determine the need for additional services.[47]

Within five days of admission, one of the following must happen:

1. The minor must be released and, when appropriate, referred to other services;

2. The minor must agree to placement or treatment as a voluntary patient; or

3. A petition for involuntary assessment or treatment must be filed with the court, thereby authorizing the treatment provider to retain physical custody of the minor.[48]

In addition, any person who believes that a minor meets the criteria for involuntary assessment and stabilization may petition the court. The petition must include the identity of the petitioner, the relationship between the petitioner and the subject of the petition, and why the petitioner believes that the minor meets the criteria for involuntary assessment and stabilization.[49]

After receiving the petition, the judge must either complete an *ex parte* order (an order issued when only one party is before the court) authorizing the involuntary assessment and stabilization of the minor or issue a summons to the minor and schedule a hearing within 10 days.[50] A minor determined by the court to meet the criteria for involuntary assessment may be admitted for a period of five days.[51]

---

44. 14 FLA. STAT. ANN. § 397.6791 (West 2002).
45. 14 FLA. STAT. ANN. § 397.6793(1) (West 2002).
46. 14 FLA. STAT. ANN. § 397.6793(3) (West 2002).
47. 14 FLA. STAT. ANN. § 397.6797 (West 2002).
48. *Id.*
49. 14 FLA. STAT. ANN. § 397.6814 (West 2002).
50. 14 FLA. STAT. ANN. § 397.6815 (West 2002).
51. 14 FLA. STAT. ANN. § 397.6819 (West 2002).

Minors also may be admitted to addictions-receiving facilities for involuntary assessment on the basis of application by their parents, guardian, or legal custodian. The application must establish the need for involuntary assessment and stabilization based on the criteria described earlier. After admission, the minor must be assessed within 72 hours to determine the need for continuing services. If, after the 72-hour period, it is determined that additional services are necessary, the minor may be kept for a period of up to five days, counting the 72-hour period.[52]

(D)(4) Criteria for Involuntary Treatment

Florida law distinguishes between involuntary assessment/stabilization and involuntary treatment of persons with substance abuse problems. Although involuntary assessment and stabilization provide for short-term assessment and intervention, involuntary treatment allows for longer-term commitment for the purpose of treating people with substance abuse problems.

An individual can be the subject of a court-ordered petition for involuntary treatment if he or she meets criteria for involuntary assessment/stabilization/treatment[53] and

1. Has undergone protective custody[54] or emergency admission[55] within the previous 10 days;

2. Has been seen by a qualified professional within the previous five days;[56] or

3. Has been the subject of involuntary assessment[57] or alternative involuntary admission[58] within the previous 12 days.

If the respondent is an adult, a petition for involuntary treatment can be filed by the respondent's spouse or guardian, any relative, a service provider, or any three adults who have personal knowledge of the respondent's substance abuse impairment and his or her course of assessment and treatment.[59] If the respondent is a minor, a petition for involuntary treatment can be filed by a parent, legal guardian, or service provider.[60] Among other things, the petition must contain the name of the respondent, the name(s) and relationship(s) between the respondent and petitioner(s), the findings and recommendations of the assessment performed by

---

52. 14 FLA. STAT. ANN. § 397.6798 (West 2002).
53. 14 FLA. STAT. ANN. § 397.675 (West 2002).
54. 14 FLA. STAT. ANN. § 397.693(2) (West 2002).
55. 14 FLA. STAT. ANN. § 397.693(3) (West 2002).
56. 14 FLA. STAT. ANN. § 397.693(2) (West 2002).
57. 14 FLA. STAT. ANN. § 397.693(4) (West 2002).
58. *Id.*
59. 14 FLA. STAT. ANN. § 397.695(1) (West 2002).
60. 14 FLA. STAT. ANN. § 397.695(2) (West 2002).

a qualified professional, and the factual allegations that form the basis of the petition.[61]

(D)(5) Involuntary Treatment Hearing

Individuals who are the subject of a petition must be appointed counsel if they do not have an attorney. The respondent must receive a copy of the petition, and the court must schedule a hearing within 10 days of the receipt of the petition.[62] At the hearing the court must consider and review all relevant evidence, including the results of an assessment completed by a qualified professional in connection with the respondent's protective custody, emergency admission, or involuntary assessment. The respondent must be present at the proceeding unless the court determines that the respondent's presence is likely to be injurious to the respondent or others, in which case the court must appoint a guardian advocate to act on behalf of the respondent.[63]

The court can order the respondent to receive involuntary treatment for substance abuse for up to 60 days[64] if it is shown, by clear and convincing evidence, that he or she[65]

1. Is substance-abuse impaired;
2. Has lost the power of self-control with regard to substance abuse;
3. Has inflicted or, unless admitted, is likely to inflict, physical harm on him- or herself or others; or
4. Refuses to accept voluntary care, and the refusal is based on judgment so impaired by the substance abuse that he or she cannot appreciate the need for, or make a rational decision about, the need for treatment.

If, during the course of treatment, treatment staff determine that the conditions justifying involuntary treatment no longer exist, the respondent must be released.[66]

(D)(6) Review and Renewal of Involuntary Treatment Orders

Treatment providers who believe that a client nearing date of release from involuntary treatment continues to meet the criteria for involuntary treatment must petition the court for renewal of the involuntary treatment order. A hearing on this request must be held within 15 days of receipt of the petition. The criteria

---

61. 14 FLA. STAT. ANN. § 397.6951 (West 2002).
62. 14 FLA. STAT. ANN. § 397.6955 (West 2002).
63. 14 FLA. STAT. ANN. § 397.6957 (West 2002).
64. 14 FLA. STAT. ANN. § 397.697 (West 2002).
65. 14 FLA. STAT. ANN. § 397.6957 (West 2002).
66. 14 FLA. STAT. ANN. § 397.697 (West 2002).

for continued involuntary treatment are the same as those used initially. If it is determined that the client continues to meet criteria for involuntary treatment by clear and convincing evidence, treatment may be continued for up to 90 days, with similar reviews occurring at the end of these 90-day periods.[67] Any time before the end of the initial 60-day involuntary treatment period or subsequent to a 90-day extension of that period, and as described earlier, a client must be discharged and referred to a more appropriate status or service if he or she no longer meets criteria for involuntary treatment.[68] A client involuntarily admitted may be released without order of the court only by a qualified professional in a hospital, detoxification facility, an addictions receiving facility, or any less restrictive treatment program. In cases of a minor, notice must be given to the applicant or to the petitioner and the court if the assessment or treatment was court-ordered.[69]

---

67. 14 FLA. STAT. ANN. § 397.6975 (West 2002).
68. 14 FLA. STAT. ANN. § 397.6971 (West 2002).
69. 14 FLA. STAT. ANN. § 397.6758 (West 2002).

4.20
Education for Gifted and Handicapped Children

All school districts in the state of Florida are required to provide special education services for exceptional students, as they are defined next.[1]

(A) Terms and Definitions

To understand the law concerning education of gifted and handicapped children, MHPs should be familiar with the following terms and their legal meanings. An *exceptional student* is

any child or youth who has been determined eligible for a special program in accordance with rules of the Commissioner of Education or the State Board of Education. The term "exceptional students" includes students who are gifted and students with disabilities who are mentally handicapped, speech and language impaired, deaf or hard of hearing, visually impaired, dual sensory impaired, physically impaired, emotionally handicapped, specific learning disabled, hospital and homebound, autistic, developmentally delayed children ages birth through five years, or children with established conditions ages birth through two years.[2]

Special education services means

instruction and such related services as are necessary for the student to benefit from education. Such services may include: transportation; diagnostic and evaluation services; social services; physical and occupational therapy; job placement; orientation and mobility training; braillists, typists, and readers for the blind; interpreters and auditory amplification; rehabilitation

---
1. 11 FLA. STAT. ANN. § 230.23(4)(m) (West Supp. 2002).
2. 11 FLA. STAT. ANN. § 228.041(18) (West Supp. 2002).

counseling; transition services; mental health services; guidance and career counseling; specified materials, assistive technology devices, and other specialized equipment; and other such services as approved by regulations of the state Board of Education.[3]

(B) Evaluation and Placement of Exceptional Students

School districts are responsible for providing instruction and special education services to exceptional students. These services include diagnostic and evaluation services and special instruction and classes.[4] Students are not to be placed in special instructional settings or receive services as exceptional students until they have been evaluated, classified, and placed in the manner prescribed by the Board of Education.

To the extent possible, exceptional students are to be mainstreamed. That is, exceptional students are to be included in the regular school facilities and classrooms with adaptations made to the extent appropriate. Segregation of exceptional students can occur only if the nature or severity of the handicap precludes education in regular classes with supplementary aides and services.[5]

The legislature has established regional Diagnostic and Learning Resource Centers that are to assist school districts in providing medical, physiological, psychological, and educational testing and other services designed to evaluate and diagnose exceptional

---

3. 11 FLA. STAT. ANN. § 228.041(19) (West Supp. 2002).
4. 11 FLA. STAT. ANN. § 230.23(4)(m) (West Supp. 2002). Eligibility criteria and special program requirements for exceptional children can be found in FLA. ADMIN. CODE ANN. r. 6A-6.03011 (2002) (mentally handicapped children); FLA. ADMIN. CODE ANN. r. 6A-6.03012 (2002) (speech- and language-impaired children); FLA. ADMIN. CODE ANN. r. 6A-6.03013 (2002) (deaf and hard of hearing students); FLA. ADMIN. CODE ANN. r. 6A-6.03014 (2002) (visually impaired students); FLA. ADMIN. CODE ANN. r. 6A-6.03015 (2002) (physically impaired students); FLA. ADMIN. CODE ANN. r. 6A-6.03016 (2002) (emotionally handicapped students); FLA. ADMIN. CODE ANN. r. 6A-6.03018 (2002) (learning-disabled students); FLA. ADMIN. CODE ANN. r. 6A-6.03020 (2002) (homebound or hospitalized students); FLA. ADMIN. CODE ANN. r. 6A-6.03021 (2002) (profoundly handicapped students), FLA. ADMIN. CODE ANN. r. 6A-6.03022 (2002) (dual-sensory-impaired students); FLA. ADMIN. CODE ANN. r. 6A-6.03023 (2002) (autistic students); FLA. ADMIN. CODE ANN. r. 6A-6.03024 (2002) (exceptional students who require physical therapy); FLA. ADMIN. CODE ANN. r. 6A-6.03025 (2002) (students who require occupational therapy); FLA. ADMIN. CODE ANN. r. 6A-6.03026 (2002) (prekindergarten children with disabilities); and FLA. ADMIN. CODE ANN. r. 6A-6.03028(3) (2002) (children ages 3 through 5 years old who are developmentally delayed).
5. 11 FLA. STAT. ANN. § 230.23(4)(m)6 (West Supp. 2002).

students, to make referrals for necessary instruction and services, and to facilitate the provision of instruction and services to exceptional students.[6] Each regional center is to provide assistance to parents, teachers, and other school personnel and community organizations in locating and identifying exceptional children and in planning educational programs; assist in providing services for exceptional children; provide orientation meetings that familiarize parents, teachers, and others with the center resources; plan, coordinate, and assist in implementing in-service training programs; assist districts in the identification, selection, acquisition, use, and evaluation of media and materials appropriate to the implementation of instructional programs based on individual educational plans for exceptional children; provide for dissemination and diffusion of significant information and promising practices derived from research and demonstration projects; and assist in the delivery, modification, and integration of instructional technology appropriate to the unique needs of exceptional students.[7]

(C) Parental Rights

Parents or guardians of students are to be notified of evaluations to determine placement and the evaluation outcomes. Parents or guardians who are dissatisfied with the outcome of the evaluations and disposition decision have the right to appeal the decision in a hearing that is conducted by an administrative law judge. These decisions can be appealed to the local circuit court.[8]

(D) Individual Education Plans for Exceptional Students

As mandated by federal law, school districts must develop an individual education plan (IEP) for every exceptional student 6 years of age and older.[9] The IEP documents and describes the student's abilities, disabilities, and needs; the school district's attempts to offer services; and the goals and objectives of interventions along with their proposed timelines. The IEP must include[10]

---

6. 11 FLA. STAT. ANN. § 229.832 (West Supp. 2002).
7. 11 FLA. STAT. ANN. § 229.832(2) (West Supp. 2002).
8. 11 FLA. STAT. ANN. § 230.23(4)(m)5 (West Supp. 2002).
9. FLA. ADMIN. CODE ANN. r. 6A-6.03028(1) (2002).
10. *Id.*

1. A statement of the student's present levels of educational performance;
2. A statement of annual goals, including short-term instructional objectives;
3. A statement of the specific special education and related services to be provided to the student and the extent to which the student will be able to participate in regular educational programs;
4. The projected dates for initiation of services and the anticipated duration of services;
5. Appropriate objective criteria and evaluation procedures and schedules for determining, at least on an annual basis, whether the short-term instructional objectives are being achieved; and
6. A statement of the transition services needed for the student to move from school to postschool activities such as vocational training, adult education, employment, or independent living.

IEPs must be developed before assigning a student to special programs and within 30 days of determining that a student qualifies as an exceptional student. Meetings must be held annually or more frequently so that the IEP can be developed, reviewed, and revised.[11] IEP meetings are to include the student's teacher, a representative of the school system other than the student's teacher, the student's parents, other professionals who are working with the student or family (at the discretion of the parents or school district), and the student (when appropriate).[12]

(E) Preschool Children With Handicapping Conditions

The Department of Education has created regional diagnostic and learning resource centers for exceptional students. These centers are to assist in providing medical, psychological, physiological, and educational testing and other services for assessing and instructing students with special conditions,[13] such as high-risk or handicapped infants and preschool children. Centers are also authorized to assist school districts in providing interdisciplinary training and resources to parents of such children and to day care and preschool programs.[14]

---

11. FLA. ADMIN. CODE ANN. r. 6A-6.03028(3) (2002).
12. FLA. ADMIN. CODE ANN. r. 6A-6.03028(4) (2002).
13. 11 FLA. STAT. ANN. § 229.832 (West Supp. 2002).
14. 11 FLA. STAT. ANN. § 229.8341 (West Supp. 2002).

(F) Gifted Pupils

School districts are also responsible for developing educational plans for students who are gifted.[15] A student may be eligible for a program for the gifted if he or she meets one of two sets of criteria.[16] First, a student is eligible if the student demonstrates

1. The need for a special program;
2. A majority of characteristics of a gifted student according to a standard scale or checklist; and
3. Superior intellectual development as measured by an intelligence quotient of two standard deviations or more above the mean on an individually administered, standardized test of intelligence.

Alternatively the student may qualify if the student is a member of an underrepresented group and meets the criteria specified by an approved school district plan for increasing the participation of underrepresented groups in programs for gifted students. Underrepresented groups for this purpose are defined as groups whose English proficiency is limited or who are from a low socioeconomic status family. Districts seeking to accomplish this goal must, among other things, indicate the criteria used for determining eligibility based on demonstrated ability or potential in areas of leadership, motivation, academic performance, and creativity.

---

15. FLA. ADMIN. CODE r. 6A-6.03019 (2002).
16. Id.

4.21
Consent, Confidentiality, and Services for Minors

With some exceptions that are described later, individuals under the age of 18 years cannot consent to treatment because they are considered to be incompetent to do so as a function of their age. Consent for medical and mental health services must be granted by a parent or guardian.[1] The MHP will need to obtain consent according to the legal rules discussed in this chapter; the MHP is also obviously concerned with and affected by confidentiality provisions of state law.

(A) Minors' Consent to Medical Services

There are a variety of exceptions to the general presumption of incompetence. Minors who have been emancipated (e.g., as a function of marrying, a court proceeding, or being adjudicated as an adult in a criminal proceeding and serving a criminal sentence in the Department of Corrections) can consent to medical treatment.[2] There are also some exceptions for some specific medical, mental health, and substance abuse treatment services (see chapter 4.22, Consent for Abortion).

When a parent or legal guardian cannot be contacted, the following persons are authorized to consent to medical services[3]

---

1. 21 FLA. STAT. ANN. § 743.07 (West Supp. 2002).
2. 21 FLA. STAT. ANN. § 743.01 (West Supp. 2002); 21 FLA. STAT. ANN. § 743.066 (West 1997); 21 FLA. STAT. ANN. § 743.015 (West Supp. 2002).
3. Surgery, general anesthesia, and administration of psychotropic medication are specifically excluded from treatments than can be consented to by someone other than the minor's parent or legal guardian. These

in the order listed: a person who possesses a power of attorney to provide medical consent for the minor, a stepparent, a grandparent, an adult sibling, or an adult aunt or uncle.[4] The DJJ, the DCF, and residential facility service program operators are also authorized to consent to medical services on behalf of a child who is in their custody when the parent or legal guardian cannot be contacted. In cases where treatment occurs without the consent of the parent or legal guardian, the parent or legal guardian must be notified as soon as possible about the intervention and the conditions surrounding the treatment, and its provision must be documented in the medical record.[5]

Children who are 17 years of age may consent to donate blood independently, unless there is a specific objection by their parents.[6] Unwed pregnant minors can consent to medical or surgical care related to the pregnancy (including abortion),[7] and minor mothers can consent to medical or surgical care or services for their children.[8] Current statutes provide that a parent or guardian of a nonemancipated pregnant women under 18 years of age seeking an abortion must be provided 48 hours notice of the minor's intention.[9] However, the minor child may petition the circuit court for waiver of the notice requirements, and the court may waive the notice requirement if it determines that the minor is sufficiently mature to make such a decision or that there is evidence that the parent or guardian has abused the minor.[10]

(A)(1) Emergency Treatment

Of course, minors can also be provided necessary emergency medical care by emergency medical technicians, paramedics, other emergency medical personnel, medical doctors, and osteopaths without parental consent if, in the opinion of the provider, delay of services would endanger the health or physical well-being of the minor. In such cases, the parents or legal guardians are to be notified as soon as possible and the conditions surrounding the treatment and its provision must be documented in the record.[11]

---

interventions require a separate court order; see 21 FLA. STAT. ANN. § 743.0645 (West Supp. 2002).
4. 21 FLA. STAT. ANN. § 743.0645(1)(b) (West Supp 2002).
5. 21 FLA. STAT. ANN. § 743.0645(4) (West Supp. 2002).
6. 21 FLA. STAT. ANN. § 743.06 (West Supp. 2002).
7. Id.
8. 21 FLA. STAT. ANN. § 743.065 (West Supp. 2002).
9. 21 FLA. STAT. ANN. § 390.01115(3) (West Supp. 2002).
10. 21 FLA. STAT. ANN. § 390.01115(4) (West 2002).
11. 21 FLA. STAT. ANN. § 743.064 (West Supp. 2002).

(B) Minors' Consent to Substance Abuse Evaluation and Treatment Services

Minors are permitted to consent to assessment and treatment for substance abuse or dependency in inpatient or outpatient settings without the knowledge, permission, or consent of their parents.[12] Parents or legal guardians, however, are not responsible for payment for services provided to the minor without their consent, unless the parent or legal guardian voluntarily participates in the treatment or is ordered to participate in the treatment.[13]

A minor can be admitted for involuntary examination and involuntary treatment for substance abuse and dependence under the same conditions as adults and using the same procedures.

(C) Minors' Consent to Mental Health Evaluation and Treatment Services

(C)(1) Outpatient Diagnostic Services, Crisis Intervention Services, Counseling, and Therapy

Minors between the ages of 13 and 17 years can consent to mental health diagnostic and evaluation services that are provided by a licensed MHP under some circumstances. These services are limited to diagnosis and assessment, cannot exceed two visits during any one-week period, and must be in response to a crisis situation. Parental participation can occur when determined to be appropriate by the MHP.[14] Parents are under no legal obligation to pay for services received by their children under these conditions.[15]

Minors can also consent to crisis intervention, individual psychotherapy, group therapy, counseling, or other forms of verbal therapy provided by a licensed MHP under some circumstances. Services cannot consist of any somatic or physical interventions (e.g., medication, use of aversive stimuli), cannot exceed two visits during any one-week period, and must be provided in response to a crisis situation. Parents are under no legal obligation to pay for services received by their children under these conditions.[16]

---

12. 14 FLA. STAT. ANN. § 397.601(4)(a) (West 2002).
13. 14 FLA. STAT. ANN. § 397.431(3) (West 2002).
14. 14 FLA. STAT. ANN. § 394.4784(1) (West 2002).
15. 14 FLA. STAT. ANN. § 394.4784(3) (West 2002)
16. Id.

Parental participation can occur when determined to be appropriate by the MHP and with the consent of the parent.[17]

(C)(2) Inpatient Assessment and Treatment

With the express and informed consent of a parent or guardian, an inpatient facility can receive for observation, diagnosis, or treatment any person under the age of 17. Before admission, however, a hearing must be held to determine the voluntariness of the consent.[18] A minor can be admitted for involuntary examination and involuntary treatment under the same conditions as adults and using the same procedures.[19]

(D) Confidentiality of Minors' Treatment

(D)(1) Mental Health Records

Release of confidential records maintained by inpatient and outpatient treatment facilities licensed by the state can be authorized by minor's parent or legal guardian.[20] This provision can be interpreted as indicating that minors' records can be accessed by their parents or legal guardians. Florida law regarding client record confidentiality in inpatient and outpatient treatment facilities operated or licensed by the state also includes a specific provision indicating that general confidentiality guarantees do not prohibit the parents or next of kin of people with mental illness from requesting and receiving information limited to the person's treatment plan and physical and mental condition. Release of such information, however, is to be in accordance with the codes of ethics of the professions involved.[21]

(D)(2) Substance Abuse Records

Noting that minors are allowed to consent to substance abuse treatment independently and without the consent of their parents,[22] Florida law also provides that the records of a minor who

---

17. 14 FLA. STAT. ANN. § 394.4784(2) (West 2002).
18. 14 FLA. STAT. ANN. § 394.4625(1)(a) (West 2000).
19. *See* 14 FLA. STAT. ANN. §§ 394.463 and 394.467 (West 2000).
20. 14 FLA. STAT. ANN. § 394.4615(2)(a) (West 2000).
21. 14 FLA. STAT. ANN. § 394.4615(8) (West 2002).
22. 14 FLA. STAT. ANN. . § 397.601(4)(a) (West 2002).

has voluntarily sought substance abuse treatment can be released only on the written consent of the minor client. This restriction covers disclosure of client identifying information to the parent, legal guardian, or custodian for the purpose of obtaining financial reimbursement.[23]

---

23. 14 FLA. STAT. ANN. § 397.501(7)(e)1 (West 2002).

4.22
Consent for Abortion

Abortions may be performed by licensed physicians during the first two trimesters of pregnancy. An abortion can be performed in the third trimester only if two physicians certify in writing that, to a reasonable degree of medical certainty, termination of the pregnancy is necessary to save the life or preserve the health of the pregnant woman or a physician certifies that a medical emergency exists and a second physician is not available for consultation.[1]

(A) Standard for Consent

An abortion may be performed only with the voluntary and informed consent of the woman or, where applicable, a court-appointed guardian. Consent is voluntary and informed, absent a medical emergency, only if the physician performing the procedure or the referring physician has informed the woman of the nature and risks of undergoing or not undergoing the procedure; the probable gestational age of the fetus at the time the abortion is to be performed; and the medical risks to the woman and fetus of carrying the pregnancy to term. The woman also is given the option of viewing materials prepared by the state that describe the fetus; a list of agencies providing alternatives to abortion; and information on the availability of medical assistance benefits for prenatal care, childbirth, and neonatal care. The patient must acknowledge in writing that this information has been made available to her.[2]

---

1. 14 FLA. STAT. ANN. § 390.0111(1) (West Supp. 2002).
2. 14 FLA. STAT. ANN. § 390.0111(3)(a) (West Supp. 2002).

(B) Notification Hearing

In the case of minors, an abortion may not be performed unless the physician performing the abortion has provided at least 48 hours notice to one parent or legal guardian of his or her intention to terminate the pregnancy.[3] Notice is not required if a medical emergency exists, notice is waived by the person entitled to receive notice, or notice is waived by a minor who is married or for some other statutory reason is considered an adult.[4] In addition, a minor may ask a court to waive the requirement for notice to a parent or guardian. If the court finds, by clear evidence, that the minor is sufficiently mature to terminate her pregnancy without notifying a parent or guardian, the court may authorize the abortion. Alternatively, if the court finds, by clear evidence, that there is evidence that the minor has been abused by one or both parents or her guardian, the court may authorize termination of the pregnancy without notice.[5] The state supreme court has created rules governing petitions by minors seeking to waive the notice requirement.[6]

---

3. 14 FLA. STAT. ANN. § 390.01115(a) (West Supp. 2002).
4. 14 FLA. STAT. ANN. § 390.01115(b) (West Supp. 2002).
5. 14 FLA. STAT. ANN. § 390.01115(c)–(d) (West Supp. 2002).
6. FLA. R. CIV. P. r. 1.840 (2002).

4.23

Evaluation and Treatment of Children at the Request of a Noncustodial Parent

When parents divorce, the court must determine who enjoys custody of the children. MHPs may be called on to provide examinations or treatment by either custodial or noncustodial parents. Regardless of who is awarded custody, the court is to order that the parents share parental responsibility unless the court finds that shared parental responsibility would be detrimental to the child.[1] If a parent has been convicted of a felony of the third degree or higher involving domestic violence, or will be incarcerated for a substantial period of the time before the child becomes 18, or has been determined by a court to be a habitual felony offender or sexual offender, then a presumption of unfitness for parental responsibility is established, and unless it is rebutted, the person will not be given shared parental responsibility.[2] If the court concludes that shared parental responsibility would be detrimental to the child, it must make a specific finding to that effect.[3] In ordering shared parental responsibility, the court may also take into account the desires of the parents and grant to one party the ultimate responsibility for specific aspects of the child's care—for example, education, medical care, and dental care.[4]

When the court orders shared parental responsibility, it is assumed that both parents will be involved in the care of the child unless otherwise specifically ordered. This means that access to records and information, including but not limited to medical, dental, and school records, is available to both parents and cannot

---

1. 5 FLA. STAT. ANN. § 61.13(2)(b)2 (West Supp. 2002).
2. Id.
3. Stelk v. Stelk, 699 So. 2d 811 (Fla. 1st D.C.A. 1997).
4. 5 FLA. STAT. ANN. § 61.13 (2)(b)2.c (West Supp. 2002).

be denied to a parent who is not the child's primary residential parent.[5]

When the parents share parental responsibility, the noncustodial parent presumably retains the right to seek evaluation and treatment of the child. However, because responsibility is shared, presumably this cannot be done unilaterally. Florida law assumes in such cases that the parents, though not living together and no longer married, will reach an accommodation between each other on these issues. If the court does not order shared parental responsibility or if the court, at the request of the parents, has given responsibility to one of the parents for medical decisions—including mental health treatment decisions—then the parent that does not share in that responsibility has no rights regarding the child's treatment.

---

5. 5 FLA. STAT. ANN. § 61.13(2)(b)3 (West Supp. 2002).

Section 5

Other Civil Matters

5.1
Mental Status of Licensed or Certified Professionals

A regulatory board or court may request that a mental health professional (MHP) evaluate a licensed professional if it is believed that the professional's mental state significantly impairs his or her ability to practice. These evaluations generally occur subsequent to initial licensing, after allegations of impropriety or inadequate practice.

Florida law provides for licensure suspension or revocation or limitation of practice when a licensed professional's ability to practice is considered to be impaired as the result of a mental disorder, substance abuse disorder, or physical impairment. This chapter addresses the evaluation of health care professionals.

(A) Licensed Professionals

(A)(1) Clinical Social Workers, Marriage and Family Therapists, and Mental Health Counselors

If the Board of Clinical Social Work, Marriage and Family Therapy, and Mental Health Counseling determines that a therapist licensed by the Board is unable to practice "with reasonable skill or competence as a result of any mental or physical condition or by reason of illness; drunkenness; or excessive use of drugs, narcotics, chemicals, or any other substance,"[1] it may impose various sanctions, including a reprimand or probation, or suspension, restriction, or revocation of licensure. The Board may also require the therapist to submit to treatment.[2] The Board of Clinical

---

1. 15 FLA. STAT. ANN. § 490.009(1)(p) (West Supp. 2002).
2. 15 FLA. STAT. ANN. § 491.009(1) (West Supp. 2002).

Social Work, Marriage and Family Therapy, and Mental Health Counseling can compel the therapist to submit to a mental or physical examination by a psychologist, physician, or other professional licensed under the statutes[3] when probable cause exists to suspect such difficulties. If a therapist's license is restricted in any way because of impairment, he or she is afforded the opportunity to demonstrate, at reasonable intervals, that he or she is able to resume competent practice with reasonable skill and safety.[4]

(A)(2) Nurses

If the Board of Nursing determines that a nurse is unable to practice with reasonable skill and safety as a result of an illness, or use of alcohol, drugs, narcotics, chemicals, or any other type of material, or as the result of any mental or physical condition,[5] it may impose various sanctions, including a reprimand or probation, or suspension, restriction, or revocation of licensure. The Board of Nursing may also require the nurse to submit to treatment.[6] The Board of Nursing can compel the nurse to submit to a mental or physical examination by a physician when probable cause exists to suspect such difficulties. If a nurse's license is restricted in any way because of impairment, he or she is afforded the opportunity to demonstrate, at reasonable intervals, that he or she is able to resume competent practice with reasonable skill and safety.[7]

(A)(3) Occupational Therapists/Occupational Therapy Assistants

If the Board of Occupational Therapy Practice determines that an occupational therapist or occupational therapy assistant is unable to practice with reasonable skill and safety as a result of an illness, or use of alcohol, drugs, narcotics, chemicals, or any other type of material, or as the result of any mental or physical condition,[8] it may impose various sanctions, including a reprimand or probation, or suspension, restriction, or revocation of licensure.[9] The Board can compel the occupational therapist or occupational therapy assistant to submit to a mental or physical examination by a physician when probable cause exists to suspect such difficulties. Failure to submit to such an examination constitutes an admission

---

3. 15 FLA. STAT. ANN. § 491 (West Supp. 2002).
4. 15 FLA. STAT. ANN. § 491.009(2)(p) (West Supp. 2002).
5. 15 FLA. STAT. ANN. § 466.018(1)(j) (West Supp. 2002).
6. 15 FLA. STAT. ANN. § 466.018(2) (West Supp. 2002).
7. 15 FLA. STAT. ANN. § 466.018(1)(j) (West Supp. 2002).
8. 15 FLA. STAT. ANN. § 462.14(1)(s) (West Supp. 2002).
9. 15 FLA. STAT. ANN. § 468.217(1) (West Supp. 2002); 15 FLA. STAT. ANN. § 468.217(1)(t) (West Supp. 2002).

of the allegations unless the failure was outside of the examinee's control. If an occupational therapist's or occupational therapy assistant's license is restricted in any way because of impairment, he or she is afforded the opportunity to demonstrate, at reasonable intervals, that he or she is able to resume competent practice with reasonable skill and safety.[10]

(A)(4) Pharmacists

If the Board of Pharmacy determines that a pharmacist is unable to practice pharmacy with reasonable skill and safety by reason of illness, use of drugs, narcotics, chemicals, or any other type of material or as a result of any mental or physical condition,[11] or that the pharmacist is incompetent or unfit to practice pharmacy as a result of habitual intoxication or misuse or abuse of scheduled medications,[12] it may impose various sanctions, including a reprimand or probation, or suspension, restriction, or revocation of licensure. The Board of Pharmacy may also require the pharmacist to submit to treatment.[13] If a pharmacist's license is restricted in any way because of impairment, he or she is afforded the opportunity to demonstrate, at reasonable intervals, that he or she is able to resume competent practice with reasonable skill and safety.[14]

(A)(5) Physical Therapists/Physical Therapist Assistants

If the Board of Physical Therapy Practice determines that a physical therapist or physical therapist assistant is unable to practice with reasonable skill and safety as a result of illness; or use of alcohol, drugs, narcotics, chemicals; or any other type of material; or as the result of a mental or physical condition, the Department of Health (DOH) may impose various sanctions, including a reprimand or probation, or suspension, restriction, or revocation of licensure.[15] The Board of Physical Therapy Practice can also compel the physical therapist or physical therapy assistant to submit to treatment.[16] If a physical therapist's or physical therapist assistant's license is restricted in any way because of impairment he or she is afforded the opportunity to demonstrate, at reasonable

---

10. 15 FLA. STAT. ANN. § 462.14(1)(s) (West Supp. 2002).
11. 15 FLA. STAT. ANN. § 465.016(1)(m) (West Supp. 2002).
12. 15 FLA. STAT. ANN. § 465.016(1)(d) (West Supp. 2002).
13. 15 FLA. STAT. ANN. § 465.016(2) (West Supp. 2002).
14. 15 FLA. STAT. ANN. § 465.016(1)(m) (West Supp. 2002).
15. 15 FLA. STAT. ANN. § 486.125(1)(a) (West Supp. 2002); 15 FLA. STAT. ANN. § 486.125(2) (West Supp. 2002).
16. 15 FLA. STAT. ANN. § 486.125(1)(a)1 (West Supp. 2002).

intervals, that he or she is able to resume competent practice with reasonable skill and safety.[17]

(A)(6) Physicians (Medical Doctors and Osteopaths)

If the Board of Medicine or the Board of Osteopathic Medicine determines that a medical doctor or osteopath is unable to practice medicine with reasonable skill and safety as a result of an illness; or use of alcohol, drugs, narcotics, chemicals; or any other type of material; or as the result of any mental or physical condition,[18] the respective Board may impose various sanctions, including a reprimand or probation, or suspension, restriction, or revocation of licensure. The Boards may also require the medical doctor or osteopath to submit to treatment,[19] and they can compel the medical doctor or osteopath to submit to a mental or physical examination by a physician when probable cause exists to suspect such difficulties. If a medical doctor's or osteopath's license is restricted in any way because of impairment, he or she is afforded the opportunity to demonstrate, at reasonable intervals, that he or she is able to resume competent practice with reasonable skill and safety.[20]

(A)(7) Psychologists

If the Board of Psychology determines that a psychologist is unable to practice "with reasonable skill or competence as a result of any mental or physical condition or by reason of illness; drunkenness; or excessive use of drugs, narcotics, chemicals, or any other substance,"[21] it may impose various sanctions, including a reprimand or probation, or suspension, restriction, or revocation of licensure. The Board of Psychology may also require the psychologist to submit to treatment.[22] The Board of Psychology can compel the psychologist to submit to a mental or physical examination by a psychologist or physician when probable cause exists to suspect such difficulties. If a psychologist's license is restricted in any way because of impairment he or she is afforded the opportunity to demonstrate, at reasonable intervals, that he or she is able to resume competent practice with reasonable skill and safety.[23]

---

17. 15 Fla. Stat. Ann. § 486.125(1)(a)2 (West Supp. 2002).
18. 15 Fla. Stat. Ann. § 458.331(1)(s) (West Supp. 2002); 15 Fla. Stat. Ann. § 459.015(1)(w) (West Supp. 2002).
19. 15 Fla. Stat. Ann. § 458.331(2) (West Supp. 2002); 15 Fla. Stat. Ann. § 459.015(2) (West Supp. 2002).
20. 15 Fla. Stat. Ann. § 458.331(1)(s) (West Supp. 2002); 15 Fla. Stat. Ann. § 459.015(1)(w) (West Supp. 2002).
21. 15 Fla. Stat. Ann. § 490.009(1)(p) (West Supp. 2002).
22. 15 Fla. Stat. Ann. § 490.009(1) (West Supp. 2002).
23. 15 Fla. Stat. Ann. § 490.009(1)(p) (West Supp. 2002).

(A)(8) Radiologic Technologists

If the DOH determines that a radiologic technologist is unable to practice "with reasonable skill and safety to patients by reason of illness; drunkenness; or excessive use of drugs, narcotics, chemicals, or other materials or as a result of any mental or physical condition,"[24] it may impose various sanctions, including a reprimand or probation, or suspension, restriction, or revocation of licensure. The DOH may also require the radiologic technologist to submit to treatment.[25] If a radiologic technologist's license is restricted in any way because of impairment, he or she is afforded the opportunity to demonstrate, at reasonable intervals, that he or she is able to resume competent practice with reasonable skill and safety.[26]

(B) Attorneys

Attorneys are regulated by the judicial system, under rules established by the state supreme court. Therefore, the impaired practitioner programs embedded in the licensing statutes of the health care professions do not apply to attorneys.

However, if an attorney who has not been adjudicated incompetent is incapable of practicing law because of physical or mental illness, incapacity, or other infirmity, the attorney may be classified as an inactive member of the Florida Bar and is to refrain from the practice of law.[27] If an allegation is made that an attorney is incapable of practicing law because of illness, incapacity, or infirmity, the allegation is handled through the ordinary disciplinary processes of the Florida Bar. The allegation is first heard by a grievance committee, which has the power to recommend a variety of dispositions, including referral to a diversion program such as a treatment program.[28] The attorney subject to the complaint may appeal any recommendation through administrative and ultimately judicial appeals. If an attorney enters a treatment program for mental illness or substance abuse, evidence of successful treatment may be introduced in a proceeding to regain his or her status as an active attorney.[29]

Individuals who report information to a lawyer assistance program in good faith are immune from civil liability for doing

---

24. 15 FLA. STAT. ANN. § 468.3101(1)(g) (West Supp. 2002).
25. 15 FLA. STAT. ANN. § 468.3101(2) (West Supp. 2002).
26. 15 FLA. STAT. ANN. § 468.3101(1)(g) (West Supp. 2002).
27. FLA. BAR. REG. r. 3-7.13 (West 2002).
28. FLA. BAR. REG. r. 3-7.4 (West 2002).
29. FLA. BAR. REG. r. 3-10 (West 2002).

so, and treatment records are confidential subject to exceptions otherwise provided by law.[30]

(C) Impaired Practitioners Program

As noted throughout this chapter, the professions of interest have discrete statutory authority to address impaired practitioner issues through their individual boards. For professions that do not have impaired practitioner programs provided in their individual practice acts, the DOH by rule is to designate approved impaired practitioner programs.[31] The DOH is also to retain a consultant on impaired practitioner issues, and the consultant is to assist in probable cause determinations in disciplinary actions involving impairment.[32] A complaint shall not give rise to disciplinary action if the sole basis of the complaint is impairment, if the probable cause panel finds[33]

1. The licensee has acknowledged the impairment problem;
2. The licensee has voluntarily enrolled in an approved treatment program;
3. The licensee has voluntarily withdrawn from or limited the scope of his or her practice as required by the DOH's consultant; and
4. The licensee has permitted access to his or her medical records.

If the person satisfactorily completes treatment the complaint may be dismissed, but if treatment is not completed then the matter may proceed to disciplinary action.

---

30. 14 FLA. STAT. ANN. §§ 397.482; 397.483; 397.486 (West 2002).
31. 15 FLA. STAT. ANN. § 456.076 (West Supp. 2002).
32. 15 FLA. STAT. ANN. § 456.076(2) (West Supp. 2002).
33. 15 FLA. STAT. ANN. § 456.076(3)(a)(1)–(4) (West Supp. 2002).

5.2
Workers' Compensation

Workers' compensation laws are designed to compensate employees expeditiously for the loss of wage-earning capacity and other economic losses associated with workplace injury. These statutes were enacted in large part because employees found it difficult to obtain compensation through the traditional tort system. In exchange for easing compensation requirements for employee loss, the employer was assured that the employee would not seek additional compensation through negligence or other tort litigation. Although these principles have been somewhat eroded, they continue to form the basis for workers' compensation statutes.

The MHP may become involved in workers' compensation by evaluating an employee who has filed a claim or by providing treatment designed to restore the employee to work. This chapter provides a brief overview of the substantive criteria under which an employee may receive workers' compensation, a discussion of recovering for "mental disability" under Florida law, and the administrative process by which workers' compensation claims are adjudicated.

(A) Scope of the Statute

Workers' compensation statutes apply to employers meeting the following criteria: "the state and all political subdivisions thereof, all public and quasi-public corporations therein, every person carrying on any employment, and the legal representative of a deceased person or the receiver or trustees of any person."[1] The statute also provides coverage rights to any "employee," which is broadly defined as "any person engaged in any employment under any appointment or contract of hire or apprenticeship, express or implied, oral or written, whether lawfully or unlawfully employed, and includes, but is not limited to, aliens and minors."[2] However, there are a number of exceptions to workers classified as employees, including[3]

1. An independent contractor under certain conditions;
2. Real estate agents if compensated solely by commission;
3. Bands, orchestras, and other performers if it is clear contractually that they are functioning as independent contractors;
4. Owner-operators of motor vehicles transporting property for others under certain conditions;
5. A person whose employment is "casual" and not in the course of the trade, business, profession, or occupation of the employer;
6. A volunteer, except a volunteer to a governmental entity;
7. A corporate officer who elects to be exempt from coverage;
8. A sole proprietor or officer of a corporation in the construction industry;
9. An exercise horse rider who works for more than one horse farm or breeder; and
10. A taxicab or limousine driver under certain conditions.

(B) Scope of Coverage

Workers' compensation laws cover accidents, injuries, or diseases arising out of the course of employment. Florida law defines *accident* as "only an unexpected or unusual event or result that happens suddenly."[4] However, coverage is not extended to a "mental or nervous injury due to stress, fright, or excitement only . . . or . . . a disease due to the habitual use of alcohol or controlled substances or narcotic drugs."[5] Before 1997, compensation could not be obtained for emotional or mental injury unless there was a physical injury that served as an antecedent to the emotional injury claim. This policy reflected a distrust of such claims in the

---

1. 14 FLA. STAT. ANN. § 440.02(15) (West 2002).
2. 14 FLA. STAT. ANN. § 440.02(14)(a) (West 2002).
3. 14 FLA. STAT. ANN. § 440.02(14)(d) (West 2002).
4. 14 FLA. STAT. ANN. § 440.02(1) (West 2002).
5. *Id.*

absence of physical evidence of injury.[6] However, the statute now permits recovery for "mental or nervous injuries" based on a showing of clear and convincing evidence, and at least one court has concluded that as a result a predicate or concomitant physical injury is no longer required.[7]

Coverage is also restricted if there is evidence that the employee had an excessive blood alcohol level or there is confirmation of the presence of controlled substances at the time of the accident. The statute creates a framework for blood testing, and the employee has the opportunity to rebut the presumption that coverage should not be made available but can do so only by showing that there is no reasonable hypothesis that the intoxication or drug contributed to the injury.[8] The statute originally created an irrebuttable presumption that recovery could not occur in such circumstances but the state supreme court ruled that provision unconstitutional in part because of the potential inaccuracy in laboratory testing for drug and alcohol levels.[9]

(C) Processing a Claim

An employee must provide notice of an injury within 30 days of the date or initial manifestation of the injury. A failure to do so will bar recovery absent the employer's actual knowledge of the injury or an inability to identify the injury without medical opinion.[10] A formal claim for benefits generally must be filed with the Division of Workers' Compensation for the Department of Labor and Employment Security within two years of the date the employee knew or should have known the injury or death arose from work performed in the course and scope of employment.[11] After a claim is filed, the statute provides for mediation in an effort to resolve the claim without resort to a hearing.[12] If mediation does not resolve the claim, a hearing is conducted before an administrative judge of compensation claims with the procedural framework for the hearing set forth in statute.[13] Appeal from the order of the administrative judge may be brought only to the district court of appeal, First District.[14]

---

6. Egan v. Florida Atlantic University, 610 So. 2d 585 (Fla. 1st D.C.A. 1992).
7. Anderson v. Wales Industries, 688 So. 2d 379 (Fla. 1st D.C.A. 1997).
8. 14 FLA. STAT. ANN. § 440.09(7)(b) (West 2002).
9. Recchi America Inc. v Astley Hall, 692 So. 2d 153 (Fla. 1997).
10. 14 FLA. STAT. ANN. § 440.185(1) (West 2002).
11. 14 FLA. STAT. ANN. § 440.19(1) (West 2002).
12. 14 FLA. STAT. ANN. § 440.25 (West 2002).
13. 14 FLA. STAT. ANN. § 440.29 (West 2002).
14. 14 FLA. STAT. ANN. § 440.271 (West 2002).

(D) Worker's Compensation Benefits

A claimant may be compensated for lost wages, impairment of earning capacity, and medical and other expenses associated with his or her injury. In an effort to make compensation predictable both to the employer and the employee, the statute creates formulas for compensating various degrees of impairment. For example, if the employee is found to have a permanent total disability, the employee will receive 66.66% of the average weekly wage during the continuance of the disability.[15] Other formulas exist for computing compensation for various degrees of impairment. In addition, in an effort to reduce costs associated with treatment for employment-related injuries, the legislature has authorized employers to enter managed care arrangements to provide treatment to employees in workers' compensation cases.[16]

---

15. 14 FLA. STAT. ANN. § 440.15 (West 2002).
16. 14 FLA. STAT. ANN. § 440.134 (West 2002).

5.3
Vocational Disability Determinations

The Division of Vocational Rehabilitation (VR) within the Department of Labor and Employment Security is responsible for providing vocational and rehabilitation services and independent living services to persons whose disabilities prevent them from obtaining or maintaining employment or from living independently. A variety of specific service programs are offered by VR, including vocational rehabilitation services,[1] independent living rehabilitation services,[2] spinal cord rehabilitation services,[3] and limiting-disabilities rehabilitation services.[4] The MHP may be called on to assess whether an individual is appropriate for such services.

(A) Definitions

The statute defines *disability* as "a physical or mental impairment that constitutes or results in a substantial impediment to employment."[5] *Person who has a disability* means an individual with an impairment that constitutes or results in a substantial impediment to employment and as a result the individual can benefit in terms of an employment outcome from vocational rehabilitation services.[6] *Rehabilitation service* means any service, provided directly or indirectly through public or private agencies, found by VR to

---

1. 14 Fla. Stat. Ann. § 413.20(34) (West 1998).
2. 14 Fla. Stat. Ann. §§ 413.371, 413.401 (West 1998).
3. 14 Fla. Stat. Ann. § 381.76 (West Supp. 2002).
4. 14 Fla. Stat. Ann. § 413.70 (West 1998).
5. 14 Fla. Stat. Ann. § 413.20 (West 1998).
6. 14 Fla. Stat. Ann. § 413.20(16) (West 1998).

be necessary to enable a person who has a limiting disability to engage in competitive employment.[7]

(B) Recipient Eligibility Requirements

To receive vocational rehabilitation services from VR, a person must have a physical or mental disability that presents a substantial handicap to employment, for which vocational rehabilitation services may reasonably be expected to prove helpful in assisting the person to engage in gainful employment.[8]

To receive independent living services from VR, a person must have a mental or physical disability that severely limits the person's ability to engage in employment and function independently in a family or community setting. In addition, the person must be able to benefit from the provision of independent living services with regard to living or functioning independently.[9]

To receive rehabilitation services for limiting disabilities, a person must have a physical condition that constitutes, contributes, or will result in an impairment in one or more activities of daily living such as personal home care, transportation, housekeeping, shopping, attending school, communicating with others, and obtaining and maintaining employment.[10]

(C) Psychological and Psychiatric Services

Once an applicant is determined to be eligible for vocational rehabilitation services, the applicant may receive any of the following benefits designed to enable the person to seek employment, including "mental restoration treatment":[11]

1. Medical and vocational diagnosis;
2. Counseling, guidance, and placement;
3. Vocational and other training services;
4. Physical and mental restoration treatment;
5. Maintenance;

---

7. 14 FLA. STAT. ANN. § 413.20(22) (West 1998).
8. 14 FLA. STAT. ANN. § 413.30(1)–(3) (West 1998).
9. 14 FLA. STAT. ANN. § 413.401 (West 1998); special services and programming are available to persons with spinal cord injuries, see 14 FLA. STAT. ANN. § 381.76 (West Supp. 2002).
10. 14 FLA. STAT. ANN. § 413.20(2) and (13) (West 1998).
11. 14 FLA. STAT. ANN. § 413.20(34) (West 1998).

6. Interpreters (for hearing-impaired persons);
7. Recruitment and training services to provide new employment opportunities in a variety of specified fields;
8. Occupational licenses;
9. Tools, equipment, and initial stocks and supplies;
10. Transportation;
11. Technological and telecommunication aids and devices;
12. Rehabilitation technology;
13. Referrals to secure services from other agencies;
14. Transition services;
15. On-the-job or related personal assistance services; and
16. Supported employment services.

Once an applicant is determined to be eligible for independent living services, he or she may receive any of the following benefits, which include mental health services:[12]

1. Psychological and psychotherapeutic counseling;
2. Independent living care services;
3. Community education and related services;
4. Housing assistance;
5. Physical and mental health treatment;
6. Personal attendant care;
7. Transportation;
8. Personal assistance services;
9. Interpreters (for hearing-impaired persons);
10. Recreational activities;
11. Services for family members of the eligible person;
12. Vocational and other training services;
13. Telecommunication services;
14. Sensory and other technological aids and devices;
15. Preventive services; or
16. Other rehabilitative services necessary to assist with independent living needs.

Once an applicant is determined to be eligible for limiting disability rehabilitation services, he or she may receive any services considered necessary by VR to engage in activities of daily

---

12. 14 FLA. STAT. ANN. § 413.20(12) (West 1998).

living for the purpose of achieving optimal functioning. If an individual requires multiple rehabilitation services over an extended period of time or also requires occupational placement services, the individual should be served by the vocational rehabilitation program or other programs offered by VR.

5.4
Emotional Distress as a Basis for Civil Liability

A party to a civil action may ask an MHP to evaluate or treat an individual claiming damages for emotional injury caused by the conduct of another individual. Courts in Florida and elsewhere have been reluctant historically to permit monetary compensation through the tort system for such claims, in the absence of evidence that reduces the likelihood that the claim is spurious. The standard for recovery in Florida varies depending on whether the individual claims the *negligent* or *intentional* infliction of emotional distress. In either case, the claimant must demonstrate that the defendant owed a duty of care, breached that duty, and because of the breach caused injury to the claimant.

(A) Negligent Infliction of Emotional Distress

Florida courts are suspicious of claims of negligent infliction of emotional distress because of concern that such claims can be fabricated. As a result, the courts have created the *impact* rule, which directs that, in general, a claimant can recover for negligent infliction of emotional distress only if he or she suffered a direct physical impact that causes the emotional injury.[1]

There are some modest exceptions to this rule. For example, the state supreme court has held that *physical* injuries resulting from *psychological* trauma may lead to recovery.[2] The court has

---

1. Gracey v. Gracey, 1999 Fla. App. LEXIS 17606 (Fla. 5th D.C.A. 1999).
2. Zell v. Meek, 665 So. 2d 1048 (Fla. 1995).

also held that a plaintiff who did not suffer direct physical impact could recover when the plaintiff was within "the sensory perception" (for example, could see or hear the injury occur) of the physical injuries that a close family member received and where the plaintiff suffered a discernible physical injury.[3] However, even in these cases, the court insists on some physical event that can be viewed as causally related to the emotional distress.

Most important for MHPs, the Florida supreme court ruled recently that the impact rule did not bar a lawsuit against a therapist who breached confidentiality. In this case, a therapist was seeing two spouses who were having marital difficulties. The therapist divulged information given separately by each spouse to the other without authorization, with the result that their marital problems were exacerbated. The supreme court permitted their claim for emotional damages to proceed, noting that "we can envision few occurrences more likely to result in emotional distress than having one's psychotherapist reveal without authorization or justification the most confidential details of one's life."[4]

(B) Intentional Infliction of Emotional Distress

In some cases, the defendant's behavior may go beyond negligence. If a defendant acts "maliciously, willfully, wantonly, or recklessly" toward the claimant, emotional injury can be compensated even without an associated physical impact. The assumption on the part of the courts is that the defendant's intentional conduct reduces the possibility that the claim is fictitious. For example, one such claim was permitted to proceed when the defendants (who were public officials) showed film and photos of a 14-year-old who had died of a drug overdose. The family members were permitted to bring suit despite the lack of physical injury.[5]

Recovery on this claim in other circumstances still may be difficult. For example, parents whose minor daughter had been sexually abused by the defendant were not able to recover for their distress because they had not been present when the abuse occurred.[6] This outcome reflects the continuing skepticism of Florida courts for emotional distress claims, a distrust ameliorated generally only when the claimant is affected physically by the

---

3. R.J. v. Humana of Florida, Inc., 652 So. 2d 360 (Fla. 1995) (this case involved a wrongful birth claim).
4. Gracey and Gracey v. Eaker, 2002 Fla. LEXIS 2662 (2002).
5. Williams v. City of Minneola, 575 So. 2d 683 (Fla. 5th D.C.A. 1991).
6. M.M. v. M.P.S., 556 So. 2d 1140 (Fla. 3d D.C.A. 1989).

defendant's conduct (when negligence is at issue), or when the claimant is present when the conduct occurs (when intentional conduct on the defendant's part is claimed), or when the behavior is considered outrageous by the courts (e.g., the public showing of autopsy films and pictures).

(C) Emotional Distress as an Element of Damages

Damages for pain and suffering may be recovered in wrongful death actions by spouses, minor children of deceased parents, and parents of deceased minor children.[7] This is one way in which damages without a physical antecedent, or intentional conduct of the plaintiff, can be recovered for emotional harm.

---

7. 21 FLA. STAT. ANN. § 768.21(2)–(4) (West Supp. 2002).

5.5
Insanity of Wrongdoers and Civil Liability

A person's mental state may have implications for legal and financial responsibility in civil cases, just as it may have implications for responsibility in criminal cases. MHPs may be asked to assess the mental state of a person at the time that he or she allegedly committed some kind of tort or civil wrong. Therefore, it is important to understand how the law addresses mental state in such actions.

(A) The Liability of an Insane Person

In Florida, a person who has a mental illness at the time he or she commits a civil wrong may be found liable for damages, despite the mental illness. In part, this is because in negligence actions it is not required that the plaintiff prove intent; therefore, because intent is not necessary, a person with mental illness can be liable for a tort, (e.g., trespass).[1] However, at least one Florida appellate court has ruled that a person who is mentally ill and institutionalized cannot be found civilly liable for injuries inflicted by the patient on staff.[2] In addition, if a person is suffering from mental illness at the time of the wrongful or tortious act, the mental illness may (but will not necessarily) preclude liability for exemplary (i.e., punitive) damages.[3]

---

1. Kaczer v. Marrero, 324 So. 2d 717 (Fla. 3d D.C.A. 1976).
2. Mujica v. Turner, 582 So. 2d 24 (Fla. 3d D.C.A. 1991); Anicet v. Gant, 580 So. 2d 273 (Fla. 3d D.C.A. 1991).
3. Jolley v. Powell, 299 So. 2d 647 (Fla. 2d D.C.A. 1974).

(B) Insanity and Liability Insurance

Insurance policies frequently exclude coverage for intentional acts committed by the insured person. This exclusion is important in civil litigation because it may deny the plaintiff the opportunity to recover from the defendant's insurer. Previously, Florida courts ruled that if the insured person was mentally ill at the time of the wrongful act, the exclusion clause did not apply (on the ground that the mental illness prevented the person from acting intentionally), and the insurance company had to compensate the injured party.[4] However, the state supreme court overturned those decisions, ruling that "an injury inflicted by an insured who is psychotic is not an 'accident' and is an intentional act within the meaning of the policy provisions at issue if the insured intends to cause the injury even if the insured's conduct is the result of the insured's mental condition."[5]

As a result, the inquiry by the MHP in such cases will focus on the relationship, if any, between the individual's mental illness and conduct, not unlike the inquiry conducted in examinations of criminal responsibility (see chapter 7.9, Criminal Responsibility).

(C) Procedural Rights of Insane Persons

If a court has adjudicated a person incapacitated to sue and be sued, the guardian is responsible for responding to and initiating legal actions on behalf of the ward.[6]

---

4. *See, e.g.,* Stone v. George, 260 So. 2d 259 (Fla. 4th D.C.A. 1972).
5. Prasad v. Allstate Insurance Company, 644 So. 2d 992 (Fla. 1994).
6. *See* chapter 4.2, Guardianship for Adults, and 21 FLA. STAT. ANN. ch. 744 (West Supp. 2000) for matters related to guardianship procedures.

5.6
Competency to Contract

A contract is enforceable only if the individuals who entered the contract have the capacity to do so. If a person not competent to do so enters a contract, it is void and has no legal effect. Some individuals are incompetent to enter contracts because of their age (see chapter 4.1, Competency to Marry). Others may be incompetent because of a judicial finding that they lack capacity for the purpose of entering a contract (see chapter 4.2, Guardianship for Adults). Still others may be incompetent because of mental illness. If a contract is challenged on this ground, an MHP may be asked to assess the individual's competency.

(A) Legal Test of Competency to Contract

Although an inquiry into competency could be conducted before entering a contract, as a preventive measure, the vast majority of such inquiries will occur after a contract has been executed. In such cases, the legal test for competency in theory varies depending on the nature and type of contract. Complex contracts (e.g., to purchase real estate or to take out a loan) may require greater sophistication and a higher degree of capacity than more simple contracts (e.g., to purchase retail goods).

(B) Determination of Competency to Contract

Florida law presumes that persons are competent to contract.[1] Mental illness or disorder does not by itself render an individual incompetent to enter a contract. As one court, considering a challenge to a contract entered into in Florida for the sale of horses, wrote, "Mere incapacity of a party is no reason for canceling a written agreement" where the party "correctly heard and evidently understood" the terms that were agreed to as part of the contracting process.[2] A contract will be invalidated only if it is shown that the individual's mental state interfered with his or her understanding of the terms of the contract and the consequences of entering the contract. This is a functional test, and it suggests that an individual may be competent to enter into one contract but may be incompetent to enter into another, usually more complex one.

---

1. Holmes v. Burchette, 766 So. 2d 387 (Fla. 2d D.C.A. 2000); Harmon v. Williams, 596 So. 2d 1142 (Fla. 2d D.C.A. 1992).
2. Feinberg v. Leach, 243 F.2d 64, 67 (5th Cir. 1957).

5.7
Competency to Sign a Will

Individuals who write or amend a will must have the mental capacity to do so. This competency is also referred to as *testamentary capacity*. The legitimacy of a will may be questioned if it is believed that the writer was suffering from some kind of mental or physical disability that affected his or her understanding of the process. As a result, MHPs are sometimes asked to assist the court in determining the writer's mental state when the will was executed or amended. Typically, this legal inquiry is conducted after the death of the person, making the inquiry a difficult one. But there is Florida case law precedent for admission of "psychological autopsies" in legal proceedings (see chapter 6.5, Psychological/Psychiatric Autopsy).[1] Although it is done rarely, testamentary capacity may also be assessed before a person executes or amends a will (as a preventive, proactive measure) or after a person writes or amends a will but before death.

(A) Legal Test of Testamentary Capacity

Florida law directs that "any person who is 18 or more years of age who is of sound mind may make a will.[2] Case law has further defined the requirements of a "sound mind." Testamentary capacity in Florida requires that testators (i.e., will-writers) know[3]

---

1. *See* Jackson v. State, 553 So. 2d 719 (Fla. 4th D.C.A. 1989).
2. 20 FLA. STAT. ANN. § 732.501 (West Supp. 2002).
3. Hamilton v. Morgan, 112 So. 80 (Fla. 1927); *In re* Estate of Bailey, 122 So. 2d 243 (Fla. 2d D.C.A. 1961); Skelton v. Dads, 133 So. 2d 432 (Fla. 3d

1. The nature and extent of their property or possessions;
2. Their rightful or natural heirs; and
3. That they are writing a will that will determine how their possessions and property will be distributed on their death.

Evidence of mental illness or disorder in and of itself does not render someone incompetent to execute a will. A clear showing must be made that the mental disorder or impairment affected the will-writer in some way that impaired the abilities identified previously.[4]

(B) Undue Influence

In addition, wills may be challenged on the grounds that the will-writer was subject to "undue influence." In cases of undue influence it is alleged that the will writer was subject to "persuasion, duress, force, coercion, or artful or fraudulent contrivances to such an extent that there is a destruction of free agency and will power."[5] A presumption of undue influence arises on a showing that a party (a) occupied a confidential relationship with the testator, (b) was a substantial beneficiary under the will and (c) was active in processing the instrument.[6]

(C) Proving Testamentary Capacity

A person is presumed to be competent to execute a will unless someone contesting a will-writer's testamentary competence can prove lack of capacity.[7] If, however, the will-writer was previously adjudicated to be lacking capacity in some sphere (e.g., via

---

D.C.A. 1962) *In re* Estate of Dunson, 141 So. 2d 601 (Fla. 2d D.C.A. 1962); *In re* Estate of Edwards, 433 So. 2d 1349 (Fla. 5th D.C.A. 1983).
4. Zinnser v. Gregory, 77 So. 2d 621 (Fla. 1955); *In re* Estate of Joiner, 147 So. 2d 563 (Fla. 3d D.C.A. 1963); *In re* Estate of Edwards, 433 So. 2d 1349 (Fla. 5th D.C.A. 1983); Murray v. Barnett National Bank, 74 So. 2d 647 (Fla. 1954).
5. Raini v. Furlong, 702 So. 2d 1273, (Fla. 3d D.C.A., 1997).
6. Bock v. Bock, 692 So. 2d 907 (Fla. 1st D.C.A., 1997).
7. Fernstrom v. Taylor, 145 So. 208 (Fla. 1933), Myers v. Pleasant, 160 So. 204 (Fla. 1935); *In re* Estate of Perez, 206 So. 2d 58 (Fla. 3d D.C.A. 1968); *In re* Estate of Witt, 239 So. 2d 902 (Fla. 2d D.C.A. 1962); Gardiner v. Goermer, 149 So. 186 (Fla. 1933); Estate of Parson, 416 So. 2d 513 (Fla. 4th D.C.A. 1982); Estate of Bailey, 122 So. 2d 243 (Fla. 2d D.C.A., 1960).

appointment of a guardian), then the burden of proof shifts to the individual who claims that the will-writer was competent.[8] Testimony of both lay persons and MHPs may be offered to the court as it attempts to determine the will-writer's mental state when the will was executed.[9]

---

8. In re Estate of Joiner, 147 So. 2d 563 (Fla. 3d D.C.A. 1963); Skelton v. Davis, 133 So. 2d 432 (Fla. 3d D.C.A. 1961); In re Estate of Supplee, 247 So. 2d 488 (Fla. 2d D.C.A. 1971); In re Estate of Ziy, 223 So. 2d 42 (Fla. 1969). American Red Cross v. Estate of Haynsworth, 7081 So. 2d 602 (Fla. 3d D.C.A. 1998).

9. In re Estate of Frank, 338 So. 2d 2098 (Fla. 3d D.C.A. 1976); In re Estate of Hammerman, 387 So. 2d 409 (Fla. 4th D.C.A. 1980); In re Estate of Edwards, 233 So. 2d 1319 (Fla. 5th D.C.A. 1983).

5.8
Competency to Vote

Although voting is a basic right, it can be removed by the court subsequent to a showing of incapacity. MHPs may be asked to evaluate individuals alleged to lack the capacity to vote or individuals adjudicated incapacitated to vote who believe they have regained their capacity to vote (see chapter 4.2, Guardianship for Adults).

(A) Voting Requirements

Anyone who is at least 18 years of age and a citizen of the United States, the state of Florida, and the county in which the person wishes to register may register to vote. However, a person convicted of a felony or a person adjudicated incapacitated to vote in Florida or any other state is ineligible to register (if not already registered) or vote.[1] If a person convicted of a felony has his or her civil rights restored or if the person adjudicated incapacitated to vote has his or her right to vote restored, then the person may vote. The voter registration form must be worded to make it clear that a person whose civil rights or competency has been restored is not required to disclose that the right to vote had been taken away in the past.[2]

---

1. 7 FLA. STAT. ANN. § 97.041 (West Supp. 2002).
2. 7 FLA. STAT. ANN. § 97.052(2)(s) (West Supp. 2002).

(B) Legal Test of Competency to Vote or Register

Florida case law provides no direction or interpretation on the issue of "competency to vote." Like the other competencies discussed in this volume, one may assume that the test is a functional one.

(C) Cancellation of Registration

Voter registration will be cancelled and the individual will become ineligible to vote in the event it is determined that the voter is deceased, has been convicted of a felony, or has been adjudicated incompetent to vote.[3] The Florida Department of State is to contract with the Florida Association of Court Clerks to create and operate an on-line electronic voter registration data base.

---

3. FLA. STAT. ANN. § 98.0987 (West Supp. 2002).

# 5.9
Competency to Obtain a Driver's License

A license to operate a motor vehicle is considered a privilege rather than a right. The state has reserved the authority to deny a driver's license to an individual on grounds set forth in statute. It is possible that an MHP may be asked to assess whether an individual is competent to drive.

The statute prohibits award of a driver's license to an individual who is "an habitual drunkard, or is an habitual user of narcotic drugs, or is an habitual user of any other drug to a degree which renders him or her incapable of safely driving a motor vehicle."[1] If a person has been adjudged to be afflicted with or to be suffering from any mental disability or disease and has not been adjudicated as restored to competence, that person also cannot obtain a license.[2]

There is no Florida case law interpreting these provisions. Florida law does permit a person to be found incompetent to drive (see chapter 4.2, Guardianship for Adults). An MHP asked to assess a person's competency to drive most likely would be asked to assess how the person's use of alcohol or narcotics or the person's mental illness and its symptoms might interfere with the person's ability to drive a vehicle. The MHP could also conceivably be asked to assess whether the effects of psychotropic medications affect the person's ability to drive. Like other competency assessments, it may be assumed that the test of competence in this area is a functional one.

---

1. 13 FLA. STAT. ANN. § 322.05 (7) (West Supp. 2002).
2. 13 FLA. STAT. ANN. § 322.05 (8) (West Supp. 2002).

5.10
Product Liability

The term *product liability* refers to liability that may be imposed on the manufacturer of a product if an individual suffers an injury while using that product. Individuals may pursue three types of liability claims in such circumstances, including claims for negligence, breach of contract, and strict liability. This chapter addresses strict liability. The MHP with appropriate credentials may be asked either to evaluate the safety of a product that has caused injury (an infrequent type of evaluation) or to assess whether a plaintiff has suffered emotional harm as part of the injury claim.

(A) Elements of a Product Liability Claim

Florida statutes define *product liability* as "liability for any personal injury, death, emotional harm, consequential economic damage, or property damage, including damages resulting from the loss of use of such property, arising out of the manufacture, design, importation, distribution, packaging, labeling, lease, or sale of a product."[1] The term does not include liability of a person in possession of the product at the time the injury giving rise to the claim occurs.[2] This distinction is drawn because the focus of product liability is on the manufacturer, lessor, or other party that has the responsibility to ensure the safety of the product, not on the consumer or user of the product.

---

1. 18 FLA. STAT. ANN. § 627.942(7) (West 1996).
2. *Id.*

For a manufacturer to be held strictly liable (that is, the defendant will have no defense to the action if the plaintiff can prove his or her claim of a defect in the product that caused injury) the plaintiff must show "the manufacturer's relationship to the product in question, the defect and unreasonably dangerous condition of the product, and the existence of a proximate causal connection between such condition and the user's injuries or damage."[3] In addition to the manufacturer, others in the "distributive chain" may be found liable because those entities "who profit from the sale or distribution of [the product] to the public, rather than an innocent person injured by it, should bear the financial burden of even an undetectable project defect."[4]

(B) Defenses to a Product Liability Claim

In product liability claims brought against a manufacturer or seller of a product, there is a rebuttable presumption that the product is not defective or unreasonably dangerous and there is no liability if the product[5]

1. Complied with federal or state codes, rules, regulations, or other applicable standards;
2. The codes or standards in question are designed to prevent the type of harm that allegedly occurred; and
3. Compliance with codes or standards is required as a condition to sell or distribute the product in question.

There are few strict liability cases involving Florida health care providers. In one case, a federal court held that if a prescribing physician is aware of the risks presented by use of a particular product (in this case, blood that might contain the HIV virus), the physician, rather than the manufacturer, may be liable for harm caused by the product because the fact that the physician knew of the risk discharges the manufacturer's legal obligation.[6] However, it is for the manufacturer to show that the physician in such a case knew of the risks in question.

---

3. West v. Caterpillar Tractor Co., 336 So. 2d 80 (Fla. 1976); Cunningham v. General Motors Corp., 561 So. 2d 656 (Fla. 1st D.C.A. 1990).
4. Samuel Friedland Family Enterprises v. Amoroso, 630 So. 2d 1067 (Fla. 1994) (holding the lessor of a sailboat at a resort hotel subject to strict liability).
5. Fla. Stat. Ann. § 768.1256(1)(a)–(c) (West Supp. 2002).
6. Walls v. Armour Pharmaceutical Co., 832 F. Supp. 1467 (M.D. Fla. 1993).

5.11
Unfair Competition

A number of statutes are designed to ensure that competition among business competitors is conducted in a manner that provides broad choice to consumers and protects one competitor from the unfair tactics of other competitors. Antitrust laws (see chapter 3.14, Antitrust Limitations to Practice) are one example of this type of legislation. Laws prohibiting unfair competition are another and are covered briefly.

Unfair competition laws are designed to prevent people from passing off their goods or business as the goods or business of a competitor.[1] MHPs and other social scientists may be asked to conduct consumer surveys to assist in determining whether a defendant's business practices caused business confusion and to testify regarding their findings.

(A) Legal Test of Unfair Competition

The core issue in determining whether an unfair competition case will succeed is the likelihood of confusion.[2] In deciding this question, the decision maker is to examine

1. The type of trademark;
2. The similarity of the two marks;
3. Similarities of the products or service in question;

---

1. 55 FLA. JUR. 2d, Trademarks, Tradenames, and Unfair Competition, § 15 (2000).
2. Tio Pepe v. El Tio Pepe De Miami Restaurant, Inc., 523 So. 2d 1158 (Fla. 3d D.C.A. 1988).

4. Similarities of retail outlets or purchasers;
5. Similarities of advertising media used;
6. The defendant's intent; and
7. Evidence of actual confusion.

According to the courts, evidence of actual confusion is the best evidence of the likelihood of confusion.[3]

(B) Types of Confusion

There are two general types of business confusion that are prohibited as constituting unfair competition.[4] One involves *product or business confusion*—that is, creating the impression among consumers that a business is really that of another, presumably more popular competitor.[5] The other involves trademark infringement.[6]

(B)(1) Trademark Infringement

A *trademark* is "any word, name, symbol, character, design, drawing or device or any other combination . . . adopted and used by a person to identify goods made or sold by him and to distinguish them from goods made or sold by others."[7] It is illegal to appropriate the trademark or other distinguishing symbols used by another business. For example, the trademark laws prohibit, absent the consent of the trademark registrant, use of a reproduction, counterfeit copy, or other imitation of another's trademark.[8]

There are other protections provided for material used by businesses in marketing and competing. For example, trademark laws also protect *service marks* (any word, name, symbol, character, design, drawing, or device, as well as distinctive advertising features used by a business to identify itself and distinguish itself from others)[9] and *trade names* (any word, name, symbol, character, design, drawing, or combination used to identify a business).[10]

(B)(2) Product Confusion

At its core, unfair competition is a form of fraud or deceit. It is illegal to attempt to create the impression that one is conducting

---

3. *Id.*
4. 16 FLA. STAT. ANN. § 495.131 (West Supp. 2002).
5. 55 FLA. JUR. 2d, Trademarks, Tradenames, and Unfair Competition, § 18 (2000).
6. 55 FLA. JUR. 2d, Trademarks, Tradenames, and Unfair Competition, § 19 (2000).
7. 16 FLA. STAT. ANN. § 495.011(1) (West Supp. 2002).
8. 16 FLA. STAT. ANN. § 495.131 (West Supp. 2002).
9. 16 FLA. STAT. ANN. § 495.011(2) (West Supp. 2002).
10. 16 FLA. STAT. ANN. § 495.011(6) (West Supp. 2002).

business or selling the product of another in an effort to trade on the good will or popularity of the other competitor. It is also illegal to use trade secrets of a business for one's own purposes. Certain practices, however, do not violate this principle. For example, the courts have ruled that it is not illegal for a health care professional who starts his or her own practice to use patient names from a previous employer, as long as the professional had legitimate access to those names in the course of his or her previous employment.[11]

---

11. Scott v. Moses, 712 So. 2d 1242 (Fla. 4th D.C.A. 1997); Blackstone v. Dade City Osteopathic Clinic, 511 So. 2d 1050 (Fla. 2d D.C.A. 1987).

5.12
Employment Discrimination

(A) Who Is Affected by Employment Discrimination Law

Federal and state laws prohibit discriminatory employment practices by employers.[1] The Americans With Disabilities Act (ADA), effective since 1992, is a federal statute that prohibits discrimination on the basis of mental and physical disability.[2] This discussion addresses only Florida law. These laws apply to MHPs and other professionals with employees. The laws also apply to management consultants who advise employers on personnel selection, discharge, and promotion of employees. MHPs who consult to employers, particularly in the areas of employee selection and job analysis, need to be aware of both Florida law and the ADA. In addition, MHPs may be asked to evaluate individuals claiming discrimination on the basis of disability and provide testimony in administrative and legal proceedings in which such claims are pursued.

(B) Florida Civil Rights Act

The Florida Civil Rights Act of 1992 bars discrimination on the basis of race, color, religion, sex, national origin, age, handicap, or marital status.[3] It is also illegal to discriminate in employment practices against an individual who has acquired immune

---
1. 42 U.S.C. § 2000(e) (West 2000); 21 FLA. STAT. ANN. § 760.10 (West 1997).
2. 42 U.S.C. §§ 12101–12213 (West 2000).
3. 21 FLA. STAT. ANN. § 760.01(2) (West 1997).

deficiency syndrome (AIDS) or has tested positive for the human immunodeficiency virus (HIV).[4] The provisions of the Civil Rights Act are enforced by the Commission on Human Relations.

The Civil Rights Act applies to any employer having 15 or more employees for each working day in each of 20 or more calendar weeks in the current or preceding calendar year, and any agent of such a person.[5] The statute does not apply to religious corporations, associations, educational institutions, or societies that condition employment on membership in a particular religion. Such corporations and other associations may also give preference in employment to individuals who are members of the religion in question.[6] State law also prohibits discrimination in employment by any county or municipal agency, board, commission, department, or office.[7] It is important for MHPs to be aware of these laws, either in the role of employer or in providing services to employees, job applicants, or employers. This is particularly important subsequent to enactment of the ADA.

(C) Unfair Employment Practices

Florida law prohibits a variety of actions by employers and others—for example, labor organizations. Unfair employment practices include[8]

1. An employer discharging, or failing or refusing to hire an individual, or to otherwise discriminate against an individual or segregate or classify individuals in compensation, terms, conditions, or privileges of employment based on race, color, religion, national origin, age, handicap, or marital status;

2. An employment agency failing or refusing to refer for employment an individual who falls into the protected classes noted previously;

3. A labor organization excluding, expelling, or otherwise discriminating against an individual in a protected class or segregating or classifying its membership by protected categories;

4. An employer, labor organization, or joint employer–labor committee discriminating in training based on membership in a protected class;

---

4. 21 FLA. STAT. ANN. § 760.50 (West Supp. 2002).
5. 21 FLA. STAT. ANN. § 760.02(7) (West 1997).
6. 21 FLA. STAT. ANN. § 760.10(9) (West 1997).
7. 21 FLA. STAT. ANN. § 112.042(1) (West 2002).
8. 21 FLA. STAT. ANN. § 760.10 (West 1997).

5. Discriminating in licensure or certification because of race or another covered status;
6. Discriminating in advertising for employment; and
7. Discriminating against a person because of that person's opposition to practices prohibited by the statute.

Employers may take into account religion, sex, national origin, age, handicap, or marital status if that condition or status is a "bona fide occupational qualification reasonably necessary for the performance of the particular employment in question."[9] An employer may create employment and training programs designed to benefit people of a particular age group and may also take marital status into account if it is necessary to do so to implement an antinepotism policy.[10]

Note that race may not be used in this fashion, because the 14th Amendment to the U.S. Constitution prohibits discrimination based on race.[11]

---

9. 21 FLA. STAT. ANN. § 760.10(8) (West 1997).
10. *Id.*
11. U.S. CONST. amend. XIV.

Section 6

Civil and Criminal Trial Matters

6.1
Jury Selection

Attorneys consider selection of a jury to be a crucial aspect of the trial. Attorneys for each side determine who, from a pool of prospective jurors, will serve on the jury. Attorneys on both sides are motivated to influence the jury panel by excluding jurors whom they believe will not be sympathetic to their case and including jurors whom they think *will* be sympathetic. Attorneys are permitted to exclude a limited number of prospective jurors without showing cause or justification (i.e., peremptory challenges), and they are allowed to challenge an unlimited number of prospective jurors if they can demonstrate that they are biased or unsuitable in some other way (i.e., challenges for cause). With regard to challenges for cause, the judge ultimately determines whether the prospective juror will be permitted to serve or not.[1]

Mental health professionals (MHPs) and other types of trial consultants (e.g., social psychologists, sociologists) sometimes assist attorneys in jury selection. These trial consultants may also establish mock or shadow juries that allow the attorney to determine how persuasive his or her argument is either before the case goes to trial or during the course of the trial. MHPs (and other social scientists) are also sometimes asked to assess community attitudes or knowledge about an upcoming trial, and this information is sometimes offered in support of, or in opposition to, requests made by the defendant or state for a change of venue (see (B)(4) Change of Venue).

1. 33 FLA. R. CRIM. P. 3.330(c) (West 1999).

(A) Juror Qualifications

Juror qualifications are identical for criminal and civil juries. A juror must be 18 years of age or older and a citizen of the state.[2] Prospective jurors may be challenged on the grounds that a mental or physical disability renders them incapable of performing the duties of a juror.[3]

However, mental illness does not, in and of itself, preclude someone from serving as a juror.[4]

(B) Criminal Trials

(B)(1) When a Jury Is Allowed

The accused is entitled to a jury trial in all criminal cases.[5] The defendant may waive the right to a jury trial (in favor of a bench trial, in which the judge decides the verdict) with the consent of the state.[6]

(B)(2) Jury Size

Juries consist of 12 people in all death penalty cases and 6 people in all other criminal cases.[7] A person who has beliefs that preclude him or her from finding a defendant guilty of an offense that is punishable by death cannot serve as a juror in a death penalty case.[8]

(B)(3) Unanimity Requirement

Jury verdicts in all criminal cases must be unanimous.[9]

(B)(4) Change of Venue

The locale in which the criminal trial is held (i.e., the venue) may be changed when the state or defendant proves to the court that a "fair and impartial trial" cannot be held in the county in which the case is pending.[10] Jurors may also be "imported" into one

---

2. 1 FLA. STAT. ANN. § 40.01 (West 1998).
3. 23 FLA. STAT. ANN. § 913.03(2) (West Supp. 2001).
4. Jefferson County v. B.C. Lewis & Sons, 20 Fla. 980 (1884).
5. 34 FLA. R. CRIM. P. 3.251 (West 1999).
6. 33 FLA. R. CRIM. P. 3.20 (West 1999).
7. 23 FLA. STAT. ANN. § 913.10 (West 2001); 33 FLA. R. CRIM. P. 3.270 (West 1999).
8. 23 FLA. STAT. ANN. § 913.13 (West 2001).
9. 34 FLA. R. CRIM. P. 3.44 (West 1999).
10. 33 FLA. R. CRIM. P. 3.210(x) (West 1999).

jurisdiction from another if it is determined that prospective jurors in the venue are biased.[11]

(B)(5) Voire Dire

After prospective jurors are sworn in, attorneys for the state and defense are permitted to examine them (orally or with a questionnaire) collectively or individually. This questioning provides the attorneys and court with information that can be used to consider the appropriateness of excluding prospective jurors either for cause or without cause (via a peremptory challenge).

The state and defense are permitted 10 peremptory challenges if the alleged offense is punishable by death or life imprisonment; 6 peremptory challenges are permitted for each side when the alleged offense is punishable by imprisonment for more than 12 months but less than life; and each side is permitted three peremptory challenges in all other criminal proceedings.[12]

Prospective jurors may be challenged for cause if they[13]

1. Do not meet minimal juror requirements;
2. Cannot be impartial;
3. Have mental or physical disabilities that render them incapable of serving;
4. Have beliefs that prevent them from finding the defendant guilty; or
5. Have had previous interactions with the defendant or are related to the defendant or to the participating attorneys.

(C) Civil Trials

(C)(1) When a Jury Is Allowed

Either the plaintiff or defendant can request a jury trial in most civil proceedings.[14] Jury trials are not guaranteed in all civil proceedings, however (e.g., divorce, child custody, delinquency, probate of wills).[15]

(C)(2) Jury Size

In civil trials a jury need only consist of six individuals.[16]

---

11. 23 Fla. Stat. Ann. § 910.03(3) (West 2001).
12. 23 Fla. Stat. Ann. § 913.08 (West 2001); 38 Fla. R. Crim. P. 3.350 (West. 1999).
13. 23 Fla. Stat. Ann. § 913.03 (West 2001); see statute for additional and more specific grounds for disqualification.
14. 30 Fla. R. Civ. P. 1.430 (West Supp. 2002).
15. Wiggins v. Williams. 18 So. 859 (1895); 47 Am. Jur. 2d, Jury, § 39 (1992).
16. 6 Fla. Stat. Ann. § 69.071 (West 1987).

(C)(3) Unanimity Requirement

The jury verdict is to be unanimous.

(C)(4) Change of Venue

A party to a civil case may apply for a change of venue if he or she believes that he or she will not receive a fair trial because the other party has "undue influence over the minds of the inhabitants of the county" or because the party seeking the change is "so odious" to county inhabitants that a fair trial is not possible.[17] A change of venue may also be granted for the convenience of the parties or witnesses or in the interests of justice.[18] Change of venue also may occur if it is impracticable to empanel a qualified jury in the county where the action is pending[19] or in the event of judicial prejudice against a party.

(C)(5) Voire Dire

After potential jurors are sworn in, attorneys for both parties are permitted to examine them (orally or with a questionnaire) collectively or individually.[20] This questioning provides the attorneys and court with information that can be used to consider the appropriateness of excluding the prospective jurors (either for cause or without cause via a peremptory challenge).

Prospective jurors can be challenged for cause if they[21]

1. Do not meet the minimal juror requirements (see earlier discussion);
2. Have an interest in the outcome of the trial and cannot be impartial;
3. Have had previous interactions with the parties that render them partial; or
4. Are related to the parties or participating attorneys.

---

17. FLA. STAT. ANN. § 47.101 (West Supp. 2001).
18. FLA. STAT. ANN. § 47.122 (West 1994).
19. FLA. STAT. ANN. § 47.121 (West Supp. 2001).
20. 30 FLA. R. CIV. P. 1.431(a) (West Supp. 2002); 30 FLA. R. CIV. P. 1.431(b) (West Supp. 2002).
21. 30 FLA. R. CIV. P. 1. 1.431(c) (West Supp. 2002); *see* rules for additional and more specific grounds for disqualification.

6.2
Expert Witnesses

MHPs may be able to assist the jury or judge to resolve issues or understand evidence (that is primarily psychological in nature) that would not otherwise be fully understood as a function of its technical or complicated nature. As a result, MHPs are sometimes called as expert witnesses in criminal and civil proceedings. Possession of specialized knowledge by the MHP does not, in and of itself, mean that the court will recognize the MHP as an expert, allow the MHP to testify about certain issues, or rely on particular information presented by the MHP.

(A) Qualifying as an Expert Witness

MHPs can be qualified as expert witnesses if it can be demonstrated that they possess "scientific, technical or otherwise specialized knowledge"[1] as a function of "knowledge, skill, experience, training or education"[2] that will assist the judge or jury to understand the evidence offered or determine a fact at issue. The party who proposes the MHP as an expert witness must establish that the MHP has specialized knowledge with respect to the particular issue at hand. The determination of whether a proffered witness is qualified to offer an expert opinion is within the discretion of the trial judge.[3]

---

1. 6 FLA. STAT. ANN. § 90.702 (West 1999).
2. *Id.*; Horowitz v. American Motorist Insurance, 343 So. 2d 1305 (Fla. 2d D.C.A. 1977).
3. Terry v. State, 668 So. 2d 954 (Fla. 1996), *reh'g denied*; McDonnell Douglas v. Holliday, 397 So. 2d 366 (Fla. 1st D.C.A. 1981).

An MHP who is qualified to testify as an expert in any proceeding might not be qualified to testify as an expert in another type of proceeding. For example, psychiatrists who work extensively with criminal populations and are trained in the area of criminal forensic psychiatry might be qualified as experts for purposes of determining a defendant's mental state at the time of the offense, but they might not be qualified as experts in a child custody hearing if they have no specialized knowledge about child rearing, parenting, and custody issues.

Before expert testimony is offered, the party against whom it is offered may examine the proposed expert witness to determine whether the expert has a sufficient basis for his or her opinion. If it is established that the expert does not have a sufficient basis for his or her opinion, then he or she can be barred from testifying.[4]

(B) When an Expert Witness May Be Called to Testify

Admissibility of expert testimony in Florida courts is guided by the *Florida Rules of Evidence*, which largely parallel the *Federal Rules of Evidence* with the exception of permitting ultimate issue testimony with regard to criminal responsibility.

The guiding principle underlying the use of expert witnesses is that they may be called to testify when "scientific, technical, or other specialized knowledge"[5] will assist the judge or jury in understanding or determining a fact that is at issue in the trial. Proffered experts can be barred from testifying when the court determines that the subject matter about which the expert will testify does not require any special knowledge or experience,[6] or that the subject matter is outside of the proffered expert's area of expertise.[7] Before the proffered expect can testify, the court must determine that the testimony will assist the trier of fact and that the witness is adequately qualified.[8]

With regard to determining what information qualifies as scientific and is accepted by the scientific community, Florida law

---

4. 6 FLA. STAT. ANN. § 90.705(2) (West 1999).
5. 6 FLA. STAT. ANN. § 90.702 (West 1999).
6. Johnson v. State, 393 So. 2d 1069 (Fla. 1980); Lewis v. State, 572 So. 2d 908 (Fla. 1990); Jordan v. State, 694 So. 2d 708 (Fla. 1997).
7. Hall v. State, 568 So. 2d 882 (Fla. 1990); Jordan v. State, 694 So. 2d 708 (Fla. 1997).
8. Terry v. State, 688 So. 2d 954 (Fla. 1996); *reh'g denied*; Pearson v. State, 254 So. 2d 573 (Fla. 3d D.C.A. 1971), *cert. denied*, 260 So. 2d 516, *cert. denied*, 409 U.S. 879.

adheres to the *Frye* test,[9] which directs that, to introduce expert testimony deduced from a scientific principle or discovery, the principle or discovery must be sufficiently established to have gained general acceptance in the particular field in which it belongs.[10] The proponent of the proffered evidence bears the burden of proving the general acceptance of the underlying principle by a preponderance of the evidence.[11]

(C) Form and Content of Testimony

Unlike "lay witnesses" or "common witnesses" who typically can testify only about facts (e.g., what they heard, saw, felt, or smelled), expert witnesses can offer testimony in the form of opinions.[12] The information on which experts may base their opinions includes personal observation, evidence presented at trial, and data presented to the expert outside of court. The expert can rely on information that might not be admissible at trial if it is information that is "reasonably relied upon" by experts in the field.[13] Thus, MHPs can base their opinions on evaluations of a particular person, other evidence presented at trial, interviews with third parties before the trial, and a review of clinical and other types of records provided that they can demonstrate that this is part of standard mental health practice. Experts, however, cannot be used as conduits simply to introduce otherwise inadmissible hearsay evidence.[14] Expert witnesses must identify all of the underlying facts or data that form the basis of their opinion, if requested to do so, on cross-examination.[15]

An ongoing issue in the consideration of expert testimony is whether MHPs (and other types of experts) should offer testimony or opinions that answer questions that are ultimately to be answered by the judge or jury (i.e., "Was the defendant sane or insane"? "Should the father or mother be granted residential

---

9. Frye v. U.S., 293 F. 1013 (D.C. Cir. 1923); Ramirez v. State, 651 So. 2d 1164 (Fla. 1995).
10. Frye v. U.S. at 1014; Ramirez v. State, 651 So. 2d 1164 (Fla. 1995); in Flanagan v. State, 1525 So. 2d 827 (Fla. 1993), the state supreme court noted that, although the U.S. Supreme Court ruled that the *Federal Rules of Evidence* superseded the *Frye* test (Daubert v. Merrell Dow Pharmaceutical, Inc., 213 S. Ct. 2786 (1993)), Florida continued to use the *Frye* standard in determining whether the proposed testimony is scientifically valid and worthy of consideration.
11. Ramirez v. State, 651 So. 2d 1164 (Fla. 1995).
12. 6 FLA. STAT. ANN. §§ 90.701 and 90.702 (West 1999).
13. 6 FLA. STAT. ANN. § 90.704 (West 1999).
14. State v. Dupont, 659 So. 2d 405 (Fla. 2d D.C.A., 1995), *review denied*, 666 So. 2d 144, *cert. denied*, 517 U.S. 1190.
15. 6 FLA. STAT. ANN. § 90.705(1) (West 1999).

custody of the children?" "Should this person be involuntarily hospitalized?"). Some contend that MHPs (and other types of expert witnesses) should not answer such questions or offer such opinions because they are ultimately legal questions not mental health questions. Florida law, however, does not preclude expert witnesses from offering opinions that include or are identical to the ultimate legal issue that is to be decided by the judge or jury.[16]

(D) Learned Treatises

Learned treatises are statements of facts or opinions on a subject of science or specialized knowledge that are contained in professional books or periodicals (e.g., scientific journals) and that may be used in the cross-examination of an expert witness if the expert witness recognizes the author of the publication to be authoritative or if the court recognizes the author to be authoritative and rules that the publication is relevant to the subject at hand.[17] Thus, on cross-examination, the opposing attorney may challenge the expert's opinions with published materials if the expert acknowledges, or the presiding judge rules, that the publication is authoritative and relevant. Authoritative work cannot be introduced as independent evidence or to bolster the expert's testimony, however.[18]

---

16. 6 FLA. STAT. ANN. § 90.703 (West 1999). *But see* Siebert v. Bayport Beach & Tennis Club, 573 So. 2d 889 (Fla. 2d D.C.A. 1990), *review denied*, 583 So. 2d 1034, for an opposing view.
17. 6 FLA. STAT. ANN. § 90.706 (West 1999).
18. Medina v. Children's Hospital; 438 So. 2d 183 (Fla. 3d D.C.A. 1983); City of St. Petersburg v. Ferguson, 193 So. 2d 648 (Fla. 2d D.C.A. 1966), *cert. denied*, 201 So. 2d 556 (Fla. 1966).

6.3
Polygraph Evidence

The use of polygraph examinations is a controversial topic. They are most commonly used in criminal investigations and employment investigations. Florida law also mandates their use as part of treatment and oversight of individuals convicted of certain types of sexual offenses (see chapter 7.21, Services for Sex Offenders).

(A) Polygraph Examination Definition

The term *polygraph* (which means "many writings") refers to the simultaneous recording of a number of physiological activities. A polygraph exam will include the collection of physiological data from at least three systems in the human body. These include recording respiratory data as well as sweat gland activity and cardiovascular activity.

(B) Licensure of Polygraph Examiners

Florida does not license or certify polygraph examiners.

(C) Admissibility of Polygraph Examinations

Polygraph examinations are not admissible to prove the guilt or innocence of a defendant.[1] Polygraph results may be admitted at trial only on the agreement or stipulation of both parties.[2]

---

1. Kaminski v. State, 63 So. 2d 339 (Fla. 1952).
2. Davis v. State, 520 So. 2d 572 (Fla. 1988).

6.4
Competency to Testify

Courts exclude testimony that is unreliable or that may mislead the judge or jury. Thus, the issue of competency to testify may be raised if it is believed that the proposed witness has some kind of disability that renders his or her testimony unreliable or invalid. Mental illness, mental retardation, or age may sometimes be offered as predicate "conditions" that render a potential witness incompetent to testify.

The judge is obligated to make inquiries into the competency of a proposed witness when the question is raised by one of the parties. The judge may seek the assistance of an MHP in assessing the allegedly incompetent witness to gauge the witness's understanding of issues relevant to testifying.

(A) Legal Test of Competency to Testify

In Florida, "every person is competent to be a witness, except as otherwise provided by statute,"[1] providing that the person understands the duty to tell the truth and is capable of expressing him- or herself in a way that is understandable to others.[2] Case law also suggests that the court can conduct an inquiry into the ability of the proposed witness to form and remember accurate

---

1. 6 FLA. STAT. ANN. § 90.601 (West 1999).
2. 6 FLA. STAT. ANN. § 90.603 (West 1999); Hawk v. State, 718 So. 2d 159 (Fla. 1998); Rutherford v. Moore, 774 So. 2d 637 (Fla. 2000).

impressions of facts and observations and that the inability to do so might be grounds for being ruled incompetent to testify.[3]

There is considerable case law establishing that mentally ill,[4] mentally retarded,[5] and drug addicted[6] persons are competent to testify, providing that they meet the criteria identified earlier. Similarly, Florida case law establishes that age, in and of itself, is not a bar to testifying.[7]

(B) Special Procedures for Victims and Witnesses Under Age 16

In accordance with the U.S. Supreme Court's decision in *Maryland v. Craig*,[8] state law allows some victims or witnesses younger than 16 years of age to testify via videotape or closed circuit television rather than testify in open court.[9] For this to be permitted, the court must determine that the minor victim or witness would suffer at least moderate emotional or mental harm as the result of coming into contact with the defendant while testifying in open court.[10] To assist the court in determining whether special procedures are necessary, MHPs may be asked to examine the minor and testify about the possible effects that testifying in open court and confronting the defendant might have on him or her.[11]

---

3. Rutherford v. Moore, 774 So. 2d 637 (Fla. 2000); Clinton v. State, 43 So. 312 (Fla. 1907); Harrold v. Schluep, 264 So. 2d 431 (Fla. 4th D.C.A. 1972); Griffin v. State, 526 So. 2d 752 (Fla. 1st D.C.A. 1988); Fuller v. State, 669 So. 2d 273 (Fla. 2nd D.C.A. 1996); Seccia v. State, 689 So. 2d 354 (Fla. 1st D.C.A. 1997); Baker v. State, 674 So. 2d 199 (Fla. 4th D.C.A. 1996).
4. Florida Power & Light Co. v. Robinson, 68 So. 2d 406 (1954).
5. McKinnies v. State, 315 So. 2d 211 (Fla. 1st D.C.A. 1975); Kaelin v. State, 410 So. 2d 1355 (Fla. 4th D.C.A. 1982).
6. Collie v. State, 267 So. 2d 352 (Fla. 3d D.C.A. 1972).
7. Cochran v. State, 117 So. 2d 544 (Fla. 3d D.C.A. 1960); Cross v. State, 103 So. 636 (Fla. 1925); Johnson v. State, 59 So. 894 (Fla. 1912); Clinton v. State, 43 So. 312 (Fla. 1907); McKinnies v. State, 315 So. 2d 211 (Fla. 1st D.C.A. 1975); Davis v. State, 264 So. 2d 31 (Fla. 4th D.C.A. 1972); Harrold v. Schluep, 264 So. 2d 431. (Fla. 4th D.C.A. 1972); Hall v. State, 260 So. 2d 881 (Fla. 2d D.C.A. 1972); Swain v. State, 172 So. 2d 3 (Fla. 3d D.C.A. 1972); Robinson v. State, 70 So. 595 (Fla. 1916); Romero v. State, 341 So. 2d 263 (Fla. 3d D.C.A. 1977); Williams v. State, 400 So. 2d 471 (Fla. 5th D.C.A. 1981), aff'd., 406 So. 2d 1115 (Fla. 1981); Rivet v. State, 556 So. 2d 521 (Fla. 5th D.C.A. 1990); Begley v. State, 483 So. 2d 70 (Fla. 4th D.C.A. 1986).
8. 497 U.S. 836 (1990).
9. 6 FLA. STAT. ANN. § 92.53 (West Supp. 2000); 6 FLA. STAT. ANN. § 92.54 (West 1999).
10. 6 FLA. STAT. ANN. § 92.53(1) (West Supp. 2000); 6 FLA. STAT. ANN. § 92.54(1) (West 1999).
11. Leggett v. State, 565 So. 2d 315 (Fla. 1990).

For these special techniques to be used, a motion must first be filed requesting that the minor testify via videotape or closed circuit television in lieu of testifying in the courtroom. The presiding judge must find that the minor will be harmed by confronting the defendant (see earlier discussion).[12] This finding must be specific to the particular witness,[13] and the judge must make a finding of fact in the record regarding the child's risk of harm.[14]

When the minor's testimony is videotaped, the defendant and his or her attorney have the right to be present during the testimony. The court may require that the defendant view the minor witness's testimony outside the presence of the minor by way of a two-way mirror or similar device, but the defendant must be able to observe and hear the witness.[15]

When the minor's testimony is offered live via closed circuit television, the court must permit the defendant to observe and hear the testimony of the minor and ensure that the minor cannot hear or see the defendant. The defendant's attorney must be able to cross-examine the child via the closed circuit process.[16]

(C) Testimony of Rape Victims

Florida has a statute, often referred to as the Rape Victim Shield Statute, that establishes certain rules governing the testimony of victims of rape. The statute provides that the victim's testimony need not be corroborated to convict the defendant.[17] A trial court may not order a psychological examination of the victim simply because there is no corroboration of her account.[18] If the defendant claims that the victim consented, then evidence of the victim's mental incapacity is admissible to prove that consent was not knowing, intelligent, or voluntary.[19]

---

12. 6 FLA. STAT. ANN. § 92.53(1) (West Supp. 2000); 6 FLA. STAT. ANN. § 92.54(1) (West 1999).
13. Gaither v. State, 581 So. 2d 922 (Fla. 2d D.C.A. 1991); Leggett v. State, 555 So. 2d 315 (Fla. 1990); Ritchie v. State, 720 So. 2d 261 (Fla. 1st D.C.A. 1998).
14. 6 FLA. STAT. ANN. § 92.53(7) (West 2000); 6 FLA. STAT. ANN. § 92.54(5) (West 1999).
15. 6 FLA. STAT. ANN. § 92.53(4) (West Supp. 2000).
16. 6 FLA. STAT. ANN. § 92.54(4) (West Supp. 2000).
17. 22 FLA. STAT. ANN. § 794.022(1) (West 2000).
18. State v. Camejo, 641 So. 2d 109 (Fla. 5th D.C.A. 1995).
19. 22 FLA. STAT. ANN. § 794.022(4) (West 2000).

6.5
Psychological/ Psychiatric Autopsy

A decedent's mental state or behavior at an earlier point in time is sometimes relevant to a legal question. The court may ask an MHP to evaluate a deceased person's mental state at an earlier point in time to help determine a legal issue. Such an evaluation is referred to as a *psychological autopsy* or *psychiatric autopsy*. Most typically, psychological autopsies may be requested to assist in determining whether a deceased person's death was accidental or a suicide (which might be relevant to disbursal of life insurance benefits) or to assist in determining whether a deceased person was competent to execute a will (see chapter 5.7, Competency to Sign a Will). Psychological autopsies have been used less frequently in criminal litigation.

(A) Admissibility of Psychological Autopsies

The admissibility of psychological or psychiatric autopsies has been addressed in only two reported Florida cases. In *Jackson v. State*,[1] the defendant allegedly forced her teenage daughter to work as a stripper, and the daughter eventually committed suicide. The prosecution retained a psychiatrist who conducted a psychiatric autopsy of the daughter and concluded that "the nature of the relationship of the defendant and her daughter was a substantial contributing factor in the daughter's decision to commit suicide."[2] The defendant mother was convicted of criminal

---
1. Jackson v. State, 553 So. 2d 719 (Fla. 4th D.C.A. 1989).
2. *Id.*

child abuse. The mother appealed, in part, on the grounds that the psychiatrist's testimony was admitted inappropriately. The appellate court affirmed the trial court's decision and ruled that "psychological autopsy is accepted in the field of psychiatry [and] the trial judge acted within his discretion in admitting the evidence at trial."[3] The court added that it did not perceive any legal distinction between psychological autopsies and mental state at the time of the offense evaluations (i.e., criminal responsibility or sanity).

In the only other reported case in Florida (*Sysn v. State*),[4] a trial court's decision to bar a psychologist's testimony based on results of a psychological autopsy was affirmed. Sandra Sysn, who was convicted of first-degree murder, contended that the victim was suicidal and provoked her into killing her, and that she (Sysn) acted in self-defense. Sysn alleged that the trial court wrongfully prevented the defense from calling a psychologist who was prepared to testify that the decedent victim was suicidal, based on the results of his psychological autopsy. The appellate court, while acknowledging that psychological autopsies were an accepted technique used by MHPs, distinguished this case from *Jackson* and affirmed the trial court's decision and verdict.

This indicates that there is some precedent in Florida courts for admitting testimony based, in part, on psychological autopsies. The courts, however, may restrict under what conditions and for what purposes such testimony may be offered.

---

3. *Id.* at 720.
4. 756 So. 2d 1058 (Fla. 4th D.C.A. 2000).

6.6

Battered Woman's Syndrome

The majority of states permit expert testimony about battered spouse syndrome either as part of an insanity defense claim or as the basis of a claim of self-defense. It has also been used to explain to the decision maker why the victim did not leave the environment in which abuse occurred. MHPs may be called on to examine and testify about a criminal defendant (usually female) who has killed or seriously injured someone (typically a spouse or partner) whom the defendant alleges has battered her or him over a period of time before the defendant responded.

(A) Legal Test of Battered Woman's Syndrome

The controlling Florida case regarding the admissibility of expert testimony on this issue is *State v. Hickson*.[1] In this case, the supreme court ruled that expert testimony regarding battered spouse syndrome is admissible as the basis for a claim of insanity or self-defense. In its decision to admit such evidence, the supreme court applied a three-part test, determining whether (a) the expert was qualified to give an opinion on the subject; (b) the state of scientific knowledge permitted a reasonable opinion to be given by the expert; and (c) the subject matter of the expert opinion was so related to some science, profession, business, or occupation as to be beyond the understanding of the average layperson. The court found that battered spouse syndrome evidence met this test, be-

---

1. 630 So. 2d 172 (Fla. 1993).

cause "the scientific principles . . . relative to the battered woman's syndrome are now firmly established and widely accepted in the scientific community . . . the syndrome has now gained general acceptance in the relevant scientific community as a matter of law."[2]

An expert can describe the syndrome generally, discuss the characteristics of a person suffering from the syndrome, and respond to hypothetical questions based on facts in evidence in the case. However, to offer an opinion about whether the defendant suffered from the syndrome, based on an examination of the defendant, the defense must first notify the state that such testimony will be offered[3] and provide the state with the opportunity to examine the defendant with its own experts.[4]

In contrast to the *Hickson* case, the state supreme court found that child sexual abuse accommodation syndrome did not meet this test and so rejected expert testimony offered on that issue (see chapter 6.10, Child Sexual Abuse Syndrome, for a discussion of syndrome testimony regarding sexual abuse).

(B) Raising the Battered Woman's Syndrome Defense

Evidence regarding the battered woman's syndrome can be raised not as a mental state defense but as part of the defense of self-defense. As an early Florida court opinion addressing the issue put it:[5]

> We think there is a difference between offering expert testimony as to the mental state of an accused in order to directly "explain and justify criminal conduct," and the purpose for which the expert testimony was offered in the instant case. In this case, a defective mental state on the part of the accused is not offered as a defense as such. Rather, the specific defense is self-defense which requires a showing that the accused reasonably believed it was necessary to use deadly force to prevent imminent death or great bodily harm to herself or her children. The expert testimony would have been offered in order to aid the jury in interpreting the surrounding circumstances as they affected the reasonableness of her belief. The factor upon which the expert testimony would be offered was secondary to the defense asserted.

---

2. *Id.* at 174.
3. FLA. R. CRIM. P. 3.201 (West 1999).
4. This requirement is similar to that described in 33 FLA. R. CRIM. P. 3.216(c) (West 1999).
5. Hawthorne v. State, 408 So. 2d 801 (Fla. 1st D.C.A. 1982).

Therefore, battered woman's syndrome is raised as part of a claim of self-defense not as a defense as to mental state—for example, diminished capacity.

(C) Standard of Proof

Because battered woman's syndrome is part of a defense of self-defense, the burden of proof in such a case is the same as it is in cases in which the defendant claims self-defense. In such cases, the state has the burden of proving its case beyond a reasonable doubt, including proving beyond a reasonable doubt that the defendant did not act in self-defense.[6] If the evidence on battered woman's syndrome raises a reasonable doubt in the fact finder's mind regarding the state's case, then the defense of self-defense should prevail.

---

6. Bolin v. State, 297 So. 2d 317 (Fla. 3d D.C.A. 1974).

6.7

Rape Trauma Syndrome

Rape trauma syndrome is considered to be a stress disorder often experienced by victims of sexual assault. Attempts have been made to introduce expert testimony regarding the presence of rape trauma syndrome in an alleged victim of a sexual assault to prove that an assault has occurred. For example, in a criminal proceeding in which the key issue is whether or not the alleged victim consented to sexual activity, the prosecution might attempt to present the expert testimony of an MHP, who has determined that the alleged victim is suffering from rape trauma syndrome, posttraumatic stress disorder, or another type of stress disorder in an attempt to prove that a sexual assault did indeed occur. A similar attempt could be made by the plaintiff in a civil proceeding in which an assault is alleged. Accordingly, MHPs may be called to examine a person with regard to whether he or she displays symptoms consistent with rape trauma syndrome, posttraumatic stress disorder, or another type of stress disorder to prove the occurrence or nonoccurrence of the alleged assault.

Although the admissibility of testimony regarding rape trauma syndrome per se has not been addressed in a reported opinion, the Fourth District court of appeals decision in *Clark v. State*[1] provides considerable direction. In this case the appellant, who was convicted of sexual battery and burglary of a dwelling, argued that the trial court improperly allowed an expert to testify that the alleged victim suffered from posttraumatic stress disorder, which, in turn, was used as evidence that the alleged victim did not consent to the sexual contact. The

---

1. 654 So. 2d 984 (Fla. 4th D.C.A. 1995).

Fourth District court of appeals affirmed the conviction. Of considerable interest is that this decision differs from the Florida supreme court's decision regarding admissibility of testimony regarding symptoms of child sexual abuse to prove the occurrence of child sexual abuse (see chapter 6.10, Child Sexual Abuse Syndrome).

6.8
Hypnosis of Witnesses

MHPs may be asked to hypnotize witnesses in an effort to improve the witness's memory. In theory, hypnosis may lead to better recall. However, the courts are reluctant to admit hypnotically refreshed testimony in Florida.

(A) Hypnotically Induced Information in a Police Investigation

Although police may find it useful to use hypnosis in eliciting evidence, the reluctance of the courts to admit it makes this a not particularly effective investigative technique. In one interesting case, a defendant argued that incriminating statements she made regarding her participation in a homicide should be excluded because earlier hypnosis by law enforcement officials (in which she did not make self-incriminating statements) rendered her psychologically vulnerable. However, the court rejected this challenge, in part because the hypnosis had occurred two months before the challenged statements.[1]

---

1. Wiley v. State, 427 So. 2d 283 (Fla. 1st D.C.A. 1983).

(B) Hypnotically Induced Courtroom Testimony

As noted, Florida courts are reluctant to admit hypnotically induced testimony. In 1985, the state supreme court ruled that hypnotically refreshed testimony was inadmissible because of its inherent unreliability.[2] The court has described hypnosis as "an altered state of awareness or perception . . . [during which] the subject is placed in an artificially induced state of sleep or trance through a series of relaxation and concentration techniques."[3]

At the same time, memories that the witness reports or relays *before* the hypnotic session may be presented in court, providing that it can be shown that those memories in fact were reported before the hypnosis occurred.[4] In addition, an MHP testifying as an expert may provide testimony that relies in part on material provided by the defendant while under hypnosis, and defendants who have been hypnotized for the purpose of assisting with their memory cannot be barred from testifying on their own behalf.[5] Hearing testimony from a defendant whose memory has been hypnotically refreshed represents an exception to the general rule, noted earlier, that bars hypnotically refreshed testimony in Florida. The supreme court, in creating this exception, described the use of hypnosis as an "evolving issue" and imposed a number of safeguards before such testimony can be permitted, including the provision of notice to the other party and the recording of the hypnosis session.

---

2. Bundy v. State, 471 So. 2d 9 (Fla. 1985), *cert. denied*, 479 U.S. 894 (1986).
3. Stokes v. State, 548 So. 2d 188, 190 (Fla. 1989).
4. *Id.*
5. Morgan v. State, 537 So. 2d 973 (Fla. 1989).

6.9
Eyewitness Identification

Eyewitness testimony is often critical in both civil and criminal trials. The state supreme court has ruled that the decision to admit such expert testimony falls within the discretion of the trial judge, and the decision by the judge to admit or exclude such testimony will be given broad latitude by appellate courts.[1]

(A) Admissibility of Expert Testimony on Eyewitness Identification

The test applied by the trial court is whether expert testimony will assist the jury in decision making by providing information ordinarily unavailable to laypersons. For example, in a recent case[2] a trial court rejected a contention by the defense that an expert could usefully provide testimony at trial on six issues, including that (a) eyewitness identifications are incorrect much more than the average person thinks; (b) a witness's confidence in the identification is unrelated to the accuracy of the identification; (c) cross-racial identifications are more difficult than same-race identifications; (d) it is easier for a person to remember a face than to remember the circumstances in which the person saw

---

1. McMullen v. State, 714 So. 2d 318 (Fla. 1998); Rodgers v. State, 511 So. 2d 526 (Fla. 1987).
2. McMullen v. State, 714 So. 2d 318 (Fla. 1998).

the face; (e) the accuracy of facial identifications decreases in stressful situations; and (f) the accuracy of identification decreases with time. The court's decision to exclude this testimony on the grounds that it was unnecessary for jury decision making was upheld by the supreme court.

6.10
Child Sexual Abuse Syndrome

In the context of a criminal proceeding, a prosecutor may attempt to introduce expert testimony from an MHP that a child exhibits evidence of this syndrome, thereby buttressing a claim that the child, in fact, had been the victim of sexual abuse. Use of such testimony may be proffered particularly when a child's testimony may be questioned because of the child's age.

The state supreme court, however, in a 1997 decision, ruled that this syndrome (called "child sexual abuse accommodation syndrome" by the court) lacked sufficient scientific acceptance to be admitted at a criminal trial.[1] Specifically, the court ruled that a qualified psychologist could not testify that an alleged victim in a sexual abuse case exhibited symptoms consistent with those of a child who had been sexually abused.

In reaching this conclusion, the court had first to consider whether the *Frye* test would be applied to expert testimony on the issue of child sexual abuse accommodation syndrome. In *Frye v. United States*,[2] a federal appellate court announced standards for determining whether scientific theories should be permitted in court. The standard governs admission of scientific evidence in the Florida courts. Under this test, the trial court must determine whether new or novel scientific evidence shall be admitted. The trial court can admit the evidence only if it has met "general acceptance" within the scientific community. In defining "general acceptance" the state supreme court means "acceptance by a clear majority of the members of the relevant scientific community, with

---

1. Hadden v. State, 690 So. 2d 573 (1997).
2. 293 F. 1013 (D.C. Cir. 1923).

consideration by the trial court of both the quality and quantity of those opinions."[3]

The supreme court applied this test to this syndrome in a case in which it considered the conviction of a man charged with sexual battery on a person under 12 (the conviction by jury was for a lesser charge of lewd assault). At trial, the court permitted testimony from a mental health counselor, over the defendant's objection, concerning symptoms and diagnostic criteria typically associated with sexually abused children. The defendant argued that there was insufficient scientific reliability underlying this expert testimony and that the expert had failed to identify enough diagnostic criteria to give an adequate description of the child's condition.

The state supreme court ruled first that the *Frye* test had to be applied by the trial court before admitting the evidence. The court then ruled that child sexual abuse accommodation syndrome "has not to date been found to be generally accepted in the relevant scientific community."[4] The court noted that there was continuing debate among experts regarding whether this syndrome was an adequate therapeutic tool for determining the presence of abuse but that there was no consensus among experts that it was useful as substantive evidence of guilt or that abuse had indeed occurred.

This gets to the heart of the hesitancy among some courts to admit new theories that rely on syndromes; the courts are concerned that when an expert describes a syndrome and suggests that the victim exhibits characteristics of that syndrome, the jury will infer that the person was in fact the victim of a crime that the defendant committed. Because in this particular case the court found no consensus in the scientific community that this particular syndrome provided evidence of the guilt of a particular defendant, the court excluded it on the ground that it did not meet standards for admitting new or novel scientific theories.

---

3. Brim v. State, 695 So. 2d 268 (1997).
4. *Id.* at 577.

6.11
Profiles or Propensity of Sexual Offenders

In some child sexual abuse and sexual assault cases, attempts have been made to introduce expert testimony regarding the psychological or behavioral characteristics or profiles of child sexual abusers or rapists and the degree to which the defendant does or does not exhibit these characteristics or does or does not match a particular profile. Such may be attempted to prove or disprove that a defendant was or was not likely to have committed the criminal act in question. MHPs may be asked to examine a defendant and offer testimony regarding the degree to which a defendant does nor does not fit such a profile. However, the courts have been reluctant to admit such testimony, as noted next.

The state supreme court has ruled that expert testimony regarding the degree to which a defendant does or does not fit a sexual abuser profile may not be admitted.[1] The court found that such evidence does not meet the *Frye*[2] requirements for the admission of expert testimony. The court wrote, "Profile testimony ... by its nature necessarily relies on some scientific principle or test, which implies an infallibility not found in pure opinion testimony. The jury will naturally assume that the scientific principles underlying the expert's conclusion are valid ... it is virtually uncontested that sex offender profile evidence cannot meet this test ... sexual offender profile evidence is not generally accepted in the scientific community."[3] Therefore, such evidence is not admissible.

---

1. Flanagan v. State, 625 So. 2d 827 (Fla. 1993).
2. *See* chapter. 6.10, Child Sexual Abuse Syndrome, for a discussion of Frye v. U.S., 293 F. 1013 (D.C. Cir. 1923), and its application to expert testimony in Florida.
3. *Flanagan*, 625 So. 2d at 827–828.

Section 7

Criminal Matters

7.1
Screening of Police Officers

Unlike some states,[1] Florida does not require that prospective law enforcement or correctional officers undergo examination by an mental health professional (MHP) as a condition of employment.

Some law enforcement agencies, however, may require evaluation by an MHP as part of the examination process for prospective law enforcement officers. The nature and scope of psychological evaluations conducted with law enforcement officers is affected by the Americans With Disabilities Act[2] and the examinee's standing with the law enforcement agency.

---

1. *See, e.g.*, TEX. GOV'T CODE ANN. § 415.057 (Vernon Supp. 1988).
2. Pub. L. No. 101-336, 42 U.S.C. §§ 12101 et seq. (West 2002).

# 7.2
Competency to Waive the Rights to Silence, Counsel, and a Jury

Individuals charged with a crime have a number of rights that are based on constitutional principles. These include the right to remain silent, the right to counsel, and the right to trial by jury. These rights may be waived, but to do so the person must be competent. This chapter discusses the issue of competency to waive these core rights.

(A) Right to Silence

The U.S. Supreme Court, in *Miranda v. Arizona*,[1] established a constitutional right to remain silent during an interrogation by the police. The case attempted to give force to the constitutional right against self-incrimination. As a result of this decision, defendants who confess to a crime without the advice of counsel sometimes challenge that confession based on an argument that their decision to waive their right to remain silent was not made voluntarily, knowingly, and intelligently.

In making such a challenge, the presence of mental disorder alone will not render a confession invalid because mental disorder does not automatically render an individual incompetent. For example, in one case, a court upheld a confession to homicide even though the defendant had an IQ of 62 and the intellectual capacity of an 11-year-old child.[2] Other courts have reached simi-

---

1. 384 U.S. 436 (1966).
2. Moore v. Dugger, 856 F.2d 129 (11th Cir. 1988). For a more in-depth discussion of the legal aspects of the *Miranda* rights process for minors, *see* Florida Bar. (1999). *Florida juvenile law and practice* (6th ed.). Tallahassee: Florida Bar Continuing Education Publications.

lar conclusions.³ Therefore, it is important for the MHP evaluating the competency of an individual who has waived the right to remain silent to distinguish between the existence of mental disorder and its impact on functioning (a caution that applies to all assessments of competency). When considering the admissibility of a confession the court considers the "totality of the circumstances." Factors that the court will consider include the defendant's age, experience with the legal system, education, background, intelligence, reading ability, state at time of the interrogation (e.g., coherence, demeanor, memory, physical condition), as well as situational factors surrounding the interrogation (e.g., time and length of interrogation).⁴

(B) Right to Counsel

The right to be represented by counsel is guaranteed by the Sixth Amendment to the Constitution and was made applicable to the states by the Supreme Court in 1963.⁵ The right is also guaranteed by the Florida constitution.⁶ An individual who wishes to waive the right to be represented by counsel must do so knowingly, voluntarily, and intelligently.⁷ The court must hold a separate hearing to determine whether a defendant who has waived the right to counsel is competent to represent him- or herself.⁸

A waiver will not be accepted if the defendant appears to the court to be unable to make a voluntary, knowing, and intelligent choice because of mental condition, age, education, experience, the nature or complexity of the case, or other factors.⁹ Therefore, before a defendant is permitted to waive the right to be represented by counsel, the court must satisfy itself that the defendant is competent to do so. Requests for MHPs to evaluate this question specifically are rare.

---

3. Hayes v. State, 581 So. 2d 121 (Fla. 1991), upholding a homicide confession by a defendant with low intellectual functioning and a history of alcohol abuse.
4. Fare v. Michael C., 442 U.S. 707 (1979); Gallegos v. Colorado, 370 U.S. 49 (1962); State v. Word, 48 Fla. Supp. 2d 182 (Fla. 2d D.C.A. 1991); T.S.R. v. State, 741 So. 2d 1142 (Fla. 3d D.C.A. 1999); State v. Crosby, 599 So. 2d 138 (Fla. 5th D.C.A. 1992).
5. Gideon v. Wainwright, 372 U.S. 335 (1963).
6. FLA. CONST. art. I, § 16.
7. Faretta v. California, 422 U.S. 806 (1975).
8. Kleinfeld v. State, 363 So. 2d 937 (Fla. 4th D.C.A. 1990).
9. 33 FLA. R. CRIM. P. 3.111(d)(3) (West 1999); Reilly v. State Dept. of Corrections, 847 Fla. Supp. 951 (M.D. Fla. 1994); Toussaiut v. State, 677 So. 2d 853 (Fla. 1st D.C.A., 1995).

(C) Right to Waive a Jury Trial

The right of a defendant to trial by jury is discussed in chapter 6.1, Jury Selection. A defendant may waive the right only with the consent of the state, and the waiver must be knowing, intelligent, and voluntary.[10] In capital cases, the defendant may waive the right to be sentenced by a jury only if the waiver is voluntary and intelligently made.[11] This represents the general rule for waiver of a jury as well: It will be permitted only if the waiver is knowing, intelligent, and voluntary.[12] As with the other waivers discussed in this chapter, mental disorder (e.g., mental retardation, mental illness) may be a factor in judging the defendant's competence to waive this right if the disorder creates functional limitations regarding the defendant's ability to assess the consequences of waiver.

---

10. 33 FLA. R. CRIM. P. R. 3.260 (West 1999); Washington v. State, 414 So. 2d 522 (Fla. 3d D.C.A. 1981); Baker v. State, 269 So. 2d 767 (Fla. 3d D.C.A. 1972).
11. Palmes v. State, 397 So. 2d 648 (Fla. 1981).
12. Smith v. State, 539 So. 2d 601 (Fla. 3d D.C.A. 1989).

7.3
Precharging and Pretrial Intervention Programs

Some persons charged with crimes may be diverted from the criminal justice system via precharging and pretrial intervention programs. These programs are designed to provide necessary mental health, substance abuse, educational, medical, and supervision services to people whose criminal behavior is considered to result from or be related to emotional, behavioral, or substance abuse problems. MHPs may be asked to evaluate persons with regard to their specific treatment needs, appropriateness for such treatment, or intervention programs. MHPs may also be involved as service providers for persons participating in these programs.

(A) Eligibility for Pretrial Intervention Programs

Defendants who are eligible for these programs include a first-time offender or a defendant previously convicted of not more than one nonviolent misdemeanor who is charged with any misdemeanor or felony of the third degree (punishable by up to five years imprisonment). Approval must be granted by the administrator of the pretrial program, as well as the victim, the state attorney, and the judge who presided at the initial appearance hearing of the offender.[1] The defendant also, after consultation with counsel, must voluntarily agree to enter the program and knowingly and intelligently waive speedy trial rights for the period in which he or she is participating in the diversion program.

---

1. 24 FLA. STAT. ANN. § 948.08(2) (West Supp. 2002).

It is impermissible for the defendant or the defendant's immediate family to contact the victim or the victim's immediate family to acquire the victim's consent for diversion.

After the defendant is released to the program, the criminal charges are continued without final disposition for a period of 90 days if the offender's participation in the program is satisfactory and for an additional 90 days on the request of the program administrator and consent of the state attorney.[2] However, if the program administrator or state attorney finds that the offender is not fulfilling his or her obligations under the diversion plan, then prosecution may be resumed.[3]

Persons charged with the purchase or possession of controlled substances and who have not been previously convicted of a felony or admitted to a pretrial intervention program are eligible for admission into an approved pretrial substance abuse education or treatment program for a period of not less than one year on the motion of the defense, state attorney, or the court. However, a person who previously rejected an offer to enter such a program or a person whom the state attorney establishes by a preponderance of the evidence was involved with selling drugs is not eligible.[4]

(B) Conditions of Pretrial Intervention Programs

Participation in the pretrial program must be voluntary. At the end of the intervention period, the program administrator is to recommend whether the case should proceed to prosecution, whether the defendant requires additional supervision, or whether prosecution is not necessary. The state attorney makes the final decision regarding whether prosecution will be continued.[5]

---

2. 24 FLA. STAT. ANN. § 948.08(3) (West Supp. 2002).
3. 24 FLA. STAT. ANN. § 948.08(4) (West Supp. 2002).
4. 24 FLA. STAT. ANN. § 948.08(6) (West Supp. 2002).
5. 24 FLA. STAT. ANN. § 948.08(5) (West Supp. 2002).

7.4
Bail Determinations

Because a defendant, before trial, has not been proven guilty, he or she generally has a right to be released pending trial. However, to ensure the defendant's appearance at trial, a court may require the defendant to post bond or bail. As described in the following sections, in making this decision, a court can consider among other factors the defendant's mental state and propensity for harming persons in the community. MHPs may be asked to provide assessments on these issues.

(A) Nature and Purpose of Bail Determinations

The purpose of a bail determination is to ensure that the defendant appears for trial and to protect the community from danger that might be presented by the defendant.[1] As a general rule, defendants in criminal proceedings in Florida have a right to be released from confinement on bail while awaiting trial, except in capital cases or when charged with an offense punishable by life in prison.[2]

(B) Right to Bail

As noted, all defendants are presumptively entitled to bail. However, the Florida constitution provides that a defendant may be

---

1. 23 FLA. STAT. ANN. § 903.046(1) (West 2001).
2. FLA. CONST. art. I, § 14.

detained pending trial when no conditions of release will protect the public from harm, ensure the defendant's appearance at trial, or preserve the integrity of the judicial process.[3] Those charged with capital offenses or with an offense punishable by life in prison may be denied bail, though the discretion to grant or withhold bail rests with the trial court.[4] A court may also order pretrial detention if it finds any of the following circumstances exists:[5]

1. The defendant has previously violated conditions of release and that no further conditions of release are reasonably likely to ensure the defendant's appearance at subsequent proceedings;
2. The defendant, with the intent to obstruct the judicial process, has threatened, intimidated, or injured any victim, potential witness, juror, or judicial officer, or has attempted or conspired to do so, and that no condition of release will reasonably prevent the obstruction of the judicial process;
3. The defendant is charged with trafficking in controlled substances, that there is a substantial probability that the defendant has committed the offense, and that no conditions of release will reasonably ensure the defendant's appearance at subsequent criminal proceedings;
4. The defendant is charged with driving under the influence of substances–manslaughter and that there is a substantial probability that the defendant committed the crime and that the defendant poses a threat of harm to the community; conditions that would support a finding by the court pursuant to this subparagraph that the defendant poses a threat of harm to the community include, but are not limited to, any of the following:
    (a) The defendant has previously been convicted of any crime involving driving under the influence;
    (b) The defendant was driving with a suspended driver's license when the charged crime was committed; or
    (c) The defendant has previously been found guilty of, or has had adjudication of guilt withheld for, driving while the defendant's driver's license was suspended or revoked;
5. The defendant poses the threat of harm to the community. The court may so conclude, if it finds that the defendant is presently charged with a dangerous crime, that there is a substantial probability that the defendant committed such crime, that the factual circumstances of the crime indicate a disregard for the safety of the community, and that there are no conditions of

---

3. *Id.*
4. State v. Perry, 605 So. 2d 94 (Fla. 3d D.C.A. 1992).
5. 23 FLA. STAT. ANN. § 907.041(4)(c)(1)-(7) (West 2001).

release reasonably sufficient to protect the community from the risk of physical harm to persons;

6. The defendant was on probation, parole, or other release pending completion of sentence or on pretrial release for a dangerous crime at the time the current offense was committed; or

7. The defendant has violated one or more conditions of pretrial release or bond for the offense currently before the court and the violation, in the discretion of the court, supports a finding that no conditions of release can reasonably protect the community from risk of physical harm to persons or ensure the presence of the accused at trial.

(C) Determining Appropriateness and Amount of Bail

In determining whether to release a criminal defendant on bail or other conditions, the court must consider[6]

1. The nature and circumstance of the offense charged;

2. The weight of the evidence against the defendant;

3. The defendant's family ties, length of residence in the community, employment history, financial resources, and mental condition;

4. The defendant's past and present conduct, including any record of convictions, previous flights to avoid prosecution, or failure to appear at previous court proceedings;

5. The nature and probability of danger that the defendant's release poses to the community;

6. The source of funds used to post bail;

7. Whether the defendant is already on release pending resolution of another criminal proceeding or whether the defendant is on probation or parole;

8. The street value of any substance or drug connected to or involved in the criminal charges;

9. The nature and probability of intimidation and danger to victims; and

10. Any other factors the court considers relevant.

---

6. 23 FLA. STAT. ANN. § 903.046(2) (West 2001).

7.5
Competency to Stand Trial

Because of the adversarial nature of the legal process, it is crucial that defendants be competent to participate in criminal proceedings. Important decisions are made throughout the criminal process, and questions about a defendant's competency may be raised at any time. A defendant must be competent to confess, waive Miranda rights, plead guilty, stand trial, waive counsel, waive an appeal, be sentenced, and be executed.

Courts have traditionally relied on MHPs to offer input about the degree to which mental illness or mental retardation affects a defendant's competency and ability to participate in the criminal process.

(A) The Importance of Competency Throughout the Criminal Process

In Florida, unlike most states, the law regarding competencies in the criminal process reflects the understanding that a defendant's competency is important throughout the criminal process, and not only with regard to competency to stand trial. Thus, Florida law refers to a generic "competence to proceed" with the criminal process.[1] However, MHPs will nearly always be asked to evaluate a defendant's competency to stand trial or competency to proceed with a probation or community control violation hearing, and the law is written primarily with those questions in mind.

---

1. 33 FLA. R. CRIM. P. 3.210 (West 1999); 23 FLA. STAT. ANN. § 916.12 (West 2001).

(A)(1) **Legal Test of Competency**

A defendant is incompetent to stand trial if he or she does not have[2]

1. Sufficient present ability to consult with a lawyer with a reasonable degree of rational understanding; and
2. A rational and factual understanding of the proceedings against him or her.

Presence of mental disorder or mental impairment alone is not enough for a finding of incompetence.[3] Rather, only in cases when an underlying mental disorder or impairment affects the defendant's understanding of or ability to participate in the criminal justice process does competence become an issue of concern for the courts.

(A)(2) **Raising the Competency Issue**

The defense attorney, the state attorney, or the judge can raise the issue of the defendant's competency to proceed.[4] Defendants whose competence to proceed is questioned may be released on bail and ordered to make themselves available for an examination. If it is believed that the defendant will not submit to an evaluation, the defendant may be taken into custody so that the evaluation can be conducted.[5]

When ordering that a competency evaluation be conducted the judge must identify the purpose of the evaluation, the legal criteria to be applied, and the date by which the report must be submitted to the court.[6] The court must appoint no fewer than two and no more than three MHPs to evaluate the defendant.[7] To the extent possible, the court should appoint experts who are licensed psychologists, psychiatrists, or physicians, who have completed forensic evaluation training approved by the Department of Children and Families (DCF).[8]

When the cause of the suspected incompetence is mental retardation, one of the evaluators must be approved by the developmental services program of the DCF.[9] All appointed examiners

---

2. 23 FLA. STAT. ANN. § 926.12(1) (West 2001).
3. Bush v. Wainright, 505 So. 2d 409 (Fla); *cert. denied*, 484 U.S. 873 (1987); James v. State, 489 So. 2d 737 (Fla. 1986); Jones v. State, 465 So. 2d 1330 (Fla. 3d D.C.A. 1985); Kent v. State. 702 So. 2d 265 (Fla. 5th D.C.A. 1997).
4. 33 FLA. R. CRIM. P. 3.210(b) (West 1999).
5. 33 FLA. R. CRIM. P. 3.210(b)(3) (West 1999).
6. 33 FLA. R. CRIM. P. 3.210(b)(4) (West 1999).
7. 23 FLA. STAT. ANN. § 916.115(1)(b) (West 2001).
8. 23 FLA. STAT. ANN. § 916.115(1)(c) (West 2001).
9. 23 FLA. STAT. ANN. § 916.12(1) (West 2001).

in these cases must be qualified to evaluate persons with retardation or autism.[10]

(B) Competency Evaluation

MHPs assessing a defendant's competency to proceed are required to make a general inquiry into whether the defendant has[11]

1. Sufficient present ability to consult with his or her lawyer with a reasonable degree of rational understanding; and

2. A rational and factual understanding of the proceedings against him or her.

In their reports and evaluations considering these issues, MHPs must assess and describe the defendant's capacity to:[12]

1. Appreciate the charges or allegations;

2. Appreciate the range and nature of possible penalties;

3. Understand the adversary nature of the legal process;

4. Disclose to his or her attorney facts pertinent to the proceeding;

5. Display appropriate courtroom behavior;

6. Testify relevantly; and

7. Any other factors that the MHP deems relevant.[13]

If the examiner offers an opinion that is supportive of a finding of incompetency, he or she must also assess and describe the following:[14]

1. The mental illness or mental retardation thought to be responsible for the incompetency;

2. The recommended treatments for the mental illness or retardation and their availability in the community and elsewhere, including a discussion of various treatment alternatives; and

3. The likelihood that the defendant will attain competence after receiving the recommended treatments and the length of time that it may take to restore the defendant to competence.

---

10. 23 FLA. STAT. ANN. § 916.301(5) (West 2001).
11. 33 FLA. R. CRIM. P. 3.211(a)(2) (West 1999); 23 FLA. STAT. ANN. § 916.12(2) (West 2001).
12. 33 FLA. R. CRIM. P. 3.212(a)(2) (West 1999).
13. Id.
14. 33 FLA. R. CRIM. P. 3.211(b) (West 1999); 23 FLA. STAT. ANN. § 916.12(4) (West 2001).

In addition to a description of the previously mentioned issues, all written reports submitted by MHPs to the court must include[15]

1. The matter referred for evaluation;

2. The evaluation procedures and techniques used and their purpose;

3. The examiner's clinical observations and opinions and their factual basis, including identification of those issues for which the examiner could not offer an opinion or conclusion; and

4. The sources of information on which the expert relied.

(C) Competency Hearing

At the competency hearing, the court is to first consider the issue of the defendant's competence to proceed.[16] Either party or the court may call the examiners who prepared the competency reports, and experts appointed by the court are considered the court's witnesses regardless of whether a party or the court calls them.[17] If the court finds the defendant incompetent to proceed or that the defendant while competent requires continuing treatment to remain competent, the court is to consider issues regarding treatment necessary to restore or maintain the defendant's competence.[18] The court may order treatment either on an inpatient basis or in the community.[19]

Treatment for competency restoration may be ordered if the court finds that[20]

1. The defendant meets the criteria for commitment as incompetent;

2. There is a substantial probability that the defendant's mental illness or retardation will respond to treatment enabling the defendant to regain competency in the reasonably foreseeable future; and

3. Treatment for competency restoration is available.

---

15. 33 FLA. R. CRIM. P. 3.211(d) (West 1999).
16. 33 FLA. R. CRIM. P. 3.212(b) (West 1999).
17. 33 FLA. R. CRIM. P. 3.212(a) (West 1999).
18. 33 FLA. R. CRIM. P. 3.212(c) (West 1999).
19. 33 FLA. R. CRIM. P. 3.212(c)(1) (West 1999).
20. 33 FLA. R. CRIM. P. 3.212(c)(3)(A)–(D) (West 1999).

(D) Confidentiality and Privilege

The Fifth Amendment privilege against self-incrimination requires that defendants be informed that their statements may be used against them at trial and that they have the right not to incriminate themselves.[21] In addition, Florida law provides that, unless the defendant uses the competence evaluation for other purposes, information gained during the course of a competency evaluation can be used only for purposes of determining competency or appropriateness for involuntary commitment, not for other purposes (i.e., prosecution).[22] Nonetheless, examiners should keep in mind that prosecutors could use information provided by the defendant related to the offense to develop investigatory leads and should tailor their reports accordingly.

The attorney–client privilege protects communications between the attorney's client and individuals employed by the attorney (including a privately retained MHP evaluating the defendant for the defense attorney). Thus, if an attorney retains an MHP to evaluate a defendant but decides not to call the MHP as a witness, the attorney–client privilege prevents the prosecutor from calling the MHP unless the defendant decides to raise a mental state defense of some type.[23] Of course, this does not apply to evaluations conducted by court-retained evaluators.

It should also be noted that if the defendant is somehow evaluated before an attorney being appointed or without notice to the defendant's attorney, then the state cannot use the examiner's report or testimony with regard to any issue.[24]

(E) Disposition of Defendants Found Incompetent to Stand Trial

As noted, if the defendant is found to be incompetent to proceed and likely to regain competence, the judge can order the defendant to undergo treatment designed to restore him or her to competency.[25]

---

21. U.S. Const. Amend. V.
22. 33 Fla. R. Crim. P. 3.211(e) (West 1999).
23. Lovette v. State, 636 So. 2d 1304 (Fla. 1994).
24. Holland v. State, 636 So. 2d 1289 (1994).
25. 33 Fla. R. Crim. P. 3.2I2(c)(l) (West 1999); 23 Fla. Stat. Ann. § 916.13(1) (West 2001).

(E)(1) Inpatient Treatment of Incompetent Defendants

An incompetent defendant can be committed to an inpatient facility (either a forensic or nonforensic hospital for treatment) if:

1. The defendant meets criteria for civil commitment[26]—that is:
   (a) The defendant is mentally ill or mentally retarded and, because of the mental illness or retardation the defendant is manifestly incapable of surviving alone or with the help of willing family and friends, including available alternative services and, without treatment, he or she is likely to suffer from neglect or refuse to care for self and this neglect or refusal poses a real and present threat of substantial harm; or
   (b) There is a substantial likelihood that in the near future the defendant will inflict serious bodily harm on self or others, as evidenced by recent behavior causing, attempting, or threatening such harm and all available, less restrictive alternatives, including treatment in community residential facilities or community inpatient or outpatient settings are inappropriate;

2. There is a substantial probability that the mental illness or mental retardation causing the defendant's incompetence will respond to treatment or training;[27] and

3. Commitment and treatment in a secure setting is the least restrictive treatment available.[28]

If the defendant is committed to a treatment facility, the facility must provide to the court a report that describes the defendant's treatment and progress and offer an opinion with regard to the defendant's competency to proceed no later than six months after the initial commitment.[29] If, during the period of commitment, the facility administrator believes that the defendant is competent to proceed or no longer meets criteria for civil commitment, the administrator must petition the court and request a hearing on this issue.[30]

---

26. 23 FLA. STAT. ANN. § 916.13(1) (West 1999).
27. 33 FLA. R. CRIM. P. 3.212(c)(3)(B) (West 1999); 23 FLA. STAT. ANN. § 916.13(1)(c) (West 2001); 23 FLA. STAT. ANN. § 916.302(1)(d) (West 2001).
28. 33 FLA. R. CRIM. P. 3.212(c)(3)(C) (West 1999); 23 FLA. STAT. ANN. § 916.13(1)(d) (West 2001); 23 FLA. STAT. ANN. § 916.302(1)(c) (West 2001).
29. 23 FLA. STAT. ANN. §. 916.1.3(2)(a) (West Supp. 2000) 33 FLA. R. CRIM. P. 3.212(c)(5) (West 1999).
30. 33 FLA. R. CRIM. P. 3.212(c)(5) (West Supp. 1999); 23 FLA. STAT. ANN. § 916.13(2) (West 2001).

(E)(2) Outpatient Treatment and Conditional Release of Incompetent Defendants

If the court determines that the defendant is incompetent to proceed but does not meet commitment criteria, the defendant can be released for a period not to exceed one year. The court can order the defendant to receive outpatient treatment designed to restore competency and order the defendant to be available for additional evaluation.[31]

Proposals for conditional release of a hospitalized incompetent defendant can be filed with the court by either the defendant or an administrator representing the DCF residential facility in which the defendant has been placed. The plan must be provided to the court, the state attorney, and the defense attorney. It must identify provisions for placement of the defendant in the community and plans for supervision, provision of outpatient mental health services, and recommendations for ancillary services, to the degree they may be necessary.[32]

When a court orders conditional release of an incompetent defendant it must identify the conditions of the release and order the appropriate treatment agencies to submit periodic reports to the court regarding the defendant's progress in treatment and compliance with the release conditions.[33] Whenever an incompetent defendant appears to have failed to comply with the conditions of release, or the defendant's condition has deteriorated so that inpatient care is required, or the release conditions should be modified, the court must hold a hearing within seven days and modify the conditions of the release or order that the defendant be involuntarily committed for additional treatment.[34]

(E)(3) Treatment of Incompetent Defendants With Psychotropic Medication

Defendants who are adjudicated incompetent to proceed are not considered to be incompetent for any other purposes including consent to medical treatment, unless such an adjudication is specifically set forth by the court.[35] Incompetent defendants, however, do not enjoy a right to refuse treatment. Incompetent defendants can be forcibly treated in jail if they do not meet commitment criteria[36] or for up to 15 days in jail while awaiting transfer to a DCF facility if they do meet commitment criteria.[37]

---

31. 33 FLA. R. CRIM. P. 3.212(d) (West 1999).
32. 23 FLA. STAT. ANN. § 916.17(1) (West 2001).
33. Id.
34. 23 FLA. STAT. ANN. § 916.172) (West 2001).
35. 33 FLA. R. CRIM. P. 3.215(b) (West Supp. 1999).
36. 33 FLA. R. CRIM. P. 3.2I2(c)(2) (West 1999).
37. 23 FLA. STAT. ANN. § 916.107(1)(a) (West 2001).

Defendants who are able to participate in the legal process because of psychotropic medication are not considered to be incompetent to proceed.[38] If a defendant goes to trial while taking psychotropic medication the jury must be informed about the nature and effects of the medication if such instructions are requested by the defense.[39]

(E)(4) Dismissal of Changes Against Incompetent Defendants

The charges against a defendant who is incompetent because of mental retardation must be dismissed if the defendant remains incompetent for two years after being adjudicated incompetent, unless the court believes that the defendant will become competent in some period of time.[40]

For defendants who are incompetent because of a mental illness and who have been charged with a misdemeanor, charges must be dismissed after one year if it is believed that the defendant will not regain competence in the near future. For defendants who are incompetent because of a mental illness and are charged with a felony, charges must be dismissed after five years if it is believed that the defendant will not regain competence in the near future. The state, however, can refile the charges at any time if the person is restored to competence.[41]

(F) Evaluation and Disposition of Defendants Found Incompetent to Be Sentenced

If a defendant is suspected of being incompetent to proceed after pleading to or being convicted of an offense or violation of probation or community control, the court must postpone sentencing and initiate a competency evaluation, with procedures to be followed as outlined in previous sections of this chapter for defendants adjudicated incompetent to stand trial.[42]

---

38. 33 FLA. R. CRIM. P. 3.215(c) (West 1999).
39. 33 FLA. R. CRIM. P. 3.215(c)(2)(a) (West 1999).
40. 23 FLA. STAT. ANN. § 916.303(1) (West 2001).
41. 33 FLA. R. CRIM. P. 3.213(a) (West 1999); 33 FLA. R. CRIM. P. 3.213(b) (West 1999); 23 FLA. STAT. ANN. § 916.145 (West 2001).
42. 33 FLA. R. CRIM. P. 3.214 (West 1999).

7.6
Provocation

Provocation is relevant in criminal proceedings in three contexts. These include its use as an affirmative defense, in mitigation of a charge of first-degree murder, and at sentencing. MHPs may provide expert testimony on the issue of provocation.

(A) Provocation as a Defense

Florida law states that homicide is excusable when committed "by accident and misfortune in the heat of passion, upon any sudden and sufficient provocation."[1] This means that in some circumstances provocation may serve as a complete defense to a charge of homicide.[2] The jury instruction on provocation defines it as the defendant acting "in the heat of passion brought on by a sudden provocation sufficient to produce in the mind of an ordinary person the highest degree of anger, rage or resentment that is so intense as to overcome the use of ordinary judgment, thereby rendering a normal person incapable of reflection."[3] Provocation is not available as a defense to a charge of assault and battery, and abusive words directed at the defendant by the victim are an insufficient basis on which to claim provocation.[4]

---

1. 22 FLA. STAT. ANN. § 782.03 (West 2000).
2. Bowes v. State, 500 So. 2d 290 (Fla. 3d D.C.A. 1986), *review denied*, 506 So. 2d 1043 (Fla. 1987).
3. Gillen v. State, 597 So. 2d 375 (Fla. 2d D.C.A. 1992).
4. Yarborough v. State, 114 So. 237 (Fla. 1927).

(B) Provocation in Mitigation

Provocation may also be claimed in an attempt to reduce a charge from first-degree homicide to a lesser charge. The underlying theory is that the defendant was sufficiently provoked to prevent him or her from forming the requisite intent to perform first-degree murder. The courts, in applying this doctrine, have required a showing of more than simple anger: "A man is not permitted to act upon any provocation . . . merely because it is sufficient to excite his anger and impulse to kill and thereby reduce his crime to manslaughter."[5]

(C) Provocation in Sentencing

A court may consider several criteria in reducing a sentence under sentencing guidelines. The court may consider whether the defendant "acted under a strong provocation" in deciding whether to imprison the defendant[6] and also may impose a sentence falling outside the statutory guidelines if the victim provoked the offense.[7]

---

5. Forehand v. State, 171 So. 241, 243 (Fla. 1936) (an assault by the victim on the defendant constituted sufficient provocation to justify a verdict other than first-degree homicide).
6. 23 FLA. STAT. ANN. § 921.005(1)(b)(3) (West 2001).
7. 23 FLA. STAT. ANN. § 921.0016(4)(f) (West 2001).

7.7
Mens Rea

Most criminal acts have two elements. A defendant can be found guilty of a criminal act[1] only if there is proof of

1. The act requirement (i.e., the defendant must have engaged in some behavior that is legally proscribed or failed to have engaged in behavior that is legally required); and
2. The mental state or mens rea requirement (i.e., the defendant must have had the particular mental state required for the proscribed behavior in question).

The reason for determining mental state is to enable the law to distinguish between accidental or inadvertent acts and those performed with a "guilty mind." MHPs may be asked to testify on the issue of mental state, or mens rea, particularly when a defendant argues that, because of mental disease or defect, he or she lacked the mental state required as a necessary element of the crime (see chapter 7.8, Diminished Capacity).

Failure to have the requisite mental state precludes conviction for most offenses. For example, an individual might kill someone with a car, but if she did not do so purposefully, recklessly, or negligently, then she would not be guilty of what might otherwise be a criminal act (e.g., murder or manslaughter).

(A) Culpable Mental States

Each criminal offense has its own required state of mind. The four mental states relevant to criminal behavior are[2]

---

1. King v. State, 95 So. 567 (Fla. 1923).
2. MODEL PENAL CODE § 2.02 (Official Draft 1962).

1. *Intentional or purposeful conduct:* conduct performed by the actor with the object or desire to cause a particular result;
2. *Knowing conduct:* conduct performed when the actor is or should be aware that the conduct is likely to cause a particular result;
3. *Reckless conduct:* conduct performed with a disregard for a substantial risk when it is or should be known that the conduct will produce a particular result; and
4. *Criminally negligent conduct:* conduct performed when the actor fails to become aware of or perceive a risk that a reasonable person would realize would create a substantial risk of a particular result.

7.8
Diminished Capacity

In some jurisdictions, MHPs may be called on to assess a defendant's mental state at the time of the alleged offense to assist the court's determination regarding whether the defendant had the requisite mental state at the time of the alleged crime.[1] Although this inquiry focuses on the mental state of the defendant at the time of the alleged offense, it differs from an insanity inquiry. In the latter, it is not alleged that the defendant lacked the requisite mental state but rather that the defendant, because of a mental disorder, should not be held criminally responsible for what otherwise would be criminal behavior.[2] In contrast, a diminished capacity defense seeks to negate proof that the defendant was able to form the mental state (for example, the intent in a specific intent crime) required by the offense—the result may be conviction on a reduced charge rather than acquittal.

(A) Legal Test of Diminished Capacity

Florida courts, as a general rule, have rejected the use of mental disorder to demonstrate that the defendant lacked the requisite mens rea, requiring instead that a defendant who wishes to use mental disorder in his or her defense plead the insanity defense.[3]

---

1. See chapter 7.7, Mens Rea, for a discussion of the different mental states required for a conviction for criminal behavior.
2. See chapter 7.9, Criminal Responsibility, for a discussion of the insanity defense.
3. Chestnut v. State, 538 So. 2d 820 (Fla. 1989).

In the past, Florida courts allowed evidence to be introduced to show that voluntary intoxication affected the defendant's ability to form specific intent required for a particular offense (an example would be to show that a defendant charged with murder was too intoxicated to form an intent to kill the other person and should therefore be convicted of manslaughter instead).[4] In 1999, however, the Florida legislature significantly limited the diminished capacity defense:

> Voluntary intoxication resulting from the consumption, injection, or other use of alcohol or other controlled substance . . . is not a defense to any offense proscribed by law. Evidence of a defendant's voluntary intoxication is not admissible to show that the defendant lacked the specific intent to commit an offense and is not admissible to show that the defendant was insane at the time of offense, except when the consumption, injection, or use of a controlled substance . . . was pursuant to a lawful prescription.[5]

---

4. *See, e.g.*, Boswell v State, 610 So. 2d 670 (Fla. 4th D.C.A. 1992); Linehan v. State, 476 So. 2d 1262 (Fla. 1985).
5. 46 Fla. Stat. 775.051 (West Supp. 2001).

7.9
Criminal Responsibility

Florida, like most other states, permits an insanity defense that provides that defendants are not to be held criminally responsible for what would otherwise be criminal actions when their mental state has impaired their capacities in specific ways. Thus, MHPs are sometimes consulted when there is a question about a defendant's mental state at the time of the alleged offense.

(A) Legal Determination of Insanity

(A)(1) Test of Insanity

Florida's insanity test is a derivation of the *M'Naghten* test. It holds that an individual is insane when, at the time of the offense, the defendant had a mental infirmity, disease, or defect and, because of this condition[1]

1. The defendant did not know what he or she was doing or its consequences; or

2. Although the defendant knew what he or she was doing and its consequences, he or she did not know that it was wrong.

Only when mental state has been impaired by "fixed and settled" *organic problems* (that is, brain injury) can alcohol or drug

---

1. *Standard Jury Instructions in Criminal Cases* § 3.04(b)(2) (1986); courts may also request that MHPs conduct sanity evaluations of persons who are accused of violating conditions of probation or community control; see 33 FLA. R. CRIM. P. 3.216 (West 1999) in general.

abuse or dependence form the basis of an insanity defense.[2] Thus, simple intoxication or addiction, in the absence of permanent organic impairment, cannot form the basis for an insanity defense.[3] The insistence that organic conditions be permanent or fixed and settled means that the defendant must demonstrate something such as permanent neurological damage to introduce alcohol or substance abuse in pursuit of an insanity defense.

(A)(2) **Burden of Proof**

The defendant must present some evidence of insanity to overcome the presumption of sanity. But once the defendant overcomes this burden, the prosecution has the burden of disproving insanity beyond a reasonable doubt.[4]

(A)(3) **Raising the Insanity Issue and Initiating Evaluations**

When a defense attorney suspects that the defendant may have been insane at the time of the alleged offense, he or she can have the defendant evaluated by an MHP. If the defendant is indigent, the attorney can petition the court to appoint one expert to examine the defendant. This confidential expert reports only to the defense attorney and communications made to the expert are protected by the attorney–client privilege. The expert cannot be deposed or called as a witness by the state unless the defense calls the expert as a witness.[5]

If the defendant intends to rely on insanity as a defense, written notice must be provided to the court.[6] After notice is filed, the court can appoint no fewer than two and no more than three MHPs to examine the defendant with respect to his or her mental state at the time of the offense, either independently or at the request of the defense or prosecution.[7] To the extent possible,

---

2. Cirack v. State, 301 So. 2d 706 (Fla. 1967); Brunner v. State, 683 So. 2d 1129 (Fla. 4th D.C.A. 1996); Hewitt v. State, 575 So. 2d 273 (Fla. 4th D.C.A. 1991).
3. Curtis v. State, 489 So. 2d 956 (Fla. 3d D.C.A. 1991).
4. Matevia v. State, 564 So. 2d 585 (Fla. 2d D.C.A. 1990).
5. 3 Fla. R. Crim. P. 3.216(a) (West 1999); Lovette v. State, So. 2d 1304 (Fla. 1994); Ursry v. State, 428 So. 2d 71.3 (Fla. 4th D.C.A. 1983); Pouncy v State, 353 So. 2d 640 (Fla. 3d D.C.A. 1977).
6. 33 Fla. R. Crim. P. 3.216(b) (West 1999).
7. 33 Fla. R. Crim. P. 3.216(d) (West 1999). It is possible that the law in this area is not followed as precisely as it should be, potentially resulting in negative outcomes for criminal defendants. In some circuits, assistant public defenders who have a question or concern about the defendant's sanity at the time of the alleged offense (and who are unsure about the feasibility of such a defense) request that the court appoint two MHPs to evaluate the defendant's sanity (and sometimes competency to proceed). On the basis of the court-appointed experts' opinions, the public defender then decides whether an insanity defense will be raised. This violates Fla. R. Crim. P. 3.21.6(b), (c), and (d) that direct that the court

the court should appoint experts who are licensed psychologists, psychiatrics, or physicians and who have completed forensic evaluation training approved by the DCF.[8]

The state can also retain its own experts to evaluate the defendant. If the defendant refuses to submit to evaluations conducted by court-appointed or state-retained MHPs, the court can bar the use of any defense experts or assertion of the insanity defense altogether.[9] If the court determines that the defendant will not appear for an evaluation in the community, the court can order that the defendant be taken into custody until the evaluation is completed.[10]

If the defendant is released from custody he or she can be ordered to be available for an evaluation.[11] Attorneys for the state and defense can be present at the sanity evaluations.[12]

(A)(4) Mental Health Defenses Other Than Insanity

If the defense notifies the court that it will use expert testimony to present a mental health defense other than insanity, the court, on the state's motion, must appoint one qualified expert to evaluate the defendant for the state regarding his or her mental state at the time of the alleged offense. Additional experts can be appointed on a showing of good cause. If the defense relies on the testimony of an expert who has not examined the defendant, then the state is not entitled to a compulsory examination.

(B) Insanity Examination and Report

MHPs who have assessed a defendant's mental state at the time of the offense and are submitting an opinion to the court are required to file a written report. The report must contain[13]

---

can appoint court-retained experts to evaluate a defendant's sanity only after notice of intent to rely on the defense has been raised. In addition to violating *Florida Rules of Criminal Procedure,* this practice risks compromising the defendant's rights by potentially providing the state with investigative leads and an admission of guilt. In some circuits, public defenders may be motivated to do this because court-appointed evaluators are paid out of the court budget, whereas confidential evaluators are paid from the public defender's budget.

8. 23 FLA. STAT. ANN. § 916.115(1)(c) (West 2001).
9. Henry v. State, 574 So. 2d 66 (Fla. 1991).
10. 33 FLA. R. CRIM. P. 3.216(i) (West 1999).
11. *Id.*
12. 33 FLA. R. CRIM. P. 3.216(d) (West 1999).
13. 33 FLA. R. CRIM. P. 3.216(g) (West 1999).

1. A description of the evaluation techniques used;
2. A description of the mental and emotional condition and mental processes of the defendant at the time of the alleged offense, including the nature of any mental impairment and its relationship to the actions and state of mind of the defendant at the time of the alleged offense;
3. A statement of all relevant factual information regarding the defendant's behavior in which the conclusions or opinions regarding his or her mental condition were based; and
4. An explanation of how the opinion regarding the defendant's mental condition at the time of the alleged offense was reached.

(C) Confidentiality and Privileged Communications

The Fifth Amendment privilege against self-incrimination requires that the defendant be informed of the risk that his or her statements may be used against him or her at trial. The attorney–client privilege protects communications between the defendant and individuals employed by the attorney (including a privately retained MHP conducting an insanity evaluation). Thus, if a defense attorney retains an MHP to evaluate a defendant but decides not to call the MHP as a witness, the attorney–client privilege prevents the prosecutor from calling the MHP as a witness without the defendant's consent.[14] Of course, this does not apply to evaluations conducted by court-appointed evaluators.

(D) Disposition of Defendants Found Not Guilty by Reason of Insanity

Because defendants found not guilty by reason of insanity are not considered criminally responsible for their actions, they do not fall under the jurisdiction of the Department of Corrections (DOC).

(D)(1) Criteria for Continuing Court Jurisdiction of Insanity Acquittees

The court retains jurisdiction over insanity acquittees who are considered to be mentally ill and, because of their mental illness,

---

14. 33 FLA. R. CRIM. P. 3.216(a) (West 1999); Lovette v. State, 635 So. 2d 1304 (Fla. 1994); Ursry v. State, 428 So. 2d 713 (Fla. 4th D.C.A. 1983); Pouncy v. State, 353 So. 2d 640 (Fla. 3d D.C.A. 1977).

"manifestly dangerous."[15] Acquittees who are determined not meet these criteria must be released and the court retains no jurisdiction over them.

For purposes of Florida law, *manifestly dangerous* is defined more broadly than the *dangerousness* criterion referred to in other commitment statutes. Insanity acquittees who are considered to pose any danger (e.g., danger to property) are considered to be manifestly dangerous. The state need only prove that the danger is more likely than not, and that the acquittee is dangerous by a "preponderance of the evidence" rather than by "clear and convincing" evidence, the stricter standard required in other types of commitment proceedings.[16]

(D)(2) Placement of Insanity Acquittees Under Court Jurisdiction

The court can involuntarily commit an insanity acquittee who is determined to be mentally ill and manifestly dangerous or it can order him or her into a community-based, residential or nonresidential treatment program.[17] The court retains jurisdiction over the acquittee until the person no longer meets the criteria for involuntary commitment or conditional release.

When a service provider believes that an acquittee who is involuntarily committed to an institution or is receiving services in the community under a conditional release order is no longer mentally ill and manifestly dangerous, he or she must notify the court with jurisdiction over the individual.[18] The court must hold a hearing to determine whether the acquittee no longer meets the criteria. Such a hearing must also be held after the first six months of commitment and every year thereafter.[19] Treatment records and comments of a person found not guilty by reason of insanity are not privileged. The parties shall have access to the acquittee's records at the treating facilities and may interview or depose personnel who have had contact with the acquittee at the treating facility.[20]

(D)(3) Conditional Release

When a court orders conditional release of an insanity acquittee, it must identify the conditions of the release and order the appropriate treatment agencies to submit periodic reports to the court

---

15. 23 FLA. STAT. ANN. § 916.15(1) (West Supp. 2000).
16. Hill v. State, 358 So. 2d 191 (Fla. 1st D.C.A. 1978).
17. 25 FLA. STAT. ANN. § 916.15(1) (West 2001); 23 FLA. STAT. ANN. § 916.17 (West 2001).
18. 23 FLA. STAT. ANN. § 916.15(2) (West 2001).
19. *Id.*
20. 23 FLA. STAT. ANN. § 916.15(3) (West 2001).

regarding the acquittee's progress in treatment and compliance with the release conditions.[21]

For acquittees initially placed in DCF institutions, proposals for conditional release can be filed with the court by either the acquittee or a DCF administrator from the residential facility in which the acquittee has been placed. The plan must be provided to the court, the state attorney, and the defense attorney for review. It must identify provisions for placement of the acquittee in the community and plans for supervision, delivery of outpatient mental health services, and recommendations for ancillary services, if they are necessary. [22]

If, at any time, it appears that an insanity acquittee has failed to comply with conditions of release, or that the acquittee's condition has deteriorated so that inpatient care is required, or that the release conditions should be modified, the court must hold a hearing within seven days and modify the conditions of the release or order that the defendant be involuntarily committed for additional treatment.[23] Any time the court determines that the acquittee no longer meets commitment criteria and no longer needs court-supervised follow-up care, the court must terminate its jurisdiction.[24]

---

21. 23 FLA. STAT. ANN. § 916.17(1) (West 2001).
22. Id.
23. 23 FLA. STAT. ANN. § 916.17(2) (West 2001).
24. 23 FLA. STAT. ANN. § 916.17(3) (West 2001).

7.10
Competency to Be Sentenced

Although Florida law provides that mental illness may be a mitigating factor in the imposition of a criminal sentence (see chapter 7.11, Sentencing), there is no separate provision of law addressing competency to be sentenced in general criminal proceedings. In general, Florida law treats the various criminal competencies (competency to plead guilty, competency to stand trial, competency to be sentenced) under the rubric of competency to proceed (see chapter 7.5, Competency to Stand Trial).

(A) Competence to Proceed in Capital Collateral Proceedings

Florida Rules of Criminal Procedure provide for specific inquiry into a death-sentenced prisoner's competence to proceed in capital collateral proceedings.[1] A death-sentenced prisoner who is found incompetent to proceed shall not be proceeded against if there are factual issues at issue that require his or her input.[2] Collateral counsel may file a motion for competence determination when there is reasonable grounds to believe that the prisoner is incompetent to proceed.[3] The motion must be in writing, identify the factual matters that the prisoner must address with counsel, and cite the basis for the attorney's belief that the prisoner may be

---
1. FLA. R. CRIM. P. 3.851(g) (West Supp. 2002).
2. FLA. R. CRIM. P. 3.851(g)(1) (West Supp. 2002).
3. FLA. R. CRIM. P. 3.851(g)(2) (West Supp. 2002).

incompetent.[4] The judge, on review of the motion, is to appoint at least two but no more than three experts to evaluate the prisoner.[5] The order must identify the purpose of the evaluation, the legal criteria to be applied, and the date by which the report should be submitted.[6] Counsel for the prisoner and state may be present during the examination.[7]

The examiners are to address whether the prisoner has "sufficient present ability to consult with counsel with a rational understanding and whether the prisoner has a rational as well a factual understanding of the pending collateral proceedings."[8] The examiners are to assess and include in their reports the prisoner's capacity to understand the adversary nature of the legal process and collateral proceedings, the prisoner's ability to disclose to counsel facts pertinent to the postconviction proceeding at issue, and any other factors deemed relevant by the examiners or court as specified in the order appointing the examiners.[9] Reports prepared by the examiners are to identify the specific matters referred for evaluation, describe the evaluation procedures and techniques used and the purpose of each, state the examiner's observations and findings, identify sources of information used by the examiners, and present a factual basis for any opinions and findings.[10]

If the examiner offers an opinion that the prisoner is incompetent to proceed, then the examiner is required to identify the nature of the disorder responsible for the incompetence, recommend appropriate treatments necessary for restoration, and describe the likelihood that the prisoner will be restored to capacity and the likely timeframe.[11] Treatment for competence restoration is to take place in a facility operated by the DOC.[12]

---

4. FLA. R. CRIM. P. 3.851(g)(4) (West Supp. 2002).
5. FLA. R. CRIM. P. 3.851(g)(5) (West Supp. 2002).
6. FLA. R. CRIM. P. 3.851(g)(6) (West Supp. 2002).
7. FLA. R. CRIM. P. 3.851(g)(7) (West Supp. 2002).
8. FLA. R. CRIM. P. 3.851(g)(8) (West Supp. 2002).
9. *Id.*
10. *Id.*
11. FLA. R. CRIM. P. 3.851(g)(9) (West Supp. 2002).
12. FLA. R. CRIM. P. 3.851(g)(13) (West Supp. 2002).

7.11
Sentencing

Following a finding of guilty or no contest, the court or jury imposes a sentence. A convicted person's current and previous adjustment and emotional functioning and related treatment needs are sometimes considered by the court when imposing a sentence. Thus, MHPs may be called on to assess persons who have been convicted of or pled guilty to a crime for purposes of sentencing.

(A) Presentence Mental Health Examination

For criminal defendants who are convicted or who pleaded guilty or no contest, the court may refer the case to the DOC for a presentence investigation and sentencing recommendation. Evaluation by an MHP may be requested by the court or the DOC.[1] In addition, the defense can conduct and submit an examination independently.

(B) Capital Sentencing

When a defendant pleads guilty to or is convicted of a felony that includes a possible penalty of death, the court must conduct a separate sentencing proceeding to determine whether the defendant should be sentenced to life imprisonment or death. The

---

1. 23 FLA. STAT. ANN. § 921.231(1)i (West 2001).

recommendation is made by a judge or jury after weighing evidence related to aggravating and mitigating circumstances.[2]

The defense attorney may seek to have an MHP examine the defendant to identify mitigating factors related to the defendant's mental health, adjustment, and emotional functioning.[3] The defendant must give written notice of the intent to present expert testimony of a mental health professional related to mitigating circumstances.[4] If the defense calls an MHP to testify about mental health issues that may serve as mitigating factors, the prosecutor may have the defendant examined by its own MHP. Within 48 hours after the defendant is convicted of capital murder, the defendant is to be examined by a mental health expert chosen by the state attorney. Attorneys for the defendant and state may be present during the evaluation, and the examination is to be limited to those mitigating factors that the defense expects to present through expert testimony.[5] If the defendant refuses to cooperate with the state's mental health expert, the court can order the defense to allow the state's expert to review all of the defense's expert's material or prohibit the defense expert from testifying at the sentencing hearing.[6]

(B)(1) Mitigating Factors

A number of statutorily identified factors can serve to mitigate against a sentence of death.[7] Those factors that might be addressed by MHPs include[8]

1. Whether the defendant committed the capital felony while under the influence of extreme mental or emotional disturbance;

2. Whether the defendant acted under extreme duress or under the substantial domination of another person; or

3. Whether the defendant's capacity to appreciate the criminality of his conduct or conform his conduct to the requirements of the law was substantially impaired.

In addition to statutorily identified mitigating factors the jury can consider any evidence in mitigation that it deems relevant.[9]

---

2. 23 FLA. STAT. ANN. § 921.141(1) (West 2001).
3. *Id.*
4. FLA. R. CRIM. P. 3.202(b) (West 1999).
5. FLA. R. CRIM. P. 3.202(d) (West 1999).
6. FLA. R. CRIM. P. 3.202(e) (West 1999).
7. 23 FLA. STAT. ANN. § 921.141(1) (West 2001).
8. 23 FLA. STAT. ANN. § 921.141(c) (West 2001). There are additional mitigating factors that are not relevant to mental state or do not require the expertise of an MHP.
9. Hall v. Wainright, 735 F. 2d 766 (1984), *cert. denied*, 749 F.2d 733.

The following psychological factors have been identified as potential mitigating circumstances in capital cases:

1. Mental retardation or intellectual capacity of the defendant;[10]
2. Emotional development or emotional maturity of the defendant;[11]
3. History of abuse and neglect;[12]
4. Alcohol or drug intoxication at the time of offense or history of alcohol and drug abuse;[13]
5. Organic impairment (i.e., neurological impairment or damage);[14]
6. Personality disorder;[15] and
7. Potential for rehabilitation.[16]

(B)(2) Aggravating Factors

A number of statutorily identified factors can serve to aggravate in favor of a sentence of death,[17] but there are none that are relevant to mental state or that require the expertise of an MHP.

---

10. Neary v. State, 384 So. 2d 881 (1980); Freeman v. State, 547 So. 2d 125 (1989); Campbell v. State, 571 So. 2d 418 (1990); Bryant v. State, 601 So. 2d 529 (1992), *opinion rev'd on denial of reh'g*.
11. Eutzy v. State, 458 So. 2d 755 (1984), *cert. denied*, 105 S. Ct. 2060, 85 L. Ed. 2d 336; Fitzpatrick v. State, 527 So. 2d 809 (1988); Scud v. State, 533 So. 2d 1137 (1988), *cert. denied*, 407 U.S. 1037.
12. Campbell v State, 571 So. 2d 415 (1990); Wickam v. State, 593 So. 2d 191 (1991), *cert. denied*, 112 S. Ct. 3003, L. Ed. 2d 878; Tomes-Arboleda v. Dogger, 636 So. 2d 1321 (1994); Blanco v. State, 706 So. 2d 7 (Fla. 1997), *reh'g denied, cert. denied*, 119 S. Ct. 96.
13. Smith v. State, 492 So. 2d 1063 (1986); Holsworth v. State, 522 So. 2d 348 (1988); Nibert v. State, 574 So. 2d 1059 (1990); Wickarri v. State, 593 So. 2d 197 (1991), *cert. denied*, 112 S. Ct. 3003, L. Ed. 2d 878; Knowles v. State, 632 So. 2d 64 (1993), *opinion corrected on denial of hearing*.
14. State v. Sired, 576 So. 2d 231 (1988).
15. Wournos v. State, 676 So. 2d 966 (Fla. 1995), *reh'g denied, cert. denied*, 519 U.S. 968.
16. Holsworth v State, 522 So. 2d 1170 (1985); Nibert v. State, 574 So. 2d 1059 (1990).
17. 23 FLA. STAT. ANN. § 921.141(5) (West 2001).

7.12
Probation

A court may determine in its discretion to place an individual on probation or community control rather than use incarceration. *Probation* is defined as "a form of community supervision requiring specified contacts with parole and probation officers and other terms and conditions" as may be required statutorily.[1] *Community control* is a "form of intensive, supervised custody in the community, including surveillance on weekends and holidays, administered by officers with restricted caseloads ... an individualized program in which the freedom of the offender is restricted within the community, home, or non-institutional residential placement and specific sanctions are imposed and enforced."[2]

While on probation or community control, the individual is subject to certain conditions for a period of time specified by the court. Failure to comply with these conditions may result in revocation of probation or community control and imposition by the court of any sentence that could originally have been imposed at the time of sentencing, including imprisonment.[3]

A court may use a variety of conditions in probation or community control that present an opportunity for involvement by an MHP. For example, the court, before ordering mental health treatment as a condition, must obtain a diagnosis and evaluation to determine the need for treatment.[4] If the court then determines treatment is necessary, it *must* require outpatient counseling for any defendant found guilty (or pleading *nolo contendere*[5]) to lewd

---

1. 24 FLA. STAT. ANN. § 948.01(5) (West Supp. 2002).
2. 24 FLA. STAT. ANN. § 948.01(2) (West Supp. 2002).
3. 24 FLA. STAT. ANN. § 948.006 (West Supp. 2002).
4. 24 FLA. STAT. ANN. § 948.03(4) (West Supp. 2002).
5. A plea of *nolo contendere* does not acknowledge the truth of the facts that underlie the criminal charge, and therefore, in contrast to a plea of guilty,

or lascivious assault on or in the presence of a child; sexual battery against a child; or exploitation of a child for prostitution.[6] In cases involving other offenses, it is within the court's discretion to require mental health treatment on an outpatient basis.

In addition, presentence reports made available to the courts are to include an offender's medical history and "as appropriate" a psychological or psychiatric evaluation.[7]

There are special provisions for individuals who have alcohol or substance abuse problems. For example, a court as a condition of probation or community control may direct an individual to submit to random testing as directed by the probation officer or professional staff of a treatment center providing treatment to determine the presence of alcohol or controlled substances.[8] In addition, individuals convicted of certain types of substance use felonies may be ordered into treatment in a community residential drug punishment center for a period not to exceed 90 days. A number of other conditions may be imposed on such offenders, including the payment of fines and restitution, the performance of public service, and participation at the offender's expense in self-help groups such as Narcotics Anonymous, Alcoholics Anonymous, or Cocaine Anonymous where appropriate and available.[9]

---

such a plea cannot be used to establish the defendant's guilt in other proceedings—for example, in a civil proceeding.
6. 24 FLA. STAT. ANN. § 948.03(4)(a)–(c) (West Supp. 2002).
7. 24 FLA. STAT. ANN. § 948.015(9) (West Supp. 2002).
8. 24 FLA. STAT. ANN. § 948.03(1)(k) (West Supp. 2002).
9. 24 FLA. STAT. ANN. § 948.034(1) (West Supp. 2002).

7.13

Dangerous Offenders

There are no statutory criteria in Florida creating a category of "dangerous offenders." A court may order the pretrial detention of a defendant if the court finds that a defendant "poses the threat of harm to the community."[1] The court may make this determination based on the fact that the defendant is charged with a "dangerous crime" (which includes a number of specifically delineated offenses such as arson, homicide, or carjacking, for example) as well as a variety of other factors, including a finding that there are no conditions of release that might protect the community from harm. There is no apparent role for an MHP in this context because the statutory criteria the court must consider in deciding to use pretrial detention do not include any for which the testimony of an MHP would be relevant.

For related topics, see chapter 7.14, Habitual Offenders. See also chapter 7.11, Sentencing, for a discussion of mental health considerations in capital sentencing.

---

1. 23 FLA. STAT. ANN. § 907.041 (4)(b)4 (West Supp. 2002).

7.14

Habitual Offenders

Criminal defendants who have been convicted previously may, as a result of those earlier convictions, be subject to more severe sanctions. In Florida, such defendants may be classified as "habitual felony offenders"; "habitual violent felony offenders"; or "violent career criminals."[1] For example, a person may be designated by a court as an habitual felony offender based on previous convictions of two or more felonies in Florida or another state, or if the offense for which the defendant is being sentenced was committed while serving a prison term, or if it is within five years of the defendant's last felony conviction or release from prison for a felony conviction.[2]

Classification as one of these types of offenders is based solely on criminal history and other statutory criteria. Such classification does not depend on individual, personality, mental health, or other emotional state factors. As a result, there is no role for MHPs in this decision-making process.

---

1. 22 FLA. STAT. ANN. §§ 775.084, 775.08401, and 775.0841–775.0843 (West Supp. 2002).
2. 22 FLA. STAT. ANN. § 775.084(1)(a) (West Supp. 2002).

7.15

Competency to Serve a Sentence

An individual must be competent to undergo a sentencing hearing.[1] However, Florida law does not require that an individual, once convicted, be competent to serve the sentence imposed. Persons requiring mental health treatment may receive such treatment in jail or prison (see chapter 7.16, Mental Health Services in Jails and Prisons).

---

1. Calloway v. State, 651 So. 2d 752 (Fla. 1st D.C.A. 1995).

7.16

Mental Health Services in Jails and Prisons

MHPs may be asked to evaluate or treat persons held in jails or prisons. In Florida, jails are county-maintained institutions that hold persons who are awaiting trial and persons who have been convicted of or pled guilty to a crime and are serving short sentences (i.e., less than one year). Prisons are state institutions operated by the DOC and house only individuals who have been convicted of or have pled guilty to a crime and are serving sentences in excess of one year.

(A) Prisons

Essentially all mental health and substance abuse services for inmates in the custody of the DOC are provided by DOC employees, health services subcontractors, or private corrections companies who have contracted with the state to manage one or more institutions.

(A)(1) Access to Mental Health and Substance Abuse Services

Inmates with mental illness in the DOC are entitled to evaluation and treatment for mental disorders via a continuum of services.[1] Inmates who have or are at risk for developing symptoms that significantly impair their ability to function adequately within the general DOC population will receive priority for treatment

---

1. 24 FLA. STAT. ANN. § 945.41 (West 2001); FLA. ADMIN. CODE 33-404.102 (2002).

services.[2] Mental health treatment in the DOC is to be provided skillfully, safely, and humanely with respect to the inmate's dignity and personal integrity.[3] Inmates are to have access to care including outpatient treatment, transitional care provided in residential settings, crisis stabilization care provided in residential settings, and hospital care if necessary for the treatment of acute psychiatric conditions.[4]

The DOC's Bureau of Substance Abuse Program Services is responsible for assessment and treatment services related to substance abuse.[5] No right to substance abuse program services is stated, intended, or implied by the DOC.[6] All inmates entering the DOC are screened to determine if they meet criteria for mandated substance abuse program participation. Factors that are considered by the DOC include presence of a substance abuse or dependence diagnosis, severity of the addiction, history of criminal behavior related to substance abuse, sentencing authority recommendations for substance abuse treatment, unsuccessful participation in community-based treatment programs, sentencing by a drug court or drug division, and other classification factors. Those inmates deemed to be in need of substance abuse program services will be assigned a priority ranking for services and will be enrolled in services as they become available.[7]

(A)(2) Confidentiality

DOC inmates' medical, mental health, and substance abuse treatment records are confidential according to Florida law,[8] but standard limitations of confidentiality associated with medical, mental health, and substance abuse treatment and treatment records presumably apply in DOC facilities as well (see chapter 3.3, Confidential Relations and Communications).

In addition, any time an inmate who has received mental health treatment while in the DOC becomes eligible for release on parole, a complete record of the inmate's treatment is to be provided to the Parole Commission and to the DCF. If the inmate is released on parole the record is to be provided to the parole officer who is to assist the inmate in applying for services in the community.[9]

---

2. FLA. ADMIN. CODE 33-404.101(2)(b) (2002).
3. 24 FLA. STAT. ANN. § 945.48 (West 2001).
4. FLA. ADMIN. CODE 33-404.101 (2002).
5. FLA. ADMIN. CODE 33-507.002 (2002).
6. FLA. ADMIN. CODE 33-507.001(3) (2002).
7. FLA. ADMIN. CODE 33-507.201(2) (2002).
8. 24 FLA. STAT. ANN. § 945.10(1)(a) (West 2001); FLA. ADMIN. CODE 33-507.401 (2000); FLA. STAT. ANN. 397.501 (West 2002).
9. 24 FLA. STAT. ANN. § 945.47(3) (West 2001).

(A)(3) Informed Consent and the Right to Refuse Treatment

Inmates who are provided psychiatric services in the DOC must provide express and informed written consent to any treatment. This requires that the inmate provide written consent after receiving an explanation of the proposed treatment and alternatives, possible side-effects of the treatment, and the expected duration of treatment.[10]

(A)(4) Involuntary Treatment of Inmates With Mental Illness

All mental health services must be administered using the least restrictive and least intrusive methods possible to accomplish the desired objectives.[11]

Involuntary mental health treatment of an inmate is permissible only when an inmate refuses treatment that is considered to be necessary for the appropriate care of the inmate and the safety of the inmate or others. It can occur only under the following conditions:[12]

1. In an emergency situation in which there is an immediate danger to the health and welfare of the inmate or others, treatment can be provided by written order of a physician for up to 48 hours, excluding weekends and legal holidays. If, after this period, the inmate does not consent to treatment and the inmate is still considered to meet criteria for involuntary treatment, the facility superintendent must petition the local circuit court and seek an order authorizing continued involuntary treatment. In the interim, treatment may be continued by the physician's written order directing that the emergency situation continues to present a danger to the safety of the inmate or others. If an inmate is to be isolated for mental health purposes, this decision must be reviewed within 72 hours by prison medical staff different than those ordering the initial isolation.[13]

2. In nonemergency situations, the facility administrator must petition the court for an order authorizing involuntary treatment of the inmate. The order can authorize involuntary treatment for a period not to exceed 90 days. This procedure is to be repeated until the inmate consents to the treatment or no longer needs treatment.

---

10. 24 FLA. STAT. ANN. § 945.48(2) (West 2001); FLA. ADMIN. CODE 33-404.105 (2002); FLA. ADMIN. CODE 33-404.210 (2002).
11. FLA. ADMIN. CODE 33-404.102(8) (2002).
12. 24 FLA. STAT. ANN. § 945.48(2)(b) (West 2001); FLA. ADMIN. CODE 33-404.210(2)(b) (2002).
13. 24 FLA. STAT. ANN. § 945.48(2)(a) (West 2001); FLA. ADMIN. CODE 33-404.210(2)(a) (2002).

To authorize involuntary treatment of DOC inmates, the court must find, by clear and convincing evidence, that[14]

1. The inmate is mentally ill;
2. The treatment is essential to the care of the inmate; and
3. The treatment is not experimental and does not present an unreasonable risk of serious, hazardous, or irreversible side-effects.

In arriving at the substituted judgment decision the court must consider at least the following:[15]

1. The inmate's expressed preferences regarding treatment;
2. The probability of adverse side-effects;
3. The prognosis for the inmates without treatment; and
4. The prognosis for the inmate with treatment.

The inmate and his or her representative must be provided with a copy of the petition and the date, time, and location of the hearing. The inmate may have an attorney represent him or her at the hearing and, if indigent, the court shall appoint the office of the public defender to represent the inmate. The inmate may testify or not, and he or she may present and cross-examine witnesses.[16]

(A)(5) Admission to Inpatient Mental Health Treatment Facilities Within the Department of Corrections

An inmate can be admitted to a residential mental health treatment facility[17] operated by the DOC if he or she is mentally ill and is in need of care or treatment. Admission can occur on recommendation of the superintendent of the facility in which the inmate is confined and the DOC director of mental health services or his or her designee. This recommendation must be supported by the expert opinion of a psychiatrist and the second opinion of a psychiatrist or psychologist. An inmate can be

---

14. 24 FLA. STAT. ANN. § 945.48(2)(c) (West 2001).
15. Id.
16. 24 FLA. STAT. ANN. § 945.48(2)(c)4. (West 2001).
17. It is noted that *mental health treatment facility* is defined narrowly in 24 FLA. STAT. ANN. § 945.42(7) and FLA. ADMIN. CODE 33-404.101 (2002) and does not include crisis inpatient crisis stabilization units or transitional care units, both of which are residential treatment program that are operated in various DOC institutions. Thus, Florida law still allows for entry of DOC inmates into residential units providing mental health services over the objection of the inmate and without judicial or quasi-judicial review. (See FLA. ADMIN. CODE 33-404.106 (2002) for specific authority for this practice.)

immediately transferred and admitted to a mental health treatment facility if the inmate waives his or her right to a hearing.[18]

Before entering a residential mental health treatment facility, the inmate is entitled to a hearing to determine his or her need for inpatient treatment and legal representation at the hearing. The hearing will occur in the county in which the inmate is housed, and one of the inmate's treating physicians must testify at trial. If the court finds that the inmate is mentally ill and in need of care and treatment, it must order that he or she be admitted to the residential mental health treatment facility or, if already there, remain in the facility for a period of up to six months. If, at the end of this time, continued treatment is necessary, the superintendent must apply to the court for an order authorizing continued placement.[19]

(B) Jails

There is no Florida law that regulates the provision of mental health services in jails. Florida does not have a well-developed mechanism for transferring jail inmates who are in need of inpatient mental health treatment to local or state hospitals. Although nothing in the law precludes jail inmates from being voluntarily or involuntarily admitted to receiving facilities (i.e., crisis stabilization units) or state hospitals for treatment, transfer usually does not occur for a number of reasons, including the criminal justice system's concern that the inmates might attempt escape if admitted to a hospital and the hospitals' reluctance to admit people with criminal charges pending. As a result, jail inmates are typically provided with outpatient and inpatient mental health services within the jail setting, and the quality and quantity of mental health services varies considerably between jails.

---

18. 24 Fla. Stat. Ann. § 945.43(1) (West 2001).
19. 24 Fla. Stat. Ann. § 945.43(2) (West 2001).

7.17
Transfer From Penal to Mental Health Facilities

Although the DOC is authorized to transfer inmates to outside facilities for necessary care,[1] all mental health services for inmates in the custody of the DOC are provided by the DOC or its private contractors.[2] Thus, transfers from DOC-operated facilities to DCF-operated facilities do not occur except in those cases where an inmate's term is expiring as he or she is considered to be in need of inpatient mental health treatment. DOC inmates whose prison terms are expiring can be transferred to a DCF-operated institution if they meet criteria for involuntary hospitalization.

(A) Initiation of Involuntary Placement Proceedings

DOC inmates who are receiving mental health treatment and who are considered to be mentally ill and, as a function of their mental illness, dangerous to themselves, dangerous to others, or unable to care for themselves, can be subject to involuntary commitment proceedings.[3] In these cases, the DOC institution superintendent is authorized to initiate procedures for involuntary placement pursuant to Florida civil commitment law. Inmates who are determined at a commitment hearing to be manifestly dangerous by

---

1. 24 FLA. STAT. ANN. § 945.12 (West 2001); 24 FLA. STAT. ANN. § 945.41(1) (West 2001).
2. 24 FLA. STAT. ANN. § 945.41 (West 2001); *see also* chapter 7.16, Mental Health Services in Jails and Prisons.
3. 24 FLA. STAT. ANN. § 945.46 (West 2001); 24 FLA. STAT. ANN. § 945.47(1)(d) (West 2001). *See also* chapter 8.4, Involuntary Commitment of Mentally Ill Adults, and 14 FLA. STAT. ANN. § 394.467 (West 2002).

clear and convincing evidence are to be transferred to a DCF inpatient facility on their release from the DOC.[4]

A DOC inmate with a history of sexual offending and who is nearing expiration of sentences and who is identified by DCF staff as eligible for involuntary commitment as a sexually violent predator is also subject to transfer from the DOC institution to a DCF institution on expiration of his or her sentence. After expiration of the sentence, the inmate is transferred from the DOC institution to a DCF-operated facility while he or she awaits a probable cause hearing and subsequent trial to determine whether they meet criteria for commitment as a sexually violent predator.[5]

(B) Referral to Outpatient Mental Health Treatment

Inmates who are receiving mental health treatment in the DOC at the expiration of their sentences but who are not considered to be in need of inpatient treatment can be released with a recommendation for outpatient treatment.[6]

(C) Mentally Retarded Inmates

There is no statutory provision for the transfer of inmates with mental retardation from correctional or mental health facilities. In fact, the statutory definition of mental illness within those provisions authorizing the transfer of inmates with mental illness excludes by its terms retardation or developmental disability, simple intoxication, or conditions manifested only by antisocial behavior or drug addiction.[7]

---

4. 24 FLA. STAT. ANN. § 945.47(2) (West 2001).
5. 24 FLA. STAT. ANN. § 394.912 (West 2002).
6. 24 FLA. STAT. ANN. § 945.47(1)(c) (West 2001).
7. 24 FLA. STAT. ANN. § 945.42 (West 2001).

7.18
Parole Determinations

Parole involves the release of a convicted individual from physical confinement before his or her sentence expires. Placement of someone on probation or community control, in contrast to parole, is the decision not to incarcerate the convicted individual (see chapter 7.12, Probation). Parole from confinement is not a right; rather, in legislative language it is considered an "act of grace."[1] The decision whether or not to grant parole is made by the Parole Commission. MHPs employed by the DOC are sometimes asked to provide the Commission with information about the convicted individual's mental health and possible adjustment to the community to assist in making judgments about early release.

(A) Eligibility for Parole

Every person convicted of a felony or one or more misdemeanors and whose sentence or cumulative sentences total 12 months or more, who is incarcerated, and who has a good record while incarcerated is eligible for parole according to statutory formulas tied to the type of sentence and number of years they are serving.[2]

---

1. 24 FLA. STAT. ANN. § 947.002(5) (West 2001).
2. 24 FLA. STAT. ANN. § 947.16 (West 2001).

(B) Parole Commission

The Parole Commission has three members, and the members are selected by the governor and cabinet and then referred to the state Senate for confirmation.[3]

(C) Parole Criteria

The Commission is to develop and implement "objective parole guidelines" for making parole decisions. The guidelines are to be developed according to an acceptable research methodology and shall be based on the seriousness of the offense and the likelihood of a favorable parole outcome,[4] as well as past criminal record.[5] If the sentencing judge files a written objection to the parole release of an inmate, the letter may be used as a basis for extending the presumptive parole release date.[6]

(D) Communication of Mental Health Treatment Information

When an inmate who has received mental health treatment in the DOC becomes eligible for release on parole, a complete record of his or her treatment is to be provided to the Parole Commission and to the DCF. If the inmate is released on parole, the mental health record is to be made available to the supervising parole officer.[7]

(E) Mental Health and Mental Retardation Treatment as a Condition of Parole

Application for continuation of mental health treatment can be a condition of parole, and the failure to participate in recom-

---

3. 24 FLA. STAT. ANN. §§ 947.01 and 947.02 (West 2001).
4. 24 FLA. STAT. ANN. § 947.165 (West 2001).
5. 24 FLA. STAT. ANN. § 947.002(2) (West 2001).
6. 24 FLA. STAT. ANN. § 947.165 (West 2001).
7. 24 FLA. STAT. ANN. § 945.47(3) (West 2001).

mended treatment can serve as the basis for a revocation of parole.[8] In addition, the Parole Commission may require inmates who are diagnosed as being mentally retarded to apply for and receive retardation services from the DCF as a condition of parole.[9]

---

8. *Id.*
9. 24 FLA. STAT. ANN. § 947.185 (West 2001).

7.19

Competency to Be Executed

The Eighth Amendment to the U.S. Constitution, which prohibits cruel and unusual punishment, also prevents the execution of incompetent persons.[1] MHPs may be called on to assess the capacity of an individual who is sentenced to death and awaits execution.

The U.S. Supreme Court, in *Ford v. Wainwright*,[2] ruled that judicial review of a governor's competency decision must be available. To accommodate this holding, the *Florida Rules of Criminal Procedure* were amended to create an avenue for judicial review.[3] The rule permits defense counsel to move for a stay of execution after the governor determines the person is competent to be executed. The motion is to be filed in the circuit court of the circuit in which the execution is to take place; counsel is also to file the expert reports submitted to the governor. The motion is also to be served on the state attorney and the Department of Legal Affairs.[4] If the court has reasonable grounds to believe that the prisoner is "insane to be executed" the court is to grant a stay of execution and may schedule a hearing.

---

1. 477 U.S. 399 (1986).
2. *Id.*
3. 33 FLA. R. CRIM. P. 3.811(d)(1)–(5) (West 1999).
4. *Id.*

(A) Legal Determination of Competency to Be Executed

(A)(1) Criteria for Competency

Florida law provides that a person understand the nature and effect of the death penalty and why it is to be imposed on him or her.[5] A rule of criminal procedure established to provide a judicial hearing on capacity states the same concept somewhat differently: A person under a death sentence is "insane for purposes of execution" if the person lacks the mental capacity to "understand the fact of the impending execution and the reason for it."[6]

(A)(2) Raising the Competency Issue

Anyone believing that an individual under sentence of death may be incompetent to be executed should inform the governor who, in turn, must stay the execution and appoint a panel of three psychiatrists to examine the inmate jointly. Attorneys for the sentenced person and for the state can be present during the evaluation. The governor must then determine whether the inmate is competent to be executed based on the results of the evaluation.[7]

(B) Competency Evaluation

The court may appoint no more than three neutral MHPs to examine the prisoner's capacity to be executed (whether the prisoner "lacks the mental capacity to understand the fact of the pending execution and the reason for it").

(C) Competency Hearing

A hearing on competency to be executed is not a review of the governor's determination but is to be conducted *de novo* (i.e., as a new hearing). At end of the hearing, the court, if it finds by clear and convincing evidence that the prisoner is insane to be executed, shall continue the stay of the death warrant. Otherwise, the stay of execution shall be dissolved.[8]

---

5. 23 FLA. STAT. ANN. § 922.07(1) (West 2001).
6. 33 FLA. R. CRIM. P. 3.811 (West 1999).
7. 23 FLA. STAT. ANN. § 922.07(10) (West 2001).
8. 33 FLA. R. CRIM. P. 3.812 (West 1999).

The rule permitting judicial review of a governor's decision on competency is apparently rarely used. According to a 1999 Florida supreme court case, only three defendants had invoked the rule.[9]

(D) Confidentiality and Privileged Communications

The topics of confidentiality and privilege are discussed in chapters 3.3, Confidential Relations and Communications, and 3.4, Privileged Communications. There are no special rules for confidentiality and privilege in this context.

(E) Disposition of Defendants Found Incompetent to Be Executed

Persons declared to be incompetent by the governor are committed to a DOC mental health facility for treatment designed to restore competency.[10] The condemned person remains in this facility until the facility administrator notifies the governor that the person has been restored to competency. At that point, the statutory provisions for review are begun again, including the appointment of a panel of psychiatrists to jointly examine the individual.[11]

---

9. Provezano v. State, 751 So. 2d 37 (1999).
10. 23 FLA. STAT. ANN. § 922.07(3) (West 2001).
11. 23 FLA. STAT. ANN. § 922.07(4) (West 2001).

7.20
Pornography

Florida law prohibits the promotion, production, and distribution of obscene materials.[1] The law also prohibits the sale or distribution of obscene materials to those under 18 years of age, including materials that depict nudity or sexual conduct, sexual excitement, sexual battery, bestiality, or sadomasochistic abuse and that is harmful to minors, or written or audio material that contains verbal descriptions of sexual material and is harmful to minors.[2] The statute also bars computer pornography directed at or depicting minors.[3]

Material is *obscene* if[4]

1. The average person, applying contemporary community standards, would find that the material, taken as a whole, appeals to prurient (i.e., matters of a sexual or improper) interest;

2. It depicts or describes, in a patently offensive way, sexual conduct as described in the statute; and

3. The material, taken as a whole, lacks serious literary, artistic, political, or scientific value.

It is possible that a court might call on social scientists (some of whom might be MHPs) to assist in assessing community standards, determining whether the materials fall within or outside of those boundaries, or determining whether the material has any

---

1. 22 FLA. STAT. ANN. § 847.011 (West 2000).
2. 22 FLA. STAT. ANN. § 847.012 (West 2000).
3. 22 FLA. STAT. ANN. § 847.0135 (West Supp. 2002).
4. 22 FLA. STAT. ANN. § 847.001(7) (West 2000).

value (particularly scientific value). However, in general, expert testimony regarding these matters is not necessary, especially given the emphasis in the statute that the "average person" is to be the frame of reference for determining whether something is obscene.

7.21
Services for Sex Offenders

Since 1999, Florida law has allowed for the civil commitment of persons with a history of sexual offending who are considered to be at increased risk for reoffending. Such persons, referred to as "sexually violent predators," can be committed to a state institution until that time when they are considered to be no longer at risk for sexual reoffending as a result of a mental disorder.[1]

(A) Criteria for Commitment

Criteria for commitment are multiple and focus on the person's offense history, risk for reoffending, mental state and condition, and need for control and treatment.[2]

(A)(1) Offense History

To be committed as a sexually violent predator a person must, at the time of the commitment, be at least 18 years of age[3] and have been convicted of a "sexually violent offense"[4] or a "sexually motivated offense." This includes persons who have been [5]

1. Adjudicated guilty of a sexually violent offense after a trial, guilty plea, or plea of no contest;

2. Adjudicated not guilty by reason of insanity of a sexually violent offense; or

---
1. 14 FLA. STAT. ANN. § 394.912 (West 2002).
2. 14 FLA. STAT. ANN. § 394.912(10) (West 2002).
3. 14 FLA. STAT. ANN. § 394.912(6) (West 2002).
4. 14 FLA. STAT. ANN. § 394.912(1)(9) (West 2002).
5. 14 FLA. STAT. ANN. § 394.912(2) (West 2002).

3. Adjudicated delinquent of a sexually violent offense after a trial, guilty plea, or plea of no contest.

Thus, persons with a history of juvenile offending are eligible for commitment (providing that they are 18 at the time of their release and subsequent commitment proceedings), as are persons with no conviction history but who have been adjudicated not guilty by reason of insanity of a qualifying offense.

Sexually violent offenses are numerous and include[6]

1. Murder of a human being while engaged in sexual battery;
2. Kidnapping of a child under the age of 13 and, in the course of that offense, committing sexual battery, or a lewd, lascivious, or indecent assault or act on or in the presence of the child;
3. Committing the offense of false imprisonment on a child under the age of 13 and, in the course of that offense, committing sexual battery or a lewd, lascivious, or indecent assault or act on or in the presence of the child;
4. Sexual battery;
5. Lewd, lascivious, or indecent assault or act on or in the presence of the child;
6. An attempt, criminal solicitation, or conspiracy to commit a sexually violent offense;
7. Any conviction for a felony offense in effect at any time before October 1, 1998, which is comparable to a sexually violent offense described earlier or any federal conviction or conviction in another state for a felony offense that in this state would be a sexually violent offense; or
8. Sexually motivated offenses.

Sexually motivated offenses are those that are committed, in part, for "sexual gratification."[7] Accordingly, a person might be eligible for sexually violent predator (SVP) status as a result of a conviction for a nonsexual offense that is considered to be sexually motivated (e.g., burglary).

At the time of the petition for civil commitment as a sexually violent predator, the person must be in "total confinement." This means that the person must be held in a physically secure facility being operated or contractually operated for the DOC, the Department of Juvenile Justice (DJJ), or the DCF.[8] A person is also considered to be in total confinement if he or she is serving a sentence

---

6. 14 FLA. STAT. ANN. § 394.912(9) (West 2002).
7. 14 FLA. STAT. ANN. § 394.912(9)(h) (West 2002).
8. 14 FLA. STAT. ANN. § 394.912(11) (West 2002).

requiring incarceration under the custody of the DOC or the DJJ and is being held in any other secure facility for any reason.[9]

(A)(2) Risk for Reoffending

To be committed as a sexually violent predator a person must be "likely to engage in acts of sexual violence."[10] What offenses or behaviors qualify as acts of sexual violence are not identified in the statute. Although the likelihood of reoffending is not specified by statute, it is offered that "the person's propensity to commit acts of sexual violence is of such a degree as to pose a menace to the health and safety of others."[11] One appellate court has determined that the term "likely" is "commonly understood by men and women of common intelligence to mean highly probable or having a better chance of existing or occurring than not. The meaning of 'likely' is sufficiently clear and definite to avoid guessing or speculation concerning its intended meaning under the act."[12]

(A)(3) Mental Disorder/Need for Treatment and Control

To be committed as a sexually violent predator a person must suffer from a "mental abnormality or personality disorder that makes the person likely to engage in acts of sexual violence if not confined in a secure facility for long-term control, care, and treatment."[13] Mental abnormality is further defined as "mental condition affecting a person's emotional or volitional capacity which predisposes the individual to commit sexually violent offenses."[14] This definition of mental disorder is more broad than the definition used in other civil commitment contexts—for example the involuntary civil commitment law (see chapter 8.4, Involuntary Commitment of Mentally Ill Adults).

(B) Commitment Petition Process

The DCF is responsible for developing a Multidisciplinary Sexually Violent Predator Team. The team must include, but is not limited to two psychiatrists, two psychologists, or a psychiatrist and psychologist. The multidisciplinary team assesses and

---

9. Id.
10. 14 FLA. STAT. ANN. § 394.912(4) (West 2002).
11. 14 FLA. STAT. ANN. § 394.9121(4) (West 2002).
12. Westerheide v. State, 767 So. 2d 637, 653 (Fla 5th D.C.A., 2000).
13. 14 FLA. STAT. ANN. § 394.912(1)(10)(b) (West 2002).
14. 14 FLA. STAT. ANN. § 394.912(5) (West 2002).

evaluates all referred persons.[15] The team is to be notified of the person's eligibility for commitment by the agency holding the person (e.g., DOC, DJJ, DCF) before release from "total confinement" (see earlier definition).[16]

Before a person is recommended by the DCF as meeting the definition of a sexually violent predator and being eligible for commitment, he or she must be offered a personal interview by a psychiatrist or licensed psychologist.[17] If the person refuses to participate in a personal interview, the multidisciplinary team may nonetheless proceed with its recommendation without a personal interview.[18] In subsequent proceedings the court may, in its discretion, order the person to allow members of the multidisciplinary team and any state mental health experts to review all mental health reports, tests, and evaluations by the person's mental health expert or experts; or prohibit the person's mental health experts from testifying about mental health tests, evaluations, or examinations of the person.[19]

Within 45 days after receiving notice, the DCF must develop a written assessment and recommendation regarding whether the person meets the definition of a sexually violent predator and provide it to the state attorney in the circuit in which the person was convicted or committed for the sexually violent offense(s). This written recommendation must include the written report(s) of the multidisciplinary team.[20]

(C) Filing of Petition, Probable Cause Hearing, and Trial

On receipt of the written assessment and recommendation from the DCF multidisciplinary team, the state attorney may choose to file a petition with the circuit court alleging that the person is a sexually violent predator and stating facts sufficient to support such allegations.[21]

The respondent is entitled to a hearing in which the judge determines whether probable cause exists to believe that the person is a sexually violent predator after receiving evidence and listening to arguments from the state attorney and respondent.

---

15. 14 FLA. STAT. ANN. § 394.913(3) (West 2002).
16. 14 FLA. STAT. ANN. § 394.913(1) (West 2002).
17. 14 FLA. STAT. ANN. § 394.913(3)(c) (West 2002).
18. 14 FLA. STAT. ANN. § 394.913(2)(c) (West 2002).
19. 14 FLA. STAT. ANN. § 394.9155(7) (West 2002).
20. 14 FLA. STAT. ANN. § 394.913(3)(e) (West 2002).
21. 14 FLA. STAT. ANN. § 394.914 (West 2002).

At this hearing the respondent has the right to be represented by counsel, present evidence, cross-examine any witnesses who testify against him or her, and view and copy all petitions and reports in the court file.[22]

If the court concludes that there is probable cause to believe that the person is a sexually violent predator the person must be held in custody in a secure facility without opportunity for pretrial release or release during the trial proceedings.[23]

Within 30 days after the determination of probable cause, the court must conduct a trial to determine whether the person is a sexually violent predator.[24] The trial may be continued on the request of either party and a showing of good cause or by the court on its own motion in the interests of justice when the person will not be substantially prejudiced.[25]

If the person is subjected to a mental health examination, the person also may retain experts or mental health professionals to perform an examination. If the person wishes to be examined by a professional of the person's own choice, the examiner must be provided reasonable access to the person, as well as to all relevant medical and mental health records and reports. In the case of a person who is indigent, the court, on the person's request, will determine whether such an examination is necessary. If the court determines that an examination is necessary, the court shall appoint a mental health professional and determine the reasonable compensation for the professional's services, which shall be paid by the state.[26] The results of this professional's examination are privileged and not discoverable until the professional is listed as a witness.[27]

The person or the state attorney has the right to demand that the trial be before a jury of six members. A demand for a jury trial must be filed, in writing, at least five days before the trial. If no demand is made, the trial will be a bench trial (that is, by the judge with no jury).[28]

(D) Disposition

The court or jury must determine by clear and convincing evidence whether the person is a sexually violent predator. If the

---

22. 14 FLA. STAT. ANN. § 394.915 (West 2002).
23. 14 FLA. STAT. ANN. § 394.915(5) (West 2002).
24. 14 FLA. STAT. ANN. § 394.916(1) (West 2002).
25. 14 FLA. STAT. ANN. § 394.916(2) (West 2002).
26. 14 FLA. STAT. ANN. § 394.916(4) (West 2002).
27. Muldrow v. State, 2001 Fla. App. Lexis 5916 (Fla. 2d D.C.A. 2001)
28. 14 FLA. STAT. ANN. § 394.916(5) (West 2002).

determination is made by a jury, the verdict must be unanimous. If the jury is unable to reach a unanimous verdict, the court must declare a mistrial and poll the jury. If a majority of the jury would find the person a sexually violent predator, the state attorney may refile the petition and proceed again according to the provisions of the SVP statute. Any retrial must occur within 90 days after the previous trial, unless the subsequent proceeding is continued. The determination that a person is a sexually violent predator may be appealed.[29]

If the court or jury determines that the person is a sexually violent predator, on the expiration of the incarcerative portion of all criminal sentences and disposition of any detainer other than a detainer for deportation by the U.S. Immigration and Naturalization Service, the person is to be committed to the custody of the DCF for control, care, and treatment until such time as the person's mental abnormality or personality disorder has so changed that it is safe for the person to be at large.[30]

Persons who are adjudicated sexually violent predators and are committed for control, care, and treatment by the DCF are housed in a secure facility at all times and are to be segregated from patients who are not committed under this section.[31] Less restrictive alternatives (e.g., outpatient commitment) are not applicable to sexually violent predator cases.[32]

A person committed as a sexually violent predator must have an examination of his or her mental condition once every year or more frequently at the court's discretion. The person may retain or, if the person is indigent and requests, the court may appoint, a qualified professional to examine the person. This examiner shall have access to all records concerning the person. The results of the examination shall be provided to the court that committed the person under this part. On receipt of the report, the court must conduct a review of the person's status.[33]

The DCF must provide the respondent with annual written notice of his or her right to petition the court for release over the objection of the director of the facility where the person is housed. The director of the facility in which the respondent is housed must forward the notice and waiver form to the court.[34]

The court must hold a limited probable cause hearing to determine whether there is probable cause to believe that the person's condition has changed so that it is safe for the person

---

29. 14 FLA. STAT. ANN. § 394.917(1) (West 2002).
30. 14 FLA. STAT. ANN. § 394.917(2) (West 2002).
31. Id.
32. 14 FLA. STAT. ANN. § 394.911 (West 2002).
33. 14 FLA. STAT. ANN. § 394.918(1) (West 2002).
34. 14 FLA. STAT. ANN. § 394.918(2) (West 2002).

to be at large and that the person will not engage in acts of sexual violence if discharged. The person has the right to be represented by counsel at the probable cause hearing, but the person is not entitled to be present. If the court determines that there is probable cause to believe it is safe to release the person, the court will set a trial date for this issue.[35]

At the subsequent trial, the person is entitled to be present and has all other constitutional protections afforded the person at the initial trial, except for the right to a jury. The state attorney represents the state and has the right to have the person examined by professionals chosen by the state. At the hearing, the state must prove, by clear and convincing evidence, that the person's mental condition remains such that it is not safe for the person to be at large and that, if released, the person is likely to engage in acts of sexual violence.[36]

If the secretary of the DCF or the secretary's designee determines, at any time, that the person is not likely to commit acts of sexual violence if discharged, the secretary or the secretary's designee shall authorize the person to petition the court for release. The petition must be served on the court and the state attorney. The court, on receiving this petition, must order a trial before the court within 30 days, unless continued for good cause. The state attorney represents the state and has the right to have the person examined by professionals of the state attorney's choice. The state bears the burden of proving, by clear and convincing evidence, that the person's mental condition remains such that it is not safe for the person to be at large and that, if released, the person is likely to engage in acts of sexual violence.[37]

(E) Rules of Procedure and Evidence

In all sexually violent predator proceedings

1. The *Florida Rules of Civil Procedure* apply unless otherwise specified;
2. The *Florida Rules of Evidence* apply unless otherwise specified;
3. The psychotherapist–patient privilege does not exist or apply for communications relevant to an issue in proceedings to involuntarily commit a person;
4. The court may consider evidence of previous behavior by a person who is subject to proceedings if such evidence is

---

35. 14 FLA. STAT. ANN. § 394.918(3) (West 2002).
36. 14 FLA. STAT. ANN. § 394.918(4) (West 2002).
37. 14 FLA. STAT. ANN. § 394.919 (West 2002).

relevant to proving that the person is a sexually violent predator; and

5. Hearsay evidence, including reports of a member of the multidisciplinary team or reports produced on behalf of the multidisciplinary team, is admissible unless the court finds that such evidence is not reliable. In a trial, however, hearsay evidence may not be used as the sole basis for committing a person.[38]

Relevant information and records that are otherwise confidential or privileged are to be released to the agency with jurisdiction, to the multidisciplinary team, or to the state attorney for the purpose of meeting the notice requirements and determining whether a person is or continues to be a sexually violent predator. A person, agency, or entity receiving information under this section, which is confidential, must maintain the confidentiality of that information. Such information does not lose its confidential status because of its release under this section.[39]

Psychological or psychiatric reports, drug and alcohol reports, treatment records, medical records, or victim impact statements that have been submitted to the court or admitted into evidence during the course of any sexually violent predator proceeding are part of the legal record but are to be sealed and may be opened only pursuant to a court order.[40]

(F) Immunity From Civil Liability

The agency with jurisdiction over the respondent before his or her referral for evaluation as a sexually violent predator, its officers and employees; the DCF and its officers and employees; members of the multidisciplinary team; the state attorney and the state attorney's employees; and those involved in the evaluation, care, and treatment of sexually violent persons committed under this law are immune from any civil liability for good faith conduct (that is, the individual did not act with malice toward the defendant).[41]

---

38. 14 FLA. STAT. ANN. § 394.9155 (West 2002).
39. 14 FLA. STAT. ANN. § 394.921(1) (West 2002).
40. 14 FLA. STAT. ANN. § 394.915(2) (West 2002).
41. 14 FLA. STAT. ANN. § 394.923 (West 2002).

7.22
Services for Victims of Crimes

Persons who suffer physical injury as a result of crime victimization and some family members and other persons close to the crime victim in cases of death can seek reimbursement for some losses from the Department of Legal Affairs, which may delegate authority to resolve such claims to its Crime Victims' Services Office.[1]

(A) Eligibility and Awards

Awards may be made on findings that a crime was committed, the crime resulted directly in personal injury or death or psychological or psychiatric injury to the victim or claimant, and the crime was promptly reported to proper authorities (a report filed more than 72 hours after the crime will not be considered prompt unless there are extenuating circumstances). The award must be made on an "actual need" basis and only after insurers and other potential payers have provided compensation. The award is considered to be the payment of last resort.[2]

An award made according to this procedure shall not exceed a total of $15,000 for all compensable cost or losses, and awards for treatment shall not exceed $10,000.[3] A minor victim may receive continuing or periodic mental health care because of the adverse impact of victimization to a maximum of $10,000. The victim's legal guardian may also seek supplemental treatment awards.[4]

---

1. 24 FLA. STAT. ANN. § 960.09 (West Supp. 2002).
2. 24 FLA. STAT. ANN. § 960.13 (West Supp. 2002).
3. 24 FLA. STAT. ANN. § 960.13(9)(a) (West Supp. 2002).
4. 24 FLA. STAT. ANN. § 960.13(9)(b) (West Supp. 2002).

(B) Information and Services Available to Victims and Their Families

Florida law provides a variety of rights to victims of crimes. Law enforcement personnel are to provide victims of crimes with notification of their rights, including the availability of compensation where available, as well as the status of the legal proceedings against the defendant and notice of the potential release of an assailant.[5] Victims may also have the right to communicate to the prosecuting attorney about the impact of the crime on them and to be informed about prosecutorial decisions.[6]

In some circumstances, counseling is available to crime victims. One example is when a victim tests positive in an HIV test administered after an offense where bodily fluids are transmitted. In such a case, face-to-face counseling must be provided to the victim.[7]

(C) Services by MHPs

As noted earlier, mental health services are available through the Crime Victims' Services Office. Therefore, MHPs may play a role in providing mental health treatment to victims of crimes who receive financial support under this state law.

---

5. 24 FLA. STAT. ANN. § 960.001 (West Supp. 2002).
6. *Id.*
7. 24 FLA. STAT. ANN. § 960.002(3) (West Supp. 2002).

Section 8

Voluntary or Involuntary Receipt of State Services

8.1

Medicaid

The Medicaid program is an extraordinarily complex program that pays for medically necessary services for indigent people meeting eligibility criteria generally established by state law. The program is established by federal statute but is administered by the states pursuant to state statutory and regulatory law. A single state agency must be designated to administer the Medicaid program on behalf of the state—in Florida, that agency is the Agency for Health Care Administration (AHCA).[1] The federal government pays a portion of the costs of the Medicaid program, with individual states paying the remainder through a formula established by federal law. Payments are made to service providers as reimbursement for providing designated services to eligible individuals. A full discussion of Medicaid as it impacts mental health professionals (MHPs) and providers is beyond the scope of this book. Therefore, this chapter discusses briefly the core elements of the Florida Medicaid program, including covered services, eligibility, and the use of managed care technologies in the Medicaid program. MHPs who provide treatment to Medicaid-eligible individuals will be affected by the general provisions governing the Medicaid program.

(A) Services Provided

States are obligated by federal law to reimburse providers for certain core, or "mandatory," Medicaid services. These are enumerated in Florida statute, and include[2]

---

1. 14 FLA. STAT. ANN. § 409.902 (West 1998).
2. 14 FLA. STAT. ANN. § 409.905 (West 2002).

1. Advanced registered nurse practitioner services;
2. Early and periodic screening, diagnosis, and treatment services;
3. Family planning services;
4. Home health care services;
5. Hospital inpatient services (note, however, that a licensed hospital maintained primarily for the care and treatment of people with mental disorders or mental diseases is not eligible for Medicaid reimbursement for adults between the ages of 22 and 64; this reflects a long-standing federal policy of not paying for care delivered in free-standing psychiatric hospitals for adults);
6. Hospital outpatient services;
7. Independent laboratory services;
8. Nursing facility services;
9. Physician services;
10. Portable x-ray services;
11. Rural health clinic services; and
12. Transportation services.

Other services, which a state may but need not provide, are called "optional services." Florida law provides coverage for the following optional services:[3]

1. Adult denture services;
2. Adult health screening services;
3. Ambulatory surgical center services;
4. Birth center services;
5. Case management services;
6. Children's dental services;
7. Chiropractic services;
8. Community mental health services;
9. Dialysis facility services;
10. Durable medical equipment;
11. Healthy start services;
12. Hearing services;
13. Home and community-based services;
14. Hospice care services;

---

3. 14 FLA. STAT. ANN. § 409.906 (West 2002).

15. Intermediate care facility for the developmentally disabled services;
16. Intermediate care services;
17. Optometric services;
18. Physician assistant services;
19. Podiatric services;
20. Prescribed drug services;
21. Registered nurse first assistant services;
22. State hospital services, for those age 65 or older in a state psychiatric hospital;
23. Visual services; and
24. Child-welfare-targeted case management.

(B) Eligibility for Services

Reimbursement is available only for covered services provided to people who meet the statutory eligibility criteria. Program eligibility focuses on needy families and elderly individuals. Individuals falling into a presumptively eligible category must also meet income and assets criteria established by federal and state law. The legislature defines people for whom mandatory services must be made available as[4]

1. Low-income families with children provided the family includes a dependent child living with a caretaker relative; the family's income does not exceed the gross income test limit; and the family's countable income and resources do not exceed the applicable Aid to Families With Dependent Children (AFDC) standards;

2. A person receiving payments from, or who is eligible for the Supplemental Security Income Program (SSI)—this includes a low-income person age 65 or older and a low-income person younger than 65 considered to be permanently and totally disabled;

3. A child under age 21 living in a low-income, two-parent family, and a child under age 7 living with a nonrelative, if the income and assets of the family or child do not exceed the limits set by the WAGES program (Work and Gain Economic Self-Sufficiency, a state program that limits the time a person receives state assistance);

---

4. 14 FLA. STAT. ANN. § 409.903 (West 2002).

4. A child eligible under the Social Security Act for subsidized board payments, foster care, or adoption subsidies and a child not eligible but who is in foster care, shelter, emergency shelter care, or subsidized adoption;

5. A pregnant woman or a child under age 1, if either is living in a family with income at or below 185% of the current federal poverty level;

6. Children meeting certain age and poverty criteria;

7. An individual older than 65 or who is determined to be disabled, whose income is at or below 100% of the current federal poverty level.

Optional payments may be made for[5]

1. A person 65 or older or who is disabled and whose income is at or below 100% of the federal poverty level;

2. A family, pregnant woman, child under age 18, a person age 65 or older, or a blind or disabled person eligible for mandatory payments, unless income exceeds established limits;

3. A person in need of the services of a licensed nursing facility, a licensed intermediate care facility for the developmentally disabled, or a state mental hospital, whose income does not exceed 300% of the SSI income standard;

4. A low-income person who meets all other requirements for Medicaid eligibility except citizenship and who needs emergency medical services, payment limited to the emergency services;

5. A postpartum woman living in a family that has an income at or below 185% of the current federal poverty level may receive family planning services for up to 24 months following a pregnancy for which Medicaid paid pregnancy services; and

6. Children meeting certain age and poverty criteria.

(C) Limitations on Payment

Other rules govern reimbursement for health care services paid for by Medicaid. Whether or not services will be reimbursed depends on whether the services are considered "medically necessary." In addition, a provider will be reimbursed only if the provider has an agreement with the AHCA. Providers must meet requirements involving licensure of staff, record-keeping, billing,

---

5. 14 FLA. STAT. ANN. § 409.904 (West 2002).

and liability insurance, among other things, to obtain a provider agreement.[6]

The statute also establishes rules governing the manner in which particular types of reimbursement will be made. For example, reimbursement for outpatient services is limited to $1500 per year, except for renal dialysis and for persons under age 21.[7] In addition, the legislation specifies that hospital payments must be made prospectively.[8] This reflects a general shift in Florida and elsewhere toward methods of reimbursement that are more predictable for the payer and are designed in part to limit cost inflation.

(D) Managed Care and the Medicaid Program

Beginning in the 1990s Florida, like many states, began to take a number of steps to control growth of Medicaid expenditures while attempting to ensure access to services. Many of those steps have fallen under the rubric of "managed care." Florida law includes most if not all of the features associated with managed care in Medicaid (and in many privately financed health care) systems, including enrollment of individuals in a managed care plan, use of a primary care physician, and a shift from fee-for-service reimbursement to prospective payment plans, including capitation.

With respect to provision of mental health services, the legislature has authorized the creation of pilot "carve-out" programs (where Medicaid funding for mental health is awarded contractually to a company that, in turn, purchases mental health services while the person's health care services are provided by the primary care system) and, most recently, has authorized the AHCA and the state Department of Children and Families (DCF) to contract with a single company to manage both Medicaid and mental health expenditures.

A section of Medicaid law dealing with managed care in general illustrates some of this evolution. For example, the legislature has required that all Medicaid recipients are to be enrolled in a managed care plan or MediPass except those Medicaid recipients who are in an institution, enrolled in the Medicaid medically needy program, or eligible for both Medicaid and Medicare. At the same time, the recipient's decision to enroll is to be voluntary,

---

6. 14 FLA. STAT. ANN. § 409.907 (West 2002).
7. 14 FLA. STAT. ANN. § 409.908(1)(b) (West 2002).
8. 14 FLA. STAT. ANN. § 409.908(1)(a) (West 2002).

and enrollment is supposed to signify a decision by the agency that the managed care plan has specific services addressing the individual's needs. State agencies are also to provide information to recipients about the characteristics of managed care plans for Medicaid recipients. In addition, any managed care plan enrolling Medicaid recipients must comply with quality-of-care standards established by statute.[9]

If the person does not enroll, he or she may be enrolled by the agency, and enrollment is supposed to be in a program that can meet individual needs. Individuals are entitled to certain rights as plan enrollees, including the right to dis-enroll from the plan under certain conditions and a right to a grievance process.

With respect to provision of mental health services, the legislature directed the AHCA to develop *provider* enrollment processes based on an assessment of service need.[10] This reflected a legislative desire to control cost, and providers are selected for participation through a competitive procurement or selective contracting process. The AHCA was authorized to use diagnostic criteria in setting reimbursement rates, preauthorize high-cost or highly used services, limit or eliminate coverage for certain services, and to take other steps to meet budget targets.

These developments, and many others not described, represent a continuing and still controversial effort to limit the growth of expenditures in the Medicaid program generally and for mental health services in particular.

---

9. 14 FLA. STAT. ANN. § 409.9122 (West 2002).
10. 14 FLA. STAT. ANN. § 409.906(8) (West Supp. 2000).

8.2

Health Care Cost Containment System

Florida has established a minimum health benefits package for individuals who are indigent and ineligible either for Medicare or Medicaid. It is called the MedAccess program, and it is administered by the AHCA.[1]

Residents of Florida with a gross family income equal to or below 250% of the federal poverty level and who have not been insured for the 12-month period before applying for the program are eligible.[2] Enrolled individuals are entitled to a minimum benefits package that includes[3]

1. Physician services, limited to 12 annual visits, excluding periodic physical examinations;

2. Hospital insurance services, up to a limit of 10 days per calendar year;

3. Hospital outpatient services, up to a limit of $1500 per calendar year per member for services that are preventive, diagnostic, therapeutic, or palliative;

4. Laboratory services;

5. X-ray services;

6. Family planning services;

7. Health appraisals, including physical examinations and well-baby and well-child screening and diagnostic services;

8. Immunizations;

9. Advanced registered nurse practitioner services; and

---

1. 14 FLA. STAT. ANN. § 408.902 (West 2002).
2. 14 FLA. STAT. ANN. § 408.903(1) and (2) (West 2002).
3. 14 FLA. STAT. ANN. § 408.904(2)(a)–(j) (West 2002).

10. Outpatient mental health visits and substance abuse treatment, up to a total of five visits per calendar year.

Services that are not covered include[4]

1. Surgery solely for cosmetic purposes;
2. Prescribed drugs;
3. Nursing home services;
4. Medical examinations and medical reports prepared either for the purchase of life insurance or for participating as a plaintiff or defendant in a civil damages action; and
5. Clinically unproven or experimental procedures.

In addition to these exclusions, MedAccess excludes coverage for preexisting conditions (other than pregnancy) for 12 months, as long as the condition manifested itself or a treatment was recommended for the condition within six months of the start of coverage, as well as coverage for outpatient prescription drugs, eyeglasses, dental services, custodial care, and emergency care for nonemergent conditions.[5]

If a person is classified by the program as "high-risk" (i.e., having a condition that may require significant amounts of health care), then a case manager is assigned to monitor the person's care.[6] In addition, a person whose care exceeds $500,000 in the program is subsequently excluded from MedAccess.[7]

---

4. 14 FLA. STAT. ANN. § 408.904(3)(a)–(e) (West 2002).
5. 14 FLA. STAT. ANN. § 408.905(2) and (3) (West 2002).
6. 14 FLA. STAT. ANN. § 408.905(4) (West 2002).
7. 14 FLA. STAT. ANN. § 408.905(5) (West 2002).

8.3
Voluntary Admission of Mentally Ill Adults

A mental health facility[1] may receive for observation, diagnosis, or treatment any person 18 years of age or older who makes application for admission by express and informed consent. If the facility finds evidence that the person has a mental illness, is competent to provide express and informed consent, and is suitable for admission, the facility may admit the person as a voluntary patient.[2] If the person is age 17 or younger, an application may be accepted from the person's guardian (including a parent) but the admission can occur only after a hearing to verify the voluntariness of the consent.[3]

(A) Differences Between Voluntary and Involuntary Admission

An individual admitted voluntarily enjoys certain rights, such as the right to leave the facility, that an individual involuntarily admitted does not. However, if the facility believes that a voluntary patient who wishes to discharge him- or herself meets involuntary admission standards, the facility may initiate a petition for civil commitment.

---

1. A *facility* is defined as any hospital, community facility, public or private facility, or receiving or treatment facility providing for the evaluation, diagnosis, care, treatment, training, or hospitalization of persons who appear to have a mental illness or have been diagnosed as having such an illness. 14 FLA. STAT. ANN. § 394.455(10) (West 2002).
2. 14 FLA. STAT. ANN. § 394.4625(1)(a) (West Supp. 2000).
3. *Id.*

(B) Evaluation and Admission

In some cases, a mental health overlay program, mobile crisis response service, or a licensed MHP authorized to initiate an involuntary examination under the civil commitment law must conduct an assessment to determine if the individual can provide express and informed consent before a voluntary admission can occur. These include an individual 60 years of age or older for whom transfer is being sought from an assisted living facility, adult day care center, or adult family-care home, if the person has been diagnosed with dementia; a person 60 years of age or older for whom transfer is being sought from a nursing home; and a person for whom health care surrogates or proxies are making decisions.[4]

A facility may not admit as a voluntary patient a person who has been adjudicated incapacitated, unless a court has removed the condition of incapacity. If a person is admitted as a voluntary patient and is later found to have been adjudicated incapacitated, the facility must discharge the patient or transfer him or her to involuntary status.[5] In addition, the health care surrogate or proxy of a voluntary patient may not consent to mental health treatment for the patient. If a voluntary patient is unwilling or unable to give express and informed consent to mental health treatment, the person must be discharged or transferred to involuntary status.[6]

(C) Discharge

A voluntary patient shall be discharged[7]

1. If the patient has sufficiently improved so that retention in an inpatient facility is no longer desirable;

2. If the patient revokes consent or requests discharge. A request for discharge may be verbal or in writing and made by the patient, relative, friend, or attorney of the patient. The patient must be discharged within 24 hours of the request, unless the request is rescinded or the patient is transferred to involuntary status. The 24-hour period can be extended for no more than three days, exclusive of holidays and weekends; or

3. If the patient admitted as voluntary refuses to consent or revokes consent to treatment, the patient shall be discharged within 24 hours of the revocation or refusal.

---

4. 14 FLA. STAT. ANN. § 394.4625(1)(b) (West Supp. 2000).
5. 14 FLA. STAT. ANN. § 394.4625(1)(d) (West 2002).
6. 14 FLA. STAT. ANN. § 394.4625(1)(e) (West 2002).
7. 14 FLA. STAT. ANN. § 394.4625(2) (West 2002).

8.4
Involuntary Commitment of Mentally Ill Adults

Adults with mental illness are subject to involuntary civil commitment under certain conditions. MHPs may become involved in the evaluation process before admission by initiating such proceedings, as witnesses at a commitment hearing, or by providing treatment after an admission or hearing.

(A) Definitions

To understand the law concerning involuntary commitment, MHPs should be familiar with the following terms and their legal meanings.[1] *Mental illness* means

> an impairment of the emotional processes that exercise conscious control of one's actions or of the ability to perceive or understand reality, which impairment substantially interferes with a person's ability to meet the ordinary demands of living, regardless of etiology . . . (with the exception of) retardation or developmental disability . . . , intoxication, or conditions manifested only by antisocial behavior or substance abuse impairment.[2]

Express and informed consent means

> consent voluntarily given in writing, by a competent person, after sufficient explanation and disclosure of the subject matter involved to enable the person to make a knowing and willful decision without any element of force, fraud, deceit, duress, or other form of constraint or coercion.[3]

---

1. 14 FLA. STAT. ANN. § 394.455 (West 2002).
2. 14 FLA. STAT. ANN. § 394.455(18) (West 2002).
3. 14 FLA. STAT. ANN. § 394.455(9) West 2002).

Clinical psychologist means a psychologist ... with 3 years of postdoctoral experience in the practice of clinical psychology, inclusive of the experience required for licensure, or a psychologist employed by a facility operated by the United States Department of Veterans Affairs that qualifies as a receiving or treatment facility. . . .[4]

Psychiatrist means "a [licensed] medical practitioner ... who has primarily diagnosed and treated mental and nervous disorders for a period of not less than 3 years, inclusive of psychiatric residency."[5] *Clinical social worker* means "a person licensed as a clinical social worker. . . ."[6] *Psychiatric nurse* means "a registered nurse with a masters degree or a doctors degree in psychiatric nursing and 2 years of post-masters clinical experience under the supervision of a physician."[7] *Receiving facility* means "any public or private facility designated by the Department of Children and Families (DCF) to receive and hold involuntary patients under emergency conditions or for psychiatric evaluation and to provide short-term treatment. The term does not include a county jail."[8]

(B) Distinction Between Examination and Placement

Civil commitment law in Florida distinguishes between the involuntary examination of allegedly mentally ill persons and involuntary placement of allegedly mentally ill persons. *Involuntary examination* refers to the process whereby a person who is believed to meet criteria for civil commitment is hospitalized for a short period of time in a community-based facility so that he or she can be evaluated and observed more closely.[9] *Involuntary placement* refers to the involuntary admission and treatment of a person to an inpatient setting for a period not to exceed six months.[10] Whereas involuntary examinations can be initiated in a number of ways, involuntary placement can occur only after an evidentiary hearing (unless the hearing is waived by the individual) and in response to a judge's order.

As indicated next, the criteria for involuntary examination and placement are essentially the same. The general requirements

---

4. 14 FLA. STAT. ANN. § 394.455(2) (West 2002).
5. 14 FLA. STAT. ANN. § 394.455(24) (West 2002).
6. 14 FLA. STAT. ANN. § 394.455(4) (West 2002).
7. 14 FLA. STAT. ANN. § 394.455(23) (West 2002).
8. 14 FLA. STAT. ANN. § 394.455(26) (West 2002).
9. 14 FLA. STAT. ANN. § 394.463 (West 2002).
10. 14 FLA. STAT. ANN. § 394.467 (West 2002).

are that the individual suffer from mental illness and, as a result of the mental illness, is likely to neglect or refuse to care for him- or herself or is likely to harm him- or herself or others.

(C) Involuntary Examination

(C)(1) Criteria for Involuntary Examination

An individual may be taken to a receiving facility for involuntary examination if there is reason to believe that[11]

1. He or she is mentally ill and, as a result of the mental illness,
   (a) Has refused voluntary examination after explanation and disclosure of the purpose of the examination; or
   (b) Is unable to determine whether examination is necessary; and
2. Without care and treatment the person is likely to suffer from neglect or refuse to care for him- or herself, and this neglect or refusal poses a real and present threat of substantial harm to his or her well-being, and it is not apparent that such harm can be avoided through the help of willing family or friends or through the provision of services; or
3. There is a substantial likelihood that without care or treatment the person will cause serious bodily harm to him- or herself or others in the near future, as indicated by recent behavior.

(C)(2) Initiating an Involuntary Examination

An involuntary examination may be initiated in three ways:[12]

1. On hearing evidence in the form of sworn testimony, a court may enter an *ex parte* order (an order entered on petition of one party but without the presence of the other party) directing that the individual appears to meet criteria for involuntary examination. This order becomes part of the clinical record. If other, less restrictive means are not available, such as voluntary appearance of the individual for outpatient evaluation, the court can direct a law enforcement officer or other designee to take the individual into custody and transport him or her to the nearest receiving facility for involuntary examination.
2. A law enforcement officer may take into custody an individual who appears to meet the criteria for involuntary examination and deliver him or her to a receiving facility for involuntary examination. The officer must submit a report that documents

---

11. 14 FLA. STAT. ANN. § 394.463(1) (West 2002).
12. 14 FLA. STAT. ANN. § 394.463(2)(a) (West 2002).

the circumstances under which the person was taken into custody and this report becomes part of the clinical record.

3. Physicians, licensed psychologists, psychiatric nurses, and clinical social workers can complete a certificate indicating that they have examined the individual within the preceding 48 hours and believe that he or she meets the criteria for involuntary examination. The certificate, which must detail the observations on which the professional's conclusions are based, becomes part of the clinical record. If other, less restrictive means are not available, a law enforcement officer can take the individual into custody and transport him or her to the nearest receiving facility for involuntary examination.

(C)(3) The Involuntary Examination Process (Emergency Admission)

A person admitted to a receiving facility for involuntary examination must be examined by a physician or clinical psychologist[13] without unnecessary delay and may, on order of a physician, be provided emergency treatment that is identified as necessary for the safety of the examinee or others. The examinee cannot be released without the documented approval of a psychiatrist or clinical psychologist.[14]

During the 72-hour examination period (excluding weekends and holidays), one of the following must happen:[15]

1. The examinee must be released, unless he or she is charged with a crime, in which case the examinee is returned to the custody of a law enforcement officer;

2. The examinee is released for outpatient follow-up treatment;

3. The examinee must agree to placement or treatment as a voluntary patient; or

4. A petition for involuntary placement must be filed with the appropriate court.

(C)(4) Change of Status

An involuntary patient who requests transfer to voluntary status must be transferred to voluntary status unless charged with a crime or involuntarily placed for examination or treatment by a court and it is determined that he or she continues to meet criteria for involuntary placement.[16]

---

13. Note that the law identifies a "clinical psychologist" (*see* 14 FLA. STAT. ANN. § 394.455(2) (West 2002) and earlier text for definition) as opposed to a "licensed psychologist."
14. 14 FLA. STAT. ANN. § 394.463(2)(f) (West 2002).
15. 14 FLA. STAT. ANN. § 394.463(2)(i) (West 2002).
16. 14 FLA. STAT. ANN. § 394.4625(4) (West 2002).

When a voluntary inpatient or his or her agent makes a request for discharge from the inpatient setting, the request for discharge must be communicated to a physician, clinical psychologist, or psychiatrist as quickly as possible, no later than 12 hours after the request is made. If the professional believes that the patient meets criteria for involuntary placement, the facility administrator must file with the court a petition for involuntary placement within two court working days, or the patient must be discharged. Pending the filing of the petition, the patient can be held and emergency treatment rendered in the least restrictive manner on the written order of a physician if it is determined that the treatment is necessary for the safety of the patient or others.[17]

(D) Involuntary Placement

(D)(1) The Involuntary Placement Hearing and Process

A hearing must be held within five days after the court receives the petition for involuntary placement, unless a continuance is granted. The subject of the petition has the following rights with regard to the involuntary placement process and hearing:

1. The right to a copy of the petition for involuntary placement;[18]
2. The right to attend the hearing unless the court determines that attendance is not in the person's best interests and the person's attorney does not object;[19]
3. The right to an attorney (the court must appoint an attorney for the individual if he or she cannot afford one);[20]
4. The right to an independent expert examination that is confidential and not discoverable unless the expert is to be called as a witness at the hearing;[21]
5. The right to refuse to testify;[22] and
6. The right to review the medical or psychiatric record and have access to witnesses (via his or her attorney).[23]

At the hearing, the recommendation for involuntary placement must be supported by the opinion of two psychiatrists or a psychiatrist and clinical psychologist who have examined the individual within the preceding 72 hours. In counties of fewer

---

17. 14 FLA. STAT. ANN. § 394.4625(5) (West 2002).
18. 14 FLA. STAT. ANN. § 394.467(3) (West 2002).
19. 14 FLA. STAT. ANN. § 394.467(6)(a)1 (West 2002).
20. 14 FLA. STAT. ANN. § 394.467(4) (West 2002).
21. 14 FLA. STAT. ANN. § 394.467(6)(a)2 (West 2002).
22. *Id.*
23. 14 FLA. STAT. ANN. § 394.467(4) (West 2002).

than 50,000 people and in which a psychiatrist or a clinical psychologist is not available to provide the second opinion, a physician with psychiatric experience or a psychiatric nurse may provide such an opinion.[24]

At the involuntary placement hearing the court is to consider testimony regarding the person's competence to consent to treatment. If the court finds that the patient is incompetent to consent to treatment, it must appoint a guardian advocate.[25] The guardian advocate can consent to medical or mental health treatment on the person's behalf subsequent to commitment and placement, but the guardian advocate may not consent to abortion, sterilization, electroconvulsive treatment, psychosurgery, or experimental treatments without express and specific approval from the court in an independent hearing.[26] The guardian advocate is discharged when the patient is returned to the community, transferred to voluntary patient status, or determined to have had his or her competence to consent to treatment restored.[27]

(D)(2) Criteria for Involuntary Placement

An individual may be involuntarily placed for treatment on a finding of the court, by clear and convincing evidence, that[28]

1. He or she is mentally ill and, because of the mental illness:
   (a) Has refused voluntary placement for treatment after sufficient and conscientious explanation and disclosure of the purpose for treatment; or
   (b) Is unable to determine whether placement is necessary; and

2. Is manifestly incapable of surviving alone or with the help of willing and responsible family or friends, including available alternatives services, and without treatment is likely to suffer from neglect or refuse to care for him- or herself, and this neglect or refusal poses a real and present threat of substantial harm to his or her well-being;

3. There is a substantial likelihood that in the near future the person will inflict serious bodily harm to him- or herself or others, as evidenced by recent behavior causing, attempting, or threatening such harm; and

4. All available, less restrictive treatment alternatives are inappropriate.

---

24. 14 FLA. STAT. ANN. § 394.467(2) (West 2002).
25. 14 FLA. STAT. ANN. § 394.467(6)(d) (West 2002).
26. 14 FLA. STAT. ANN. § 394.4598(6) (West 2002).
27. 14 FLA. STAT. ANN. § 394.4598(7) (West 2002).
28. 14 FLA. STAT. ANN. § 394.467(1) (West 2002).

(D)(3) Disposition of Persons Who Meet Criteria for Involuntary Placement

If the court determines that the examinee meets the criteria for involuntary placement by clear and convincing evidence, then it must order that the person be transferred to a treatment facility for a period of up to six months. A patient must be released from the treatment facility or transferred to voluntary status whenever facility staff believe that the person no longer meets the criteria for involuntary placement.[29] If, after six months, it is believed that the patient continues to meet criteria for involuntary placement, another hearing must be held to determine this issue. The request for continued commitment must be accompanied by a statement from the patient's physician or clinical psychologist justifying the request, a brief description of the patient's treatment during the period of involuntary placement, and an individualized treatment plan.[30] Subsequent placements are for a six-month period.[31] In those cases where the patient has previously been found incompetent to consent to treatment, the hearing officer will consider testimony and evidence regarding the patient's competence. If the hearing officer finds evidence that the patient is competent to consent to treatment, he or she may issue a recommended order to the court that found the patient incompetent to consent to treatment that the patient's competence be restored and that any previously appointed guardian advocate be discharged.[32]

(E) Discharge

An involuntary patient who requests transfer to voluntary status must be transferred to voluntary status unless charged with a crime or involuntarily placed for examination or treatment by a court and it is determined that he or she continues to meet criteria for involuntary placement.[33]

When a voluntary inpatient or his or her agent makes a request for discharge from the inpatient setting, the request for discharge must be communicated to a physician, clinical psychologist, or psychiatrist as quickly as possible, no later than 12 hours after the request is made. If the professional believes that the patient meets criteria for involuntary placement, the facility administrator must file with the court a petition for involuntary

---

29. 14 FLA. STAT. ANN. § 394.467(6)(b) (West 2002).
30. 14 FLA. STAT. ANN. § 394.467(7)(b) (West 2002).
31. 14 FLA. STAT. ANN. § 394.467(7)(d) (West 2002).
32. 14 FLA. STAT. ANN. § 394.467(7)(f) (West 2002).
33. 14 FLA. STAT. ANN. § 394.4625(4) (West 2002).

placement within two court working days or the patient must be discharged. Pending the filing of the petition, the patient can be held and emergency treatment rendered in the least restrictive manner on the written order of a physician if it is determined that the treatment is necessary for the safety of the patient or others.[34]

(F) Patient Rights

Individuals with mental illness have the following rights under state law:[35]

1. A right to individual dignity and to not be incarcerated in a jail unless charged with a criminal offense;
2. A right to not be denied treatment or to have services delayed because of an inability to pay;
3. A right to receive the least restrictive appropriate available treatment based on individual needs and the best interests of the person, consistent with optimum improvement of the person's condition;
4. A right to a physical examination within 24 hours of arrival at a treatment facility if the person is at the facility for longer than 12 hours;
5. A right in a treatment facility to participate in activities designed to enhance self-image;
6. A right to a treatment plan no more than five days after admission, with an opportunity to assist in preparation of the plan and an opportunity to review before implementation;
7. A right to give informed consent to treatment;
8. A right to services suited to his or her needs, administered skillfully, safely, and humanely, including such medical, vocational, social, educational, and rehabilitative services as his or her condition requires to bring about an early return to the community;
9. A right to be free from the use of restraint or seclusion for punishment or for the convenience of staff;
10. A right to communicate freely with persons outside the facility absent a determination that such communication would be harmful to the person or others;
11. A right to receive and send unopened mail absent a finding of harm to the person or others;

---

34. 14 FLA. STAT. ANN. § 394.4625(5) (West 2002).
35. 14 FLA. STAT. ANN. § 394.459 (West 2002).

12. A right to visitation by family or legal representatives or guardian or guardian advocate;
13. A right to the use of a telephone and the right to report abuse;
14. A right of access to personal effects and clothing; and
15. A right to vote if otherwise qualified.

(G) Civil Liability

Individuals who act in good faith (that is, without malice or intent to do harm) in complying with the provisions of law discussed in this chapter are immune from civil or criminal liability for their actions in connection with the admission, diagnosis, treatment, or discharge of an individual to a facility.[36] However, liability may be imposed for negligence.[37] Individuals involved with the evaluation, care, and treatment of individuals committed as sexually violent predators are also immune from civil liability if they act in good faith.[38]

---

36. 14 FLA. STAT. ANN. § 394.459(10) (West 2002).
37. *Id.*
38. 14 FLA. STAT. ANN. § 394.923 (West 2002).

8.5
Voluntary Admission and Involuntary Commitment of People With Substance Problems

In 1993, the legislature combined the laws regulating the provision of voluntary and involuntary examination and treatment of persons with alcohol and other drug disorders.

(A) Definitions

To understand the law concerning assessment and treatment of persons substance abuse problems, MHPs should be familiar with the following terms and their legal meanings.[1] *Assessment* means

> the systematic evaluation of information gathered to determine the nature and severity of the client's substance abuse problem and the client's need and motivation for services. Assessment entails the use of a psychosocial history supplemented, as required by rule, by medical examinations, laboratory testing, and psychometric measures.

Habitual abuser means "a person who is brought to the attention of law enforcement for being substance impaired, who meets the criteria for involuntary admission, and who has been taken into custody for such impairment three or more times during the preceding twelve months." *Qualified professional* means "a licensed physician; a professional licensed under Florida law; or a person who is certified through a Department of Children and Families (DCF)-recognized certification process for substance abuse treatment services and who holds, at a minimum, a bachelor's degree." *Stabilization* means "alleviation of a crisis condition or prevention of further deterioration, and connotes short-term emergency treat-

---

1. 14 FLA. STAT. ANN. § 397.311 (West 2002).

ment." *Substance abuse impaired* means "a condition involving the use of alcoholic beverages or any psychoactive or mood-altering substance in such a manner as to induce mental, emotional, or physical problems and cause socially dysfunctional behavior."

(B) Voluntary Treatment and Admission

A person who wishes to enter treatment for substance abuse may apply to a service provider (i.e., any public agency, private agency, private practitioner, or hospital)[2] for voluntary treatment or admission for treatment. The service provider must emphasize the least restrictive alternative necessary given the person's treatment needs.[3]

Persons under the age of 18 years may consent to substance abuse treatment without the knowledge or consent of their parents, legal guardians, or legal custodians,[4] but their parents, legal guardians, or legal custodians are not responsible for payment for services unless they have voluntarily participated in such services or they have been ordered to participate in such services.[5]

(C) Protective Custody

A law enforcement officer who discovers a minor or adult who appears to meet criteria for involuntary admission (see section D, Involuntary Admissions) may implement protective custody measures. Such assistance includes transporting the person home, to a hospital, or to a licensed detoxification or addictions receiving facility, whichever the officer believes to be most appropriate.[6] If the person refuses assistance from the law enforcement officer and the law enforcement officer has determined that a hospital or licensed detoxification or addictions receiving facility is the most appropriate place for the person, the law enforcement officer can take the person to such a facility against his or her will or, in the case of an adult, detain him or her in a jail or other detention facility for protection of the person.[7] A person who is in protective

---

2. 14 FLA. STAT. ANN. § 397.311(28) (West 2002).
3. 14 FLA. STAT. ANN. § 397.601(1) (West 2002); 14 FLA. STAT. ANN. § 397.601(3) (West 2002).
4. 14 FLA. STAT. ANN. § 397.601(4)(a) (West 2002).
5. 14 FLA. STAT. ANN. § 397.431(3) (West 2002).
6. 14 FLA. STAT. ANN. § 397.6771 (West 2002).
7. 14 FLA. STAT. ANN. § 397.6772 (West 2002).

custody must be released by a qualified professional when the person no longer meets criteria for involuntry admission, a 72-hour period has elapsed, or the client has consented to remain voluntarily at the licensed facility.[8] A client involuntarily admitted may be released only by a qualified professional. In cases of a minor, notice must be given to the applicant or to the petitioner and the court if the assessment or treatment was court-ordered.[9] A person can only be retained in protective custody beyond the 72-hour period when a petition for involuntary assessment or treatment has been initiated, and the person can be retained if the petition is filed in a timely manner.[10]

(D) Involuntary Admissions

Substance abusing or dependent people are subject to involuntary commitment under certain conditions. MHPs may become involved in the evaluation process before admission by initiating such proceedings, as a witness at a hearing, or by providing treatment after an admission.

Similar to the distinction regarding involuntary examination and involuntary placement for treatment of mental disorders,[11] Florida law distinguishes between involuntary assessment/stabilization and involuntary treatment of persons with substance abuse problems. Criteria for involuntary assessment/stabilization and involuntary treatment are essentially the same. The most significant distinction between assessment/stabilization and treatment are the processes by which, and the length of time for which, someone can be detained in a facility over their objections and without their consent. Involuntary assessment and stabilization provide for short-term assessment and intervention, and involuntary treatment allows for longer term commitment for the purpose of treating people with substance abuse problems.

(D)(1) Criteria for Involuntary Assessment and Stabilization

A person meets the criteria for involuntary assessment/stabilization/protective custody if there is reason to believe that the person[12]

---

8. 14 FLA. STAT. ANN. § 397.6773(1) (West 2002).
9. 14 FLA. STAT. ANN. § 397.6758 (West 2002).
10. 14 FLA. STAT. ANN. § 397.6773(2) (West 2002).
11. *See* chapter 8.4, Involuntary Commitment of Mentally Ill Adults.
12. 14 FLA. STAT. ANN. § 397.675 (West 2002).

1. Is substance-abuse impaired and, because of this impairment he or she
   (a) Has lost the power of self-control with respect to substance abuse;
   (b) Has inflicted, threatened, or attempted to inflict, or unless admitted is likely to inflict physical harm on himself or herself or others; or
2. Is in need of substance abuse treatment and, as a result of substance abuse impairment, the person's judgment is so impaired that he or she is cannot appreciate the need for, or make a rational decision about, the need for treatment. However, mere refusal of services does not constitute lack of judgment with respect to the need for treatment.

(D)(2) **Initiating Involuntary Assessment and Stabilization in a Residential Facility**

With adults, involuntary assessment and stabilization may be initiated in two ways. The first is that, on an emergency basis, a physician can certify that the person meets the criteria for involuntary assessment and stabilization. This can be initiated independently by the physician or at the request of any person who has personal knowledge of the person's substance abuse impairment, but requires that the physician has examined the person within five days of the application date.[13] The physician's certificate for emergency admission must identify how the person meets the criteria for involuntary assessment/stabilization. This certificate becomes part of the clinical record.[14]

Within 72 hours after emergency admission to a hospital or other residential facility, the person must be assessed by the attending physician to determine the need for additional services, and one of the following must happen:[15]

1. The client must be released and, when appropriate, referred to other services;
2. The client must agree to placement or treatment as a voluntary client; or
3. A petition for involuntary assessment or treatment must be filed with the court, thereby authorizing the treatment provider to retain physical custody of the client.

The second way involuntary assessment and stabilization may be initiated is that anyone who believes that a person meets

---

13. 14 FLA. STAT. ANN. § 397.6791 (West 2002).
14. 14 FLA. STAT. ANN. § 397.6793 (West 2002).
15. 14 FLA. STAT. ANN. § 397.6797 (West 2002).

criteria for involuntary assessment and stabilization can petition the court and request that the person be involuntarily assessed and stabilized. The petition must include the identity of the petitioner, the relationship between the petitioner and the subject of the petition, and how the subject of the petition meets the criteria for involuntary assessment and stabilization.[16]

After receiving the petition the judge must complete an *ex parte* order (an order entered on the application of a party but without the presence of the other party) authorizing the involuntary assessment and stabilization of the person or issue a summons to the person and schedule a hearing within 10 days.[17] An individual determined by the court to meet the criteria for involuntary assessment can be admitted to a hospital, licensed detoxification facility, or addictions receiving facility for five days for involuntary assessment and stabilization.[18]

Minors can be admitted for purposes of involuntary assessment and stabilization by these procedures. In addition, minors can be admitted to Addictions Receiving Facilities (ARFs) for involuntry assessment based on the application of a parent, guardian, or legal custodian. The parent, guardian, or legal custodian must demonstrate that the minor meets the criteria for involuntary assessment and stabilization as set out earlier. After admission, the minor must be assessed within 72 hours to determine the need for continuing services. If, after the 72-hour period, it is determined by the attending physician that additional services are necessary, the minor may be kept for up to five days, counting the 72-hour period.[19] In cases where minors are admitted involuntarily, the "disability of minority" for purposes of treatment decision making is not removed, so that the parent, guardian, or legal custodian may be involved in decision making.[20]

A client involuntarily admitted may be released without order of the court only by a qualified professional in a hospital, detoxification facility, an ARF, or any less restrictive treatment program. In cases of a minor, notice must be given to the applicant or to the petitioner and the court if the assessment or treatment was court-ordered.[21]

---

16. 14 FLA. STAT. ANN. § 397.6811 (West 2002); 14 FLA. STAT. ANN. § 397.6814 (West 2002); FLA. STAT. ANN. § 397.6815 (West 2002).
17. 14 FLA. STAT. ANN. § 397.6815 (West 2002).
18. 14 FLA. STAT. ANN. § 397.6811 (West 2002).
19. 14 FLA. STAT. ANN. § 397.6798 (West 2002).
20. 14 FLA. STAT. ANN. § 397.601(4)(b) (West 2002).
21. 14 FLA. STAT. ANN. § 397.6758 (West 2002).

(E) Involuntary Treatment

As noted, substance-abusing or dependent people are subject to involuntary commitment under certain conditions. MHPs may become involved in the evaluation process before admission by initiating such proceedings, as a witness at a hearing, or by providing treatment after an admission.

Also noted, Florida law distinguishes between involuntary assessment/stabilization and involuntary treatment of persons with substance abuse problems. Although involuntary assessment and stabilization provide for short-term assessment and intervention, involuntary treatment allows for longer term commitment for the purpose of treating people with substance abuse problems.

(E)(1) Criteria for Involuntary Treatment

An individual can be the subject of a court-ordered petition for involuntary treatment if he or she meets criteria for involuntary assessment/stabilization/treatment[22] and

1. Has undergone protective custody[23] or emergency admission[24] within the previous 10 days; or

2. Has been seen by a qualified professional within the previous five days;[25] or

3. Has been the subject of involuntary assessment[26] or alternative involuntary admission[27] within the previous 12 days.

If the respondent is an adult, a petition for involuntary treatment can be filed by the respondent's spouse or guardian, any relative, a service provider, or any three adults who have personal knowledge of the respondent's substance abuse impairment and his or her course of assessment and treatment.[28] If the respondent is a minor, a petition for involuntary treatment can be filed by a parent, legal guardian, or service provider.[29] Among other things, the petition must contain the name of the respondent, the name(s) and relationship(s) between the respondent and petitioner(s), the findings and recommendations of the assessment performed by

---

22. *See* earlier text discussion, 14 Fla. Stat. Ann. § 397.675 (West 2002), and later text discussion.
23. 14 Fla. Stat. Ann. § 397.693(2) (West 2002).
24. 14 Fla. Stat. Ann. § 397.693(3) (West 2002).
25. 14 Fla. Stat. Ann. § 397.693(2) (West 2002).
26. 14 Fla. Stat. Ann. § 397.693(4) (West 2002).
27. *Id.*
28. 14 Fla. Stat. Ann. § 397.695(1) (West 2002).
29. 14 Fla. Stat. Ann. § 397.695(2) (West 2002).

a qualified professional, and the factual allegations that form the basis of the petition.[30]

(E)(2) Involuntary Treatment Hearing

Individuals who are the subject of a petition must be appointed counsel if they do not have an attorney. The respondent must receive a copy of the petition, and the court must schedule a hearing within 10 days of the receipt of the petition.[31] At the hearing the court must consider and review all relevant evidence, including the results of an assessment completed by a qualified professional in connection with the respondent's protective custody, emergency admission, or involuntary assessment. The respondent must be present at the proceeding unless the court determines that the respondent's presence is likely to be injurious to the respondent or others, in which case the court must appoint a guardian advocate to act on behalf of the respondent.[32]

The court can order the respondent to receive involuntary treatment for substance abuse for up to 60 days[33] if it is shown, by clear and convincing evidence, that he or she[34]

1. Is substance-abuse impaired;
2. Has lost the power of self-control with regard to substance abuse; and
3. Has inflicted or, unless admitted, is likely to inflict, physical harm on him- or herself or others; or
4. Refuses to accept voluntary care and the refusal is based on judgment so impaired by the substance abuse that he or she cannot appreciate the need for, or make a rational decision about, the need for treatment.

If, during the course of treatment, the conditions justifying involuntary treatment no longer exist, the respondent must be released.[35]

(E)(3) Review and Renewal of Involuntary Treatment Orders

Treatment providers who believe that a client nearing date of release from involuntary treatment continues to meet the criteria for involuntary treatment must petition the court for renewal of the involuntary treatment order. A hearing on this request must be held within 15 days of receipt of the petition. The criteria

---

30. 14 Fla. Stat. Ann. § 397.6951 (West 2002).
31. 14 Fla. Stat. Ann. § 397.6955 (West 2002).
32. 14 Fla. Stat. Ann. § 397.6957 (West 2002).
33. 14 Fla. Stat. Ann. § 397.697 (West 2002).
34. 14 Fla. Stat. Ann. § 397.6957 (West 2002).
35. 14 Fla. Stat. Ann. § 397.697 (West 2002).

for continued involuntary treatment are the same as those used initially. If it is determined that the client continues to meet criteria for involuntary treatment by clear and convincing evidence, treatment may be continued for up to 90 days, with similar reviews occurring at the end of these 90-day periods.[36] Any time before the end of the 60-day involuntary treatment period or subsequent to a 90-day extension of that period, a client must be discharged and referred to a more appropriate status or service if he or she no longer meets criteria for involuntary treatment.[37] A client involuntarily admitted may be released without order of the court only by a qualified professional in a hospital, detoxification facility, an ARF, or any less restrictive treatment program. In cases of a minor, notice must be given to the applicant or to the petitioner and the court if the assessment or treatment was court-ordered.[38]

(F) Confidentiality

Records of service providers that pertain to the identity, diagnosis, and prognosis of and service provision to any client are confidential according to state and federal law on the confidentiality of substance use information (state law mirrors federal law). Such records can be disclosed only with client consent except[39]

1. To medical personnel in a medical emergency;
2. To service provider personnel who need to know the information to serve the client;
3. To the secretary of the DCF or designee, for scientific research, with written agreement that the client's name and other identifying information will not be disclosed;
4. During a record review or audit on behalf of any third-party payer, but reports produced from the audit may not disclose names or identifying information on clients;
5. Pursuant to court order on application showing good cause for disclosure. The court must weigh whether the public interest and need for disclosure outweigh the potential injury to the client, to the service provider–client relationship, and the service provider;
6. Law enforcement officials may communicate with treatment staff if the communications relate to commission of a crime on

---

36. 14 FLA. STAT. ANN. § 397.6975 (West 2002).
37. 14 FLA. STAT. ANN. § 397.6971 (West 2002).
38. 14 FLA. STAT. ANN. § 397.6758 (West 2002).
39. 14 FLA. STAT. ANN. § 397.501(7) (West 2002).

the premises of the provider or against provider personnel or a threat to commit a crime;

7. The communications must be limited to the circumstances of the incident, including the client status of the individual committing or threatening to commit the crime, name and address of the individual, and last known whereabouts; and

8. Child abuse and neglect allegations may be reported.

Because minors may voluntarily apply for substance abuse treatment, the minor has sole authority (when the minor has voluntarily sought service) to provide written consent for disclosure.[40] If the parent or guardian is required for the minor to obtain services, then both the minor and the parent or guardian must provide written consent to disclose otherwise confidential information.[41]

(G) Client Rights

Individuals receiving substance use services have a number of rights in addition to a right to confidentiality. These include[42]

1. A right to individual dignity and a right (if not charged with a crime) to not be held in jails, detention centers, or training schools, except for purposes of protective custody;

2. A right to nondiscriminatory access to services, without being denied access solely on grounds of race, gender, ethnicity, age, sexual preference, HIV status, leaving service previously against medical advice, disability, or number of relapses. In addition, service may not be denied solely because the client is taking a physician-prescribed medication or for inability to pay;

3. A right to participation in the formulation and periodic review of his or her treatment plan;

4. A right to service in the least restrictive and most appropriate manner possible;

5. A right to participate in activities designed to enhance self-image;

6. A right to services suited to the client's needs, administered skillfully, safely, and humanely;

---

40. 14 FLA. STAT. ANN. § 397.501(7)(e)(1) (West 2002).
41. 14 FLA. STAT. ANN. § 397.501(7)(e)(2) (West 2002).
42. 14 FLA. STAT. ANN. § 397.501 (West 2002).

7. A right to communication, though communications of all types may be monitored and restrictions set with the goal of maintaining a substance-free environment;
8. A right of access to personal effects and clothing; and
9. A right on the part of minors to education.

(H) Civil Liability

Service providers who violate or abuse a client's rights or privileges as protected by law are liable for damages under standard tort principles. However, all persons acting in good faith, reasonably, and without negligence in connection with the preparation or execution of petitions, applications, certificates, or other documents relevant to the apprehension, detention, discharge, examination, transportation, or treatment of a person under the provisions discussed in this chapter shall be free of civil and criminal liability for such acts.[43]

---

43. 14 FLA. STAT. ANN. § 397.501(10) (West 2002).

8.6 Voluntary and Involuntary Commitment of Drug Addicts

Florida has no separate law for treatment of individuals addicted to drugs. However, Florida does have a statute that addresses the admission and involuntary confinement of individuals with substance abuse problems, some of whom may be addicted to drugs (see chapter 8.5, Voluntary Admission and Involuntary Commitment of People With Substance Problems).

8.7
Services for People With Developmental Disabilities

People with developmental disabilities may receive various treatments and services at state expense, and there is a legislative preference that such treatments be noninstitutional.[1] The courts may ask MHPs to evaluate individuals for developmental disabilities to determine their appropriateness for programs, for involuntary placement, or for appointment of a guardian advocate.

(A) Definitions

MPHs need to understand the following terms in working with the law regarding developmental disability services.[2] *Developmental disability* means "a disorder or syndrome that is attributable to retardation, cerebral palsy, autism, spina bifida, or Prader-Willi syndrome and that constitutes a substantial handicap that can reasonably be expected to continue indefinitely."[3] *Guardian advocate* means "a person appointed by the circuit court to represent a person with developmental disabilities but excludes the use of the term as applied to a guardian advocate for mentally ill persons."[4] *Retardation* means "significantly subaverage general intellectual functioning existing concurrently with deficits in adaptive behavior and manifested during the period from conception to age 18." *Significantly subaverage general intellectual functioning*, for the purpose of this definition, means performance that is two or more standard deviations from the mean score on a standardized

---

1. 14 FLA. STAT. ANN. § 393.062 (West 2002).
2. 14 FLA. STAT. ANN. § 393.063 (West 2002).
3. 14 FLA. STAT. ANN. § 393.063(12) (West 2002).
4. 14 FLA. STAT. ANN. § 393.063(25) (West 2002).

intelligence test specified in the rules of the department. *Adaptive behavior*, for the purpose of this definition, means the effectiveness or degree with which an individual meets the standards of personal independence and social responsibility expected of his or her age, cultural group, and community.[5]

(B) Voluntary Admission to Services

The DCF is responsible for administering programs for individuals with developmental disabilities. Any resident of the state with a developmental disability is eligible to receive services. Application for services is made to the DCF, which may conduct a diagnostic evaluation if necessary.[6] Application for services is to be made in writing to the DCF, and the application is to be reviewed within 45 days for children under 6 years of age and within 60 days for all other applicants. Only individuals domiciled in Florida are eligible for services.

(B)(1) Habilitation Plans

The DCF must develop and implement an appropriate individualized habilitation plan for each developmental services client. The client (if competent) or client advocate must be consulted in developing the plan. The ultimate goal of each plan is to enable the client to live in the least restrictive setting, which is to be the community or home when possible.[7] For clients who are public school students, the habilitation plan must be integrated with the individual education plan (IEP; see chapter 4.20, Education for Gifted and Handicapped Children, for a discussion of students with special needs).[8]

(B)(2) Treatment Programs

Residential and institutional services must be made available by the DCF for those clients in need of such services. Community-based services are to be emphasized over institutional services to the extent possible.[9]

Community-based services, to the extent possible, are to include developmental training services, family care services, guardian advocate referral services, medical and dental services, parent training, recreation, residential services, respite services,

---

5. 14 FLA. STAT. ANN. § 393.063(42) (West 2002).
6. 14 FLA. STAT. ANN. § 393.065(1) (West 2002).
7. 14 FLA. STAT. ANN. § 393.0651 (West 2002).
8. 14 FLA. STAT. ANN. § 393.0651(2) (West 2002).
9. 14 FLA. STAT. ANN. § 393.13(2)(b) (West 2002).

social services, specialized therapies, supported employment, supported living, behavioral programming, and transportation.

(C) Involuntary Admission

(C)(1) Criteria for Involuntary Admission

The court can order the involuntary admission of a person with a developmental disability to a residential facility if it is proven that[10]

1. The person is mentally retarded or autistic;
2. Placement in a residential setting is the least restrictive and most appropriate alternative to meet the person's needs; and
3. Because of the person's degree of mental retardation or autism, the person:
   (a) Lacks sufficient capacity to give express and informed consent to a voluntary application for services and lacks basic survival and self-care skills to such a degree that close supervision and habilitation in a residential setting is necessary and, if not provided, would result in a real and present threat of substantial harm to the person's well-being; or
   (b) Is likely to physically injure others if allowed to remain at liberty.

If the court does not find the person meets these criteria, the court may recommend voluntary admission.

(C)(2) Examination and Petitioning Process

A petition for involuntary admission to residential services is to be executed by the petitioning commission, which consists of three people, one of whom must be a licensed physician.[11] The petition must[12]

1. State the name, age, and present address of the three commissioners and their relationship to the person with mental retardation or autism;
2. State the name, age, county of residence, and present address of the person with mental retardation or autism;

---

10. 14 Fla. Stat. Ann. § 393.11(8) (West 2002).
11. 14 Fla. Stat. Ann. § 393.11(2)(b) (West 2002).
12. 14 Fla. Stat. Ann. § 393.11(2)(C) (West 2002).

3. Allege that the commission believes the person needs involuntary residential services and specify the factual information on which such belief is based;

4. Allege that the person lacks sufficient capacity to give express and informed consent to a voluntary application for services and lacks the basic survival and self-care skills to provide for the person's well-being or is likely to physically injure others if allowed to remain at liberty; and

5. State which residential setting is the least restrictive and most appropriate alternative and specify the factual information on which such belief is based.

(C)(3) Developmental Services Program Evaluation

Once a petition is filed, the court must immediately direct the DCF developmental services program to examine the individual and report the results of the evaluation to the court not less than 10 working days before a hearing is scheduled.[13]

(C)(4) Examining Committee

Once a petition is filed, the court must also appoint an examining committee to evaluate the individual being considered for involuntary admission to residential services. The committee shall consist of no less than three people with expertise in mental retardation. The committee must include one licensed physician, one licensed psychologist, and one professional with a minimum of a master's degree in social work, special education, or vocational rehabilitation counseling. The committee must prepare and submit a written report to the court that documents[14]

1. The degree of the person's mental retardation;
2. Whether, because of the degree of mental retardation, the person:
   (a) Lacks sufficient capacity to give express and informed consent to a voluntary application for services;
   (b) Lacks basic survival and self-care skills to such a degree that close supervision and habilitation in a residential setting is necessary and if not provided would result in a real and present threat of substantial harm to the person's well-being; or
   (c) Is likely to physically injure others if allowed to remain at liberty;
3. The purpose served by residential care;

---

13. 14 FLA. STAT. ANN. § 393.11(4) (West 2002).
14. 14 FLA. STAT. ANN. § 393.11(5) (West 2002).

4. A recommendation on the type of residential placement that would be the most appropriate and least restrictive for the person; and

5. The most appropriate care, habilitation, and treatment.

(D) Rights of the Mentally Retarded and Developmentally Disabled

Individuals receiving mental retardation/developmental disabilities services from the DCF have the following rights:[15]

1. A right to dignity, privacy, and humane care, including the right to be free from sexual abuse in residential facilities;

2. A right to religious freedom and practice;

3. A right to receive services, within available resources, that protect personal liberty and are provided in the least restrictive conditions necessary to achieve the goals of treatment;

4. A right to participate in an appropriate educational and training program, within available resources;

5. A right to social interaction and to participate in community activities;

6. A right to physical exercise and recreational opportunities;

7. A right to be free from harm, including unnecessary physical, chemical, or mechanical restraint, isolation, excessive medication, abuse, or neglect;

8. A right to consent to or refuse treatment;

9. A right to not be excluded from participation in, or denied the benefits of, or be subject to discrimination under any program or activity receiving public funds; and

10. A right to vote in public elections if otherwise qualified.

Individuals served in facilities licensed by the DCF also have rights to[16]

1. Receive, send, and mail sealed, unopened correspondence unless there is reason to believe that it contains items or substances that may be harmful to the client, in which case the mail may be examined and regulated;

---

15. 14 Fla. Stat. Ann. § 393.13(3) (West 2002).
16. 14 Fla. Stat. Ann. § 393.13(4) (West 2002).

2. Have reasonable opportunities for telephone communication, subject to restriction if there is reason to believe that there may be harm to the client or others;

3. Unrestricted visitation;

4. Possession and use of personal effects and clothing, except where the use of some of these items is essential as reinforcers in the individual's behavioral training program;

5. Medication administered only on written order of a physician;[17]

6. Informed consent of the client (if competent) or legal guardian to surgery;[18]

7. Individual storage space in residential facilities;[19]

8. Humane discipline;[20]

9. Freedom from treatment programs designed to eliminate certain behaviors without an earlier exam by a physician to determine whether the behaviors are organically caused;

10. Freedom from noxious or painful stimuli; and

11. Compliance with minimum wage and fair labor standards for work done in programs that must comply with federal wage and hour laws.

(E) Appointment of Guardian Advocates

In general, the issue of the capacity of an individual with mental retardation or a developmental disability is a separate issue from that of placement and is to be determined by procedures established in the *Florida Probate Rules*.[21] However, a probate court can appoint a guardian advocate for a person without an adjudication of incapacity if the person lacks capacity to do some, but not all, of the tasks necessary to care for his or her person, property, or estate, or if the person has voluntarily petitioned for the appointment of a guardian advocate.[22]

---

17. 14 FLA. STAT. ANN. § 393.13(4)(c)(1) (West 2002).
18. 14 FLA. STAT. ANN. § 393.13(4)(c)(6) (West 2002).
19. 14 FLA. STAT. ANN. § 393.13(4)(d) (West 2002).
20. 14 FLA. STAT. ANN. § 393.13(4)(f)–(k) (West 2002).
21. 14 FLA. STAT. ANN. § 393.12(1) (West 2002).
22. 14 FLA. STAT. ANN. § 393.12(2)(a) (West 2002).

(E)(1) Allegations of the Petition

Any adult person who is a resident of Florida can petition for appointment of a guardian advocate for an individual with developmental disabilities. The petition, among other things, must[23]

1. State the name, age, and present address of the petitioner and his or her relationship to the person with developmental disabilities;
2. State the name, age, and present address of the person with developmental disabilities;
3. Allege that the person needs a guardian advocate and specify the factual information on which that belief is based;
4. Specify the exact areas in which the person lacks the capacity to make informed decisions about his or her care and treatment services or to meet the essential requirements for his or her physical health or safety;
5. Specify the legal disabilities to which the person is subject; and
6. State the name of the proposed guardian advocate, the relationship of that person to the person with developmental disabilities, and the reason why this person should be appointed. If a willing and qualified guardian advocate cannot be located, the petition must state this as well.

(E)(2) Rights of the Subject of the Petition

Notice of filing of the petition must be provided to the subject of the petition, his or her legal guardian, and counsel. The individual is entitled to a copy of the petition, to counsel, to be present at the hearing, to remain silent, to present evidence, to cross-examine witnesses, and to have the hearing open or closed as he or she chooses.[24]

(E)(3) Appointing Guardian Advocates

If the court determines a guardian advocate is needed, the court on entering an order appointing a guardian advocate must make findings on[25]

1. The nature and scope of the person's incapacity;
2. The exact areas in which the individual lacks capacity to make informed decisions about care and treatment services or to

---

23. 14 FLA. STAT. ANN. § 393.12(2)(b) (West 2002).
24. 14 FLA. STAT. ANN. § 393.12(2)(e) (West 2002).
25. 14 FLA. STAT. ANN. § 393.12(2)(f) (West 2002).

meet the essential requirements for his or her physical health and safety;
3. The specific legal disabilities to which the person with developmental disabilities is subject; and
4. The powers and duties of the guardian advocate.

8.8
Hospice Care

The legislature has found that terminally ill individuals who are no longer pursuing curative medical treatment should have the opportunity to "select a support system that permits the patient to exercise maximum independence and dignity during the final days of life."[1] *Terminally ill* in this context means that the patient has a medical prognosis that his or her life expectancy is one year or less if the illness runs its normal course.[2] The legislature further characterized hospice care as providing a cost-effective and less intrusive form of medical care that meets the social, psychological, and spiritual needs of terminally ill patients and their families. Florida law defines hospice care, describes who may provide it and under what circumstances, and provides for the licensing of hospice care providers.

A *hospice* is defined as a "centrally administered corporation not for profit . . . providing a continuum of palliative and supportive care for the terminally ill patient and his or her family."[3] The AHCA licenses hospices. The initial application must contain a plan providing for the delivery of home, residential, and homelike inpatient services to terminally ill patients and their families. The plan must contain at a minimum information regarding the estimated number of terminally ill patients to be served monthly; the geographic area the hospice will serve; a list of services to be provided directly or through contract; the implementation of hospice care within three months and homelike inpatient care within 12 months after licensure; number and discipline of staff; name and qualifications of any contractee; a plan for attracting

---

1. 14 FLA. STAT. ANN. § 400.6005 (West 2002).
2. 14 FLA. STAT. ANN. § 400.601(10) (West 2002).
3. 14 FLA. STAT. ANN. § 400.601(3) (West 2002).

and training volunteers; the projected annual cost of the hospice; and a statement of financial resources and available personnel.[4]

If a hospice claims to provide special care for Alzheimer's disease or related disorders, special rules apply. The hospice must disclose in its advertisements or other documents that care is especially applicable to, or suitable for, such patients. Any advertisements or documents noting the availability of such care must be retained by the hospice as part of a license renewal procedure.[5]

The hospice must provide a continuum of services tailored to the specific needs and preferences of the patient and family while care is provided to the patient and during a bereavement period after death. Services must be available 24 hours per day, 7 days per week. Services include[6]

1. Core services include physician services, nursing services, social work services, pastoral or counseling services, dietary counseling, home health aide services, and bereavement counseling services. A hospice also must arrange or provide any additional services needed to meet the palliative and support needs of the patient and family, including physical therapy, speech therapy, massage therapy, infusion therapy, provision of medical services and equipment, day care, homemaker and chore services, and funeral services. Core services must be provided directly by the hospice and cannot be contracted out.[7]

2. Hospice home care services are those provided in a private home and are supposed to be the primary form of care provided by hospice. The goal is to provide adequate training and support to encourage self-sufficiency and allow the patient to remain at home as long as possible.

3. Hospice residential care may be provided by the hospice care team to a patient living in an assisted living facility, nursing home, hospice residential unit, or other nondomestic living place.

4. Hospice inpatient care is considered a short-term adjunct to home care, and is to be used only for pain control, symptom management, or respite care. The total number of inpatient days provided by the hospice in any 12-month period cannot exceed 20% of the total number of hospice days provided by the hospice. Inpatient rooms are supposed to be as homelike as possible and must be limited to no more than double occupancy to encourage overnight stays by family.

---
4. 14 FLA. STAT. ANN. § 400.606(1) (West 2002).
5. 14 FLA. STAT. ANN. § 400.6045 (West 2002).
6. 14 FLA. STAT. ANN. § 400.609(1)–(5) (West 2002).
7. 14 FLA. STAT. ANN. § 400.6085 (West 2002).

5. The bereavement counseling program must be under professional supervision and provide supportive services to families when they desire them for a minimum of one year after the patient's death.

The statute also provides staffing standards. Each hospice must have a medical director, a full-time registered licensed nurse, and a care team with a minimum of a nurse, physician, social worker, and pastoral or other counselor. A trained volunteer staff must be maintained as well.[8]

Hospice services are to be made available to all terminally ill patients, regardless of age, gender, national origin, disability, diagnosis, cost of therapy, or ability to pay.[9] Admission occurs based on a diagnosis and prognosis of terminal illness by a licensed physician.[10] The hospice is to inquire on admission whether a patient has an advanced directive and, if not, to provide information on that topic.[11]

A plan of care is to be created for each patient.[12] The plan at a minimum must identify the primary caregiver; provide a diagnosis, prognosis, and patient preferences regarding care; assess patient and family needs; identify services to meet those needs and the manner in which services will be provided; have plans for instructing the family and patient in care; and identify the nurse responsible for coordinating care.

Patient records are confidential. They must contain pertinent past and current medical, social, and nursing information. When services are terminated, the record must reflect the date and reason for termination.[13] Records may be released only on the express written informed consent of the patient or guardian; or pursuant to court order; or to a state or federal agency requiring submission of aggregate data.[14]

---

8. 14 FLA. STAT. ANN. § 400.6105 (West 2002).
9. 14 FLA. STAT. ANN. § 400.6095(1) (West 2002).
10. 14 FLA. STAT. ANN. § 400.6095(2) (West 2002).
11. 14 FLA. STAT. ANN. § 400.6095(3) (West 2002).
12. 14 FLA. STAT. ANN. § 400.6095(5)(a)–(e) (West 2002).
13. 14 FLA. STAT. ANN. § 400.611(1) (West 2002).
14. 14 FLA. STAT. ANN. § 400.611(3) (West 2002).

Appendix

Table of Cases

Table of Statutes

Table of Rules of Court

Table of Administrative Rules and Regulations

Table of References to Constitution

Table of Cases

References are to page numbers in this book.

A

Alderman v. Winn, 191
American Red Cross v. Estate of Haynsworth, 312
Anderson v. Wales Industries, 297
Anicet v. Gant, 306
Arzola v. Reigosa, 142

B

Baker v. State, 338, 360
Begley v. State, 338
Belair v. Belair, 191
Bernard v. Kee Mfg. Co., 81
BL v. Department of Health and Rehabilitative Services, 204
Blackstone v. Dade City Osteopathic Clinic, 320
Blanco v. State, 390
Blosser v. Blosser, 193
Bock v. Bock, 311
Bolin v. State, 344
Boswell v. State, 379
Bowes v. State, 374
Boyle v. Thebaut, 143
Boynton v. Burglass, 131, 137, 138
Bradshaw v. Ultra-Tech Enter., Inc., 107
Brim v. State, 352
Brooks v. Serrano, 157
Brunner v. State, 381
Bryant v. State, 390
Bundy v. State, 348
Bush v. Wainright, 367

C

Caddy v. State, 165
Calloway v. State, 395
Campbell v. State, 390
Caraballo v. Hernandez, 191
Caso v. HRS, 217
Central Florida Clinic for Rehabilitation, Inc. v. Citrus County Hosp. Board, 171
Chaifair v. Chaifair, 191
Chant v. Chant, 194
Chestnut v. State, 378
Cirack v. State, 381
City of St. Petersburg v. Ferguson, 334
Clark v. State, 345
Clay v. State, 234
Clinton v. State, 338
Cochran v. State, 338
Collie v. State, 338
Courtney v. Courtney, 187
Crews v. Norris, 187
Cross v. State, 338
Cunningham v. General Motors Corp., 317
Curtis v. State, 381

D

Daubert v. Merrell Dow Pharmaceutical, Inc., 333
Davis v. State, 336, 338
Department of Health and Rehabilitative Services v. Cox, 228
Dinardo v. State, 115, 151
D.K. v. Parents of D.K., 142, 188
Doody v. C.I.R., 109

E

Egan v. Florida Atlantic University, 297
Enyeart v. Stull, 194
Estate of Bailey, 311
Estate of Parson, 311
Eutzy v. State, 390

F

Fare v. Michael C., 359
Faretta v. California, 359
Feinberg v. Leach, 309
Feller v. Kisiel, 187
Fernstrom v. Taylor, 311
Fitzpatrick v. State, 390
Flanagan v. State, 333, 353
Flint v. Fortson, 193
Florida Power & Light Co. v. Robinson, 338

Ford v. Wainwright, 406
Forehand v. State, 375
Freeman v. State, 390
Freshwater v. Freshwater, 143
Frye v. United States, 333, 351, 353
FTC v. Hospital Board of Directors of Lee County, 171
Fuller v. State, 338

G

Gaither v. State, 339
Gallegos v. Colorado, 359
Gardiner v. Goermer, 311
Gibbs v. Gibbs, 194
Gideon v. Wainwright, 359
Gillen v. State, 374
Goldberg v. Goldberg, 189
Goldfarb v. Virginia State Bar, 170
Gracey v. Gracey, 303
Green v. Ross, 138
Griffin v. State, 338

H

Hadden v. State, 351
Hall v. State, 332, 338
Hall v. Wainright, 389
Hamilton v. Morgan, 310
Harmon v. Williams, 309
Harrold v. Schluep, 338
Hawk v. State, 337
Hawthorne v. State, 343
Hayes v. State, 359
Henry v. State, 382
Hewitt v. State, 381
Hill v. State, 384
Holland v. State, 370
Holmes v. Burchette, 309
Holsworth v. State, 390
Horowitz v. American Motorist Insurance, 331
Humana Medical Plan, Inc. v. Erdely, 129

I

In re BW, 216
In re D.B., 233
In re DJ, 217
In re D.S., 233
In re Estate of Bailey, 310
In re Estate of Dunson, 310
In re Estate of Edwards, 310, 311, 312
In re Estate of Frank, 312
In re Estate of Hammerman, 312
In re Estate of Joiner, 311, 312
In re Estate of Perez, 311
In re Estate of Shadow, 176
In re Estate of Supplee, 312
In re Estate of Witt, 311
In re Estate of Ziy, 312
In re RDD, 217
In re RH, 216
In re W.W., 243

J

Jackson v. State, 310, 340, 341
James v. State, 367
Jefferson County v. B.C. Lewis & Sons, 328
Johnson v. State, 332, 338
Jolley v. Powell, 306
Jones v. State, 367
Jordan v. State, 332
J.R. v. State, 243

K

Kaczer v. Marrero, 306
Kaelin v. State, 338
Kaminski v. State, 336
K.D. v. Department of Juvenile Justice, 246
Kent v. State, 367
Kilgore v. Kilgore, 194
King v. State, 376
Kleinfeld v. State, 359
Knowles v. State, 390
Kuehmsted v. Turnwall, 187
Kuharcik v. Kuharcik, 191

L

Leggett v. State, 338, 339
Leonard v. Leonard, 143, 188
Lewis v. State, 332
Linehan v. State, 379
Lovette v. State, 250, 370, 381, 383

M

Mack v. Bristol-Myer Squibb Co., 170
Mahan v. Mahan, 176, 187

Martin v. Martin, 176, 187, 191
Maryland v. Craig, 338
Matevia v. State, 381
Mauldin v. C.I.R., 85
McDonnell Douglas v. Holliday, 331
McGregor v. McGregor, 194
McKinnies v. State, 338
McMullen v. State, 349
Medina v. Children's Hospital, 334
Metcalfe v. Metcalfe, 194
Miranda v. Arizona, 358
M.M. v. M.P.S, 304
M.O. McC. v. Department of Health and Rehabilitative Services, 204
Moore v. Dugger, 358
Morgan v. State, 348
Mujica v. Turner, 306
Muldrow v. State, 415
Murray v. Barnett National Bank, 311
Myers v. Pleasant, 311

N

Neary v. State, 390
Nelson v. Womble, 142
Nibert v. State, 390
Nova University v. Wagner, 139

O

O'Keefe v. Orea, 139

P

Paddock v. Chacko, 138
Palm Beach County School Board v. Morrison, 143
Palmer v. HRS, 217
Palmes v. State, 360
Parker v. Parker, 191
Parkway General Hospital v. Allinson, 160
Pearson v. State, 332
Perez v. Perez, 193, 194
Porter v. Commissioner, 110
Pouncy v. State, 250, 381, 383
Prasad v. Allstate Insurance Co., 307
Provezano v. State, 408

R

Raini v. Furlong, 311
Ramirez v. State, 333

Recchi America Inc. v. Astley Hall, 297
Reilly v. State Dept. of Corrections, 359
Richardson v. Richardson, 191
Ritchie v. State, 339
Rivet v. State, 338
R.J. v. Humana of Florida, Inc., 304
Robinson v. Shands Teaching Hospital, 106
Robinson v. State, 338
Rodgers v. State, 349
Romero v. State, 338
Rush Prudential HMO v. Moran, 107
Russell v. Stardust Cruisers, 142, 143
Rutherford v. Moore, 337, 338

S

Samuel Friedland Family Enterprises v. Amoroso, 317
Sanifel v. Department of Health, 134
Santa Cruz v. Northwest Dade Community Health Center, 138
Savage v. Olson, 187
Schweinberg v. Click, 194
Scott v. Moses, 320
Scud v. State, 390
Seccia v. State, 338
Siebert v. Bayport Beach & Tennis Club, 334
Skelton v. Dads, 310
Skelton v. Davis, 312
Smith v. Koolidge, 191
Smith v. State, 360, 390
State v. Camejo, 339
State v. Crosby, 359
State v. Dupont, 333
State v. Hickson, 342, 343
State v. Jett, 143
State v. Perry, 364
State v. Porter, 234
State v. Sired, 390
State v. Winters, 204
State v. Word, 359
Stelk v. Stelk, 284
Stepien v. Bay Memorial Medical Center, 157
Stokes v. State, 348
Stone v. George, 307
Sullivan v. Sullivan, 194
Swain v. State, 338
Sysn v. State, 341

T

Tarasoff v. Regents of the University of California, 137
TB v. Department of Children and Family Services, 217
Terry v. State, 331, 332
Tio Pepe v. El Tio Pepe De Miami Restaurant, Inc., 318
Tomes-Arboleda v. Dogger, 390
Toussaint v. State, 359
T.S.D. v. State, 359

U

Ursry v. State, 250, 381, 383

V

Vaughan v. Guardianship of Vaughan, 189
Villazon v. Prudential Health Care Plan, 107
Vinton v. State, 9
Voigt v. Commissioner, 110
Von Eiff v. Azicri, 191

W

Walls v. Armour Pharmaceutical Co., 317
Washington v. State, 360
Weinstock v. Groth, 157
Welch v. Helvening, 109
West v. Branham, 125
West v. Caterpillar Tractor Co., 317
Westerheide v. State, 413
Wickam v. State, 390
Wickarri v. State, 390
Wiggins v. Williams, 329
Wiley v. State, 347
Wilking v. Reiford, 191
Williams v. City of Minneola, 304
Williams v. State, 338
Wournos v. State, 390

Y

Yarborough v. State, 374
Young v. Young, 194
Younger v. State, 146

Z

Zediker v. Zediker, 194
Zell v. Meek, 304
Zinnser v. Gregory, 311

Table of Statutes

References are to page numbers in this book.

Florida Statutes

Section	Page
11.61	75
11.62	74
11.62(3)(a)-(d)	74
11.62(4)(a)-(k)	74
18.627.942(7)	316
39.001	222
39.001(1)(h)	222
39.001(1)(j)	222
39.001(3)(a)-(h)	222
39.01(1)	204
39.01(2)	202
39.01(7)(b)	203
39.01(12)	202, 204
39.01(46)	203
39.01(64)	203
39.044(4)	237
39.201	131, 205
39.201(1)	204
39.201(3)(d)	210
39.201(g)-(h)	205
39.202	205
39.202(2)(a)	205
39.202(2)(d)	205
39.202(2)(e)	206
39.202(2)(f)	205
39.202(2)(h)	205
39.202(3)	206
39.202(4)	206
39.203	205
39.204	204
39.205	206
39.205(2)	206
39.205(3)	206
39.303(1)	206
39.395	208
39.401(1)	207
39.401(2)	208
39.402(1)	208
39.402(2)	209
39.402(7)	209
39.402(8)	209
39.402(8)(a)	209
39.402(8)(h)	209
39.402(13)(a)	209
39.501(1)-(3)	224
39.501(2)	210
39.501(3)	210
39.504	210
39.507(1)	211
39.507(1)(b)	224
39.507(4)	211, 225
39.507(5)	225
39.507(7)	225
39.521	225
39.521(1)	211
39.521(1)(b)	225
39.521(1)(b)(3)	225
39.521(1)(d)(9)(f)	225
39.521(2)	211
39.521(9)	212
39.521(9)(5)	213
39.601(1)	213
39.601(2)	214
39.601(3)	214
39.601(3)(k)	214
39.701(1)(a)	225
39.701(2)(b)	225
39.701(6)(a)	226
39.701(7)	226
39.806(1)	215
39.811(2)	217
39.811(3)	217
39.811(7a)	217
39.811(7b)	218
39.811(9)	217
40.01	328
47.101	330
47.121	330
47.122	330
61.13(2)(b)	191
61.13(2)(b)2	191, 192, 284
61.13(2)(b)2.b	192, 194
61.13(2)(b)2.c	284
61.13(2)(b)3	194, 285
61.13(2)(d)	193
61.13(3)	192
61.13(4)(a)	194
61.13(4)(b)	194
61.13(4)(c)2	191
61.20	193, 195
61.20(2)	195
61.20(3)	195
61.20(5)	228
61.021	188
61.052	176

Section	Page	Section	Page
61.052(1)(b)	189	92.54(5)	339
61.052(2)	188, 189	95.11(4)(a)	157
61.052(2)(b)1	189	95.11(4)(b)	157
61.052(2)(b)2	189	97.041	313
61.121	191	97.052(2)(s)	313
61.1302	190	98.0987	314
61.401	210	110.123(3)(h)(2)(a)	104
63.042(2)	228	112.042(1)	322
63.042(3)	228	119.01	149
63.052(2)	231	119.07(v)	149
63.062(1)(a)	227	120.57(1)(b)	12, 21, 42, 51, 59, 67
63.062(1)(b)	227		
63.062(1)(c)	227	120.57(1)(l)	13, 21, 29, 42, 51, 59, 67
63.072	228		
63.082(4)(b)	230	120.68(2)(a)	13, 21, 29, 42, 52, 59, 68
63.088	229		
63.089(2)	229	120.569	12, 20, 58
63.089(3)	229	120.569(1)	29, 41
63.092(1)	229	228.041(18)	272
63.092(2)	228	228.041(19)	273
63.092(2)(i)	228	229.832	274, 275
63.092(3)	229	229.832(2)	274
63.102	230	229.8341	275
63.102(1)	228	230.23(4)(m)	272, 273
63.112(3)	229	230.23(4)(m)5	274
63.122(1)	230	230.23(4)(m)6	273
63.125	230	231.15(1)	48
63.142	230	231.17(2)	49
63.162(1)	231	231.261(1)	50
63.162(2)	231	231.2615	49
63.162(4)	231	231.262	50
63.162(4)(d)	232	231.262(1)	50
63.0427	229	231.262(3)	50
69.071	329	231.262(4)	50
90.503	134, 142, 143	231.262(5)	50, 51
90.503(1)(a)	141	231.262(7)(a)-(g)	52
90.503(2)	141	322.05(7)	315
90.503(3)	142, 143	322.05(8)	315
90.601	337	381.76	299, 300
90.603	337	390.0111(1)	282
90.701	333	390.0111(3)(a)	282
90.702	331, 332, 333	390.01115(3)	278
90.703	334	390.01115(4)	278
90.704	333	390.01115(a)	283
90.705(1)	333	390.01115(b)	283
90.705(2)	332	390.01115(c)-(d)	283
90.706	334	393.11(2)(b)	455
92.53	338	393.11(2)(c)	455
92.53(1)	338, 339	393.11(4)	456
92.53(4)	339	393.11(5)	456
92.53(7)	339	393.11(8)	455
92.54	338	393.12	181
92.54(1)	338, 339	393.12(1)	458
92.54(4)	339	393.12(2)(a)	458

Section	Page	Section	Page
393.12(2)(b)	459	394.467(7)(d)	265, 439
393.12(2)(e)	459	394.467(7)(f)	266, 439
393.12(2)(f)	459	394.911	416
393.13(2)(b)	454	394.912	402, 411
393.13(3)	457	394.912(1)(9)	411
393.13(3)(h)	152	394.912(1)(10)(b)	413
393.13(4)	457	394.912(2)	411
393.13(4)(c)(1)	458	394.912(4)	413
393.13(4)(c)(6)	458	394.912(5)	413
393.13(4)(d)	458	394.912(6)	411
393.13(4)(f)-(k)	458	394.912(9)	412
393.13(4)(g)(1)	152	394.912(9)(h)	412
393.13(4)(g)(3)	152	394.912(10)	411
393.062	453	394.912(11)	412
393.063	244, 453	394.913(1)	414
393.063(12)	453	394.913(2)(c)	414
393.063(25)	453	394.913(3)	414
393.063(42)	454	394.913(3)(c)	414
393.065(1)	454	394.913(3)(e)	414
393.0651	454	394.914	414
393.0651(2)	454	394.915	415
394.455	260, 433	394.915(2)	418
394.455(2)	260, 262, 434, 436	394.915(5)	415
		394.916(1)	415
394.455(4)	260, 434	394.916(2)	415
394.455(9)	260, 433	394.916(4)	415
394.455(10)	431	394.916(5)	415
394.455(18)	260, 433	394.917(1)	416
394.455(21)	97	394.917(2)	416
394.455(23)	261, 434	394.918(1)	416
394.455(24)	260, 434	394.918(2)	416
394.455(26)	261, 434	394.918(3)	417
394.459	440	394.918(4)	417
394.459(3)	152	394.919	417
394.459(3)(a)	114, 150	394.921(1)	418
394.459(3)(b)	115, 150	394.923	418, 441
394.459(3)(c)	115	394.4598(6)	264, 438
394.459(10)	161, 441	394.4598(7)	264, 438
394.463	280, 434	394.4615	131, 146
394.463(1)	261, 435	394.4615(1)	131
394.463(2)(a)	262, 435	394.4615(2)	131
394.463(2)(f)	263, 436	394.4615(2)(a)	280
394.463(2)(i)	263, 436	394.4615(3)	131
394.467	261, 280, 401, 434	394.4615(6)	132
		394.4615(7)	132
394.467(1)	265, 438	394.4615(8)	280
394.467(2)	264, 438	394.4625(1)(a)	259, 280, 431
394.467(3)	264, 437		
394.467(4)	264, 437	394.4625(1)(b)	432
394.467(6)(a)1	264, 437	394.4625(1)(d)	432
394.467(6)(a)2	264, 437	394.4625(1)(e)	432
394.467(6)(b)	265, 439	394.4625(2)	432
394.467(6)(d)	264, 438	394.4625(4)	263, 266, 436, 439
394.467(7)(b)	265, 439		

Section	Page	Section	Page
394.4625(5)	263, 266, 437, 440	397.6798	269, 446
394.4784(1)	279	397.6811	446
394.4784(2)	280	397.6814	268, 446
394.4784(3)	279	397.6815	268, 446
394.4785(1)(a)	259	397.6819	268
394.4785(1)(b)	260	397.6951	270, 448
394.4785(2)	260	397.6955	270, 448
394.9121(4)	413	397.6957	270, 448
394.9155	418	397.6971	271, 449
394.9155(7)	414	397.6975	271, 449
395.0191(4)	97	399.463	261
395.0193	170	400.601(3)	461
395.0193(1)	98	400.601(10)	461
395.0193(2)	98	400.606(1)	462
395.0193(3)	98	400.609(1)-(5)	462
395.3025	121	400.611(1)	463
397.311	267, 442	400.611(3)	463
397.311(28)	443	400.6005	461
397.431(3)	266, 279, 443	400.6045	462
397.482	294	400.6085	462
397.483	294	400.6095(1)	463
397.486	294	400.6095(2)	463
397.501	397, 450	400.6095(3)	463
397.501(7)	131, 132, 449	400.6095(5)(a)-(e)	463
397.501(7)(b)	133	400.6105	463
397.501(7)(e)1	134, 281, 450	408.902	429
397.501(7)(e)2	450	408.903(1)	429
397.501(7)(j)	133	408.903(2)	429
397.501(10)	451	408.904(2)(a)-(j)	429
397.601(1)	443	408.904(3)(a)-(e)	430
397.601(3)	443	408.905(2)	430
397.601(4)(a)	266, 279, 280, 443	408.905(3)	430
397.601(4)(b)	446	408.905(4)	430
397.675	267, 269, 444, 447	408.905(5)	430
397.693(2)	269, 447	409.166	231
397.693(3)	269, 447	409.166(4)	231
397.693(4)	269, 447	409.175(3)(a)	223
397.695(1)	269, 447	409.175(3)(d)	223
397.695(2)	269, 447	409.175(4)(a)	223
397.697	270, 448	409.175(5)(a)	224
397.6758	271, 444, 446, 449	409.175(5)(c)	224
397.6771	443	409.175(5)(i)	224
397.6772	443	409.175(5)(j)	224
397.6773(1)	444	409.175(8)(b)	224
397.6773(2)	444	409.902	423
397.6791	268, 445	409.903	425
397.6793	445	409.904	426
397.6793(1)	268	409.905	423
397.6793(3)	268	409.906	424
397.6797	268, 445	409.906(8)	428
		409.907	427
		409.908(1)(a)	427
		409.908(1)(b)	427
		409.1671	223

Section	Page	Section	Page
409.9122	428	455.225(4)	11, 20, 41, 58
413.20	299	455.667(4)	122, 125, 128
413.20(2)	300	455.671(1)	124
413.20(12)	301	455.2273	13
413.20(13)	300	455.2425	138
413.20(16)	299	456.057	117, 125
413.20(22)	300	456.057(4)	118, 128
413.20(34)	299, 300	456.057(5)	118
413.30(1)-(3)	300	456.057(5)(6)	124
413.70	299	456.057(5)(a)	124
413.371	299	456.057(5)(b)	124
413.401	299, 300	456.057(5)(c)	124, 147
415.102(1)	197	456.057(5)(d)	124
415.102(10)	198	456.057(6)	118
415.102(12)	198	456.057(7)	119
415.102(14a)	198	456.057(7)(a)	147
415.102(22)	198	456.057(7)(b)	118, 147
415.103(2)	200	456.057(9)	118, 121, 124, 127
415.104(e)	201		
415.105(1)	201	456.057(10)	118
415.107	200	456.057(17)	118
415.111(1)	201	456.059	131, 134, 136, 141
415.111(5)(b)	200		
415.1034	199	456.061	139
415.1034(1)	199	456.063	164
415.1034(1)(b)1-8	199	456.065	73
415.1034(1)(b)7	199	456.072(2)	13, 22, 30, 42, 60, 68
415.1045(5)	199		
415.1055	200	456.073	135
419.001(1)(a)	99	456.076	294
419.001(2)	101	456.076(2)	294
419.001(3)(a)	100	456.076(3)(a)(1)-(4)	294
419.001(3)(b)	100	458.305	4
419.001(3)(c)(1)-(3)	100	458.305(3)	5
419.001(5)	100	458.307	4
419.001(6)	100	458.307(2)	4
419.001(7)	101	458.307(3)	5
419.001(9)	101	458.309(1)	5
440.02(1)	296	458.310	5
440.02(14)(a)	296	458.310(2)-(3)	5
440.02(14)(d)	296	458.311(1)	5
440.02(15)	296	458.313(1)	5
440.09(7)(b)	297	458.315	7
440.15	298	458.317	7
440.19(1)	297	458.319(1)	7
440.25	297	458.319(2)	7
440.29	297	458.320	7
440.134	298	458.323	7
440.185(1)	297	458.325	115
440.271	297	458.325(2)	116
455.209(2)	168	458.327(1)	8
455.225	11, 20, 40, 58	458.327(2)	8
455.225(2)	11, 20, 40, 58	458.331(1)	8
455.225(3)	11, 20, 41, 58	458.331(1)(j)	164

Section	Page	Section	Page
458.331(1)(m)	125	485.003(4)	70
458.331(1)(s)	292	486.125(1)(a)	291
458.331(2)	292	486.125(1)(a)1	291
458.341	146	486.125(1)(a)2	292
458.343	147	486.125(2)	291
458.3115	5	490.003	25
458.3124	5	490.003(3)(b)(1)	24
458.3165	4, 7	490.003(3)(b)(2)	24
459.015(1)(o)	125	490.003(3)(b)(3)	25
459.015(1)(w)	292	490.003(4)	23
459.015(2)	292	490.003(5)(a)-(d)	44
459.015(l)	164	490.004	23
462.14(1)(s)	290, 291	490.004(1)	23
464.003(3)(a)	15	490.004(2)	23
464.003(3)(b)	15	490.005	24
464.003(3)(c)	15	490.005(2)	45
464.004	14	490.006	25
464.004(1)	14	490.007(1)	26
464.004(2)	14	490.009(1)	292
464.008(1)(a)-(c)	16	490.009(1)(p)	289, 292
464.008(1)(c)-(d)	16	490.009(2)(a)-(w)	27
464.009(1)(a)	16	490.012(1)(a)	27, 33
464.009(1)(b)	16	490.014(2)	26, 33
464.009(3)	16	490.014(2)(a)-(e)	34
464.012(1)(a)-(c)	16	490.0051	26
464.012(2)	17	490.0121	46
464.013	16	490.0141	31
464.014	16	490.0143	30, 76
464.015	17	490.0145	31
464.015(2)	17	490.0147	120, 131, 134, 135, 141
464.015(3)	17		
464.015(4)	17	490.0147(2)	120
464.015(5)	17	490.0148	121
464.015(7)	17	490.339(1)	129
464.016(1)(a)-(d)	18	491	290
464.017	18, 164	491.003	35, 53
464.018(1)(c)	17	491.003(7)	35, 36
464.018(1)(d)	18	491.003(7)(c)	36
464.018(1)(e)	18	491.003(8)	54
464.018(1)(f)-(l)	18	491.003(9)	62
464.018(1)(m)	18	491.003(9)(c)	62
465.016(1)(d)	291	491.004	35, 53
465.016(1)(m)	291	491.004(1)	35, 53, 61
465.016(2)	291	491.004(2)	61
466.018(1)(j)	290	491.005	62
466.018(2)	290	491.005(1)	36
468.217(1)	290	491.005(3)	54
468.217(1)(t)	290	491.006	37, 55, 63
468.3101(1)(g)	293	491.007	37, 55, 64
468.3101(2)	293	491.009(1)	289
485.002(2)	70	491.009(1)(a)-(w)	38, 56, 65
485.002(3)	69	491.009(2)(p)	290
485.003	69	491.012(1)(a)	38, 55
485.003(3)	70	491.012(1)(b)	56

Section	Page	Section	Page
491.012(1)(c)	65	627.644	102, 104
491.012(3)	38, 56, 65	627.668(1)	105
491.014(4)	37, 55, 64	627.668(2)	90, 105
491.0046	64	627.668(2)(a)	90
491.0046(3)	63	627.669	106
491.0046(4)	64	627.6471(1)(b)	92
491.047	141	627.6471(1)(c)	92
491.0065	37	627.6471(2)	92
491.0112	40, 57	627.6471(4)(a)-(h)	92
491.0112(1)	164, 165, 166	627.6471(5)	94
491.0141	127	627.6472	93
491.0143	77	627.6472(4)	93
491.0145	38	627.6472(4)-(5)	93
491.0147	127, 134, 136	627.6472(13)	93
491.0148	127	627.6472(15)	94
495.011(1)	319	627.6685	105
495.011(2)	319	627.65625	104
495.011(6)	319	641.19(13)	89
495.131	319	641.31	90
542.15 *et seq.*	169	641.185	91
542.18	169	641.225	90
542.19	169	641.309	90
544.22(1)	171	641.315(1)	91
544.22(2)	171	641.315(2)(a)(2)	91
607.0120	83	641.315(5)	91
607.0831	84	732.501	310
608.401-514	83	741.04	175
617.01201	84	741.0405	175
617.1401	84	743.01	277
617.1420	84	743.06	278
620.102(6)	85	743.07	277
620.108	86	743.015	277
620.129	87	743.064	278
620.137	86	743.0645	277
620.157	87	743.0645(1)(b)	278
620.158	88	743.0645(4)	278
620.8101(7)	85	743.065	278
620.8105	86	743.066	277
620.8202(3)	86	744	307
620.8305	87	744.102	219
620.8306	87	744.301(1)	219
620.8401	87	744.301(4)(a)	221
620.8404	87	744.304	181, 219
620.8801	88	744.312(2)(d)	181
620.8803	88	744.312(3)(c)	181
620.8806	88	744.331(1)	179
621.02	82	744.331(2)(a)	179
621.03(1)	83	744.331(3)(a)	179
621.03(2)	83	744.331(3)(b)	179
621.03(3)	83	744.331(3)(d)	179
621.06	83	744.331(3)(r)	179
621.07	84	744.331(5)(a)	179
621.12	83	744.331(5)(b)	179
627.643(2)	102	744.331(6)	180

Section	Page	Section	Page
744.341	181	782.07	167
744.361	180	782.08	167
744.464(2)(a)	183	784.011(1)	167
744.464(2)(c)	183	794.011(1)(b)	164
744.464(2)(l)	183	794.011(4)(d)	163
744.464(3)	183	794.011(4)(e)	164
744.1012	177	794.022(1)	339
744.3021	219, 220, 221	794.022(4)	339
744.3031	180	847.001(7)	409
744.3045(3)	180	847.011	409
744.3201	178	847.012	409
744.3215	177, 189	847.0135	409
744.3215(2)	177, 178	903.046(1)	363
744.3215(3)	177, 178	903.046(2)	365
744.3215(4)	182	907.041(4)(b)4	393
744.3725	182	907.041(4)(c)(1)-(7)	364
747.01	184	910.03(3)	329
747.031-.052	184	913.03	329
747.035	184	913.03(2)	328
752.01(1)(a)	191	913.08	329
760.01(2)	321	913.10	328
760.02(7)	322	913.13	328
760.10	321, 322	916.12	366
760.10(8)	323	916.12(1)	367
760.10(9)	322	916.12(2)	368
760.50	322	916.12(4)	368
765.104(2)	186	916.13(1)	370, 371
766.101(2)	154	916.13(1)(c)	371
766.101(3)(a)	154	916.13(1)(d)	371
766.101(5)	154	916.13(2)	371
766.101(7)(a)	154	916.13(2)(a)	371
766.101(7)(a)1-2	154	916.15(1)	384
766.101(7)(c)	129, 154	916.15(2)	384
766.101(a)(1)(c)	154	916.15(3)	384
766.101(g)-(h)	154	916.17(1)	372, 385
766.102(1)	157	916.17(2)	372, 385
766.102(4)	157	916.17(3)	385
766.104	156	916.107(1)(a)	372
766.106	156	916.107(3)	150
766.106(3)(a)1-4	158	916.107(3)(b)	115, 150
766.110(1)	153	916.107(3)(c)	115, 151
766.110(1)(a)-(c)	153	916.115(1)(b)	367
768.1256(1)(a)-(c)	317	916.115(1)(c)	367, 382
768.21(2)-(4)	305	916.145	373
775.051	379	916.301(5)	368
775.082	8, 256	916.302(1)(c)	371
775.082(3)(a)3	216	916.302(1)(d)	371
775.082(4)(a)	8	916.303(1)	373
775.082(4)(b)	201	921.005(1)(b)(3)	375
775.084	394	921.0016(4)(f)	375
775.084(1)(a)	394	921.141(1)	389
775.0841	394	921.141(5)	390
775.0841-.0843	394	921.141(c)	389
782.03	374	921.231(1)i	388

Section	Page	Section	Page
922.07(1)	407	984.10(1)	240
922.07(3)	408	984.10(3)	241
922.07(4)	408	984.11	241
926.12(1)	367	984.12(1)	241
933.01	145	984.12(8)	241
933.02	145	984.13(1)	239
933.04	145	984.14(1)	240
933.18	145	984.21	241
945.10(1)(a)	397	984.21(2)	240
945.12	401	984.22	241
945.41	396, 401	984.22(6)	242
945.41(1)	401	985	233
945.42	402	985.01(1)(c)	234
945.42(7)	399	985.03(6)	252
945.43(1)	400	985.03(9)	234
945.43(2)	400	985.03(15)	234
945.46	401	985.03(57)	252
945.47(1)(c)	402	985.21	235
945.47(1)(d)	401	985.21(2)	236
945.47(2)	402	985.21(4)(a)	234
945.47(3)	397, 404	985.21(4)(d)	234
945.48	397	985.201(1)	234
945.48(2)	398	985.201(4)	239
945.48(2)(a)	398	985.203	237
945.48(2)(b)	398	985.207(1)	235
945.48(2)(c)	399	985.207(2)	235
945.48(2)(c)4	399	985.211	236
947.002(2)	404	985.213	236
947.002(5)	403	985.214	236
947.01	404	985.218	237
947.02	404	985.223(1)	244
947.1405(7)(b)(1)	72	985.223(1)(b)	244, 245
947.16	403	985.223(1)(d)	244
947.165	404	985.223(1)(e)	244
947.185	405	985.223(1)(f)	243
948.01(2)	391	985.223(1)(f)1-6	244
948.01(5)	391	985.223(1)(g)	246
948.015(9)	392	985.223(1)(h)	246
948.03(1)(k)	392	985.223(2)	246
948.03(4)	391	985.223(3)	245
948.03(4)(a)-(c)	392	985.223(4)	246
948.034(1)	392	985.223(4)(d)	246
948.06	391	985.223(4)(e)	246
948.08(2)	361	985.223(5)(a)	246
948.08(3)	362	985.223(5)(b)	246
948.08(4)	362	985.223(5)(c)	247
948.08(5)	362	985.223(6)(a)	246
948.08(6)	362	985.224(1)	239
960.001	420	985.224(2)	237, 239
960.002(3)	420	985.224(3)	239
960.09	419	985.224(5)	239
960.13	419	985.226(1)	253
960.13(9)(a)	419	985.226(2)(a)	254
960.13(9)(b)	419	985.226(2)(b)	257

Section	Page
985.226(2)(b)1	253
985.226(2)(b)2	254
985.226(3)	254
985.226(3)(b)	255
985.226(4)(a)	253
985.226(4)(b)	253
985.227(1)(a)	255
985.227(1)(b)	256
985.227(2)(a)	256, 257
985.227(2)(b)	256, 257
985.227(2)(c)	256
985.227(3)(a)	255
985.227(3)(c)	258
985.228(1)	237
985.228(2)	237
985.228(2)(a)	237
985.229(1)	238
985.229(2)	238
985.229(3)	238
985.231	238
985.231(1)(d)	238
985.231(3)	239
985.233(1)(a)	257
985.233(1)(b)	257
985.233(3)	257
985.233(3)(b)	258
985.233(5)(b)	257

United States Code

Section	Page
5 U.S.C. §§ 11101 et seq.	153
26 U.S.C. § 162(a)	109
26 U.S.C. § 213(a)	108
26 U.S.C. § 213(d)(1)	108
26 U.S.C. § 213(d)(2)(A)(B)	108
29 U.S.C. §§ 1001–1461	107
42 U.S.C. § 2000(e)	321
42 U.S.C. §§ 12101 et seq.	357
42 U.S.C. §§ 12101–12213	321

Table of Rules of Court

References are to page numbers in this book.

Florida Bar, Rules Regulating

Rule	Page
3-7.4	293
3-7.13	293
3-10	293

Florida Rules of Civil Procedure

Rule	Page
1.360	118
1.430	329
1.431(a)	330
1.431(b)	330
1.431(c)	330
1.840	283

Florida Rules of Criminal Procedure

Rule	Page
3.20	328
3.44	328
3.111(d)(3)	359
3.201	343
3.202(b)	389
3.202(d)	389
3.202(e)	389
3.210	366
3.210(b)	367
3.210(b)(3)	367
3.210(b)(4)	367
3.210(x)	328
3.211(a)(2)	368
3.211(b)	368
3.211(d)	369
3.211(e)	370
3.212(a)	369
3.212(a)(2)	368
3.212(b)	369
3.212(c)	369
3.212(c)(1)	369, 370
3.212(c)(2)	372
3.212(c)(3)(A)–(D)	369
3.212(c)(3)(B)	371
3.212(c)(3)(C)	371
3.212(c)(5)	371
3.212(d)	372
3.213(a)	373
3.213(b)	373
3.214	373
3.215(b)	372
3.215(c)	373
3.215(c)(2)(a)	373
3.216	380
3.216(a)	250, 381, 383
3.216(b)	381
3.216(c)	343, 381
3.216(d)	381, 382
3.216(g)	382
3.216(i)	382
3.220(a)	148
3.220(b)	148
3.220(c)	148
3.251	328
3.260	360
3.270	328
3.330(c)	327
3.350	329
3.811	407
3.811(d)(1)–(5)	406
3.812	407
3.851(g)	386
3.851(g)(1)	386
3.851(g)(2)	386
3.851(g)(4)	387
3.851(g)(5)	387
3.851(g)(6)	387
3.851(g)(7)	387
3.851(g)(8)	387
3.851(g)(9)	387
3.851(g)(13)	387

Florida Rules of Juvenile Procedure

Rule	Page
8.095(b)	249
8.095(b)(1)	249
8.095(c)(1)	249
8.095(c)(3)	249
8.095(e)	250
8.095(e)(2)	250
8.095(e)(2)(A)	250
8.095(e)(2)(B)	250
8.095(e)(2)(C)	250
8.095(e)(2)(D)	250
8.095(e)(2)(F)	250, 251
8.095(e)(2)(G)	251

Table of Administrative Rules and Regulations

References are to page numbers in this book.

Florida Administrative Code

Rule	Page
4-154.106	103
4-154.106(2)	103
4-191.024(12)	95
6A-4.0181	48
6A-6.03011	273
6A-6.03012	273
6A-6.03013	273
6A-6.03014	273
6A-6.03015	273
6A-6.03016	273
6A-6.03018	273
6A-6.03019	276
6A-6.03020	273
6A-6.03021	273
6A-6.03022	273
6A-6.03023	273
6A-6.03024	273
6A-6.03025	273
6A-6.03026	273
6A-6.03028(1)	274
6A-6.03028(3)	273, 275
6A-6.03028(4)	275
28-5.111	12, 20, 41, 58
28-106.206	12, 21, 29, 41, 51, 59, 67
28-106.208	12, 21, 29, 41, 51, 59, 67
28-106.209	12, 21, 29, 41, 51, 59, 67
28-106.212	12, 21, 29, 41, 51, 59, 67
28-106.216	12, 21, 29, 42, 51, 59, 67
28-106.217	12, 21, 29, 42, 51, 59, 67
33-404.101	397, 399
33-404.101(2)(b)	397
33-404.102	396
33-404.102(8)	398
33-404.105	398
33-404.106	399
33-404.210	398
33-404.210(2)(a)	398
33-404.210(2)(b)	398
33-507.001(3)	397
33-507.002	397
33-507.201(2)	397
33-507.401	397
59A-12.012(2)	96
61F66-2101	136
64-10.002	164
64B-6.001(2)(a)	64
64B-6.001(2)(b)	64
64B-6.001(2)(c)	64
64B-6.001(3)	64
64B-7.006	196
64B4-5	136
64B4-7.002	71
64B4-7.004	77
64B4-9.001(1)	127
64B4-9.001(2)	127
64B4-9.001(3)	128
64B4-9.001(4)	128
64B4-9.002(2)	114, 127
64B8-9.008(2)	166
64B8-9.008(5)	166
64B8-10.001	126
64B8-10.002(3)	125
64B8-10.002(4)	126
64B8-10.003	125
64B9-8.005	19
64B9-8.006	22
64B10.003(2)	167
64B10.003(3)-16.003	167
64B15-15.001	126
64B15-15.002	126
64B15-15.002(3)	126
64B15-15.003	125
64B15-15.004(1)	125
64B15-15.004(3)	125
64B19-9.002(3)	126
64B19-9.008(4)	166
64B19-10.004	164
64B19-10.004(3)	164
64B19-11.001	25
64B19-11.005	25
64B19-11.0035	24
64B19-13.001	26
64B19-13.003(3)	26
64B19-15.001	26

Rule	Page
64B19-15.003	26
64B19-16.003	165
64B19-17.002	135
64B19-18.002	30, 76
64B19-18.003	31, 70
64B19-18.004(2)	31
64B19-18.004(3)	123
64B19-18.006	31, 195
64B19-18.007	195
64B19-18.007(1)	32
64B19-18.007(2)	32
64B19-18.0025	31
64B19-19.002	119
64B19-19.003	122
64B19-19.004(1)	123
64B19-19.004(2)	123
64B19-19.005(1)	122
64B19-19.005(2)	122
64B19-19.006	135
64B19-19.006(1)	120
64B19-19.006(2)	120
64B19-19.006(3)	121
64B19-19.006(5)	120

Rule	Page
64B19-19.0025	122
64B19-19.0025(2)	114
64B21-500.005	45
64B21-500.009	45
64B21-500.013	45
64B21-500.013(6)	46
64B21-501.003	46
64B21-502.001	46
64B21-502.004	46
64B25-28.015	38
65B-6.013(5)(d)	152
65E-5.1703	150

Treasury Regulations

Regulation	Page
1.162-5(a)	110

Revenue Rulings

Ruling	Page
Rev. Rul. 53-143	109
Rev. Rul. 63-91	109

Table of References to Constitution

References are to page numbers in this book.

Florida Constitution

Article	Page
art. I, § 12	144
art. I, § 14	363
art. I, § 24	149
art. I, § 16	359

U.S. Constitution

Amendment	Page
amend. 5	370
amend. 14	323

Index

References are to chapters.

A

ABORTION
  Consent for minors, 4.22
ABUSE OF PROCESS
  Professional liability, 3.11(A)(4)
ABUSED ADULTS
  Mandated reporting, 4.7
ABUSED/NEGLECTED CHILDREN
  Child protection teams, 4.8(H)
  Legal procedure, 4.9
  Mandated reporting, 4.8
ADOPTION
  Generally, 4.14
ADVERTISING
  Unfair competition, 5.11
AIDS
  Partner notification of status, 3.3(D)
ANTITRUST LAW
  Generally, 3.14
ASSAULT
  Criminal liability, 3.12(B)
ASSISTED SUICIDE
  Manslaughter, 3.12(C)
ATTORNEYS
  Attorney-client privilege, 7.5(D), 7.9(C)
  Mental status, 5.1(B)
  Waiver of right to, 7.2(B)
AVERSIVE/AVOIDANCE CONDITIONING
  Regulation, 3.8

B

BAIL DETERMINATIONS
  Generally, 7.4
BATTERED WOMAN'S SYNDROME
  As legal defense, 6.6
BEHAVIOR TREATMENT
  Regulation, 3.8
BUSINESS REGULATION
  Antitrust limitations, 3.14
  Employment discrimination, 5.12
  Health maintenance organizations, 2.4
  Individual practice associations, 2.6
  Mental health education as business deduction, 2.11(C)
  Mental health services as business deduction, 2.11(B)
  Partnerships, 2.3
  Preferred provider organizations, 2.5
  Product liability, 5.10
  Professional corporations, 2.2
  Sole proprietorships, 2.1
  Unfair competition, 5.11

C

CAPITAL PUNISHMENT
  Generally, 7.19
  Sentencing hearing, 7.11(B)
CERTIFICATION AND REGULATION. *See also* LICENSURE AND REGULATION
  Credentialing boards
    Liability of, 3.13
    Sunset laws, 1.14(B)
  Foster care, 4.13(A)
  Mental status of professionals, 5.1
  School psychologists, 1.7
  Social workers, 1.8
  Subdoctoral/uncertified psychologists, 1.5
CHILD CUSTODY
  Generally, 4.6
  Rights of noncustodial parents, 4.23
  Temporary, in abuse/neglect cases, 4.9(A)
CHILDREN
  Abused and neglected, 4.9
  Adoption, 4.14
  Competency to stand trial, 4.16
  Consent for abortion, 4.22
  Conservatorship, 4.12
  Custody after marital dissolution, 4.6
  Delinquency, 4.15
  Foster care, 4.13
  Gifted and handicapped, 4.20
  Guardianship, 4.11
  Involuntary commitment, 4.19(B)
  Medical decision-making for, 4.21
  In need of services, 4.15(B)
  Nonresponsibility defense, 4.17
  Reporting abuse of, 4.8
  Rights of noncustodial parents, 4.23

Runaways, 4.15(B)
Sexual abuse syndrome, 6.10
Termination of parental rights, 4.10
Tried as adults, 4.18
Voluntary admission and commitment, 4.19

CIVIL LAW
Emotional distress as basis for liability, 5.4
Insanity of wrongdoers, 5.5
Intentional torts, 3.11(A)
Jury selection, 6.1(C)
Liability, 3.11
Product liability, 5.10

CIVIL RIGHTS ACT
Generally, 5.12(B)

COMMITMENT
Of alcoholics and drug abusers, 8.5
Of drug addicts, 8.6
Of mentally ill adults, 8.4
Of minors, 4.19

COMMUNITY HOMES
Zoning, 2.8

COMPETENCY
Admission and commitment of substance abusers, 8.5
To be executed, 7.19
To be sentenced, 7.10
Of children to stand trial, 4.16
Conservatorship for adults, 4.3
To contract, 5.6
Diminished capacity defense, 7.8
To execute a will, 5.7
Guardianship for incapacitated adults, 4.2
Involuntary commitment of mentally ill adults, 8.3(A), 8.3(D), 8.4
To marry, 4.1
To obtain driver's license, 5.9
Pretrial intervention programs, 7.3
To serve sentence, 7.15
To stand trial, 7.5
To testify, 6.4
Voluntary admission of mentally ill adults, 8.3
To vote, 5.8
To waive legal rights, 7.2

CONDITIONING
Avoidance/aversion, 3.8

CONFIDENTIALITY
Admission and commitment of substance abusers, 8.5(F)
Adoption records, 4.14(F)
Adult abuse reporting, 4.7(B)(1), 4.7(F)
Child abuse reporting, 4.8(B)(1), 4.8(F)
Generally, 3.3
Insanity defense, 7.9(C)
Juvenile competency hearings, 4.16(D)
Juvenile delinquency records, 4.15(E)
Prisoners' medical records, 7.16(A)(2)
Privileged communications, 3.4
Public records, 3.6
Search and seizure of records, 3.5

CONSERVATORSHIP
For adults, 4.3
For minors, 4.12

CONTRACT LAW
Competency issues, 5.6
Professional liability, 3.11(B)(2)

COUNSELORS. *See* MENTAL HEALTH COUNSELORS

CREDENTIALING BOARDS
Generally, 1.14
Liability, 3.13

CRIMINAL LAW. *See also* JUVENILE JUSTICE
Bail determinations, 7.4
Competency to be sentenced, 7.10
Competency to serve sentence, 7.15
Competency to stand trial, 7.5
Competency to waive rights, 7.2
Dangerous offenders, 7.13
Diminished capacity defense, 7.8
Habitual offenders, 7.14
Insanity defense, 7.9
Jury selection, 6.1(B)
Mens rea determination, 7.7
Pornography, 7.20
Pretrial intervention programs, 7.3
Probation, 7.12
Professional liability, 3.12
Provocation defense, 7.6
Sentencing, 7.11
Sex offenders, 7.21
Victim's services, 7.22

D

DANGEROUS OFFENDERS
Generally, 7.13

DEATH SENTENCE
Generally, 7.19
Sentencing hearing, 7.11(B)

DEFAMATION OF CHARACTER
  Professional liability, 3.11(A)(2)
DELINQUENCY
  Generally, 4.15
DEVELOPMENTAL DISABILITIES
  Services for people with, 8.7
DIMINISHED CAPACITY DEFENSE
  Generally, 7.8
DISABLED PERSONS. *See also*
  VOCATIONAL REHABILITATION
  Vocational disability, 5.3
DISCRIMINATION
  Employment, 5.12
DIVORCE
  Annulment of marriage, 4.4
  Child custody, 4.6
  Generally, 4.5
DOMESTIC VIOLENCE
  Adult abuse, 4.7
  Battered woman's syndrome as legal defense, 6.6
DRIVER'S LICENSE
  Competency issues, 5.9
DRUG ABUSE. *See* SUBSTANCE ABUSE
DUTY TO PROTECT OR WARN
  Generally, 3.3(C)

E

EDUCATIONAL SYSTEM
  Services for gifted and handicapped children, 4.20
EMOTIONAL DISTRESS
  As personal injury, 5.4
EMPLOYMENT DISCRIMINATION
  Generally, 5.12
EMPLOYMENT SCREENING
  Police officers, 7.1
EXPERT WITNESSES
  On eyewitness identification, 6.9
  Rules of evidence, 6.2
EYEWITNESS IDENTIFICATION
  Expert testimony on, 6.9

F

FALSE IMPRISONMENT
  Professional liability, 3.11(A)(4)
FAMILY THERAPISTS. *See* MARRIAGE AND FAMILY THERAPISTS
FIDUCIARY DUTY
  Breach of, 3.11(B)(1)
FOSTER CARE
  Generally, 4.13

FREEDOM OF INFORMATION
  Generally, 3.6

G

GIFTED/HANDICAPPED CHILDREN
  Education for, 4.20
GUARDIANSHIP
  For adults, 4.2
  For minors, 4.11
GUILTY BUT INSANE. *See* INSANITY

H

HABITUAL OFFENDERS
  Generally, 7.14
HEALTH MAINTENANCE ORGANIZATIONS
  Regulation, 2.4
HIV-POSITIVE/AIDS
  Partner notification of status, 3.3(D)
HOSPICE CARE
  Generally, 8.8
HOSPITAL MEDICAL REVIEW BOARDS
  Generally, 3.2(E)
HOSPITALS
  Medical review committees, 3.9(B)
  Quality assurance, 3.9
  Records maintenance, 3.2
  Staff privileges, 2.7
HYPNOSIS
  Licensure and regulation of hypnotists, 1.11
  Of witnesses, 6.8

I

IMMUNITY. *See* LIABILITY OF PROFESSIONALS
INCARCERATED PERSONS
  Competency to be executed, 7.19
  Confidentiality of medical records, 7.16(A)(2)
  Consent to and right to refuse medical treatment, 7.16(A)(3)
  Mental health services, 7.16
  Parole determinations, 7.18
  Transfer to mental health facility, 7.17
INCOMPETENCY. *See* COMPETENCY
INDIVIDUAL PRACTICE ASSOCIATIONS
  Regulation, 2.6

INFORMED CONSENT
    Generally, 3.1
    Services for minors, 4.21
INSANITY
    Civil liability and, 5.5
    Legal defense, 7.9
    Liability insurance and, 5.5(B)
INSURANCE
    Insanity defense and, 5.5(B)
    Reimbursement for mental health services, 2.9
    State plans, 2.10
    Workers' compensation, 5.2
INVASION OF PRIVACY
    Professional liability, 3.11(A)(3)

J

JURY SELECTION
    Generally, 6.1
JURY TRIAL
    Right to waive jury trial, 7.2(C)
JUVENILE JUSTICE
    Competency to stand trial, 4.16
    Delinquency, 4.15
    Nonresponsibility defense, 4.17
    Transfer to stand trial as adult, 4.18

L

LAW ENFORCEMENT
    Employment screening, 7.1
    Rights of detained individuals, 7.2
LIABILITY OF PROFESSIONALS
    Civil, 3.11
    Credentialing boards, 3.13
    Criminal, 3.12
    Immunity
        Reporting of abuse, 4.7(E), 4.8(E)
        Treatment of sexually violent persons, 7.21(F)
        Involuntary commitment proceedings, 8.4(G)
    Malpractice, 3.10
    Review committees, 3.10(C)
LICENSURE AND REGULATION. *See also* CERTIFICATION AND REGULATION
    Credentialing boards, 1.14
        Liability of, 3.13
        Sunset laws, 1.14(B)
    Generally, 1.1, 1.10
    Hypnotists, 1.11
    Liability of credentialing boards, 3.13
    Marriage and family therapists, 1.9
    Mental health counselors, 1.10
    Mental status of professionals, 5.1
    Polygraph examiners, 1.12
    Psychiatric nurses, 1.3
    Psychiatrists, 1.2
    Psychologists, 1.4
    Sex therapists, 1.15
    Social workers, 1.6
    Sunset laws, 1.14(B)
    Unlicensed mental health professionals, 1.13

M

MALICIOUS PROSECUTION
    Professional liability, 3.11(A)(4)
MALPRACTICE
    Generally, 3.10
    Statute of limitations, 3.10(A)(5)
MANAGED CARE
    Medicaid and, 8.1(D)
MANDATED REPORTING
    Adult abuse, 4.7
    Child abuse, 4.8
MANSLAUGHTER/MURDER
    Criminal liability, 3.12(C), 3.12(D)
    Provocation defense, 7.6
MARRIAGE. *See also* DIVORCE
    Annulment, 4.4
    Competency to marry, 4.1
    Voiding, 4.4
MARRIAGE AND FAMILY THERAPISTS
    Confidentiality issues, 3.3(B)(3)
    Licensure and regulation, 1.9
    Mental status, 5.1(A)(1)
    Privileged communications, 3.4(A)
    Records maintenance, 3.2(D)
    Sex therapists, 1.15(C)
    Sexual misconduct, 3.12(A)(2)(c)
MEDICAID
    Generally, 8.1
    Managed care, 8.1(D)
MEDICAL CARE
    Admission and commitment of substance abusers, 8.5, 8.6
    Conservatorship for adults, 4.3
    Cost containment, 8.2
    Decision-making for minors, 4.21
    Guardianship for incapacitated adults, 4.2
    Hospice care, 8.8
    Mental health services as tax medical deduction, 2.11(A)

Quality assurance, 3.9
Right to refuse treatment, 3.7
　Prisoners, 7.16(A)(3)
Rights of noncustodial parent, 4.23
MEDICAL PROFESSIONALS
　Mental status, 5.1
MENS REA
　Generally, 7.7
MENTAL HEALTH COUNSELORS
　Confidentiality issues, 3.3(B)(3)
　Licensure and regulation, 1.10
　Mental status, 5.1(A)(1)
　Sexual misconduct, 3.12(A)(2)(c)
MENTAL HEALTH PROFESSIONALS
　(MHPs). *See also specific profession*
　Agency and administrative
　　positions, 2.7(A)
　Civil liability, 3.11
　Confidentiality issues, 3.3
　Criminal liability, 3.12
　Hospital staff privileges, 2.7(B)
　Licensure and regulation, 1.1, 1.10
　Malpractice liability, 3.10
　Mental status, 5.1
　Privileged communications, 3.4
　Records maintenance, 3.2
　Unlicensed, 1.13
MENTAL ILLNESS
　Competency to stand trial, 7.5
　Competency to testify, 6.4
　Conservatorship for adults, 4.3
　Diminished capacity criminal
　　defense, 7.8
　Evaluation of licensed professionals,
　　5.1
　Guardianship for adults, 4.2
　Guardianship for minors, 4.11
　Involuntary admission/commitment
　　of minors, 4.19(B)
　Involuntary commitment of
　　mentally ill adults, 8.3(A), 8.3(D),
　　8.4
　Legal liability and, 5.5
　Services for people with
　　developmental disabilities, 8.7
　Services for prisoners, 7.16
　Transfer of incarcerated persons,
　　7.17
　Vocational disability, 5.3
　Voluntary admission/commitment
　　of minors, 4.19
　Voluntary admission of adults, 8.3
　Workers' compensation, 5.2(B)
MENTAL RETARDATION. *See*
　DEVELOPMENTAL DISABILITIES

N

NONRESPONSIBILITY DEFENSE
　Generally, 4.17
NURSES. *See also* PSYCHIATRIC
　NURSES
　Mental status, 5.1(A)(2)

O

OCCUPATIONAL THERAPISTS
　Mental status, 5.1(A)(3)

P

PARENTAL RIGHTS
　Consent for minor's abortion, 4.22
　Education for gifted and
　　handicapped children, 4.20(C)
　Guardianship for minors, 4.11
　Noncustodial parents, 4.23
　Services for minors, 4.21
　Termination of, 4.10
PAROLE
　Generally, 7.18
PARTNERSHIPS
　Regulation, 2.3
PATIENT RIGHTS
　Admission and commitment of
　　substance abusers, 8.5(G)
　Developmentally disabled persons,
　　8.7(D)
　Involuntary commitment of
　　mentally ill adults, 8.4(F)
　Refusal to treatment, 3.7
　Incarcerated persons, 7.16(A)(3)
　Voluntary admission of mentally ill
　　adults, 8.3
PEER REVIEW
　Hospitals, 3.9(B)
PENAL SYSTEM. *See* INCARCERATED
　PERSONS
PHARMACISTS
　Mental status, 5.1(A)(4)
PHYSICAL THERAPISTS
　Mental status, 5.1(A)(5)
PHYSICIANS
　Mental status, 5.1(A)(6)
POLICE OFFICERS
　Employment screening, 7.1
POLYGRAPH TESTING
　As legal evidence, 6.3
　Licensure and regulation of
　　examiners, 1.12

PORNOGRAPHY
  Generally, 7.20
PREFERRED PROVIDER
  ORGANIZATIONS
  Regulation, 2.5
PRETRIAL INTERVENTION
  PROGRAMS
  Generally, 7.3
PRIVILEGED COMMUNICATIONS
  Attorney-client privilege, 7.5(D), 7.9(C)
  Generally, 3.4
  Insanity defense, 7.9(C)
  Reporting of adult abuse, 4.7(B)(1), 4.7(F)
  Reporting of child abuse, 4.8(B)(1), 4.8(F)
PROBATION
  Generally, 7.12
PRODUCT LIABILITY
  Generally, 5.10
PROFESSIONAL CORPORATIONS
  Regulation, 2.2
PSYCHIATRIC NURSES
  Licensure and regulation, 1.3
PSYCHIATRISTS
  Confidentiality issues, 3.3(B)(2)
  Licensure and regulation, 1.2
  Privileged communications, 3.4(A), 7.9(C)
  Records maintenance, 3.2(C)
  Sex therapists, 1.15
  Sexual misconduct, 3.12(A)(2)(a)
PSYCHOLOGICAL AUTOPSY
  Admissibility of, 6.5
PSYCHOLOGISTS
  Confidentiality issues, 3.3(B)(1)
  Licensure and regulation, 1.4
  Mental status, 5.1(A)(7)
  Privileged communication, 3.4(A), 7.9(C)
  Records maintenance, 3.2(B)
  School, 1.7
  Sex therapists, 1.15(A)
  Sexual misconduct, 3.12(A)(2)(a)
  Subdoctoral/uncertified, 1.5
PUBLIC RECORDS
  Access, 3.6

Q

QUALITY ASSURANCE
  For hospital care, 3.9

R

RADIOLOGIC TECHNOLOGISTS
  Mental status, 5.1(A)(8)
RECORDS MAINTENANCE
  Access to public records, 3.6
  Generally, 3.2
  Privileged communications, 3.4
  Search and seizure of records, 3.5
REFUSAL OF TREATMENT
  Generally, 3.7
  Prisoner's right, 7.16(A)(3)
REGULATION. *See* CERTIFICATION
  AND REGULATION; LICENSURE
  AND REGULATION
RULES OF COURT
  Jury selection, 6.1
RULES OF EVIDENCE
  Expert witnesses, 6.2
  Sexually violent predator proceedings, 7.21(C)

S

SCHOOL PSYCHOLOGISTS
  Certification and regulation, 1.7
SEARCH AND SEIZURE
  Of records, 3.5
SENTENCING
  Competency to be executed, 7.19
  Competency to be sentenced, 7.10
  Competency to serve sentence, 7.15
  Of dangerous offenders, 7.13
  Generally, 7.11
  Of habitual offenders, 7.14
SEX THERAPISTS
  Licensure and regulation, 1.15
SEXUAL ASSAULT
  Child sexual abuse syndrome, 6.10
  Competency of rape victim to testify, 6.4(C)
  Professional liability, 3.12(A), 3.12(B)
  Profiles or propensity of offenders, 6.11
  Rape trauma syndrome, 6.7
  Treatment of offenders, 7.21
SEXUAL ASSAULT COUNSELORS
  Privileged communications, 3.4(B)
SEXUAL MISCONDUCT
  Professional liability, 3.12(A)
SOCIAL WORKERS
  Confidentiality issues, 3.3(B)(3)
  Licensure and regulation, 1.6
  Mental status, 5.1(A)(1)
  Privileged communications, 3.4(A)

Records maintenance, 3.2(D)
School, 1.8
Sex therapists, 1.15(C)
Sexual misconduct, 3.12(A)(2)(c)
SOLE PROPRIETORSHIPS
  Regulation, 2.1
SUBPOENA
  For search and seizure of records, 3.5(B)
SUBSTANCE ABUSE
  Admission and commitment of substance abusers, 8.5, 8.6
  Diminished capacity defense, 7.8(A)
  Treatment of minors, 4.19(C)
    Confidentiality, 4.19(D)
    Consent, 4.21(B)
SUNSET LAWS
  Generally, 1.14(B)

T

"TARASOFF ISSUES," 3.3(C)
TAX LAW
  Deductions for mental health service payments, 2.11

U

UNFAIR COMPETITION
  Generally, 5.11

V

VICTIM'S SERVICES
  Generally, 7.22
VOCATIONAL DISABILITY
  Evaluation for, 5.3
VOCATIONAL REHABILITATION
  Evaluation for services, 5.3
VOTING
  Competency for, 5.8

W

WARRANTS
  For search and seizure of records, 3.5
WILLS
  Competency of testator, 5.7
WORKERS' COMPENSATION
  Generally, 5.2

Z

ZONING
  For community homes, 2.8

About the Authors

John Petrila, JD, LLM, is chair and professor in the Department of Mental Health Law and Policy in the Louis de la Parte Florida Mental Health Institute at the University of South Florida. He holds a joint appointment at the University of South Florida College of Public Health and an adjunct appointment at the Stetson University College of Law. He received his law degree and an advanced degree in mental health law from the University of Virginia. He served as general counsel to the New York State Office of Mental Health and was the first director of forensic services in the Missouri Department of Mental Hygiene. He was also the first Fellow in mental health law at the University of Virginia. He is coauthor of *Psychological Evaluations for the Courts: A Handbook for Mental Health Professionals and Lawyers* (1997) and coeditor of *Mental Health Services: A Public Health Perspective* (1996). He has written extensively on mental disability law, including forensic mental health, confidentiality, managed care, and the Americans With Disabilities Act. He is coeditor of the journal *Behavioral Sciences and the Law*. He is also a member of the MacArthur Foundation Network on Mandated Community Treatment.

Randy K. Otto, PhD, is an associate professor in the Department of Mental Health Law and Policy in the Louis de la Parte Florida Mental Health Institute at the University of South Florida. He holds adjunct faculty appointments at Stetson University College of Law as well as in the Department of Psychology and the Department of Rehabilitation and Mental Health Counseling at the University of South Florida. In addition to his research and training activities, he has a private practice limited to forensic evaluation. He has served as corresponding secretary of the American Board of Forensic Psychology, president of the American Academy of Forensic Psychology, and president of the American Psychology–Law Society. He serves on the editorial boards of the journals *Law and Human Behavior, Behavioral Sciences and the Law,* the *Journal of Behavioral Health Services and Administration*, and the *Correctional Mental Health Report*. He has published numerous articles and book chapters in the areas of forensic assessment and forensic practice in general. *Adjudicative Competence: The MacArthur Studies,* a book he coauthored with Norman Poythress, John Monahan, Richard Bonnie, and Steven Hoge, was published in 2002.